Contents

UNIT II : SECONDARY EDUCATION IN INDIA— PROBLEMS AND ISSUES

UNIT I : Development of Secondary Education in India

1

Nomenclature of Secondary Education and the Characteristics of Learners at this Stage

1.1 NOMENCLATURE OF SECONDARY EDUCATION/SCHOOL—WORLD OVERVIEW

On account of the variety of educational patterns in different parts of the world, it is not easy to say at which age a pupil normally enters the secondary school and the period of the school stage that can be properly designated as 'Secondary'.

According to the 'Regulations for Secondary Schools' issued by the Board of Education (England), a secondary school is one which makes provision for pupils between the age of twelve and seventeen. As a matter of fact, however, schools retain their pupils up to the age of nineteen, that is, until they are prepared to enter the university.

Secondary education in the U.S.A. normally comprises the junior high school and senior high school and in some cases the junior college.

UNESCO's survey of world education takes the 14 to 19 age range as the second level of schooling, i.e. secondary education.

In many countries of the world, the term higher secondary school does not occur in the educational literature. Usually the term high school is used.

1.2 NOMENCLATURE OF SECONDARY EDUCATION/SECONDARY SCHOOL IN INDIA

I. *The Wood's Despatch (1859) mentions the high school stage.*

II. *Post-War Educational Development in India, Sargent Report 1944:*
High school education for six years for selected children between the ages of 11 and 17.

III. *Report of the Committee on Secondary Education in India (1948)*:
1. Junior basic stage of 5 years.
2. Senior basic or pre-secondary stage of 3 years.
3. Secondary stage of 3 years.

IV. *Report of the Secondary Education Commission (1952–53)*:
1. Primary or Junior Basic Stage of 4 or 5 years.
2. Middle or Junior Secondary or Senior Basic Stage of 4 years.
3. Higher Secondary Stage of 4 years.

V. *Report of the Education Commission 1964-66:*
- A pre-school stage of one to three years.

- A primary stage of seven or eight years divided into two sub-stages—a low primary stage of four or five years and a higher primary stage of three years.
- A lower secondary or high school stage of three or two years of general education or of one to three years in vocational education.
- A higher secondary stage of two years of general education or one to three years of vocational education.
- A higher education stage having a course of three years or more for the first degree, followed by courses of varying durations for the second or research degree.

Note: The Education Commission has not used the term higher secondary education or higher secondary school.

VI. *National Policy on Education (1986 and 1992)*:
1. Elementary Education.
2. Secondary Education.

VII. *NPE Programme of Action (1992)*:

The secondary stage is divided into two very distinct sub-stages—Secondary (up to Class X) which is the stage of general education and higher secondary (Classes XI and XII) which is marked by differentiation and diversification.

The term 'higher secondary' refers to all post-secondary (high school, Class XI) and pre-degree education and includes higher secondary of the 10+2 pattern, pre-university (one year course), pre-Degree/pre-University (Two Year Course) and Intermediate Junior College.

VIII. *'National Curriculum Framework for School Education', NCERT (2000)*:
1. Secondary Stage (Classes IX and X).
2. Higher Secondary Stage (Classes XI and XII).

IX. *'Seventh All India School Education Survey'-NCERT (2002)*:
1. Secondary Schools (Classes IX and X).
2. Higher Secondary Schools (Classes XI and XII).

X. *'National Curriculum Framework-2005' – NCERT (2005)*:
1. Secondary School (Classes IX and X).
2. Higher Secondary School (Class XI and XII).

Summing Up. For all purposes, the term secondary education is generally used to denote education for students of the age group 14 to 18 and classes IX to XII.

1.3 CHARACTERISTICS OF THE SECONDARY STAGE

Sensitive Stage. This stage is characterised by the process of maturity, both of body and minds. It is at this stage that abstract thinking and logic develop predominantly. Goal fixation and symbolisation are the other characteristics that mark this stage in a big way. Similarly, traits like self-consciousness, self-assertion resulting in an emergence of identity of self indicating personal preferences and choices, and ideal formation are typical of this stage. The students also show strong likes and dislikes, reactions and adventurism and have strong peer group influences. There is a tendency to imitate adult

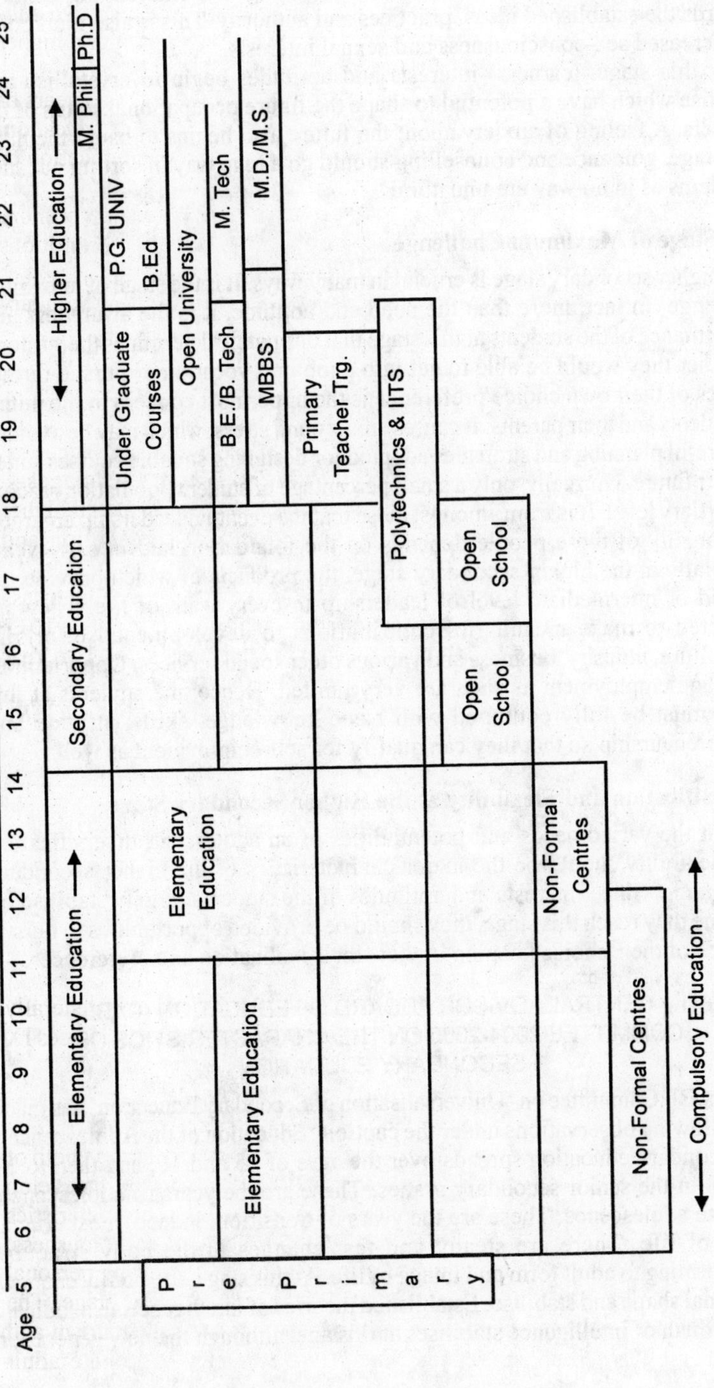

Fig. 1.1: Structure of Secondary Education in India in the Overall Structure of Education.

behaviour and roles, defiance, moral reasoning and challenging attitude towards the established ideas, practices and authority. This is also marked by an increased sex-consciousness and sexual interests.

At this stage, learners' interests and aptitudes begin to crystallise and stabilise which have a potential to shape the future occupational status of the learners. A feeling of anxiety about the future also begins to haunt them. At this stage, guidance and counselling should go a long way in sorting out such problems as in no way are unnatural.

The Stage of Maximum Challenge

The higher secondary stage is crucial in many ways. It is the stage of maximum challenge. In fact, more than the need and aptitude, it is the awareness and performance of the students at this stage that ultimately determines their future. Whether they would be able to get into a job or a vocation or pursue further studies of their own choice/preference is the uppermost concern in the minds of students and their parents. It causes anxiety and stress, which may be avoided by careful planning and strategies adopted for designing suitable courses suited to their future. Normally, only a small percentage of student population reaches the tertiary level. It is from amongst these that the eventual leadership emerges. The quality of these people depends on the foundation laid in early years especially at the higher secondary stage, the products of which provide the second or intermediate level of leadership in every walk of life. They are expected to make meaningful contributions to developmental efforts in agriculture, industry, business and various other social services. Opportunities for wage employment as such are very limited. Hence, the students at this stage must be fully equipped with basic knowledge, skills, attitude and entrepreneurship so that they can qualify for self-employment as well.

Diversification and Flexibility at the Higher Secondary Stage

To suit the varied needs and potentialities of an adolescent, diversification and flexibility should be the major characteristics of the higher secondary curriculum. Since interests and aptitudes of the students largely stabilise by the time they reach this stage, they should be provided opportunities to pursue courses of their choice keeping in view their inclination and preferences.

1.4 CENTRAL ADVISORY BOARD OF EDUCATION (CABE) COMMITTEE 2004-2005 ON THE CHARACTERISTICS OF SECONDARY EDUCATION

The CABE Committee on 'Universalisation of Secondary Education' has made the following observations under the caption 'Education of the Adolescence':

Secondary education spreads over the ages of 15 and 16, and then to 17 and 18 in the senior secondary grades. These are the years of adolescence, and late adolescence. These are the years of transition; indeed, most crucial years of life. There are steady and fast changes in the body structure transforming to adult form and image of life. At this stage, the bodily changes take final shape and stabilise. Established theories of intelligence also indicate that growth of intelligence stabilises at this age, although the new generation brain research indicates that because of continuous reorganisation of brain neurons, intelligence may continue to grow beyond this age. From the angle of multiple intelligence, this age is the most significant since the potentialities unfold faster and stabilise. The childhood voice cracks and takes the final shape (important for budding musicians); majority of the players show their final promise at this stage, and so on. This is also the stage of emotional transformation and maturity that swings between joy and trauma. Secondary education essentially has to be the education of the adolescence. Experiences in schooling have to be designed to be responsive to the needs of transition and stabilisation. Since large number of students are likely to transit from education to the world of work, it is also the stage of transition to work. Secondary education must foster skills of transition.

Though both boys and girls experience transition, there is a special case for girls and it needs special attention. Because of prejudices, taboos and social stigma, phase of transition for girls is more difficult. Child marriage, still prevalent in many parts of the country is a stumbling block for girls' education. Also, it will be necessary to develop a gender friendly curriculum.

2

Significant Developments in Secondary Education in India During the Pre-Independence Period

2.1 IMPORTANT DOCUMENTS AND POLICY DECISIONS HAVING BEARING ON SECONDARY EDUCATION

With a view to have a clear perspective of the secondary education system as it existed in India during the pre-independence period, it seems necessary to have a quick review of the various resolutions of the Government and reports of Committees and Commissions. In this context, following documents provide us useful information and insight:

- The Charter Act of 1813.
- Macaulay's Minute of 1835.
- Lord William Bentinck's Resolution (March 7, 1835).
- The Despatch of 1854.
- The Hunter Commission of 1882.
- The University Commission of 1902.
- Indian Universities Act of 1904.
- National Education Movement and National Council of Education of 1906.
- The Calcutta University Commission or Sadler Commission of 1917.
- The Hartog Committee of 1929.
- The Sapru Committee of 1934.
- The Abbot Wood Report of 1936-37.
- The Sargent Report of 1944.

2.2 CHARTER ACT OF 1813

The beginning of the system of education in India under the British rule may be traced back to the Clause 43 of the Charter Act of 1813, which governed the functioning of the East India Company. It is stated that a sum of not less than one lakh of rupees in each year shall be set apart and applied to the revival and improvement of literature and the encouragement of the learned natives of India and for the introduction and promotion of a knowledge of the sciences among the inhabitants of the British territories in India. The Act did not specify the term 'learned natives of India' and 'knowledge of the sciences'. It was silent on the medium in which knowledge was to be imparted. As a matter of fact the Clause 43 was of a general nature. It led to a lot of confusion and controversies. No action was taken on this issue till 1835.

2.3 MACAULAY'S MINUTE OF 1835: MACAULAY AS THE ARCHITECT OF THE BRITISH SYSTEM OF EDUCATION IN INDIA

Lord Macaulay (1800-1859) was an English essayist, historian and politician. He is known for his Minute on Education (1835), which was accepted by Lord William Bentinck, the Governor-General of India (1828-1835). He came to India as a Law Member of the Council of Governor-General on 10th June 1835. He was also appointed the Chairman of the Committee of Public Instructions of Bengal by Lord William Bentinck, the Governor-General. Macaulay was asked to give his opinion on the policy of education to be followed in India. He gave his views, which are known as Lord Macaulay's Minute. This minute was accepted by the Governor-General and it became the policy document on education.

Macaulay's Views on Indian and European Literature: Macaulay in his Minute made the following observations:

1. "A single shelf of a good European literature was worth the whole native literature of India and Arabia".
2. Regarding imparting instruction through the media of Arabic, Persian and Sanskrit, he wrote, "We are to teach false history, false astronomy, false medicine, because we find them in the company of false religion".
3. About the claim of English language, he stated, "It stands pre-eminent even among the languages of the West. ...It is likely to become language of commerce throughout the seas of the East".

Main Aim of Introducing English System of Education in India: Macaulay wrote in his Minute, "We must at present do our best to form a class of persons, Indian in blood and colour, but English in taste, in opinions, in morals and in intellect".

Macaulay's Arguments in Favour of English: Macaulay rejected the claims of Arabic and Sanskrit as against English, because he considered that English was better than either of them. His arguments in favour of English were:

1. It is the key to modern knowledge and is, therefore, more useful than Arabic or Sanskrit.
2. It stands pre-eminent even among the languages of the West. In India, English is the language sponsored by the ruling class. It is likely to become the language of commerce throughout the seas of the East.
3. It would bring about renaissance in India, just as Greek or Latin did in England or just as the languages of Western Europe did in civilising Russia.
4. The natives are desirous of being taught English and are not eager to learn Sanskrit or Arabic, and that demand of the latter was maintained artificially through, "bounty money".
5. It is possible to make the natives of this country good English scholars, and to that end our efforts ought to be directed.

2.4 LORD WILLIAM BENTINCK'S RESOLUTION (MARCH 7, 1835)

The Minute of Macaulay was accepted by Lord William Bentinck, the Governor-General of India (1825-1835). The resolution included the following policy decisions on education:

First: The great object of the British Government was the promotion of European literature and science among the natives of India.

Second: All the funds appropriate for the purpose of education would be best employed on English education alone.

2.5 FORMULATION OF THE EDUCATION POLICY IN INDIA

The Government Resolution of 1813, the Macaulay's Minute of 1835 and Lord William Bentinck's Resolution 1835, related to policy matters on education. They were not specifically concerned with any level of education, i.e. primary, secondary and higher.

Important changes in the type of education to be imparted to the youth of the country were introduced in the first half of the 19th century. The minute of Lord Macaulay and subsequent resolutions passed by the Government (in 1835) led to the establishment of schools teaching European literature and science. These schools became immediately popular because of the great interest shown in English education by some of the educated Indians and more particularly by leaders like Raja Ram Mohan Roy and others.

2.6 LORD HARDING'S PROCLAMATION (1844)

The education imparted in these schools became a passport for entrance into Government services. This was mainly due to the Proclamation issued by Lord Hardinge in 1844 that for service in public offices preference should be given to those who were educated in English schools. In consequence thereof education was imparted with the limited object of preparing pupils to join the service and not for life. In the new High Schools the standard of achievement in literary subjects was from the very beginning high but little or no progress was made in training the pupils in the practical side of science.

2.7 THE DESPATCH OF 1854 AND ITS IMPACT ON SECONDARY EDUCATION

By 1853 a number of problems had arisen which required immediate solution. As a result of an enquiry made, a despatch (known as 'Wood's Despatch') was issued in 1854 reviewing the development of education to date, and proposing certain new schemes for adoption. Sir Charles Wood was the President of the Board of Control in the Coalition Ministry of Earl of Aberdeen (1852-55) in England. Among these the following may be mentioned: Departments of Public Instruction under an important officer to be called the Director of Public Instruction were to be created; a scheme to establish Universities was to be formulated, whose functions were to hold examinations and confer degrees. It is interesting to note that the Despatch recommended that a number of high schools should be set up. The Despatch observed: "Our attention should now be directed to a consideration, if possible still more important and one which has been hitherto, we are bound to admit, too much neglected, namely, how useful and practical knowledge suited to every station of life, may be best conveyed to the great mass of the people who are utterly incapable of obtaining any education worthy of the name by their unaided effort; and we desire to see the active measures of Government more especially directed for the future to this object, for the attainment of which we are ready to sanction a considerable increase of expenditure".

Impact of Despatch

The Despatch included the following policy decisions which had a great bearing on Secondary Education in India:

1. Education should spread European knowledge.
2. English should be medium for higher education.
3. Anglo-Vernacular high schools should be set up at the district level.
4. A system of grant-in-aid should be introduced.
5. Vernacular languages should be encouraged at the school stage.
6. Vocational and technical schools should be set up.
7. Department of Public Instruction should be set up in each of the five provinces, under the charge of a Director.
8. Universities on the model of London University should be set up at Calcutta, Bombay and Madras.

The establishment of Universities in the year of 1857 had far-reaching consequences especially on the content, range and scope of Secondary Education. The Universities dominated secondary schools in every respect. Secondary Education instead of being a self-sufficient course-preparing students to enter life after completing the course became merely a step towards the Universities and University colleges with the result that schools could not function with an independent programme of their own.

Certain specific defects grew out of the system of secondary education in vogue during the years 1854-1882: the mother-tongue was completely neglected as a medium of instruction; nothing was done to train teachers for the secondary schools; and the course of study became too academic and unrelated to life mainly because there was no provision for vocational or technical courses. One further defect that had now taken concrete shape was that the Matriculation Examination began to dominate not only secondary education but even the education imparted in primary schools.

2.8 THE HUNTER COMMISSION (1882) AND ITS IMPACT ON SECONDARY EDUCATION

Important Recommendations of the Commission

In 1882 an Education Commission, known as the Hunter Commission, was appointed by the Government to report on the whole question of education in the country. The following instructions regarding Secondary education were given: "The Commission was directed to enquire into the quality and character of the instructions imparted in schools of this class. The great majority of those who prosecute beyond the primary stage will never go beyond the curriculum of the middle, or farthest of the high schools. It is therefore of the utmost importance that the education they received should be as thorough and sound as possible. There are grounds for doubting whether there is not, in some provinces at any rate, much room for improvement in this respect".

Since it was very costly for the Government to maintain secondary schools it was thought that the Government should take over the entire responsibility of primary education, leaving secondary education to private enterprise. The Commission recommended that "Secondary Education as far as possible, be provided on the grant-in-aid basis and that the Government should withdraw as early as possible from the direct management of Secondary Schools".

Important recommendations of the Commission were as under:

1. Primary education should be encouraged.
2. Grant-in-aid should be encouraged in the field of secondary education.
3. The Government should withdraw from secondary education.
4. There should be two type of courses at the secondary stage: (i) Technical leading to university education, (ii) Technical for commercial and vocational careers.
5. Female education should be encouraged.
6. Certificates should be awarded after school education.

Impact of the Commission's Report

The report of the Hunter Commission of 1882 is a valuable document, which not only gave an excellence survey of the position of secondary schools at that time, but made certain fundamental recommendations concerning the type of education to be given at this stage. It anticipated what has come to be recognised later as diversified courses of instruction in the secondary stage of education. With regard to vocational and technical education, the Commission recommended that in a particular class of high school there should be two avenues, one leading to the entrance examination of the University and the other of a more practical character intended to fit the youth for commercial, vocational or non-literary pursuits. In spite of such specific recommendations, neither the public nor the Government seem to have appreciated the value of the suggestions, with the result that the recommendations were practically ignored.

During the period 1882-1902, there was considerable expansion in the field of secondary education. It was due partly to the enthusiasm of private enterprise and partly to the system of grant-in-aid. The unwieldy expansion without proper consolidation led to certain obvious defects.

2.9 THE UNIVERSITY COMMISSION OF 1902 AND ITS IMPACT ON SECONDARY EDUCATION

In 1902 a University Commission was appointed, the main purpose of which however, was to review the position of the Universities regarding the higher grades of examination. As a result of the recommendations of this Commission, secondary education came to be even more under the domination of the Universities. Under the Indian Universities Act of 1904 schools had to be recognised by the Universities, and rules and regulations were framed for this purpose.

Creation of Boards of Secondary Education

The feeling that the Universities were dominating secondary education and that an attempt should be made to see that secondary education was conducted independently of the universities led to the creation, in certain States, of Boards of Secondary Education which were responsible for laying down syllabuses and for conducting examinations at the school final stage. The Secondary School Leaving Certificate was expected to furnish full information as to the progress of the pupil during the whole period of the school course as well as in the Public Examination conducted at the end of that course. On the basis of these records it was left to employers and to principals of University colleges to entertain them in service or to admit them to college for such courses of study as in the opinion of the Principals concerned the pupils were best fitted.

2.10 NATIONAL EDUCATION MOVEMENT AND NATIONAL COUNCIL OF EDUCATION (1906)

Political developments and especially the partition of Bengal (1905) gave impetus to National Education Movement.

The National Council of Education, registered in 1906, was devoted to the spread education on national lines. Its scheme of studies included primary stage (extending over three yeas), secondary stage—lower (extending over five yeas), secondary stage—upper (extending over two years) and collegiate stage (excluding over four years).

2.11 THE CALCUTTA UNIVERSITY COMMISSION OR THE SADLER COMMISSION OF 1917 AND ITS IMPACT ON SECONDARY EDUCATION

Observations and Recommendations

The next important stage was the appointment of the Calcutta University Commission in 1917 under the chairmanship of the late Sir Michael Sadler. This Commission went into the question of secondary education and held the view that the improvement of secondary education was essential for the improvement of university education. It observed, "No satisfactory reorganisation of university system will be possible until a radical reorganisation of the system of secondary education upon which university on system depends is carried into effect." The Commission made certain important recommendations among which were the following:

1. The school course should be of 12 years.
2. Diversified courses should be provided at the secondary stage.
3. The medium of instruction at the school stage should be the mother tongue.
4. A Board of Secondary and Intermediate Education consisting of the representatives of Government, University, high schools and intermediate colleges to be established and entrusted with the administration and control of Secondary Education.
5. The dividing line between the University and Secondary courses is more properly to be drawn at the Intermediate examination than at the Matriculation.
6. Government should, therefore, create a new type of institutions called the intermediate colleges which would provide for instruction in Arts, Science,

Medicine, Engineering, Teaching etc.; these colleges might either be run as independent institutions or might be attached to selected high schools.

7. The admission test for universities should be the passing of the Intermediate Examination.

Evaluation of the Report

Though the Sadler Commission was appointed to enquire into the conditions of the Calcutta University and to make recommendations, the report was so comprehensive that many of the universities in India began to implement the suggestions contained therein. For the first time a Commission had recommended the attachment of intermediate classes to the high schools and the setting up of a Board of Education to control High School and Intermediate Education.

During the subsequent period there was a great expansion of secondary education and the number of secondary schools began to increase both in rural and urban areas largely owing to the interest evinced by the public and the generous donations of individuals and institutions.

But problems relating to the training of teachers, their salaries, and conditions of service were left unsolved. The unprecedented expansion of the academic type of secondary schools resulted in a failure to provide for technical schools or for bifurcated courses of studies in high schools.

2.12 THE HARTOG COMMITTEE 1929 AND ITS IMPACT ON SECONDARY EDUCATION

In 1929, as auxiliary to the Indian Statutory Commission, a Committee was appointed known as the Hartog Committee, to review the position of education in the country. In the opinion of this Committee, Matriculation examination of the University still dominated the whole of the secondary course. In order to obviate this defect, the Committee recommended that a large number of pupils intending to follow certain avocations should stop at the middle school stage. There should be "more diversified curricula in the schools". The Committee also recommended "diversion of more boys to industrial and commercial careers at the end of the middle stage, preparatory to special instruction in technical and industrial schools". It is interesting to note that the Committee reviewed the position of the training of teachers and the service conditions of secondary school teachers and remarked "that enough cannot be done in the short space of nine months which is all that is usually available, to uproot the old methods of teaching to which many of the students are accustomed". The best pupils were not attracted to the teaching profession, the Committee held, because the best type of men cannot be attracted to the profession so long as the general conditions remain unsatisfactory and "only too frequently the teachers have no heart in their work", and "in no province is the pay of the teacher sufficient to give him the status which his work demands".

2.13 THE SAPRU COMMITTEE OF 1934 AND ITS IMPACT ON SECONDARY EDUCATION

The Sapru Committee appointed in 1934 by the U.P. Government which enquired into the causes of unemployment in Uttar Pradesh (United Provinces) came to the conclusion that much of the unrest was primarily due to mass unemployment and that the system of education commonly prevalent prepared pupils only for examinations and degrees and not for an avocation in life. "In a situation like this, the Committee remarked, "the real remedy is to provide diversified courses of study at the secondary stage and to make that stage more practical and complete in itself and more closely related to the vocational requirements of different types of students. At the secondary stage, side by side with the general course leading to the University, there should be parallel courses offering instruction in technical, commercial, industrial and other vocational subjects".

The main suggestions made by the Committee were—

1. Diversified courses at the secondary stage should be introduced—one of these courses leading to the university degree.
2. The intermediate stage be abolished and the secondary stage be extended by one year; the secondary stage to consist of six years to be divided into two, the higher and lower, each covering a period of three yeas, the whole course thus covering 11 years, 5 for the primary and six for the secondary the general course to be of 8 years, i.e. up to the lower secondary course.
3. Vocational training and education should begin after the lower secondary stage.
4. The Degree course at the university should extend over a period of three years.

2.14 THE ABBOT-WOOD REPORT (1936-37) AND ITS IMPACT ON SECONDARY EDUCATION

In 1936-37, two expert advisers, Messrs. Abbot and Wood were invited to advise the Government "on certain problems of educational reorganisation and particularly on problems of vocational education". One of the basic reasons for instituting this inquiry was "the fact that a large number of University graduates were not securing employment of a kind for which their education qualified them". The terms of reference included:

"(1) Whether any vocational or practical training should be imparted in primary, secondary and higher secondary schools, and if so what should be its nature and extent?

(2) Whether the technical or vocational institutions already in existence can be improved and whether new institutions for vocational or technical training would be required, and if so, to suggest the type of institutions required for the purpose; the stage at which divergence from the ordinary secondary schools (lower or higher secondary) to such schools should be effected; and the means to be adopted for effecting such diversion".

The report of Mesrs. Abbott and Wood suggested a complete hierarchy of vocational institutions parallel with the hierarchy of institutions imparting general education.

One important result of their recommendations has been that "a new type of technical institution called the Polytechnic came into existence". The provinces also started technical, commercial or agricultural high schools conducting non-literary courses.

2.15 THE SARGENT REPORT 1944 AND ITS IMPACT ON SECONDARY EDUCATION

Major Recommendations

In 1944, the Central Advisory Board of Education which is an all-India advisory body set up by the Government of India, submitted a comprehensive report on Post-War Educational Development containing certain important recommendations. The report, more popularly known as the Sargent Report after Sir John Sargent who was Educational Adviser to the Government of India, visualised a system of universal, compulsory and free education for all boys and girls between the ages of 6 and 14, the Senior Basic or the Middle School being the final stage in the school career of majority of the future citizens. It was also recommended by this Committee that at the Middle School stage, provision should be made for a variety of courses extending over a period of five years after the age of 11. These courses while preserving an essentially cultural character should be designed to prepare the pupils for entry into industrial and the commercial occupations as well as into the universities. It was recommended that the High School course should cover 6 years, the normal age of admission being 11 years and that the High Schools should be of two main types (a) academic, and (b) technical. The objective of both should be to provide a good all-round education combined with some preparation in the latter stages for the careers, which pupils will pursue on leaving schools.

Recommendations of the Sargent Report relating to secondary education may be summarised as under:

1. The normal age for admission to secondary/high stage should be 11 years.
2. The duration of high schools should be of six years.
3. The admission to high schools should be selective.
4. There should be two types of high schools:
   (i) Academic high schools providing courses related to arts and sciences.
   (ii) Technical high schools providing courses related to applied sciences and commerce.
5. Mother tongue (Hindustani) should be the medium of instruction.
6. Girls education should be recommended.
7. Scholarships should be provided on a large school.
8. The curriculum should be flexible.
9. Out of a total annual expenditure of Rs. 312, 60 lakhs, an expenditure of Rs. 7,900 was meant for high school education.

Evaluation

The Report did not make any impact on education on account of the financial constraints developed as a huge amount was incurred during the Second World War. Besides the political situation in India was very fluid as negotiations for independence of the country were in full swing.

2.16 EXPANSION OF SECONDARY EDUCATION

Table 2.1: Enrolment by Stages (1855-56 to 1946-47)

	1855-56	*1901-02*	*1921-22*	*1946-47*
1. University				
(i) Total	4,355	23,007	58,837	237,546
(ii) Girls	N.A.	264	1,529	23,207
2. Secondary Stage:				
(i) Total	33,801	82,312	218,606	370,812
(ii) Girls	N.A.	1,677	5,818	83,270
3. Middle School Stage:				
(i) Total	—	1,080,670	385,372	2,036,109
(ii) Girls	—	8,133	24,655	281,606
4. Primary School Stage:				
(i) Total	885,624	3,564,122	6,404,200	14,105,418
(ii) Girls	—	380,282	1,297,643	3,728,793
5. Total Enrolment of All Stages:				
(i) Total	923,780	3,886,493	7,207,308	17,750,263
(ii) Girls	N.A.	393,161	1,340,842	4,156,742

Sources: (1) Basu, Aparna, *Essays in the History of Indian Education*, 1981.

(2) Nurullah and Naik in '*A Students' History of Education in India*' 1949 gives the number of universities as 19 with 241,794 students.

(3) The Education Commission 1964-66 puts the number of universities at 20.

Table 2.2: Number of Secondary Schools, Number of Pupils in Secondary Schools and Cost Per Pupil in Secondary School (1870-71 to 1946-47)

Year	*No. of Secondary Schools*	*No. of Pupils in Secondary Schools*	*Cost Per Pupil in Secondary School (in Rs.)*
1870-71	464	64,873	NA
1881-82	512	65,477	28.8
1891-92	831	172,463	NA
1896-97	930	192,995	35.0
1901-02	1,170	262,859	30.3
1906-07	1,277	298,276	31.5
1911-12	1,354	407,765	32.6
1916-17	1,750	572,261	36.9
1921-22	2,248	594,910	54.0
1926-27	2,687	794,201	55.2
1931-32	3,125	955,051	54.8
1936-37	8,652	1,132,713	52.5
1941-42	4,035	1,333,948	48.7
1946-47	3,659	1,571,541	56.8

Source: NCERT, *The Fourth Indian Yearbook of Education: Secondary Education*, NCERT, New Delhi, 1973.

Table 2.3: Progress of Girls Education in India at the Secondary Stage (1901-02 to 1946-47)

Year	*No. of Secondary Schools for Girls*	*No. of Girls Enrolled in Secondary Schools*		
		For Boys	*For Girls*	*Total*
1901-02	100	647	9,662	10,309
1906-07	112	1,200	10,685	11,885
1911-12	135	—	—	—
1916-17	166	2,942	22,006	24,948
1921-22	170	4,668	32,030	36,698
1931-32	324	17,660	74,938	92,598
1936-37	410	32,708	101,582	1,34,290
1941-42	539	30,894	1,36,645	1,67,539
1946-47	586	53,729	1,74,720	2,28,449

Sources: *The Fourth Indian Yearbook of Education*, 1973.

2.17 AN OVERVIEW OF THE SYSTEM OF SECONDARY EDUCATION IN INDIA DURING THE BRITISH PERIOD

For having a clear understanding of the State of Secondary Education during the British period in India, we may have a quick look at the merits and demerits of the entire system of education. These, by and large, are applicable to secondary education also. A perusal of Tables 2.2 and 2.3 indicates that expansion of secondary education was very slow and extremely inadequate.

Merits of the System of Secondary Education

1. The system promoted Western knowledge and science among the Indians, which broadened their outlook in life.
2. English education brought about a reawakening and a desire among the people of India to recapture their past glory.
3. Contact with Western thought helped to develop democratic and liberal ideas among the Indians.
4. English education rekindled in the people the spirit of nationalism. By and large, national movement was led by leaders who had received their education through the English medium and were well-versed with Western political thoughts.
5. A uniform system of education through English medium educational institutions brought the people of different provinces together and they waged the freedom struggle.

Demerits of the System of Secondary Education

1. It was an urban system of education in a rural country.
2. English dominated the curriculum and other aspects of education.
3. System was too literary and bookish.
4. Education system was examination-oriented.
5. It stressed knowledge aspects only and ignored other aspects of education.

6. It emphasised rote-memory.
7. It neglected technical and vocational education.
8. It was a single-track system that emphasised humanities.
9. It was unplanned.
10. It was very expensive.
11. It was not in accordance with the economic and social needs of India.
12. It was confined to a few sections of the society.
13. It was beyond the reach of common man.
14. Co-curricular activities were neglected.
15. It neglected girl's eduation.
16. It created a gulf between the English educated upper and middle classes and the masses.
17. It neglected democratic values.

In the words of Gandhiji, "The present system of education does not meet the requirements of the country in any shape or form. English has created a permanent bar between the highly educated few and the uneducated many. The excessive importance given to English has cast upon the educated classes a burden, which has maimed them mentally for life and made them strangers in their own land. Absence of vocational training has made the educated class almost unfit for productive work and harmed them physically. Money spent on primary education is a waste of expenditure".

Summing Up

In the words of University Education Commission (1948-49), "Our secondary education remains the weakest link in our educational machinery and needs urgent reforms".

3

Secondary Education Commission (1952-53)

3.1 PATTERN OF EDUCATION INCLUDING SECONDARY EDUCATION AS IT EXISTED AT THE TIME OF THE APPOINTMENT OF THE SECONDARY EDUCATION COMMISSION

There was wide variation in the pattern of education in different States not only with regard to the different stages of education but also with regard to the particular types of institutions imparting education at each of the stages.

Broadly speaking, different types of educational institutions at the various stages were as under:

Pre-Primary Stage

At the pre-primary stage, Nursery Schools of various types existed in some States but on a very small scale. At this stage, the child was introduced to the joy of learning through companionship and recreational activities and it was slowly guided in proper habits of life, cleanliness and healthy modes of living as well as in the cultivation of social habits so necessary later for a community life. In several States there were a few such nursery schools run by private organisations or by missions; and where they had been so established, they had done good work. The age of admission to Nursery Schools varied: in some States it was between 3 and 5 in some, children were trained up to the age of 7.

Primary and Post-Primary Stage

This stage extended in some States to 4 years and in others to 5 years, the age period being 6 or 7 to 10 or 11. Under the system of Basic Education, the States had introduced Junior Basic Schools corresponding to the primary schools, but their number was still very small in proportion to the total number of primary schools in the different States.

Higher Elementary Schools

In a few States, a type of institution known as the Higher Elementary or Vernacular Middle School existed where all subjects were taught through the mother tongue and no other language was taught. These schools catered to the students of the post-primary stage, the duration of the course being three years. The number of such schools was on the decline.

Secondary Schools

At the Secondary School level, there were two divisions, the Junior and the Senior. The junior stage of secondary schools was known in some cases as middle schools or lower secondary schools and in some as the Senior Basic Schools. It covered a period varying in different areas, between 3 and 4 yeas. In the majority of States, the pattern was one of three years.

High Schools corresponded to the senior school stage of secondary schools. In the large majority of cases this stage extended over a period of three years. In a few States the High School period was limited to two years, the Middle School being of four years' duration.

Higher Secondary Schools

The Higher Secondary School was the latest type of institution, where the education imparted was in some cases of 3 years, and in some cases 4 years, depending upon the period of study required for the high schools in the State. The higher secondary schools had been formed by the addition of one year, which was taken from the Intermediate stage of the University.

Higher Education

At the University level, the degree course was generally of four years, comprising two years of Intermediate and two years of the degree course. In Delhi State, however, where the Higher Secondary Schools had been established, the degree stage was of three years' duration, the Intermediate having been abolished. It was of interest to note that in some other States also, like Mysore and Travancore, the experiment of a three-year degree course has been tried, but owing largely to lack of cooperation and coordination from their universities, the experiment could not be continued.

Intermediate Colleges

Consequent upon the recommendations of the Sadler Commission, an impetus was given to the starting of Intermediate colleges more particularly in certain States in the North. These colleges had a two-year course and came under the purview of the Board of Secondary an Intermediate Education and not under the control of the Universities. In other States, however, the four-year degree course was divided into two separate units, one for the Intermediate standard and the other for the degree standard. While the great majority of colleges had a four-year course, the recent increase in the number of students seeking admission to university courses of study after their school final stage had led to the starting of Intermediate colleges of two years' duration in many States.

3.2 BACKGROUND TO THE APPOINTMENT OF THE SECONDARY EDUCATION COMMISSION (1952-53)

Recommendations of the Central Advisory Board of Education

The Central Advisory Board of Education at its 14th meeting held in January, 1948, considered the question of secondary education in the country. In view of its importance in the educational system in the country, the Board resolved that a Committee be appointed by the Government of India to:

(a) review the present position of Secondary Education in India, and
(b) make recommendations in regard to the various problems related thereto.

This resolution was endorsed by the All India Education Conference convened by the Hon'ble Minister of Education in January 1948. In pursuance of these recommendations, the Government of India appointed a Committee under the Chairmanship of Dr. Tara Chand, the then Educational Adviser to the Government of India. This Committee made some important recommendations on different aspects of secondary education. The Report of this Committee was further considered by the Central Advisory Board of Education at its 15th meeting held at Allahabad in 1949 when it was resolved that the Government of India be requested to appoint a Commission for Secondary Education to which the questions raised by some of the conclusions drawn in the Report be referred and that it should, in addition to these items, go into the wider question of the aim, objective and purpose of secondary education and the relation of Secondary Education to Basic and University Education. The Board again at its meeting held in January, 1951, reiterated its conviction that the reorganisation of secondary education in the country was of such vital importance that the Government of India should appoint a Commission at an early date.

University Education Commission of 1948

In the meantime in pursuance of the recommendations of the Central Advisory Board of Education and also of the Inter-University Board, the Government of India appointed a University Education Commission in 1948 under the Chairmanship of Dr. S. Radhakrishnan. The Commission which had to report primarily on University Education in India had necessarily to review the position of Secondary Education as well and it made certain notable suggestions. The Commission recommended that the standard of admission to University courses should correspond to that of the present Intermediate examination, i.e. after 12 years of the study at School and Intermediate College. The Commission thought it unfortunate that neither the public or the Government had realised the importance of Intermediate colleges in the Indian educational system, and remarked that "our Secondary Education remains the weakest link in our educational machinery and needs urgent reforms.

Framing of the Constitution and Aspirations of the Society

The Constitution of India had come into force on January 26, 1950. Accordingly, educational needs had to be studied in this context.

Significance of Secondary Education

It is the secondary school that supplies teachers to the primary schools and students to the universities. An inefficient system of secondary education is bound to affect adversely the quality of education at all stages.

It was felt that one of the major defects of the prevailing system of secondary education was its unilinear and predominantly academic character. The need for the reorganisation of secondary education with diversified courses had become more urgent as a result of acceptance by the Government of Basic Education as the pattern of education at the elementary stage. There had been no comprehensive examination of the problems pertaining to secondary education, while the problems of elementary and university education had been surveyed and steps taken to improve.

3.3 APPOINTMENT OF THE SECONDARY EDUCATION COMMISSION (1952-53)

In view of above considerations, the Government of India set up the Secondary Education Commission by Resolution dated 23rd September, 1952. The Commission was inaugurated on October 6, 1952. It submitted its report in June 1953.

Members of the Commission

The Commission consisted of 9 members including the Chairman, Dr. A. Lakshmanaswami Mudaliar, Vice-Chancellor, Madras University and A.N. Basu, Principal, Central Institute of Education, Delhi, was its Member-Secretary. Two foreign educators, namely, Principal John Christie, Jesus College, Oxford (U.K.) and Dr. Kenneth Rast Williams, Associate Director, Southern Regional Educational Board, Atlanta (USA) were also members of the Commission. Sixteen eminent educationists were co-opted members.

3.4 TERMS OF REFERENCE

Under the terms of reference, the Commission was asked:

"(a) to enquire into and report on the present position of Secondary Education in India in all its aspects; and

(b) suggest measures for its reorganisation and improvement with particular reference to:
   - (i) the aims, organisation and content of Secondary education;
   - (ii) its relationship to Primary, Basic and Higher education;
   - (iii) the inter-relation of Secondary Schools of different types;
   - (iv) other allied problems.

so that a sound and reasonable uniform system of Secondary Education suited to our needs and resources may be provided for the whole country".

3.5 FUNCTIONING OF THE COMMISSION

The Commission interviewed a large number of educationists, members of universities, representatives of teachers' organisations, representatives of managements, high officials of the Department of Education, Ministers of the States and Centre and leading representatives of the public.

The Commission issued a Questionnaire covering a wide field of enquiry. It consisted of 8 sections, which had a number of questions:

1. Aims of education.

2. Organisation.
3. Administration and supervision.
4. Curriculum.
5. Methods of instruction.
6. Teachers and conditions of service.
7. Finances.

Contents of the Report

The Report is divided into 15 Chapters, Conclusion, Summary of Recommendations and 10 Appendices.

3.6 MAJOR RECOMMENDATIONS OF THE COMMISSION

I. *Needs, Aims and Objectives of Secondary Education*: The Commission took note of the changed political, social and economic conditions of the country and accordingly formulated the following main objectives of secondary education:
   1. Development of democratic citizenship.
   2. Improvement of vocational efficiency.
   3. Development of personality.
   4. Development of qualities for leadership.

II. *Duration of Secondary Education*: Under the new organisational structure, education should commence after a four or five years' period of Primary or Junior Basic Education and should include: (a) the Middle or Senior Basic or Junior Secondary Stage of 3 years, and (b) Higher Secondary stage of 4 years.

III. *Multi-purpose Schools and Vocational Schools*:
   1. Multi-purpose schools should be established wherever possible to provide varied courses of interest to students with diverse aims, aptitudes and abilities.
   2. Those who have successfully completed such course should be given opportunities to take up higher specialised courses in polytechnics or technological institutions.

IV. *Diversified Curriculum*: There should be seven groups out of which students could select anyone besides languages and core curriculum.

V. *Guidance and Counselling*: The Commission suggested a comprehensive programme for guidance and counselling at the secondary stage.

VI. *Technical Schools*: Technical Schools should be started in large numbers either separately or as a part of multi-purpose schools.

VII. *Agricultural Schools*: The Commission observed that as agriculture is the most important industry, it must receive its due attention.

VIII. *Other Types of Schools*:
   1. Public schools should continue to exist for the present and the pattern of education given in them should be brought into reasonable conformity with the general pattern of national education.

2. A number of residential schools should be established, more particularly in certain rural areas.
3. A large number of schools should be established to meet the needs of handicapped children.

IX. *Co-education*:

1. While no distinction need be made between education imparted to boys and girls, special facilities for the study of home science should be made available in all girls' schools and co-education of mixed schools.
2. Efforts should be made by State Governments to open separate schools for girls wherever there is demand for them.

X. *Textbooks*:

1. With a view to improving the quality of textbooks prescribed, a high power Textbooks Committee should be constituted.
2. The Textbooks Committee should lay down clear criteria for the type of paper, illustration, printing and format of the books.
3. A single textbook should not be prescribed for every subject of study, but a reasonable number of books which satisfy the standards laid down should be recommended leaving the choice to the schools concerned. In the case of languages, however, definite textbooks should be prescribed for each class to ensure proper gradation.
4. No book prescribed as a textbook or as a book for general study should contain any passage or statement which might offend the religious or social susceptibilities of any section of the community or might indoctrinate the minds of the young students with particular political or religious ideologies.
5. Frequent changes in textbooks and books prescribed for study should be discouraged.

XI. *Dynamic Methods of Teaching*:

1. The methods of teaching in schools should aim not merely at imparting of knowledge in an efficient manner, but also at inculcating desirable values and proper attitudes and habits of work in the students.
2. The emphasis in teaching should shift from verbalism and memorisation to learning through purposeful, concrete and realistic situation and, for this purpose, the principles of 'Activity Method' and 'Project Method' should be assimilated in school practice.
3. In the teaching of all subjects special stress should be placed on clear thinking and expression both in speech and writing.
4. A well thought-out attempt should be made to adopt methods of instruction to the needs of individual students as much as possible so that dull, average and bright students may all have a chance to progress at their own pace.
5. Students should be given adequate opportunity to work in groups and to carry out-group projects so as to develop in them the qualities necessary for group life and cooperative work.

6. Every Secondary School should have a well-equipped school library, class libraries and subject libraries should also be utilised.

XII. *Discipline*:

1. The education of character should be envisaged as the responsibility of all teachers.
2. In order to promote discipline, personal contact between the teacher and the pupils should be strengthened; self-government in the form of house system with perfects or monitors and student councils, whose responsibility will be to draw up a code of conduct and enforce its observance, should be introduced in all schools.

XIII. *Religious and Moral Instruction*: Religious instruction may be given in schools only on a voluntary basis outside the regular school hours; such instruction being confined to the children of the particular faith concerned and given with the consent of the parties and the managements.

XIV. *Extra-curricular Activities*: Extra-curricular activities should form an integral part of education imparted in the school and all teachers should devote a definite time to such activities.

XV. *Guidance and Counselling in Secondary Schools*: Educational guidance should receive much greater attention on the part of the educational authorities. The services of trained guidance officers and career masters should be gradually made available to all schools.

XVI. *Health Education*: A properly organised school medical service should be built up in all States. A thorough medical examination of all pupils and necessary follow-up treatment where necessary should be carried out in all schools.

XVII. *Physical Education*:

1. All teachers below the age of 40 actively participate in many of the physical activities of students and thus make them a lively part of the school programme.
2. Full records of physical activities of the students must be maintained.

XVIII. *A New Approach to Examination and Evaluation*: The number of examinations should be reduced and the element of subjectivity in the essay-type tests should be minimised by introducing objective tests. In the final assessment of the pupils due credit should be given to the internal tests and the school records of the pupils. The system of symbolic rather than numerical marking should be adopted. There should be only one public examination at the completion of the secondary school course.

XIX. *Improvement of the Teaching Personnel*:

1. The normal period of probation for a trained teacher should be one year.
2. The teachers possessing the qualifications and performing the same type of work should be treated at par in the matter of grades of salary irrespective of the type of institution in which they are working.

3. The system of triple benefit scheme, pension-cum-provident fund-cum-insurance should be introduced in all States.
4. Arbitration Boards of Committees should be established to look into the appeals and grievances of teachers.
5. The age of retirement in the case of physically fit and competent teachers may be extended to 60 with the approval of the Director of Education.
6. The children of teachers should be given free education throughout the school stage.
7. Through a system of cooperative house building societies teachers should be provided with quarters so as to enable them to live near the school.
8. The practice of private tuitions by teachers should be abolished.

XX. *Teacher Training*:

1. There should be only two types of institutions for teacher training:
   (i) For those who have taken the School Leaving Certificate or Higher Secondary School Leaving Certificate; for them the period of training should be two years; and
   (ii) For graduates for whom the training may, for the present, be of one academic year, but extended as a long-term programme to two academic years.
2. During the period of training all the student-teachers should be given suitable stipend by the State.
3. All Training Colleges should provide adequate residential facilities.

XXI. *Organisation and Administration*:

1. There should be a Board of Secondary Education consisting of not more than 25 members with the Director of Education as its Chairman to deal with all matters of education at the secondary stage and to lay down general policies. A Sub-Committee of the Board should deal with the conduct of examinations.
2. State Advisory Boards should be constituted in each State to advise the Department of Education on all matters pertaining to education.

XXII. *Inspection of Schools*:

1. The true role of an Inspector should be to study the problems of school and view them comprehensively in the context of educational objectives, to formulate suggestion for improvement and help the teachers to carry out his advice and recommendations. The Commission prepared the term 'Educational Adviser'.
2. In addition to direct recruitment, Inspectors should also be drawn from (i) teachers of ten years' experience, (ii) headmasters of High Schools, and (iii) duly qualified staff of Training Colleges who may be allowed to work as such for a period of three to five years.

XXIII. *Management of Schools*:

1. The Managing Boards of all schools should be registered and should consist of a limited number of persons with the Headmaster as an ex-officio member.
2. No member of the Managing Board should directly or indirectly interfere with the internal administration of the school.

XXIV. *School Building and Equipment*:

1. The open spaces available in cities must be conserved to be utilised as playground by groups of schools.
2. Normally, in designing buildings for schools, care should be taken to see that an area of not less than 10 sq. ft. is provided per student in the classroom.
3. The optimum number of boys to be admitted to any class should be 30 and the maximum should not in any case exceed 40; the optimum number in the whole school should be 500 while the maximum should not exceed 750.

XXV. *Hours of Working and Vacation*:

1. As a rule the total number of working days in a school should not be less than two hundred, the working hours per week should be at least thirty-five periods of about forty-five minutes each; the schools should work regularly for six days in the week. One of the days being a half day when the teachers and students might meet informally and work together on various extra-curricular and social projects.
2. Normally, during the year there should be a summer vacation of two months and two breaks of ten to fifteen days at suitable periods during the year.

XXVI. *Finance*:

1. A cess called the Industrial Education Cess be levied, the amount collected to be utilised for the furtherance of technical and vocational education at the secondary stage.
2. The Centre should assume certain amount of direct responsibility for the contemplated reorganisation of secondary education and give financial aid for the purpose.

XXVII. *The Education of Character*: "We should like to emphasise, as strongly as we can, the basic principle that 'character is forged on the anvil of action'—of every kind of action, academic, social, manual or moral—and the way in which the student performs his manifold duties in school or at home leaves an indelible impression on him. This would require the setting before him of high standards of work and conduct—both personal and impersonal—and creating the desire to approximate to those standards. It would also call for the rejection of any work—and depreciation of any form of behaviour—that falls below the standard that may be expected from the particular student concerned. If all school work and activities are made psychologically interesting and exacting—in the sense of challenging the full powers of the adolescents—and if they are trained to take them up in the right spirit, the most congenial conditions will be created for the right training of character".

3.7 EVALUATION OF THE REPORT AND ITS IMPACT

Impact of the Report. A 'Discussion Paper' of the Education Commission (1964-66), observed that the impact of the recommendations of the Secondary Education Commission (1952-53) during the period 1953-1964, had been very little and the progress in the implementation of the recommendations was hardly visible. It remarked, "In fact, it may be said that the major defects pointed out by the commission still persist in a majority of schools today. The education imparted in these institutions continues to be more or less isolated from life. The curriculum is still, generally speaking, narrow and one-sided and not designed to develop the full personality of adolescents. The methods of teaching are by and large dreary and unimaginative and do not aim at inculcating desirable values and proper attitudes and habits of work among the students".

It is observed that in 1963-66, out of nearly 22,600 Secondary Schools, there were only about 2000 multipurpose schools.

Merits

First: The Commission's suggestions regarding the levy of 'Industrial Educational Cess' was rightly conceived.

Second: The Commission rightly laid stress upon the need of providing higher secondary education according to 3 A's, i.e. Age, Ability and Aptitude.

Third: The Commission underlined the need for providing educational and vocationai guidance to students.

Fourth: The Commission's suggestion for laying emphasis on agricultural education was very valuable.

Fifth: The Commission fully realised the need for using dynamic and progressive methods of education.

Sixth: The Commission's concept of curriculum including subjects, experiments and co-curricular activities was quite modern.

Seventh: The Commission made significant recommendations regarding the necessity of raising the economic and social status of teachers.

Eighth: Recommendations of the Commission on improving the system of examination were very valuable. Now objective types of tests have become an integral part of evaluation.

Cumulative records cards are increasingly being used.

Ninth: Several tax exemption were suggested for the promotion of educational facilities.

Tenth: Recommendations on the thorough medical check-up was quite timely.

Shortcomings and Drawbacks of the Report

Before discussing the shortcomings of the recommendations, a few words may be said regarding the composition of the Secondary Education Commission. The Commission was male-dominated. There was only one representative of women. No representation to agriculture/commerce and trade was given. The most glaring defect was the omission of any educator associated with the running of state-run or state-aided schools. Representation of any Education Board was also missing. Thus the Commission's composition was lop-sided and university/higher education dominated.

Following were the major shortcomings of the recommendations:

1. *No Programme of Action*: The Commission did not suggest either any long term or short term plan for the implementation of recommendations.

2. *No Financial Estimates*: The Commission lamented on the non-implementation of the recommendations of the earlier Education Commission. It observed, "It has been pointed out…the recommendations of the previous Commissions have not been given effect to largely because the necessary financial resources could not be made available either by the State or by the Centre". It is an irony of fate that the recommendations of this Commission also met the same fate. The Secondary Education Commission itself did not give thought to the financial aspect of the various reforms.

3. *Vague Recommendations on the Structure of Secondary Education*: It has used several terms like primary school stage, middle school stage, high school stage, and secondary school stage without defining each stage.

4. *No Clear-cut Duration of the School Course*: The Commission's recommendations use the term 'either' several times while mentioning the duration of each stage. This led to a good deal of confusion.

5. *Post-Graduate Qualifications of Teachers*: The Commission suggested that the minimum qualification required for teaching in the last two years of the higher secondary school should be an M.A. degree or a first class B.A. degree with a degree in teaching. An adequate number of qualified post-graduate teachers were not readily available.

6. *Core Subjects*: The introduction of core-subjects like crafts and general science in the curriculum of the higher secondary school created further difficulties regarding staff requirements.

7. *Difficulties in Upgrading Higher Secondary Schools*: The serious difficulties in the process of implementing the recommendations of establishing multipurpose schools could not be foreseen with the result that out of 22,581 higher secondary schools in 1963-64, there were only 2,000 multipurpose schools. Subsequently their number began to dwindle. Thus we find that schools remained as bookish and stereotype as at the time of the recommendations of the Secondary Education Commission.

8. *Unpopularity of Multipurpose Schools*: The multipurpose schools benefited neither the school leavers nor the seekers of higher education.

9. *Expansion without Quality*: A close scrutiny of the implementation of the recommendations of the Commission reveals that the quantitative expansion of secondary education had not been simultaneously accompanied by qualitative improvement.

10. *Vague Recommendations on Vocational Education*: The Commission did not suggest a clear-cut path of vocationalised education. In no way education facilitated the task of finding suitable manpower for various sectors of development of industries and other services.

11. *Lack of Coordination*: The Commission did not suggest methods of coordination between growth of economy, manpower needs, employment opportunities and the output of secondary schools.

12. *No Definite Guidelines for Conversion of Schools*: The selection of high schools for conversion into higher secondary schools was to be governed by strict and carefully defined conditions. The Commission's Report stated that only those schools would develop into efficient higher secondary institutions which satisfied definite criteria prescribed regarding accommodation, equipment, qualification of the staff, salaries and grades and adequate finances, and that such conditions had to be fulfilled scrupulously before the schools were recognised as higher secondary schools. The establishment of higher secondary schools in several areas unfortunately became a matter of prestige for the people concerned. Social and political pressures were sometimes used for getting the necessary conversion and recognition for their institutions. This resulted in the upgrading of a number of schools which did not satisfy the minimum criteria regarding accommodation, equipment, qualifications of staff, etc.

3.8 IMPACT OF THE REPORT OF THE SECONDARY EDUCATION COMMISSION

In view of a large number of shortcomings of the Report as cited above, it could not make any worthwhile impact on Secondary Education. The greatest demerit of the Report was that it did not work out the financial implications of the proposals. No "Programme of Action' was formulated for implementation. Implementation remained haphazard and ad hoc.

The Commission, however made its impact on two issues. It formulated the aims of secondary education in the light of the Constitution of India.

It also led to increased interest in providing guidance services in schools.

3.9 SECONDARY EDUCATION COMMISSION ON THE CONSTRUCTION OF THE CURRICULUM AT THE HIGHER SECONDARY STAGE

Major Defects of the Curriculum

The SEC pointed out the following defects in the existing curriculum:

1. The curriculum is narrowly conceived.
2. It is bookish and theoretical.
3. It is over-crowded.
4. It does not provided rich and significant contents.
5. It makes inadequate provision for practical and other kinds of activities.
6. It does not educate the whole of the personality.
7. It is dominated too much by examinations.
8. It does not include technical and vocational subjects which are necessary for training the students to take part in industrial and economic development of the country.

Principles of Curriculum Construction

The Commission recommended that the following considerations should be kept in mind while constructing the curriculum:

(i) *Principle of Students Abilities*: The curriculum at the Higher

Secondary Stage should be, as far as possible, framed on the basis of the abilities and interests of the students.

(ii) *Principle of Diversification*: Varied courses with a fairly wide latitude for choice should be provided for. There should be diversification of courses.

(iii) *Principle of Vocational bias*: The educational programme should not be narrowly vocational but should have a definite vocational bias.

(iv) *Principle of Core Subjects*: The curriculum should provide for certain core subjects, common to all, and certain optional subjects.

In the words of the Secondary Education Commission, "It must be clearly understood that according to the best modern educational thought, curriculum in this context does not mean only the academic subjects traditionally taught in the school but it includes the totality of experiences that a pupil receives through the manifold activities that go on in the school, in the classroom, library, laboratory, workshops, playgrounds and in the numerous informal contacts between teachers and pupils. In this sense, the whole life of the school becomes the curriculum which can toughen the life of the students at all points and help in the evolution of a balanced personality".

Curriculum Suggested by the Secondary Education Commission

The curriculum should consist of the following:

I. *Languages*

1. Mother tongue or Regional language or a Composite course of the mother tongue and a Classical language.
2. One other language to be chosen from among the following:

(a)Hindi (for those whose mother-tongue is not Hindi).
(b)Elementary English (for those who have not studied it in the middle stage).
(c)Advanced English (for those who have studied English in the earlier stage).
(d)A modern Indian language (other than Hindi).
(e)A modern foreign language (other than English).
(f)A Classical language.

II. *Compulsory Subjects*

(i) Social Studies—general course (for the first two years only).
(ii) General Science including Mathematics—general course (for the first two years only).

III. *Craft*

One Craft to be chosen from the following list (which may be added to according to local needs):

(a) Spinning and Weaving; (b) Wood-work; (c) Metal work; (d) Gardening; (e) Tailoring; (f) Typography; (g) Workshop Practice; (h) Sewing, Needlework and Embroidery; (i) Modelling.

IV. *Elective Subjects*

Three subjects from one of the following groups:

Group 1. (*Humanities*): (a) A classical language or a third language from (a) not already taken; (b) History; (c) Geography; (d) Elements of Economics and Civics; (e) Elements of Psychology and Logic; (f) Mathematics; (g) Music; (h) Domestic Science.

Group 2. (*Sciences*): (a) Physics; (b) Chemistry; (c) Biology; (d) Geography; (e) Mathematics; (f) Elements of Physiology and Hygiene (not to be taken with Biology).

Group 3. (*Technical*): (a) Applied Mathematics and Geometrical Engineering; (b) Applied Science; (c) Elements of Mechanical Engineering; (d) Elements of Electrical Engineering.

Group 4. (*Commercial*): (a) Commercial Practice; (b) Book-keeping; (c) Commercial Geography or Elements of Economics and Civics; (d) Shorthand and Typewriting.

Group 5 (*Agriculture*): (a) General Agriculture; (b) Animal Husbandry; (c) Horticulture and Gardening; (d) Agricultural Chemistry and Botany.

Group 6. (*Fine Art*): (a) History of Art; (b) Drawing and Designing; (c) Painting; (d) Modelling; (e) Music; (f) Dancing.

Group 7. (*Home Science*): (a) Home Economics; (b) Nutrition and Cookery; (c) Mother Craft and Child Care; (d) Household Management and Home Nursing.

Besides the above a student may take at his option one additional subject from any of the above groups irrespective of whether or not he has chosen his other options from that particular group.

Observations

As already stated only a few States/Union Territories accepted the curriculum. The proposal remained on paper only. Post-graduate teachers were required to teach secondary classes for which no adequate training facilities were available.

3.10 SECONDARY EDUCATION COMMISSION ON DIFFERENT TYPES OF SECONDARY SCHOOLS INCLUDING MULTIPURPOSE SCHOOLS

Multipurpose or Multilateral Schools

We have recommended the introduction of diversified courses which will be provided in multilateral or multipurpose schools. A multipurpose school seeks to provide varied types of courses for students with diverse aims, interests and abilities. It endeavours to provide for each individual pupil suitable opportunity to use and develop his natural aptitude and inclinations in the special course of studies chosen by him. The main advantages claimed for it are:

1. It removes all invidious distinctions between students preparing for different courses of studies, breaking down the sense of inferiority that is associated with vocational subjects and makes it possible to plan the educational system on a truly democratic basis.

2. It provides a greater variety of educational media and thereby facilitates proper educational guidance in the choice of studies.
3. It helps to solve the problem of the wrongly classified pupil, because transfer within the same school is easier to arrange than transfer from one school to another.

While we advocate the starting of a certain number of multi-purpose schools, it is not our intention to suggest that all should be of the same type. There will be room for unilateral schools also where intensive training will be provided in particular types of vocational courses according to the occupational needs of the community and the locality.

Agricultural Education in Secondary Schools

Realising the importance of agriculture in India, the Commission recommended that all States should provide greater opportunities for agricultural education in rural schools so that more students may take to it and adopt it as a vocation. As the training in agriculture has to be largely provided in the field, the student should have an opportunity to work under realistic conditions for a considerable part of his study so that he may acquire the right approach to agriculture.

With agriculture two other allied subjects should be closely integrated—Horticulture and Animal Husbandry. If the study of Agriculture is to lead to any positive results, the student must be trained not merely in the mechanics of agricultural operations but also in those subsidiary occupations that a farmer should know in order to utilise his leisure profitably in the off-season. So far not much attention has been given to horticulture in the scheme of secondary education. It goes without saying that, in all schools offering agriculture as a special subject, adequate plots of land should be available for cultivation and students should be trained to carry out all the operations necessary for the purpose. Moreover, the teaching should be so planned as to bring out its scientific aspect properly so that pupils may gain adequate knowledge of the allied sciences of Botany, Climatology, the nature of the soils and seed, and the different pests that affect agricultural plants.

Public Schools: It is, however, essential that certain definite principles should be borne in mind in the working of the public schools.

1. The public school should not be a special or exclusive institution. It must have its roots in the soil of the country and must generally conform to the normal pattern of national education.
2. Public Schools should place due stress not only on the spirit of sportsmanship but also on all other important aspects of citizenship, the dignity of labour and a social sense. They should also take care to see that their general educational life is in conformity with Indian culture, traditions and outlook.

So far as the financing of these schools is concerned, we are of the opinion that public schools should depend less and less on grants made by the Centre or the State concerned and should become self-supporting as soon as possible. We believe that, in principle, in so far as they are expensive schools, largely meant for the richer classes, they have no claim to receive State aid and the Government grants that are at present given to them should be steadily reduced.

Residential Schools: Residential schools have a definite place in any scheme of secondary education. It is true that the best education up to the age of adolescence can be provided in an environment in which the home, the school and the local community all pay their respective parts.

Residential Day Schools: This is a type of school—not common in our country so far—where the pupils can come early in the morning and stay till late in the evening, i.e., between 8 a.m. and 6 p.m. The advantage of this Residential Day School, as it may be called, is that many of the children will be able to utilise the facilities of the school for the greater part of the day. Such facilities will include the full use of the playgrounds and the library, opportunities for supervised study and extra-curricular activities. As in the case of the residential schools, there will be greater teacher-pupil contact which is so necessary for the education of character.

4

Indian Education Commission or Kothari Commission (1964-66) on Secondary Education

4.1 BACKGROUND OF THE APPOINTMENT OF THE EDUCATION COMMISSION

It was hoped that Indian education would make rapid strides in independent India but the results were not satisfactory. In spite of a number of Committees and Commissions on different aspects of education, situation remained stagnant and far below the aspirations, ideals and values of democratic, socialist and secular India. It was felt that in place of piecemeal reforms in different sectors of education, comprehensive evaluation of the entire system of education was needed to make meaningful changes in it.

Secondly, in the post-Independence period, a good deal of expansion had taken place in the field of education, but all this was mostly at the expense of quality. This needed a detailed study.

Thirdly, the Commission was appointed to bring home to the people that they should also have a share in the reconstruction of the country through education, the government of course shouldering the main responsibility.

Fourthly, there was an explosion of knowledge, particularly in science and technology. The appointment of a Commission was consequently felt to consider educational reforms in this context.

Fifthly, in the past, several Commissions and Committees had examined specific sectors and specific aspects of education. A Commission was needed to survey the entire field of educational development as the various parts of the educational system strongly interact with and influence one another. Education needed to be considered as a whole and not in fragments.

Sixthly, the system of education could not be strengthened without eliciting the cooperation of teachers. The teacher community had hitherto been neglected to a considerable extent. All these years, the teachers had been subjected to great economic hardships. A positive approach to the problems of the teacher was, therefore, urgently needed.

4.2 COMPOSITION OF THE KOTHARI COMMISSION

The Commission included 16 members including the Chairman, Dr. D.S. Kothari, who was the Chairman of the University Grants Commission. Shri

J.P. Naik, Head of the Department of Educational Planning Administration and Finance, Gokhale Institute of Politics and Economics, Poona, was the Member-Secretary of the Commission. The Commission included a few foreign experts also.

4.3 TERMS OF REFERENCE

The Commission will advise the Government on national pattern of education and on the general principles and politics for the development of education at all stages and in all aspects. It need not, however, examine the problems of medical or legal education, but such aspects of these problems as are necessary for its comprehensive enquiry may be looked into.

4.4 ESSENCE OF THE REPORT — NEEDED EDUCATIONAL REVOLUTION

Role of Education: Education and National Development. The report begins with these observations, "The destiny of India is now being shaped in her classrooms. This, we believe, is no mere rhetoric. In a world based on science and technology, it is education that determines the level of prosperity, welfare and security of the people. On the quality and number of persons coming out of our schools and colleges will depend our success in the great enterprise of national reconstruction whose principal objective is to raise the standard of living of our people."

Need for the Educational Revolution: The Commission felt, "The present system of education, designed to meet the needs of an imperial administration within the limitations set by a feudal and traditional society, will need radical changes if it is to meet the purposes of a modernising democratic and socialistic society—changes in objectives, in content, in teaching methods, in programmes, in the size and composition of the student body, in the selection and professional preparation of teachers, and in organisation. In fact, what is needed is a revolution in education which in turn will set in motion the much desired social, economic and cultural revolution".

Relating Education to the Life, Needs and Aspirations of the People: In this regard, the Commission said, "In our opinion, therefore, no reform is more important or more urgent than to transform education, to endeavour to relate to it to the life, needs and aspirations of the people and thereby make it a powerful instrument of social, economic and cultural transformation necessary for the realisation of our national goals. This can be done if education:

- is related to productivity;
- strengthens social and national integration, consolidates democracy as a form of government and helps the country to adopt it as a way of life; and
- hastens the process of modernisation.

The role of Secondary Education was examined by the Commission and made recommendations accordingly.

4.5 IMPORTANT ISSUES IN SECONDARY EDUCATION (CLASSES VIII-XII)

The Commission considered class VIII to XII comprising secondary education in Chapter 7 of its Report. Among the major issues it looked into, following deserve special mention:

1. Structure of education
2. Expansion of Secondary Education (Discussed separately)
3. Vocational Education and Work Experience (Discussed separately)
4. Curriculum Reforms (Discussed separately)
5. Language Formula (Discussed separately)
6. Religious and Secular Education, Moral, Social and Spiritual Values.
7. Teachers
8. Common School System
9. Equalisation of Educational Opportunities

4.6 NATIONAL STRUCTURE OF EDUCATION—PROPOSED BY KOTHARI COMMISSION

The new educational structure to consist of:

1. *Duration*:
   (a) One to three years of pre-school education.
   (b) A primary stage of 7 to 8 years divided into a lower primary stage of 4 or 5 years and a higher primary stage of 3 or 2 years.
   (c) A lower secondary stage of 3 to 2 years.
   (d) A higher secondary stage of two years of general education or one to three years of vocational education.
   (e) A higher education stage having a course of three years or more for the first degree and followed by a course for the second or research degree of varying durations.
2. *Ten Years of Schooling of General Education*: The first ten years of schooling should cover a primary stage of seven or eight years and a lower secondary stage of three or two years providing a course of general education without any specialisation.
3. *Admission Age*: Age of admission to class I ordinarily not to be less than 6.
4. *Public Examination*: First public examination to come at the end of first ten years of schooling.
5. *Diversification of Courses*: The system of streaming in school of general education to be made beyond class X.
6. *Types of Secondary Schools*: Two types of secondary schools, high schools providing a ten-year course and higher secondary schools providing a course of 11 or 12 years.
7. *Upgrading of Schools*: Bigger schools and more efficient schools—about one-fourth of the total number to be upgraded and attempts to upgrade every secondary school to the higher secondary stage to be abandoned.

8. *Location of Pre-university Course*: Transfer of the pre-university course from the universities and affiliated colleges to secondary schools by 1975-76 and the duration of the course to be lengthened to two years by 1985-86; U.G.C. being responsible for effecting the transfer of all pre-university or intermediate work from university and affiliated colleges to schools.
9. *Boards of Education*: Reconstituting Boards of Secondary Education to accept the responsibility for the higher secondary stage also.
10. *Vocational Courses*: Vocationalisation at the secondary stage at two points at the end of Class VII (VIII) and at the end of Class X and provision to be made for the introduction of different types of vocational courses at the lower and higher secondary stages, the duration of these courses to vary from one to three years which would prepare young persons for employment.
11. *Two Years Duration of Higher Secondary Stage*: The Higher Secondary stage should be extended to cover a period of two years and to be located exclusively in schools.

Steps to be taken to implement this reform through a phased programme spread over the next 20 years, 1965-85.

Then Existing and Proposed Nomenclatures for Various Stages of Education

Nomenclatures Proposed	*Existing Nomenclatures*
School Education	
1. Pre-primary	1. Pre-primary 2. Pre-basic 3. Kindergarten 4. Montessori, etc.
2. Primary (Classes I-VII or I-VIII)	
(a) *Lower Primary* Classes I-IV or I-V	1. Primary in some States (e.g. Punjab) 2. Lower primary in some States (e.g. Gujarat) 3. Junior basic 4. Lower Elementary in some States (e.g. Madras)
(b) *Higher Primary* Classes V-VII or VI-VIII	1. Middle in some States (e.g. Punjab) 2. Junior High School (e.g. U.P.) 3. Upper Primary in some States (e.g. Gujarat) 4. Senior Basic 5. Higher Elementary in some States (e.g. Madras)
3. Secondary Classes VIII-XII or IX-XII	High School; Higher Secondary School
(a) *Lower Secondary Education* *Classes VIII-X or IX-X*	High School

(Contd.)

(Contd.)

Nomenclatures Proposed	*Existing Nomenclatures*
(b) *Higher Secondary Education Classes XI-XII*	This will include Class XI or PUC in some States (e.g. Rajasthan). It will include Junior Colleges in Kerala. It will include Intermediate Classes in Uttar Pradesh. It will also include terms like pre-professional, pre-medical and pre-engineering.
4. Higher Education	
1. *Professional Degrees*	All degrees which lead in a professional qualification (e.g. M.A.; M.Sc., M. Com.; B.E.; M.B.B.S.; B.T.; LL. B.; B.Ag.; etc.
2. *General Degrees*	All degrees other than professional ones.
3. *Undergraduate*	All courses leading to the first degree
4. *Post-graduate*	All courses beyond the first degree (excluding certain first degrees given after the first degree, e.g. B.Ed.).
5. General	
First Level of Education	This will include pre-school and primary education
Secondary Level of Education	This will include high school and higher secondary education
Third Level of Education	This will include undergraduate and post-graduate education and research.

Evaluation: Why 12 Years of Schooling Before a Three-Year First Degree

The present educational structure popularly known as the 10+2+3 finds its origin in the recommendations of the Kothari Commission Report. It is observed that since 1975, (the beginning year of the introduction of the new pattern of education), it has been gradually introduced in all parts of the country. The duration of secondary education was increased by one year with the introduction of the New Pattern of Education, popularly called 10+2 in 1975 by the Central Board of Secondary Education in its affiliated schools. Since then it has been adopted almost by all States and Union Territories. Under this pattern, there is 12 years of schooling (8 years of elementary and 4 years of secondary) and three years of the first degree. Previously, secondary education structure consisted of 3 years.

Now, why 15 years! It was felt that the standard of education must be raised if India has to take her rightful place among other nations. No advanced country in the world honours a young man with the award of a first degree in less than 15 years of preparation and hard work. In the U.S.A., the high school is up to 12th grade which is followed by a 4-year course in a college or university leading to a bachelor's degree. In the erstwhile U.S.S.R., the complete secondary education ended with grade 10 and then began 5 years of higher education in a university. In England, after 13 years of schooling, three years are needed in a college or university to obtain the first degree. Thus it will take total 16 years in U.S.A., 15 years in U.S.S.R. and 16 years in England to be awarded the first degree. Which is why a graduate from India was not considered equivalent to a graduate in U.K. and therefore a graduate needed to graduate again in U.K. before pursuing higher education for which B.A. is the minimum qualification. The 10+2+3 pattern or extension of one year in secondary education provides the answer.

The new structure of secondary education does not envisage mere addition of one year to the total period of secondary education. It envisages raising the standard of education.

Observations

The Commission's recommendations on the structure of education including secondary education popularly known as 10+2+3 were accepted by the Government of India in its National Policy on Education (1968). However, for about seven years, the proposal remained on paper. A National Committee on 10+2+3 (1973) was formed to work out the details. On its recommendations a beginning was made in 1975 when the Central Board of Secondary Education decided to introduce this pattern in some of the schools affiliated to it. Gradually it was introduced in almost all States and Union Territories.

4.7 EDUCATION COMMISSION ON CURRICULUM REFORM

Need for an Enrichment and Improvement in the Quality of the Curriculum. The Commission stated: "The explosion of knowledge in recent years and the reformulation of many concepts in the sciences have highlighted the inadequacy of existing school programmes and brought about a mounting pressure for a radical reform of school curriculum. A unified approach should be taken to the framing of the entire school curriculum, a new definition of the content of general education and a new approach to the place of specialisation".

The Commission noted the following defects in the existing curriculum at the school stage:

1. It was narrowly conceived.
2. It was largely out-of date.
3. Education is a three-fold process of:
   (i) Imparting knowledge
   (ii) Developing skills
   (iii) Inculcating proper interests, attitudes and values. However, our schools are mostly concerned with imparting knowledge and that too in an unsatisfactory manner.
4. It places overemphasis on rote learning.
5. It makes inadequate provision for practical activities and experiences.
6. The curriculum neglects modern knowledge.
7. The curriculum is out of tune with the life of the people.
8. Most of the curriculum revisions are of an adhoc nature.
9. No research is done in the field of curriculum.
10. Curriculum is not based on any research.
11. Curriculum is prepared at the state level and it cramps the freedom of headmasters and teachers.

Essentials of Curriculum

The Commission suggested:

(1) *Research in Curriculum*: The first is the need for systematic curricular research so that the revision of the curriculum may be worked as a well co-ordinated programme of improvement on the basis of the findings of experts instead of being rushed through haphazardly and in a piecemeal fashion, as often happens in many States today. Facilities for such research should be established in the universities, in the secondary training colleges, in the State Institutions of Education and in the State Boards of School Education. It would also be advantageous to have some experts in curriculum on the staff of the State Boards of School Education who would work in close collaboration with the state evaluation Organisation and the State Institutes of Education.

(2) *Preparation of Text-Books and Other Teaching Aids*: Basic to the success of any attempt at curriculum improvement is the preparation of suitable text-books, teachers' guide and other teaching and learning materials. These define the goals and the content of the new programmes in terms meaningful to the school, and as actual tools used by the teacher and pupil, they lend substance and significance to the proposed changes.

(3) *In-Service Education of Teachers*: In addition to this, it is necessary to make the teacher understand the chief features of the new curriculum with a view to developing improved teacher competence, better teaching skills, and a more sensitive awareness of the teaching learning process in the changed situation. Accordingly, an extensive programme of the in-service education consisting of seminars and refresher courses, should be arranged to orient the teachers to the revised curriculum.

(4) *Relating Curricula to the Available Facilities*: A curriculum should be related to the quality of teachers, the facilities available in the school and the needs of the students with reference to their socio-economic background. These vary immensely from one institution to another. Consequently, a simple State curriculum designed to serve the needs of average school ceases to be meaningful for the large variety of institutions and fails to provide an adequate challenge to the better ones. The solution lies in making it possible to device and adopt curricula suited to their own needs and to vie with one another in upgrading them.

(5) *Freedom of Schools*: Schools should be given the freedom to devise and experiment new curricula suited to their needs. A lead should be given in the matter by training colleges and universities through their experimental schools.

(6) *Preparation of Advanced Curricula*: Advanced curricula should be prepared by State Boards of School Education in all subjects and introduced in a phased manner in schools which fulfil certain conditions of staff and facilities.

(7) *Formation of Subject Teacher Associations*: The formation of subject teacher association will help to stimulate experimentation and in the upgrading of curricula. The State Education Departments, State Institutes of Education and NCERT should help the Associations in their educational activities and co-ordinate their work.

Standards of Attainment at Different Stages

Though the curriculum of the first ten years of general education covering seven years of primary education (four years of lower primary and three years of upper primary) and two or three years of lower secondary education should be organised as a continuous programme of studies. The standard of attainment at the end of each sub-stage in the total course should be clearly indicated. These standards should be defined in terms of the knowledge, skills, abilities and attitudes to be developed with reference to the overall objectives of school education.

Organisation of the Curriculum

The Commission made the following recommendations:

1. *Common Curriculum for Ten Years*: In general, a common curriculum of general education should be provided for the first ten years of school education, and diversification of studies and specialisation should begin only at the higher secondary stage.
2. *Curriculum at Higher Secondary Stage*: At the higher secondary stage of general education, courses to be diversified in such a manner as to enable pupils to study a group of any three subjects in depth with considerable freedom and elasticity in the grouping of subjects. A student, for example, may specialise in any three subjects of the science group or in combination of subjects from the science and the humanities. In order to ensure the balanced development of the adolescent's total personality, the curriculum at this stage should provide half the time to the electives, one-fourth of the time to the language, and one-fourth to physical education, arts and crafts, and moral and spiritual education.
3. *Standards of Attainment at Different Stages*: Though the curriculum of the first ten years of general education covering seven years of primary education (four years of lower primary and three years of upper primary and three years of lower secondary education should be organised as a continuous programme of studies, the standard of attainment at the end of each sub-stage in the total course should be clearly indicated. The standards should be defined in terms of the knowledge, skills, abilities and attitudes to be developed with reference to the overall objectives of school education.

Subjects at Different Stages

Lower Secondary Stage (Classes IX-X)

(a) Three languages
(b) Mathematics
(c) Science
(d) History, Geography and Civics
(e) Art
(f) Work Experience and Social Service
(g) Physical Education
(h) Education in Moral and Spiritual Values

Higher Secondary Stage (Classes XI-XII)

1. Any two languages, including any modern Indian language, any modern foreign language and any classical language
2. Any three subjects from (a) An Additional Language, (b) History, (c) Geography, (d) Economics, (e) Logic, (f) Psychology, (g) Sociology, (h) Art, (i) Physics, (j) Chemistry, (k) Mathematics, (l) Biology, (m) Geology, (n) Home Science
3. Work-Experience and Social Service
4. Physical Education
5. Art or Craft
6. Education in Moral and Spiritual Values

Observations: The curriculum suggested by the Commission was considered to be quite meaningful and appropriate. It was based on the consideration that there should be a uniform structure up to Class X and as such there need not be any diversified curriculum at this stage.

One of the major weaknesses in the scheme as suggested by the Secondary Education Commission was that specialisation of studies began too early. At the age of 13 or 14, the students were classified as belonging to the pre-engineering or the pre-medical section. The streaming of pupils in this way into specialised groups from Class IX upwards is undesirable. The world trends in secondary education are in the direction of lengthening the period of general education and postponing diversification and specialisation to the second cycle or senior stage of secondary education.

Emphasis on Science and Mathematics: The Kothari Commission laid emphasis on these two subjects on account of their special importance in the technological age.

Work Experience: This was included to initiate students into the 'world of work'.

With slight modifications of the curriculum, this pattern of curriculum is still being followed as this is considered to be broad based.

4.8 RELIGIOUS EDUCATION AND SECULAR EDUCATION

Secularism and Religion: Religious Education and Education About Religious

The adoption of a secularist policy means that political, economic and social matters, all citizens, irrespective of their religious faith, will enjoy equality of rights, that no religious community will be favoured or discriminated against, and the instruction in religious dogmas will not be provided in State schools. But it is not an irreligious or anti-religious policy; it does not belittle the importance of religion as such. It gives to every citizen the fullest freedom of religious belief and worship.

The Commission made a distinction between 'religious education' and 'education about religions'. The former is largely concerned with the teaching of the tenets and practices of a particular religion, generally in the form in which the religious group envisages them, whereas the latter is a study of religious and religious thought from a broad point of view—the eternal quest of the spirit. It would not be practicable for a secular State with many religions to provide education in any one religion. It is, however, necessary for a multireligious democratic State to promote a tolerant study of all religions so that its citizens can understand each other better and live amicably together. It must be remembered that, owing to the ban placed on religious instruction in schools and the weakening of the home influences which, in the past, often provided such instruction, children are now growing up without any clear ideas of their own religion and no chance of learning about others. In fact, the general ignorance and misunderstanding in these matters are so widespread in the younger generation as to be fraught with great danger for the development of a democracy in which tolerance is rated at a high value. We suggest that a syllabus giving well chosen information about each of the major religions should be included as a part of the course in citizenship or as part of general education to be introduced in schools and colleges up to the first degree. It should highlight the fundamental similarities in the great religions of the world and the emphasis they place on the cultivation on certain broadly comparable moral and spiritual values.

Science and Spiritualism

If science and *ahimsa* join together in creative synthesis of belief and action, mankind will attain a new level of purposefulness, prosperity and spiritual insight. In this context we cannot do better than to quote Pandit Jawaharlal Nehru:

'Can we combine the progress of science and technology with this progress of the mind and spirit also? We cannot be untrue to science because that represents the basic fact of life today. Still less can we be untrue to those essential principles for which India has stood in the past throughout the ages. Let us then pursue our path to industrial progress with all our strength and vigour and, at the same time, remember that material riches without toleration and compassion and wisdom may well turn to dust and ashes'.

Social, Moral and Spiritual Values

The Commission has observed that the expanding knowledge and the growing power which it places at the disposal of modern society must, therefore, be combined with strengthening and deepening of the sense of social responsibility and keener appreciation of moral and spiritual values.

4.9 EDUCATION COMMISSION AND TEACHERS

Important recommendations regarding teachers are briefly given here.

Stimulating Conditions for Teachers

The Commission observed, "In creative work like teaching or research, the provision of stimulating conditions of work and adequate opportunities for professional advancement are extremely important and can play a very significant role in attracting and retaining the right type of persons in the profession. The conditions of work in educational institutions should be such as to enable teachers to function at their highest level of efficiency".

The Commission, therefore, made several suggestions for enhancing the status of teachers and their salary scales.

Teachers	Remuneration	Rs.
1. Teachers who have com-pleted the secondary course and have received two years of professional training	Minimum for trained teachers	150
	Maximum salary (to be reached in a period of about 20 years)	250
	Selection grade (for about 15 p.c. of the cadre)	250-300
2. Graduates who have received one year's professional training	Minimum for trained graduates	220
	Maximum salary (to be reached in a period of 20 years)	400
	Selection grade (for about 15 p.c. of the cadre)	300-500
3. Teachers working in second-dary schools and having post-graduate qualifications		300-600
4. Heads of secondary schools	Depending upon the size and quality of the school and also on their qualifications, the headmasters should have one or other of the scales of pay for affiliated colleges recommended below.	
		Rs.
5. Teachers in affiliated colleges	1. Lecturer, Junior scale	300-25-600
	2. Senior Scale	400-30-640-40-800
	3. Senior Lecturer/Reader	700-40-1100
	Principal I	700-40-1100
	II	800-50-1500
	III	1000-50-1500
6. Teachers in university departments	Lecturer	500-40-800-50-950
	Reader	700-50-1250
	Professor	1000-50-1300-60-1600

Note: These scales are exclusively of allowances.

Training/Education of Secondary Teachers

1. The staff of secondary training colleges should have a double Master's degree in an academic subject and in education. A fair proportion of them should hold doctorate degrees. They should all have taken induction or orientation courses in teacher education.
2. Qualified specialists in subjects like psychology, sociology, science or mathematics may be appointed on the staff even if they have not had professional training.
3. No student should be allowed to specialise in the teaching of a subject unless he has studied it for his first degree or obtained an equivalent qualification prior to training.
4. Attempts should be made to recruit first and good second class students to teacher-training institutions and adequate scholarships should be given to them.
5. Introducing integrated courses of general and professional education in universities.
6. Visualising professional studies and basing them on Indian conditions through the development of educational research.
7. Using improved methods of teaching which leave greater scope for self-study and discussion and improved methods of evaluation which

include continuous internal assessment of practical and sessional work as well as practice teaching.

8. Improving practice-teaching and making it a comprehensive programme of internship.
9. Developing special courses and programmes.
10. Revising the curricula and programmes at all levels of teacher education in the light of the fundamental objectives of preparing teachers for their varied responsibilities in an evolving system of education.
11. Summer institute should be organised for the in-service training of staff.
12. States and Union Territories should adopt a rule that teachers in secondary schools will ordinarily teach only those subjects which they studied for a university degree. If they are required to teach subjects other than those they have studied, they should take a special course therein either by correspondence or in the summer institutes.

4.10 COMMON SCHOOL SYSTEM

The Commission observed, "In a situation of the type we have in India, it is the responsibility of the educational system to bring the different social classes and groups together and thus promote the emergence of an egalitarian and integrated society".

The Commission stated that if educational system is to become a powerful instrument of national development in general and social and national integration in particular, we must move towards the goal of a common school system of public education.

Characteristics of the Common School System

1. It will be open to all children irrespective of caste, creed, community, religion, economic sanctions or social status;
2. In this system access to good education will depend, not on wealth or class, but on talent.
3. It will maintain adequate standards in all schools and provide at least a reasonable proportion of quality institutions.
4. In this system no tuition fee will be charged; and
5. It would meet the needs of the average parent so that he would not ordinarily feel the need to send his children to expensive school outside the system.

Observations

It is really very sad that the words of wisdom of the Kothari Commission have not been headed by the policy makers and administrators. There is very little hope that the present system of education having public schools, semi-public schools, aided schools, state schools, local bodies schools, sainik schools, Navodaya schools, etc. would cater to different categories of society—admission generally speaking depending upon monetary considerations.

4.11 EQUALISATION OF OPPORTUNITIES

(a) The target is to provide free education for all up to Higher Secondary stage and provision of free text-books, etc. and provision of scholarships to increasing percentage to be made.
The supply of free text-books does not imply the permanent possession of the text-books by students as in some Western countries. Books can be used for a year and then returned to school for use by others. This will naturally reduce the finance involved in providing books.

(b) To equalise opportunities scholarships should be increasingly provided to cover the cost of books and other expenses, etc.

(c) The provision of free education up to Higher Secondary stage as recommended may not be possible immediately. It is, therefore, made the following suggestions:
   (i) The first step may be that we extended the freeships to all those who cannot afford to pay fees.
   (ii) Merit Scholarships can be made available to 5% to begin with and this can be increased to 20% in the course of 10 years.
   (iii) Free books can be made available to very deserving students.
   (iv) Book banks can be opened from where books can be deposited and drawn by those who need them.

4.12 VOCATIONALISATION AT THE HIGHER SECONDARY STAGE

We must emphasize particularly the need to vocationalize higher secondary education and to expand the vocational courses to cover about half of the total enrolment at this stage. A large variety of terminal courses should be organized, varying in duration from one to three years. They will include courses for the training of primary and pre-primary teachers; courses conducted by the industrial training institutions for a large number of trades for which the completion of studies in class X is the minimum qualification; courses in agriculture and industry which will train the middle level of personnel needed, courses for training para-medical/health personnel, courses for secretariat work; and, courses in home science. It is such courses that will make secondary education mainly terminal. (Chapter 2-28)

Development of Vocational Education

At the lower secondary level, leading to matriculation, we must realize that manpower data available gives little guidance on the extent of vocationalization. Manpower needs are expressed in terms of matriculates only or in terms of pupils successfully completing courses of general education. Pupils in schools for technical or industrial education, arts and crafts training, or for music, dancing and other fine arts are not represented in the man-power data. How far these courses should expand and what new courses of a vocational or practical nature should be started are questions which can be answered only after further study. (Chapter V)

At the higher secondary level, leading to intermediate or its equivalent, considerable guidance is given by the manpower fore-casts. These suggest that by 1985-86 there should be 2,413,000 enrolments in vocational schools and perhaps 600,000 in vocational colleges out of total enrolments of 6,875,000. This is equivalent to 43 per cent of the total. We are of the view that vocational education at this level has to be emphasized. We have therefore, assumed that enrolments in vocational courses at this level would be about 50 per cent of the total.

4.13 IMPLEMENTATION OF THE RECOMMENDATIONS OF THE EDUCATION COMMISSION

1. *National Policy Resolution* (*1968*): Recommendations of the Education Commission 1964-66 were considered by various educational organisations and institutions. These were also discussed by educators all over the country. Many educational conferences were held to deliberate over these recommendations. Meetings of Vice-Chancellors, State Education Secretaries, Directors of Education were convened. All these discussions and debates resulted in the adoption of a Resolution on the National Policy on Education in 1968.

2. *Introduction of the New Pattern of Education*: On the recommendations of the Education Commission and in accordance with the National Policy on Education (adopted by Parliament in 1968) the Central Advisory Board of Education adopted a resolution in its meeting held in November 1974 recommending the introduction of the 10+2+3 pattern of education all over India during the Fifth Plan. Now almost all States and Union Territories have adopted this pattern.

3. *Vocationalisation of Higher Secondary Education*: A Centrally-sponsored Scheme for Vocationalisation was formulated during 1976-77. Under it the State Governments were provided with Central assistance during the Fifth Five-Year Plan period and thereafter the programme was run on a regular basis as a State scheme.

4. *Work Experience*: As recommended by the Education Commission, work experience has been made an integral part of the new scheme of studies under the pattern 10+2+3.

5. *Book Banks*: Book banks have been established in educational institutions which provide books to the students belonging to the weaker sections of the society.

6. *Two Levels of Courses*: Under the new pattern of education, provision made for the students to select courses in some subjects at two levels, i.e., ordinary and advanced, depending upon their capacity to work and comprehend.

7. *Revised Pay Scale of Teachers*: The pay scale of teachers working in schools were revised almost in all the States as a result of the recommendations of the Education Commission.

8. *National Institute of Educational Planning and Administration, New Delhi*: The Working Party on Educational Planning, Administration and Evaluation in the Fourth Five-Year Plan set up by the Planning Commission

reiterated the recommendation of the Kothari Commission for the setting up of the National Staff College. The Government of India accepted this recommendation. The National Staff College for Educational Planners and Administrators began to function on 1st January, 1971.

The Staff College was renamed as National Institute of Educational Planning and Administration in 1980. It acquired the status of a deemed University in 2006 and renamed National University of Educational Planning and Administration.

Recommendations which Received Little Attention

Following areas have remained ignored by and large. They have not received the due attention they deserved:

1. Creation of school complexes.
2. Development of 'neighbourhood' concept of educational institutions.
3. Creation of Indian Education Service.
4. Creation of District School Boards.
5. Strengthening of the Offices of the District Educational Officers.
6. National Education Act.
7. Creation of a National Board of School Education.
8. Establishment of a Farm University in each State.
9. Freedom to Headmasters.
10. Making Institutional Plans as an integral part of District, State and National Plan of Education.
11. Developing partnership between educational authorities and industry.
12. Spending 6 per cent of GNP on education.

Contribution of the Report of the Education Commission (1964-66)

There is no exaggeration in the statement that there is no report of any educational commission and committee in India which has made such a valuable contribution to the role of education, its contents, development, expansion and planning, etc. as the report of the Education Commission (1964-66). The present educational system in India is, by and large, draws its inspiration from this report. The report, no doubt, has brought about radical changes in education in India. The National Policy of Education (1986) is based on it.

The report provided not only sound philosophical and sociological bases of education but also a reasonable working programme for implementation.

The most notable feature of the educational programme is that it also took note of the financial aspects of various programmes it suggested.

5

NPE (1986), Ramamurti Committee (1990-91) and Programme of Action (1992)

5.1 SECONDARY EDUCATION AND NATIONAL POLICY ON EDUCATION (1986)

Formation and implementation of NPE is a landmark in the history of education in India.

5.2 NEED FOR THE FORMULATION OF NPE (1986)

The Education Commission 1964-66 recommended that the Government of India should issue a statement on the National Policy on Education which should provide guidance to the State Governments and the local authorities in preparing and implementing educational plans. In 1967 the Government of India constituted a committee of Members of Parliament on Education to prepare the draft of a statement on the National Policy of Education. The Committee brought together, for the first time in recent history, leading members of almost all the political parties in the country and prepared a draft which was considered by the Central Advisory Board of Education. A general consensus on the national policy on education emerged in the course of the Board's deliberations. Thereafter the Government of India issued the Resolution on National Policy on Education in 1968.

The National Policy on Education (1968) stipulated that the implementation of the various educational programmes undertaken in accordance with its directions should be reviewed every five years. However, no such review was done in the next 17 years. It was, therefore, felt that a review should be made. The then Prime Minister Rajiv Gandhi took the initiative in this regard.

5.3 PROCESS FOR THE FORMATION OF THE NPE

As a first step a Document entitled *Challenge of Education: A Policy Perspective* was prepared. The contents of the document were debated in the country at various conferences, seminars and study circles, etc. It is of great interest to note that the document was translated practically into all the regional languages. 5,80,000 copies of this document in English, 2,40,000 in Hindi and 4,000 in Urdu were distributed by the Ministry, inviting suggestions and comments from all sections of the people. As a part of the nation-wide debate for the formulation of the new policy on education, 12 National Seminars and 17 sponsored seminars were organised by the Ministry of Education and its national organisations. All State Governments and Union Territories also organised seminars, workshops and symposia. A detailed analysis was made of all the communications and recommendations received in the Ministry. Thereafter, the Ministry of Human Resource Development brought out a revised document 'National Policy on Education 1986—A Presentation'. This paper was discussed at the meetings of the State Ministers of Education, the National Development Council and the Central Advisory Board of Education. It was revised in the light of these discussions and the 'Draft National Policy on Education 1986' was finally laid on the table of Parliament in the first week of May, 1986.

The National Policy on Education was adopted by the Lok Sabha on May 8, 1986 and the Rajya Sabha on May 13, 1986.

Contents of the NPE. The NPE contains XII Parts and 157 paragraphs on different aspects of education.

5.4 SALIENT FEATURES OF NPE

1. *Essence of Education*: Education for all and for the all-round development of the individual.
2. *National System of Education*: (i) Common educational structure of 10+2+3.
   (ii) National Curriculum Framework.
3. Education for quality and equality.
4. Child-centred education.
5. Operation black-board.
6. Pace-setting schools.
7. Vocational education.
8. Delinking degrees from jobs.
9. Investment on education to exceed 6 per cent of the national income.
10. Making the system to work.

In sum, education is a unique investment in the present and the future. This cardinal principle is the key to the National Policy on Education".

Future

1. "The future shape of education in India is too complex to envision with precision, yet, given our tradition which has almost always put a high premium on intellectual and spiritual attainment, we are bound to succeed in achieving our objectives".
2. "The main task is to strengthen the base of the pyramid, which might touch a billion people at the turn of the century. Equally, it is important to ensure that those at the top of the pyramid are among the best in the world".

5.5 NPE ON SECONDARY EDUCATION

Secondary education is dealt with in PART V and PART VIII of the Document

Extracts on Secondary Education (Paras in the Report)

Secondary education begins to expose students to differentiated roles of science, the humanities and social sciences. This is also an appropriate stage to provide children with a sense of history and national perspective and give them opportunities to understand their constitutional duties and rights as citizens. Conscious internalisation of a healthy work ethos and of the values of a humane and composite culture will be brought about through appropriately formulated curricula. Vocationalisation through specialised institutions or through the refashioning of secondary education can, at this stage, provide valuable manpower for economic growth. Access to secondary education will be widened to cover areas unserved by it at present. In other areas, the main emphasis will be on consolidation. (5.13)

5.6 PACE-SETTING SCHOOLS

It is universally accepted that children with special talent or aptitude should be provided opportunity to proceed at a faster pace, by making good quality education available to them, irrespective of their capacity to pay for it. (5.14)

Pace-setting schools intended to serve this purpose will be established in various parts of the country on a given pattern, but with full scope for innovation and experimentation. Their broad aims will be to serve the objective of excellence, coupled with equity and social justice (with reservation for SCs and STs), to promote national integration by providing opportunities to talented children largely rural, from different parts of the country, and most important7ly, to become catalysts of a nation-wide programme of school improvement. The schools will be a residential and free of charge. (5.15)

5.7 VOCATIONALISATION

The introduction of systematic, well planned and vigorously implemented programmes of vocational education is crucial in the proposed educational reorganisation. These elements are meant to enhance individual employability, to reduce the mis-match between the demand and supply of skilled manpower, and to provide an alternative for those pursuing higher education without particular interest or purpose. (5.16)

Vocational education will be a distinct stream, intended to prepare students for identified occupations spanning several areas of activity. These courses will ordinarily be provided after the secondary stage, but keeping the scheme flexible, they may also be made available after Class VIII. In the interests of integrating vocational education better with their facilities the Industrial Training Institutes will also conform to the larger vocational pattern. (5.17)

Health planning and health service management should optimally interlock with the education and training of appropriate categories of health manpower through health-related vocational courses. Health education at the primary and middle levels will ensure the commitment of the individual to family and community health, and lead to health-related vocational courses at the +2 stage of higher secondary education. Efforts will be made to devise similar vocational courses based on agriculture, marketing, social services, etc. An emphasis in vocational education will also be on development of attitudes, knowledge, and skills for entrepreneurship and self-employment. (5.18)

The establishment of vocational courses or institutions will be the responsibility of the Government as well as employers in the public and private sectors; the Government will, however, take special steps to cater to the need of women, rural and tribal students and the deprived sections of society. Appropriate programmes will also be started for the handicapped. (5.19)

Graduates of vocational courses will be given opportunities, under predetermined conditions, for professional growth, career improvement and lateral entry into courses of general, technical and professional education through appropriate bridge courses. (5.20)

Non-formal, flexible and need based vocational programmes will also be made available to neoliterates, youth who have completed primary education, school drop-outs, persons engaged in work and unemployed or partially employed persons. Special attention in this regard will be given to women. (5.21)

Tertiary level courses will be organised for the young who graduate from the higher secondary courses of the academic stream and may also require vocational courses. (5.22)

It is proposed that vocational courses cover 10 per cent of higher secondary students by 1990 and 25 per cent by 1995. Steps will be taken to see that a substantial majority of the products of vocational courses are employed or become self-employed. Review of the courses offered would be regularly undertaken. Government will also review its recruitment policy to encourage diversification at the secondary level. (5.23)

5.8 REORIENTING THE CONTENT AND PROCESS OF EDUCATION (PART 8)

The Cultural Perspective

The existing schism between the formal system of education and the country's rich and varied cultural traditions needs to be bridged. The preoccupation with modern technologies cannot be allowed to sever our new generations from the roots in India's history and culture. De-culturisation, dehumanisation and alienation must be avoided at all costs. Education can and must bring about the fine synthesis between change-oriented technologies and the country's continuity of cultural traditions. (8.1)

The curricula and processes of education will be enriched by cultural content in as many manifestations as possible. Children will be enabled to develop sensitivity to beauty, harmony and refinement. Resource persons in the community, irrespective of their formal educational qualifications, will be invited to contribute to the cultural enrichment of education, employing both the literate and oral traditions of communication. To sustain and carry forward the cultural tradition, the role of old masters, who train pupils through traditional modes will be supported and recognised. (8.3)

Linkages will be established between the university system and institutions of higher learning in art, archaeology, oriental studies, etc. Due attention will also be paid to the specialised disciplines of Fine Arts, Museology, Folklore, etc. Teaching, training and research in these disciplines will be strengthened so as to replenish specialised manpower in them. (8.3)

Value Education

The growing concern over the erosion of essential values and an increasing cynicism in society has brought to focus the need for readjustments in the curriculum in order to make education a forceful tool for the cultivation of social and moral values.

In our culturally plural society, education should foster universal and eternal values, oriented towards the unity and integration of our people. Such education should help eliminate obscurantism, religious fanaticism, violence, superstition and fatalism. (8.5)

Apart from this combative role, value education has a profound positive content, based on our heritage, national goals and universal perceptions. It should lay primary emphasis on this aspect. (8.6)

Languages: The Education Policy of 1968 had examined the question of the development of languages in great detail; its essential provisions can hardly be improved upon and are as relevant today as before. The implementation of this part of the 1968 Policy has, however, been uneven. The Policy will be implemented more energetically and purposefully. (8.7)

Work Experience: Work experience, viewed as purposive and meaningful manual work, organised as an integral part of the learning process and resulting in either goods or services useful to the community, is considered as an essential component at all stages of education, to be provided through well structured and graded programmes. It would comprise activities in accordance with the interests, abilities and needs of students, the level of skills and knowledge to be upgraded with the stages of education. The experience would be helpful on entry into the workforce. Pre-vocational programmes provided at the lower secondary stage will also facilitate the choice of the vocational courses at the higher secondary stage. (8.14)

Education and Environment: There is a paramount need to create a consciousness of the environment. It must permeate all ages and all sections of society, beginning with the child. Environmental consciousness should inform teaching in schools and colleges. This aspect will be integrated in the entire educational process. (8.15)

Mathematics Teaching: Mathematics should be visualised as the vehicle to train a child to think, reason, analyse and to articulate logically. Apart from being a specific subject, it should be treated as a concomitant to any subject involving analysis and reasoning. (8.16)

With the recent introduction of computers in schools, educational computing and the emergence of learning through the understanding of cause-effect relationships and the interplay of variables, the teaching of mathematics will be suitably redesigned to bring it in line with modern technological devices. (8.17)

Science Education: Science education will be strengthened so as to develop in the child well defined abilities and values such as the spirit of inquiry, creativity, objectivity, the courage to question, and an aesthetic sensibility. (8.18)

Science education programmes will be designed to enable the learner to acquire problem solving and decision-making skills and to discover the relationship of science with health, agriculture, industry and other aspects of daily life. Every effort will be made to extend science education to the vast numbers who have remained outside the pale of formal education. (8.19)

Sports and Physical Education: Sports and physical education are an integral part of the learning process, and will be included in the evaluation of performance. A nation-wide infrastructure for physical education, sports and games will be built into the educational edifice. (8.20)

The Evaluation Process and Examination Reform: Assessment of performance is an integral part of any process of learning and teaching. As part of sound educational strategy, examinations should be employed to bring about qualitative improvements in education. (8.23)

The objective will be to re-cast the examination system so as to ensure a method of assessment that is a valid and reliable measure of student development and a powerful instrument for improving teaching and learning. In functional terms, this would mean:

(i) The elimination of excessive element of change and subjectivity.
(ii) The de-emphasis of memorisation;
(iii) Continuous and comprehensive evaluation that incorporates both scholastic and non-scholastic aspects of education, spread over the total span of instructional time;
(iv) Effective use of the evaluation process by teachers, students and parents;
(v) Improvement in the conduct of examinations;
(vi) The introduction of concomitant changes in instructional materials and methodology;
(vii) Introduction of the semester system from the secondary stage in a phased manner; and
(viii) The use of grades in place of marks. (8.24)

The above goals are relevant both for external examinations and evaluation within educational institutions. Evaluation at the institutional level will be streamlined and the predominance of external examinations reduced. (8.25)

5.9 NATIONAL POLICY ON EDUCATION, 1986: PROGRAMME OF ACTION (POA) (1986)

Introduction

With a view to implement the National Policy on Education 1986, the Ministry of Human Resource Development, prepared a Programme of Action. Twenty-three Task Forces were constituted and each was assigned a specific topic covered by NPE. Eminent educationists, experts, senior bureaucrats und representative of the Central and State Governments were associated with these Task Forces. The Task Forces projected the necessary action and indicated the broad targets. Their reports were further considered in a series of meetings of the Education Secretaries of the State Governments and the Union Territories and of the Central Advisory Board of Education. The Lok Sabha and the Rajya Sabha discussed and approved POA on August 22 and 23, 1986 respectively.

Extracts from the Chapter III—Secondary Education and Navodaya Vidyalayas

It is known that the secondary and higher secondary schools are under-provided particularly in the rural areas in terms of buildings, teachers and school facilities but the extent of these shortages have not been surveyed in all aspects. The programme of consolidation envisaged in the policy will have the following components of which the cost cannot be precisely estimated:

(a) Adequate playground facilities where needed will have to be provided by making available nearby vacant land and in other places by arranging for sharing of such facility with neighbouring school as a priority programme during the 7th Plan.

(b) A programme of construction of additional classroom and laboratory facilities in schools to the extent they are deficient will be taken up. School education is mainly looked after by the State Governments and local bodies. If possible the Central Government may consider supplementation of resources.

(c) Every school must have laboratories and other facilities as specified in the terms of recognition of the Board of Secondary/Higher Secondary Education to which it is affiliated. These norms have been developed by the NCERT and KVS also. Taking into consideration the past experience that the equipment once given is not replaced and even maintained it is suggested that community participation by way of student contribution at the rate of Rs.10 to 15 per month should be levied, except from girls and others exempt from payment of tuition fee. This collection should remain in the school for replacement and maintenance purposes.

(d) The teacher competencies would be improved by attracting better qualified people to the profession as envisaged in the policy and by improving the pre-service and in-service training programmes through strengthened secondary teacher training institutions. The process will begin straight away and will be continued for consistently upgrading teachers' competencies.

(e) As envisaged in the Policy the core-curriculum will play an important role in educational consolidation. This will be followed by overall improvement in curriculum, the textual material, teaching practices and examination/evaluation methods.

(f) The Kothari Commission suggested that the ratio of higher secondary and secondary schools should be 1:3. This should be ensured. A large number of higher secondary schools have only one or two streams out of humanities, science and commerce and most do not have vocational stream. As an important programme in the process of consolidation, schools should be helped to have all the three streams and a vocational stream in selected schools. This will be the responsibility of the State Government concerned. Vocational stream would be set up with the assistance of the Government of India as may be determined.

The programme for bright children has two parts—one is for potentially high achievers particularly in the areas who are substantially left uncovered by the present system and the other is the programme for the gifted students who can be expected to make original contribution in their subject areas if properly nurtured.

Under the scheme of Navodaya Vidyalayas for catering to the category of high achievers one such Vidyalaya will be set up in each district during the 7th Five Year Plan period. These schools will make available good quality education irrespective of the parents capacity to pay and their socio-economic background. In these schools there will be 75% reservation for children from rural areas. There will be reservation for SC and ST as per their actual population in the district subject to a minimum of nationally prescribed figure of 15 and 7½ for SC & ST respectively. An effort will be made to cover girls to the extent of 1/3 in a school. Education will be free including boarding and lodging in these schools. These schools will be affiliated to the Central Board of Secondary Education.

The gifted students frequently have pronounced competence in a limited subject area accompanied by indifference in certain other areas. Therefore, arrangements for such students cannot be fitted into regular courses of study. Special arrangements for such students will have to provide teaching/learning on modular basis for every small group of students in a small number of subjects of interest to them. Such arrangements will be characterised by large facilities, higher teacher-student ratio and regular participation by professionals in teaching programmes. A detailed project for this purpose should be worked out by a specially constituted group within one year. Arrangements will be designed for implementation within the present system for such students.

5.10 EVALUATION AND OBSERVATIONS ON NPE 1986 AND PROGRAMME OF ACTION 1986

Significance and Merits

The most significant aspect of the NPE is that for the first time in the history of India, an education policy was formulated at the initiative of a Prime Minister.

The *second aspect* is that a nation-wide debate was held on different aspects of education before the NPE came into being.

The *third aspect* is that it was discussed in the Parliament.

Fourthly, a Programme of Action was chalked out for its implementation.

Fifthly, it included the outline of the national system of education.

Sixthly, at the secondary stage, following schemes were introduced:

(i) Pace-setting schools or Navodaya Vidyalayas now known as Jawahar Vidyalayas.
(ii) Vocationalisation of secondary education.
(iii) Reconstruction of the curriculum.

Missing Links and Limitations

1. Financial aspects of the proposals were not worked out.
2. No reference was made to the basic system of education.
3. It was silent on the existence of public schools.

Important Recommendations on which Action has not been initiated so far:

1. Delinking degrees from jobs.
2. Constitution of an Indian Education Service.

5.11 COMMITTEE FOR REVIEW OR RAMAMURTI COMMITTEE ON NATIONAL POLICY ON EDUCATION, 1986

Introduction

In pursuance of its election manifesto, the National Front Government headed by Shri V.P. Singh, appointed on May 7, 1990, a Committee comprising 17 members, with Acharya Ramamurti as its Chairman to review the National Policy on Education (NPE), 1986. The Committee submitted its report to the Minister of State for Education in the Ministry of Human Resource Development on December 26, 1990. The report was tabled in the Parliament on January 9, 1991. With the fall of the National Front Government, the report could not be given its due attention.

Terms of Reference of the Review Committee

(a) To review the NPE, 1986 and its implementation;
(b) To make recommendations regarding revision of the policy;
(c) To recommend action necessary for implementation of the revised policy within a time frame.

Extracts from the Report

Approach

The approach of the Committee in reviewing the National Policy on Education, 1986 and its implementation has been guided by the following principal concerns:

1. Equity and social justice.
2. Decentralisation of educational management at all levels.
3. Establishment of a participative educational order.
4. Inculcation of values indispensable for creation of an enlightened and humane society.
5. Empowerment of work.

Recommendations Relating to Secondary Education: Navodaya Vidyalays

The Ramamurti Review Committee did not find favour with the scheme of Navodaya Vidyalays as visualised in the National Policy on Education, 1986. It recommended that the Government may decide from out of the following three alternatives:

(i) No further Navodaya Vidyalaya need be opened. The existing 261 Navodaya Vidyalayas may be restructured and continued with provision of adequate resources. The scheme may also be reviewed at the end of 1992-93.
(ii) All the existing 261 Navodaya Vidyalayas may be transferred to the State Sector for the States to run them as residential centres on the Andhra Pradesh model.

(iii) The Navodaya Vidyalaya scheme may be transformed into a Navodaya Vidyalaya programme of broad based talent nurturing and pace-setting. (A day-school each under the Common School System can function in the premises of Navodaya Vidyalayas). (4.5.10)

Vocational Education and Structural Changes in Secondary Education

In order to make vocationalisation a success, substantial structural changes may be introduced in secondary education on the principles of modular courses and credit accumulation, at the same time providing flexibility for multiple exit and entry points for the students. In other words, students opting for any particular vocational course should have the facility of acquiring credits for specific modules of courses, go out into the world of work and come back later at their convenience for earning further credits by pursuing further modules. This would make it possible for the schools to offer vocational courses in varying combinations with subjects, such as, Languages, Mathematics, Sciences and Social Studies. No doubt, vocational and non-vocational subjects should be inter-woven both at the level of content and pedagogy. For those students taking up vocational courses at the secondary stage leading to direct job placements, provision should also be made for further education in those vocations or other fields, and, if necessary, bridge courses may be provided. These arrangements are necessary in the expanding world of knowledge and technology, which requires continuing and updating of education for all. What is required for long term viability of vocationalised education is to make provision not merely for specific skill training but also for necessary theoretical background to enhance transferability of well planned and logically designed open learning and distance learning programmes at the school and University levels should be established as the same would be a good support system for vocationalisation of education. (8.7.0)

Vocational Programmes in NPE

For those who do not go in for formal secondary education in the school system, vocational programmes should be organised in non-formal stream through TRYSEM and community polytechnics and in the formal stream through the ITIs, Rural Institutions etc. (8.7.0)

Removal of Anomalies in Vocational Courses

Several vocational courses get sex stereotyped. That is, they are considered predominantly relevant in the domain of women. This stereotyping should be carefully availed, and girls given access to increasingly diversified courses not discriminated in terms of relevance to men or women. Access for Scheduled Castes and Scheduled Tribes to vocational courses should be enhanced too. (8.7.0)

Work Benches and Practice Schools

In order that the process of vocational education is enriched by a meaningful combination of teaching of theory and practice and effective linkages are established with the 'World of work', 'Work benches' and 'Practice schools' may be identified and involved.

- Work benches or practice schools are work situations selected for purpose of giving vocational training and direct experience to students within production units or developmental activities of official agencies.
- Education at these work places would be through student involvement in work activities which would be clearly identified. (8.8.4)

Resources for Education

The first step, therefore, should be to provide for at least 6% of the GNP for education which has not so far been provided, though this has been repeatedly urged for over quarter of a century. (15.13.5)

All technical and professional education should be made self-financing, education being viewed as involving the use of resources (inputs) that should be necessarily paid for by the beneficiaries as it confers on them greater employability (output). (15.13.5)

The tuition fees now prevalent in educational institutions, by and large are those fixed many years ago. In 1950-51, income from fees accounted for 20% of the total expenditure on education. This proportion has now come down to 5%. In the circumstances, a justifiable strategy is to bring about an appropriate increase in the fees paid by students going in higher education. (15.13.5)

5.12 OBSERVATIONS ON THE REPORT

The observations and recommendations of the report were not given any consideration in view of the change of the Government at the Centre. It may be observed that the NPE, 1986, was formulated by the Congress Government at the Centre. The Janata Government formed in 1989 had its own agenda almost on every issue including education. The Janata Government was short-lived. The recommendations of the Committee were examined by another Committee constituted by the Congress Government and were, by and large, rejected.

5.13 REVISED NATIONAL POLICY ON EDUCATION (1992)

Introduction

The Janata Dal lost power at the Centre to the Congress. It appointed the CABE Committee to review the recommendations of the Ramamurti Committee on NPE. The Committee was headed by Shri Janardhana Reddy, Chief Minister and Minister of Education, Andhra Pradesh. This committee found little substance in the recommendations of the Ramamurti Committee. On the basis of the Janardhana Committee Report, the NPE 1996 was revised.

Presenting the revised National Policy on Education in both Houses of Parliament on May 7, 1992, the Human Resource Development Minister, Shri Arjun Singh said though the policy formulated in 1986 had stood the test of time, the developments during the last few years had necessitated certain alterations.

The Human Resource Development Minister also stated that the 1986 Policy enunciated a comprehensive framework to guide the development of education in the country. However, the experience in implementation of the policy has necessitated certain modifications.

Extracts from the Revised Policy

Revised Para 5.13: Secondary education begins to expose students to the differentiated roles of science, the humanities and social sciences. This is also an appropriate stage to provide children with a sense of history and national perspective and give them opportunities to understand their constitutional duties and rights as citizens.

Access to secondary education will be widened with emphasis on enrolment of girls, SCs and STs, particularly in science, commerce and vocational streams. Boards of Secondary Education will be reorganised and vested with autonomy so that their ability to improve the quality of secondary education is enhanced. Effort will be made to provide computer literacy in as many secondary level institutions as possible so that the children are equipped with necessary computer skills to be effective in the emerging technological world. A proper understanding of the work ethos and of the values of a humane and composite culture will be brought about through appropriately formulated curricula. Vocationalisation through specialised institutions or through the refashioning of secondary education will, at this stage, provide valuable manpower for economic growth.

Pace Setting Schools: (*Revised Para* 5.15): Pace-setting residential schools, Navodaya Vidyalayas, intended to serve this purpose have been established in most parts of the country on a given pattern, but with full scope for innovation and experimentation. Their broad aim will continue to be to serve the objective of excellence coupled with equity and social justice with reservation for the rural areas, SCs and STs, to promote national integration by providing opportunities to talented children from different parts of the country, to live and learn together, to develop their full potential, and, most importantly, to become catalysts of a nationwide programme of school improvement.

Vocationalisation: The introduction of systematic, well planned and rigorously implemented programme of vocational education is crucial in the proposed educational reorganisation. These elements are meant to develop a healthy attitude amongst students towards work and life, to enhance individual employability, to reduce the mismatch between the demand and supply of skilled manpower, and to provide an alternative for those intending to pursue higher education without particular interest or purpose. Efforts will be made to provide children at the higher secondary level with generic vocational courses which cut across several occupational fields and which are not occupation specific.

Revised Para 5.17: Vocational education will also be a distinct stream, intended to prepare students for identified occupations spanning, several areas of activity. These courses will ordinarily be provided after the secondary stage, but keeping the scheme flexible, they may also be made available after class VIII.

Revised Para 5.23: It is proposed that vocational courses cover 10 per cent of higher secondary students by 1995 and 25 per cent by 2000. Steps will be taken to see that a substantial majority of the products of vocational courses are employed or become set-employed. Review of the courses offered would be regularly undertaken. Government will also review its recruitment policy to encourage diversification at the secondary level.

5.14 NPE AND PROGRAMME OF ACTION 1992

Introduction

For the implementation of the NPE, 1992, a Programme of Action was formulated by the Department of Education, Ministry of Human Resource Development, Government of India. Twenty-two Task Forces were constituted on different subject areas. A Steering Committee was also set up.

Secondary Education and Programme of Action (POA)

Issues relating to secondary education are elaborated in Chapter 8 entitled 'Secondary Education'.

The issues relating to computer literary, Navodaya Vidyalayas, vocationalisation of education, open learning systems, examination reforms and teacher training, through linkage with secondary education have been discussed in Chapters 9, 10, 12, 21 and 22 respectively.

Broad Parameters of Strategy Envisaged

1. *Widening Access to Secondary Education*: This is to be done setting new schools in the unserved areas and by extending and consolidating the existing facilities with particular emphasis on ensuring substantially increased enrolment of girls, the SCs and the STs.
2. *Uniformity in Pattern of Secondary Education*: Progressively bringing in the higher secondary stage (and all the equivalents—pre-university one year degree course, pre-university two-year course, intermediate colleges) as part of the school system in all the States.
3. *Curriculum Reforms*: (i) Formulating a National Curriculum Framework for the higher secondary stage as well as the development of new curricula and instructional packages based on the semester system.
   (ii) Reviewing and revising the curricula of secondary education.
4. *Examination Reform*: Implementing a comprehensive scheme of examination reform.
5. *Infrastructure*: Improving considerably the physical and infrastructural facilities in secondary and higher secondary schools.
6. *Teacher Education*. (i) Reviewing afresh the existing system of pre-service teacher education for the secondary stage and formulating and implementing the improved teacher education system.
   (ii) Institutionalising in-service teacher training.
7. *Boards of Secondary Education*: Transforming the role of the Boards of Secondary Education.

8. *Navodaya Vidyalayas*: (i) Covering all districts.
   (ii) Increasing the validity and reliability of the admission.
9. *Vocational Education*: (i) Setting up of Joint Council of Vocational Education (JCVE).
   (ii) Strengthening Boards of Apprenticeship Training.
   (iii) Vocational Education. Vocational education to be strengthened at the college stage.
   (iv) Facilities for vocational guidance to be expanded.
   (v) Giving financial preference to States with adequate management structure.
10. *Teachers*: (i) Opening teacher's resource centres.
   (ii) Providing autonomous states to National Council for Teacher Education (NCTE).
   (iii) Organising special in-service training programme for teachers teaching subjects like work experience, art education, and health and physical education.

5.15 OBSERVATIONS AND IMPLEMENTATION OF THE PROGRAMME OF ACTION

Following programmes were initiated after the Programme of Action:

I. *Navodaya Vidyalayas*: The scheme initiated in 1986 with two schools was expanded and there were 513 such schools as on March 2005, covering 513 districts in 34 States/Union Territories.

II. *National Council for Teacher Education* (*NCTE*): The NCTE was given a statutory recognition in 1995 in pursuance of the NCTE Act, 1993. It has prepared norms for establishing different types of teacher education institutions.

III. *Education of Girls*: The scheme of providing boarding and hostel facilities for girls was initiated in 1993.

IV. *Vocational Education*: (i) A Joint Council for Vocational Education (JCVE) has been set up for policy formulation and coordination at national level.

(ii) In 1993, Pt. Sunderlal Sharma Central Institute of Vocational Education was set up at Bhopal to provide technical and academic support to vocational education programme.

V. *Reconstitution of CABE*: The Central Advisory Board of Education, the highest advisory body to advise the Central and State Governments in the field of education was reconstituted in July 2004. The Board in its meeting held in August 2004, *inter alia* constituted the following committees having bearing on secondary education:

1. Girls education and the common school system.
2. Universalisation of secondary education.
3. Integration of culture education in the school curriculum.
4. Regulatory mechanism of the textbooks and parallel textbooks.

The Committees submitted their reports and action was initiated on them.

VI. *National Curriculum Framework*: The National Curriculum Framework (NCF) 2005 was formulated. This is discussed separately under 'Curriculum'.

VII. *Evaluation of Textbooks*: Action in this field has been initiated and new textbooks introduced in a phased manner with effect from the academic session 2006-2007 in Classes I, III, VI, IX and XI.

VIII. *Examination Reforms*: The Central Board of Secondary Education (CBSE) and other Boards have taken several steps for reforming the secondary and senior secondary examinations.

Missing Links

The programme relating to the Vocationalisation of Secondary education has not made much headway. It needs in-depth analysis. These has been a mushroom growth of Secondary teachers training colleges resulting in lowering of standards of teacher education. Corrective measures must be taken immediately to arrest deterioration. Hasty Changes in curriculum and textbooks lead to confusion. A well-thought out and planned programme on the basis of try-out should be followed.

6

Constitutional Obligations Related to Education (With Special Reference to Secondary Education)

6.1 EDUCATION IN THE CONCURRENT LIST

Education was a State subject till 1976. With 42nd Amendment in the Constitution which received President's assent on December 18, 1976, it was put on the concurrent list which implies that both the Central Government and the State Governments can take appropriate action in matters concerning education. However, in case of clash on any policy or action, the Central Government has overriding powers.

Entry 25 of the Concurrent List states, "Education including technical education, medical education and university education subject to entries 63, 64, 66 of list 1, vocational and technical training of labour".

6.2 VARIOUS CONSTITUTIONAL PROVISIONS RELATING TO EDUCATION

Article 21A. *Right to Education*: The State shall provide free and compulsory education to all children of the age of six to fourteen years in such a manner as the State may, by law determine. [Inserted by the Constitution (Eighty-sixth Amendment) Act, 2002].

Article 28: *Freedom as to Attendance at Religious Instruction or Religious Worship in Certain Educational Institutions*: (1) No religious instruction shall be provided in any educational institution wholly maintained out of State funds.

(2) Nothing in Clause (1) shall apply to an educational institution which is administered by the State but has been established under any endowment or trust which requires that religious instruction shall be imparted in such institution.

(3) No person attending any educational institution recognised by the State or receiving aid out of State funds shall be required to take part in any religious instruction that may be imparted in such institution or to attend any religious worship that may be conducted in such institution or in any premises attached thereto unless such person or, if such person is a minor, his guardian has given his consent there to.

Article 29. *Protection of Interests of Minorities*: (1) Any section of the citizens residing in the territory of India or any part thereof having a distinct language, script or culture of its own shall have the right to conserve the same.

(2) No citizen shall be denied admission into any educational institution maintained by the State or receiving aid out of State funds on grounds only of religion, race, caste, language or any of them.

Article 30. *Right of Minorities to Establish and Administer Educational Institutions*: (1) All minorities, whether based on religion or language, shall have the right to establish and administer educational institutions of their choice.

(2) In making any law providing for the compulsory acquisition of any property of an educational institution established and administered by a minority, referred to in clause (1), the State shall ensure that the amount fixed by or determined under such law for the acquisition of such property is such as would not restrict or abrogate the right guaranteed under the clause.

(3) The State shall not, in granting aid to educational institutions, discriminate against any educational institution on the ground that it is under the management of a minority, whether based on religion or language.

Article 45. *Provision for Early Childhood Care and Education to Children Below the Age of Six Years*: The State shall endeavour to provide early childhood care and education for all children until they complete the age of six years. (Substituted for the original Article 45 by the Constitution (Eighty-Sixth Amendment) Act, 2002).

Provision for Free and Compulsory Education for Children: The State shall endeavour to provide, within a period of ten years from the commencement of this Constitution, for free and compulsory education for all children until they complete the age of fourteen years. (Original Article which was amended in 2002).

Article 96. *Promotion of Educational and Economic Interests of Scheduled Castes, Scheduled Tribes and Other Weaker Sections*: The State shall promote with special care the educational and economic interests of the weaker sections of the people, and in particular, of the Scheduled Castes and the Scheduled Tribes, and shall protect them from social injustice and all forms of exploitations.

Article 51A. *Fundamental Duties*: It shall be the duty of every citizen of India who is a parent or guardian to provide opportunities for education to his child or as the case may be, ward between the age of six and fourteen years. [Inserted by the Constitution (Eighty-sixth Amendment) Act, 2002].

Article 350A. *Facilities for Instruction in Mother-Tongue at Primary Stage*: It shall be the endeavour of every State and of every local authority within the State to provide adequate facilities for instruction in the mother-tongue at the primary stage of education to children belonging to linguistic minority groups; and the President may issue such directions to any State as he considers necessary or proper for securing the provision of such facilities.

Article 350B. Special Officer for Linguistic Minorities: (1) There shall be a Special Officer for linguistic minorities to be appointed by the President.

(2) It shall be the duty of the Special Officer to investigate all matters relating to the safeguards provided for linguistic minorities under this

Constitution and report to the President upon those matters at such intervals as the President may direct, and the President shall cause all such reports to be laid before each House of Parliament, and sent to the Government of the States concerned.

Article 351. *Directive for Development of the Hindi Language*: It shall be the duty of the Union to promote the spread of the Hindi language, to develop it so that it may serve as a medium of expression for all the elements of the composite culture of India and to secure its enrichment by assimilating without interfering with its genius, the forms, style and expressions used in Hindustani and in the other languages of India specified in the Eighth Schedule, and by drawing, wherever necessary or desirable for its vocabulary, primarily on Sanskrit and secondarily on other languages.

Higher Education and Research: Parliament has the exclusive rights to enact legislation in respect of institutions and Union Agencies mentioned in entries 62, 63, 64, 65 and 66 of list-I, Union List.

Educational and Cultural Relations with Foreign Countries

Entry 13 of the Union List. Participation in international conferences, associations and other bodies and implementing of decisions made thereat.

6.3 EDUCATIONAL ADMINISTRATION AT THE NATIONAL LEVEL

A perusal of the constitutional provisions reveals that Central Government is expected to play a significant role in the field of education. Though Ministry of Human Resource Development, through its Department of Education, Government of India, (Before 1985, the Ministry was known as the Ministry of Education) discharges the major responsibility in the field of Education on behalf of the Government of India, yet there are other Ministries at the Centre which also perform functions in the field of education.

The origin of the Education Department dates back to pre-Independence days when for the first time a separate Department was created in 1910 to look after education. However, soon after India achieved its independence on 15th August, 1947, a full-fledged Ministry of Education was established on 29th August, 1947. The nomenclature and responsibilities of the Education Department have undergone changes from time to time since independence. Since 1986, the Ministry has been known as Ministry of Human Resources Development. At present, the Ministry has three departments, namely 1. Department of Secondary and Higher Education, 2. Department of Elementary Education and Literacy, 3. Department of Women and Child Development.

Broadly speaking, following are the major functions performed by the Ministry of Human Resource Development, Government of India.

1. *Planning*: Educational planning is a part and parcel of the total planning of the country. The Central Government determines targets and prepares the educational plan to be implemented by the country as a whole. Of course it consults State Governments.
2. *Educational Reforms*: From time to time, the Government of India has set up Commissions which have gone into the various aspects of

education at different levels and have provided valuable recommendations and suggestions. These recommendations have further been considered by the experts and the States requested to implement the recommendations of the expert bodies.

3. *Organisation*: For carrying out educational plans, Government of India has set-up institutions like All-India Council of Technical Education, the National Council of Educational Research & Training, National Institute of Educational Planning and Administration which provide guidance to the States in the field of Education.
4. *Direction*: The Central Government also directs and guides the State Governments, local bodies and private enterprise so as to encourage education on right lines. This is being done by the Ministry through the Central Advisory Board of Education.
5. *Control*: As the State Governments require financial help from the Centre for supporting their educational programmes, they look for grants to the Central Government. The Central Government allocates suitable grants to the States, local bodies and private agencies. Thus, it exercises considerable control on education.
6. *Equalisation of Educational Opportunities*: The Government of India is wedded to the establishment of an egalitarian society and therefore has taken many steps to provide equal educational opportunities to the weaker sections of the society. It has initiated a large number of programmes in this direction.
7. *Pilot Projects*: The Ministry of Human Resource Development, Government of India, has undertaken a large number of pilot projects like rural universities, regional institutes, curriculum reform and textbooks, etc. By starting these projects, the Ministry aims at providing enlightened leadership all over the country.
8. *Administration of Education in the Union Territory and Centrally Administered Areas*: Centre is directly responsible for education in various Union territories and other centrally-administered areas.
9. *Clearing House Function*: The Department of Education serves as a depository of information and ideas of education, research, training and statistics. From time to time it brings out useful information on various aspects of education. The Department of Education also published a few educational journals which have proved to be very helpful in disseminating information in the country.

6.4 A MEANINGFUL PARTNERSHIP

The National Policy on Education (1986) revised in 1992 has described the relationship between the Central Government and State Governments as that of 'a meaningful partnership'. The 1986 policy in Part 3, para 13, has observed, "The Constitutional Amendment of 1976, which includes education in the Concurrent List, was a far-reaching step whose implications—substantive financial and administrative—require a new sharing of responsibility between the Union Government and the States in respect of this vital area of national life. While the role and responsibility of the States in regard to education will remain essentially unchanged, the Union Government would accept a larger responsibility to reinforce the national and integrative character of education, to maintain quality and standards (including those of the teaching profession at all levels), to study and monitor the educational requirements of the country as a whole in regard to manpower for development, to cater to the needs of research and advanced study, to look after the international aspects of education, culture and human resource development and, in general, to promote excellence at all levels of educational pyramid throughout the country. Concurrency signifies a partnership which is at once meaningful and challenging; the National Policy will be oriented towards giving effect to it in letter and spirit".

6.5 CONSTITUTIONAL PROVISIONS AND DESIGNED CHANGES IN SECONDARY EDUCATION

According to the constitutional provisions, secondary education is also in the concurrent list. In other words, the Central Government and State Governments have an important role to play in this sector. As stated in 6.4, the partnership between the central government and the state Governments is quite meaningful, the major role in the secondary education is played by the state governments and the central role is limited and the major responsibility for the quantitative and qualitative improvement rests with the State Government.The situation is quite encouraging.

The role of the Central Government in secondary education is discharged by the Department of Secondary Education and Higher Education, Ministry of Human Resource Development, Government of India.

(i) *The Ministry appoints Commissions and Committees on Secondary Education*: To give an instance, it appointed the Secondary Education Commission (1952-53). The Education Commission (1964-66) also went into all aspects of Secondary Education.

(ii) *Central Advisory Board of Education* (*CABE*): It is the highest apex body to guide the Ministry. It appoints several Committees on the very dimensions of secondary education. The CABE Committee (2004-2005) went into the issue of Universalisation of Secondary Education.

(iii) *NCERT*: The National Council of Educational Research and Training is the 'Academic Wing' of the Ministry of Human Resources Development (MHRD).

(iv) *NIEPA*: The National Council of Educational Administration and Planning organises training programmes for educational administrator, planners and supervisors. NIEPA was declared a Deemed University in August, 2006 and now it is known as National University of Educational Planning and Administration.

(iv) *CBSE*: Central Board of Secondary Education.

(v) Navodaya Vidyalaya Samiti.

(vi) Kendriya Vidyalaya Sangathan.

Centrally Sponsored Schemes

The Central Government has sponsored a number of schemes known as 'Centrally Sponsored Schemes' for the improvement of education in secondary schools and higher secondary schools in States.

1. Promotion of Science Laboratories.
2. Environmental Orientation to School Education.
3. Promotion of Yoga.
4. Population Education Project.
5. Environmental Education.
6. International Mathematical Science Olympiad.
7. Computer Education and Literacy in Schools (CLASS).
8. Educational Technology (IT).
9. Computer Education Plans (CEP).

Policy Decisions of the Ministry of Human Resource Development (MHRD) on Secondary Education; the National Policy on Education 1968, 1986 and 1992 covered secondary education also.

Administration of Secondary Education.

(*Discussed in a Separate Chapter*)

UNIT II : SECONDARY EDUCATION IN INDIA—PROBLEMS AND ISSUES

7

General Aims of Secondary Education

7.1 SIGNIFICANCE OF SECONDARY EDUCATION AND NEEDS OF INDIA

While discussing the aims of secondary education in India, two points must be kept in mind:

1. Significance of Secondary Education.
2. Needs of the Nation.

Significance of Secondary Education

The Secondary Education Commission (1952-53) has pointed out the significance of secondary education: "We have to bear in mind that secondary education is a complete unit in itself and not merely a preparatory stage; that at the end of this period, the student should be in a position, if he wishes, to enter on the responsibility of life and take up some useful vocation". It helps individuals to become useful members of a complex modern society. Since our needs are to transform the Indian State into a democratic, secular and socialist one, the secondary education being a terminal stage must discharge this function effectively. It is of interest to note that just 5 to 6 per cent of the college-age students, enter the portals of higher education. Thus a good quality of secondary education is very essential to meet the needs of the country.

Providing Teachers for Primary Schools: Secondary education provides teachers for the primary schools. Now the qualification for training in an elementary teacher training institute or school is the completion of the secondary schooling. Secondary education must fulfil this need adequately.

Preparing Mature Students for Higher Education: Secondary education leads to higher education. It is expected that students completing this stage should have the requisite maturity to pursue higher education.

Needs of a Nation as the Determining Factor in the Formulation of Aims of Education Including Secondary Education

While formulating the aims of secondary education, the Commission observed, "As political, social and economic conditions change and new problems arise, it becomes necessary to re-examine carefully and restate clearly the objectives which education at each stage, should keep in view. Moreover, this statement must take into account not only the facts of the existing situation but also the direction of its development and the nature and type of the social order that we envisage for the future to which education has to be geared".

The Secondary Education Commission pointed out the following needs of India:

(a) Transformation of India into a secular democratic republic.
(b) Improvement of productive efficiency.
(c) Stimulation of a cultural renaissance.

7.2 SECONDARY EDUCATION COMMISSION ON AIMS OF SECONDARY EDUCATION IN INDIA

In the light of the above mentioned needs the Secondary Education Commission stated the following aims of secondary education:

1. Developing democratic citizenship.
2. Improvement of vocational efficiency.
3. Development of personality.
4. Development of qualities of leadership.

1. *Developing Democratic Citizenship*: Citizenship is a very exacting and challenging responsibility for which every citizen has to be carefully trained. For democratic citizenship, education should develop in them the following five qualities:

(i) *Capacity for clear thinking*: The first requisite in this connection is to develop capacity for clear thinking and receptivity to new ideas. This is the hall-mark of educated mind. A democratic citizen should be able to sift fact from fiction and reject what is bad.

(ii) *Clearness in speech and writing*: It is an essential prerequisite for successful living in a democracy which is based not on force but on free discussion, persuasion and peaceful exchange of ideas.

(iii) *Education for living*: Education should initiate the students into the many-sided art of living in a community graciously. This art should be imbibed. Amongst the qualities which should be cultivated for this purpose are: (a) discipline, (b) cooperation, (c) social sensitiveness, and (d) tolerance.

(iv) *Sense of true patriotism*: The concept of patriotism is three fold: (a) a sincere appreciation of the social and cultural achievement of one's country, (b) a readiness to recognise its weaknesses frankly and work for its eradication, and (c) an earnest resolve to serve it to the best of one's ability. Education should develop these.

(v) *Sense of world citizenship*: Lastly, education must instil in an individual sense of one world and we must discharge our duties accordingly. 'My country—right or wrong' is a dangerous slogan these days. These are the days of internationalism.

2. *Improvement of Vocational Efficiency*: The second important aim is technical and vocational efficiency of our students. This includes:

(a) creating a new attitude that implies an appreciation of the dignity of all work, however, slowly;

(b) making the students realise that self-fulfilment and national prosperity are only possible through work in which everyone must participate and a conviction that when our educated men take any piece of work in hand they will try to complete it as efficiency and artistically as their powers permit;

(c) making attempts by all the teachers to ensure that such an attitude on the part of the students finds expression in every activity of the school; and

(d) promotion of technical skill and efficiency at all stages of education so as to provide trained and efficient personnel to work out schemes of industrial and technological advancement.

3. *Development of Personality*: The third aim of education includes:

(i) to release the sources of creative energy in the students so that they may be able to appreciate their cultural heritage; and

(ii) to cultivate rich interests.

4. *Development of Qualities of Leadership*: The special function of the secondary school in this context, is to train persons who will be able to assume the responsibility of leadership—in the social, political, industrial and cultural fields—in their own groups of community or locality.

7.3 AIMS OF SECONDARY EDUCATION AND EDUCATION COMMISSION (1964-66)

Education Commission did not formulate specifically the aims of secondary education.

However, since secondary education stage is one of the stages in the long-drawn process of education, overall aims of education are also applicable to this stage. According to the Commission, these are as under:

1. Relating education (secondary also) to productivity.
2. Strengthening emotional and national values.
3. Consolidating democratic values.
4. Developing social, moral and spiritual values.
5. Modernising society through developing scientific temper, awakening of curiosity, development of attitudes and values through essential skills. The Education Commission observed, "We are at a critical stage in the process of development and transformation and in this context the role of science is of the utmost importance. Science education must become an integral part of school education.
6. Balancing the claim of science (materialism) and spiritualism.

The Education Commission has struck a balance between materialism and spiritualism. The Commission has aptly remarked, "If science and *Ahimsa* join together in creative synthesis of belief and action, mankind will attain to a new level of purposefulness, prosperity and spiritual insight". The Kothari Commission has further supplemented this statement by quoting Jawaharlal Nehru, 'can we combine the progress of science and technology with this progress of the mind and spirit also? We cannot be untrue to science because that represents the basic fact of life today. Still less can we be untrue to those essential principles for which India has stood in the past throughout the ages. Let us then pursue our path to industrial progress with all our strength and vigour and at the same time remember that material riches without toleration and compassion and wisdom may turn to dust and dashes'.

7.4 AIMS OF SECONDARY EDUCATION ACCORDING TO ISHWAR BHAI PATEL COMMITTEE (1977)

1. Promoting an understanding and appreciation of our cultural heritage while simultaneously stimulating desirable changes in our traditional culture-pattern.
2. Moulding the learner after the image of the citizen as visualised in the Constitution.
3. Releasing learning from bookishness and elitist character so as to relate it closely to socially productive manual work and the socio-economic situation of the country.
4. Encouraging rationalism and the scientific attitude.
5. Developing the qualities of simplicity, integrity and tolerance.
6. Enabling the learners to combine 'work' and 'learning'.

7.5 AIMS OF SECONDARY EDUCATION AS STIPULATED IN THE NATIONAL COMMITTEE ON HIGHER SECONDARY EDUCATION OR +2 COMMITTEE OR ADISESHIAH COMMITTEE (1977-78)

The Report of the Committee is entitled '*Learning to Do Towards a Learning and Working Society*'.

One of the primary objectives of the Committee was to recommend a plan of action for introduction of vocationalisation of the secondary/higher secondary stage.

The Committee suggested the following aims:

1. Making the learners aware of the need for rural development.
2. Enabling the learners to understand the place of agriculture in the national economy.
3. Developing the skills and managerial skills to run small-scale and cottage industries.
4. Developing insight into the problems of unemployment, under-employment and economic backwardness of India.

7.6 AIMS OF SECONDARY EDUCATION ACCORDING TO NPE, 1986

The NPE 1986 indicated the following aims of secondary education in Part 5.

1. Exposing students to the differentiated roles of science, the humanities and social sciences.
2. Providing children with a sense of history and national perspective.
3. Giving opportunities to the learners to understand their constitutional duties and rights as citizens.
4. Developing consciousness of a healthy work ethos.
5. Developing values of a humane and composite culture.
6. Preparing learners for a vocation.
7. Developing manpower for economic growth.

7.7 AIMS AS FORMULATED BY THE INTERNATIONAL COMMISSION FOR THE TWENTY-FIRST CENTURY (1993-96)

1. '*Learning to Know*' or '*Learn a number of subjects*'.
2. '*Learning to Do*', in order to acquire not only occupational skills but

also, more broadly, the competence to deal with many situations and work in teams.

3. '*Learning to Live Together*', by developing an understanding of other people and an appreciation of interdependence.
4. '*Learning to be*', so as to better to develop one's personality and be able to act with greater autonomy, judgment and personal responsibility. In that regard education must not disregard any aspect of a person's potential – memory, reasoning, aesthetic sense, physical capacities and communication skills.

7.8 AIMS OF SECONDARY EDUCATION IN BEHAVIOURAL OR FUNCTIONAL OR OPERATIONAL TERMS

'*National Curricular Framework for School Education*' (2002), NCERT envisages to promote the following among the learners:

1. *Developing Language Abilities*: Language abilities of listening, speaking, reading, writing and thinking and communication skills—verbal and visual—needed for social living and effective participation in the day to day activities.

2. *Developing Mathematical Abilities*: Mathematical abilities to develop a logical mind that would help learners perform mathematical operations and apply them in every day life.

3. *Developing Scientific Temper*: Scientific temper characterised by the spirit of enquiry, problem-solving, courage to question and objectivity leading to elimination of obscurantism, superstition and fatalism, while at the same time, sustaining and emphasising the indigenous knowledge ingrained in the Indian tradition.

4. *Creating Environmental Understanding*: Understanding of the environment in its totality both natural and social, and their interactive processes, the environmental problems and the ways and means to preserve the environment.

5. *Appreciating Unity in Diversity*: Understanding of the diversity in lands and people living in different parts of the country and the country's composite cultural heritage.

6. *Developing Admiration for Freedom Fighters*: Appreciation of the sacrifices and contributions made by the freedom fighters and social workers from rural, tribal and weaker sections from all the regions of the Indian society, particularly from the North-East and the Andaman and Nicobar Islands, in India's freedom struggle and social regeneration, and readiness to follow their ideals.

7. *Balanced Attitude Between the Past and Present*: Appreciation for the need of a balanced synthesis between the change-oriented technologies and the continuity of the country's traditions and heritage.

8. *Developing Respect for National Symbols*: Knowledge of and respect for the national symbols and the desire and determination to uphold the ideals of national identity and unity.

9. *Developing Balanced Attitude Towards Nationalism and Internationalism*: Deep sense of patriotism and nationalism tempered with the spirit of *Vasudhaiva Kutumbakam*.

10. *Developing Right Understanding of the Globalisation Impact*: Understanding of the positive and the negative impact of the processes of globalisation, liberalisation and localisation in the context of the country's needs.

11. *Inculcating Values*: Qualities clustered around the personal, social, moral, national and spiritual values that make a person humane and socially effective, giving meaning and direction to life.

12. *Developing 'Self-Learning Qualities*: Qualities and characteristics necessary for self-learning, self-directed learning and life-long learning leading to the creation of a learning society.

13. *Developing Insight*: Capacity not only to process information but also to understand, reflect and internalise and develop insight.

14. *Developing Dignity of Labour*: Willingness to work hard, entrepreneurship and dignity of manual work necessary for increasing productivity, obtaining job-satisfaction and creating wealth generating systems.

15. *Developing Sensitiveness to Population Concerns*: Appreciation of the various consequences of large families and over-population and need for checking population growth.

16. *Cultivating Healthy Sex Attitude*: Cultivating proper understanding and attitude toward healthy sex related issues and respectful attitude toward members of the opposite sex.

17. Ensuring the minimum essential level of the acquisition of knowledge, understanding and skill at all stages, commensurate with the learners' abilities and the societal context.

18. Nurturing and sustaining of multiple talents and creativity among all learners in various domains of knowledge.

19. Shifting of emphasis from information-based and teacher centred education to process centred and learner friendly education.

7.9 BROAD AIMS OF EDUCATION INCLUDING SECONDARY EDUCATION AS VISUALISED IN THE NATIONAL CURRICULUM FRAMEWORK 2005 (NCERT)

1. Developing independence of thought and action.
2. Developing sensitivity to others' well-being and feelings.
3. Enabling the learners to learn to respond to new situations in a flexible and creative manner.
4. Developing predisposition towards participation in domocratic processes.
5. Developing the ability to work and contribute to economic process.
6. Developing the ability to work towards social change.
7. Enabling students to connect knowledge to life outside the school.
8. Nurturing an overriding identity informed by caring concerns within the democratic polity of the country.

7.10 SUMMING UP THE AIMS OF SECONDARY EDUCATION

1. Development of values of democratic citizenship.
2. Development of vocational efficiency.

3. Development of balanced and harmonious personality.
4. Development of qualities of leadership as well as followership.
5. Assisting the students make proper career choices.
6. Preparing the students for leading a moral life.
7. Preparing the students to imbibe the art of living together.
8. Preparing the learner to become an autonomous learner.
9. Providing knowledge of subjects which is essential for day-to-day life.
10. Developing scientific temper as well as spiritual values.
11. Preparing the learners for the effective utilisation of scientific development and technology.
12. Enabling the learners to understand the various dimensions of liberalisation and globalisation and their implications.

In short, secondary education should aim at the balanced and harmonious development of the learner so that he is culturally refined, emotionally stable, ethically sound, mentally alert, morally upright, nationally patriotic, physically strong, socially efficient, spiritually enlightened, vocationally self-sufficient and worldly humane.

8

Quality of Secondary Education

8.1 MEANING OF QUALITY IN SECONDARY EDUCATION

Although, quality in education has become the touchstone of education, yet it has not been defined precisely. Terms like quality in education, efficiency, effectiveness and standards in education are very bewildering and deny all efforts to define and explain them in a uniform way. It is sometimes stated, "You cannot define these terms but you understand when you observe".

Wider Concept of Quality in Education

The quality in education need to be defined in the wider sense of the overall aim of education as the all-round development of the individual and his commitment to social objectives; and viewed in this context, there is no doubt that vigorous efforts will have to be made to improve these to suit the changing needs of the country. It has become increasingly evident that the relevance of education, its significance, its validity for personal aspiration, its link with societal needs and goals, its efficiency and impact are the basic parameters of every educational system.

Narrow View of Quality in Education

According to narrow interpretation, educational standards are judged from examination results. Taking students coming out of an educational institution as its outputs, their quality can be considered from the following variables or characteristics:

1. Percentage of passing students in terms of divisions and distinctions secured.
2. The magnitude of wastage and retention.
3. The earning capacity of the qualified students.
4. Achievement of students in the domain of co-curricular activities like athletics, dramatics, debates, etc.
5. Admission of students into reputed institutions or professions, etc.

Quality of what students learn or more correctly, what they carry with them out of an institution, is largely dependent upon the variables like (i) students—their ability, interest, level of motivation, family background, attitudes, expectations, etc. (ii) teachers—their qualities and qualifications, and (iii) equipments which students and teaches are given to work with. Given the same level of other facilities to an identical group of students in two different institutions, one institution significantly excels the other because of its teacher competencies, calibre and professional responsibility.

1. *Quality of the Staff.* This implies:
   (a) Acceptable social and financial status of teachers.
   (b) A will to reduce inequalities, such as relating to gender.
   (c) A concern to manage the staff in accordance with the merit principle.
   (d) A desire to provide them with the in-service training they need to fulfil their role in a changing society.
   (e) A system of the establishment of incentives and structures to encourage research to work in multidisciplinary teams and thematic projects, thus breaking with the habit of exclusively solitary scientific work.

2. *Quality of Curricula.* This implies:
   (a) Taking special care in the definition of the objectives of the training provided in relation to the requirements of the world of work and the needs of the society.
   (b) Adaptation of teaching methods to make students more active and to develop an enterprising spirit in them.
   (c) Expansion and greater flexibility in training so as to make the full use of the possibilities afforded by information technology (IT).
   (d) Internationalisation and networking of curricula, students and teachers.

3. *Quality of the Students who Constitute the Raw Material of Secondary Education.* It is dependent upon:
   (a) Giving special attention to their problems of access in the light of the criteria related to merit (abilities and motivation).
   (b) Adopting proactive policies for the benefit of the disadvantaged.
   (c) Undertaking exchanges with secondary education and with the bodies involved in the transition from secondary to higher education to ensure that education is an unbroken chain.
   (d) Regulating admissions.

4. *Quality of Infrastructure.* This implies:
   (i) Provision of well-equipped libraries and reading rooms.
   (ii) Adequate use and development of Information Technology.
   (iii) Provision of guidance and counselling.
   (iv) Provision of co-curricular activities.

6. *Methodology of Teaching-Learning*:

   Degree of student involvement in the teaching-learning process.

8.2 QUALITY OF SECONDARY EDUCATION IN TERMS OF AIMS

Taking all the factors into consideration, it is generally said that the quality of the State run schools is far inferior to the quality of public schools.

Way back the University Education Commission (1948-1949) observed that secondary education is the weakest link in the structure of education in India. To a considerable extent, this is true even today.

It is generally observed that students completing their secondary education do not possess the 'art of living together'. Those who do not go beyond secondary education they are not able to play their role as envisaged in the system of education. They are not proficient in any language.

The quality suffers on account of the following:

1. The secondary education curriculum is not very challenging.
2. It is largely bookish and theoretical.
3. For a long time, its duration remained very short.
4. It is dominated by college requirements.
5. It does not have adequate rich and significant control.
6. It is dominated by the examination system.
7. A large number of secondary schools suffer from lack of infrastructure.
8. It does not adequately meet the individual differences of students.
9. Quite a large number of teachers remain without teachers.
10. There is no specific programme of teacher education for the teachers taking +2 classes.
11. Very little use is made of communication and information technology (CIT).

8.3 IMPROVING THE QUALITY OF SECONDARY EDUCATION

Knowledge has been increasing very rapidly. At the same time population in India has also been increasing at an alarming rate. Apart from 'Knowledge Explosion', and 'Population Explosion', there is the 'Expectation Explosion'—people want more and more quality education. Then there are the requirements of globalisation. Therefore, a balance has to be struck against competing demands. Following are some of the suggestions to bring about qualitative and quantitative improvements in secondary education:

1. *Provision of Adequate Facilities in State Managed Schools and Rise in their Educational Standards*: The roles of local bodies and private organisations in school education should be properly integrated with those of the State Governments to ensure that the minimum conditions necessary for the successful working of educational institutions are provided in every institution within the common system of public education, irrespective of its management. For instance, every such institution should be intimately involved with its local community. Each should be regarded as an individuality and given adequate freedom. A continuous attempt should be made to develop each school to the best extent possible in accordance with a plan to be prepared and implemented jointly by the management, parents, teachers and students and the department; and every institution should be assured of adequate financial support to discharge its responsibilities to its student body.

2. *Liberal Scholarship*: On grounds of social and national integration all the children of the country should study in the common school system of public education, because this experience is extremely significant for their development as citizens. To encourage this trend in the national interest, it is recommended that the public scholarships at the school stage, i.e. those given by government and local authorities, should be tenable only in a school functioning within the

common school system of public education, which will ultimately charge no fees and to which every child shall have access. This will not cause any hardship, because it is mostly the children of the rich persons who will be attending the independent schools and they will not be in need of any such scholarships.

3. *Curriculum Reforms*: (Discusssed Separately—Chapter 11)

4. *Strengthening Boards of Secondary Education*: Boards of Secondary Education will be reorganised and vested with autonomy so that their ability to improve the quality of secondary education is enhanced.

- Efforts should be made to provide computer literacy in as many secondary schools as possible.
- Secondary stage should expose students to the differential roles of Science, the Humanities and Social Sciences.
- Secondary stage is an appropriate stage to provide children with a sense of history and national perspective.
- Secondary stage should give students opportunities to understand their constitutional duties.
- Secondary stage should develop work ethos.
- Secondary stage should inculcate values of a humane and composite culture. (See also chapter)

5. *Adoption of the Neighbourhood School Plan*: The neighbourhood school plan should be adopted as a step towards eliminating the segregation that now takes place between the schools for the poor and the underprivileged classes and those for the rich and the privileged ones.

6. *Tuition-Free System in a Phased Manner*: The ultimate goal should be to provide tuition-free education at the school stage. From this point of view, tuition fees will have to be abolished in a phased programme.

7. *Admission Policy at the University Stage*: At the university stage also, it is essential to see that children coming up from the common school system of public education are not at a disadvantage in comparison with those appearing from the independent schools. It is, therefore, suggested that ninety per cent of the scholarships awarded from public funds at the university stage should be open only to those students who have received their secondary education in schools functioning within the common school system of public education.

8. *No Discrimination in Teachers' Service Conditions*: The first is to ensure that the undesirable discrimination that now exists between teachers working under different managements—government, local authority and private organisations—should be done away with. In this regard following steps to be taken:

- all teachers should have equality of privileges irrespective of the different managements under whom they serve;
- teachers with similar qualifications and responsibilities should have a similar system of remuneration;
- there should be a uniform system of retirement benefits for all teachers;
- the conditions of work and service under the different types of managements should be similar; and
- the methods of recruitment of teachers in institutions of different categories should also be essentially similar.

9. *Dynamic and Progressive Methods of Teaching*: There is a great need to use new techniques of teaching. Emphasis should be on developing the capacity of students 'how to learn by their own efforts'. (See Chapter 12)

10. *Evaluation System*: Evaluation should be made more challenging as well as objective. (See Chapter 13)

11. *Strengthening of Boarding and Hostel Facilities for Girl Students*: With a view to expand secondary education and also to improve quality, increasing facilities should be provided to girls.

12. *More Central and Navodaya Schools*: It is observed that these schemes have proved to be quite helpful in providing better quality education than other State-run schools.

13. *Human and Physical Resources*: (See Chapter 13)

Conclusion: If the proposals made above are implemented, we will have created a common school system of public education embracing three categories of educational institutions—government, local authority and private-aided—which form the vast bulk of all the educational institutions at this stage. The residual responsibility for the financial support of this system will be borne entirely by the State, although the local authorities and private management will be raising some resources of their own to supplement State effort. Within this set-up, the existing 'caste' system on the basis of management will largely disappear and a number of common features will be maintained for all schools, such as parity with regard to teachers, common admission policies which will prevent segregation of classes and ensure admissions to all quality institutions on the basis of merit, involvement with local communities, and freedom for experimentation and creativity.

Recent Schemes for Qualitative Improvement in Secondary Education

The key issues in this area apart from access are: (i) Quality, (ii) Relevance, (iii) Modernisation, (iv) Diversification, (v) Vocationalisation, (vi) Information Technology. Accordingly, the Central Government has sponsored several schemes for the qualitative improvement of secondary education and minimising drop-outs, stagnation and wastage. A brief account of these schemes is given below:

1. *Vocationalisation of Secondary Education*: The scheme introduced in February 1988 aims at enhancing individual employability, reducing mis-match between demand and supply of skilled manpower and providing an alternative for those who are pursuing higher education without particular interest or purpose. Details of the scheme are given in a separate chapter.

2. *Improvement of Science Education in Schools*: The scheme has been operational since 1987-88. Under this 100 per cent assistance is provided to the States/Union Territories for provision of Science Kits to primary schools, upgradation of science laboratories and libraries in secondary/senior secondary schools and training of science and mathematics teachers. The scheme also provides for assistance to voluntary organisations for undertaking innovative projects in the field of science education.

3. *Environmental Orientation to School Education*: The scheme initiated in 1988-89 envisages grants and assistance to States/UTs and voluntary organisations for various activities related to the promotion of environmental

education. The scheme includes programmes like review of textbooks and development of teaching-learning material relating to environmental education.

4. *International Science Olympiads*: With a view to identifying and nurturing talent in Mathematics and Physics at school level, India has been participating in the International Mathematical Olympiad (IMO) and International Physics Olympiad (IPO), since 1989 and 1998 respectively.

5. *Educational Technology*: Six autonomous State Institutes of Educational Technology (SIETs) have been set up in Uttar Pradesh, Bihar, Orissa, Maharashtra, Gujarat and Andhra Pradesh.

6. *Computer Literacy and Studies in Schools*: Realising that students, who are the work-force of tomorrow, need to be exposed to utility and applications of computers, the Department of Electronics, in collaboration with the Ministry of Human Resource Development, introduced this scheme in 1984-85.

Quality Secondary Education

Recommendations on the Functioning of Boards of Secondary Education

1. The Boards should think in terms of universalisation of secondary education.
2. In addition to the conduct of examinations and related matters, the Boards should advise the Government on all matters relating to secondary education.
3. Education Boards should be modernised through information technology.
4. The Boards should support schools in undertaking innovative activities and in offering high quality education.
5. The Boards must think regarding curriculum not only in the context of national level but also from the global level.
6. Industries, science laboratories and service sectors need to be actively involved in curriculum designing and updating.
7. The curriculum must accommodate any number of basic disciplines and has to provide learner-friendly inputs. The learner would have the freedom and choice to select his own discipline.
8. Strong coordination between with Directorates and the Boards needs to be developed for monitoring school education.
9. Standards in curriculum and evaluation of students should be comparable among all the State Education Boards.
10. The curriculum needs to be evaluated periodically. The curriculum development should be on the basis of national level framework and local area needs. The stress should be given on vocational programmes.
11. Examination should be subordinate to teaching and it should follow the curriculum.
12. Apart from academic performance, non-scholastics subjects should be given weightage at the secondary school certificate exam.
13. The flexibility in number of attempts to appear for the Board's examination may be increased to reduce stress on students.
14. System of coordination with industries, universities, higher educational institutions, etc. may be developed.

9

Qualitative Expansion and Universalisation of Secondary Education: Financing in India

9.1 REASONS FOR EXPANSION OF SECONDARY EDUCATION

On account of the reasonable success of efforts to universalise elementary education, lakhs of students are likely to knock on the doors of secondary schools and put education system under constant pressure to meet their demands for further education.

There are several grounds for expanding secondary education.

First, providing learning after elementary education is essential to consolidate what has already been learnt.

Second, at secondary level students can develop reasoning and thinking skills that are inaccessible to younger children. It is at this level that youngsters can be expected to acquire the common culture that will allow them to be useful citizens, to build knowledge through experience and experiments and to learn essential subjects, such as, health education, science and technology. It is here that large number of youngsters can be taught how to work, how to work in teams and how to live together.

Third, expanding quality secondary education is essential to ensure a better educated teaching force at the first level.

Fourth, opening learning opportunities beyond elementary education is necessary to motivate elementary school learners to complete their elementary education.

Fifth, as illustrated by the experience of the fast developing countries, the highest level of economic growth in the past decade was achieved by making substantial investment in their secondary education.

Table 9.1: Expansion of Secondary Education Since1950-51

Year	*No. of High/Hr. Sec./Inter/Junior Colleges/Pre-Degree*	*No. of Students (In lakhs)*
1950-51	7416	15.0
1960-61	17,257	28.9
1968-69	33,487	61.5
1978-79	46,874	84.1
1988-89	72,635	185.2
1990-91	79,796	249.0

(Contd.)

Contd.

Year	*No. of High/Hr. Sec./Inter/Junior Colleges/Pre-Degree*	*No. of Students (In lakhs)*
1998-99	1,12,438	277.6
1999-2000	1,16,820	282.1
2001-2002	1,33,000	305.0
2002-2003	1,37,207	332.0

As observed in the Tenth Five Year (2002-2003), "The number is not adequate to accommodate the out-of-school children and the growing number of upper primary school pass outs".

9.2 OBSERVATIONS AND RECOMMENDATIONS OF THE CABE COMMITTEE ON UNIVERSALISATION OF SECONDARY EDUCATION (2004-05)

Introduction

The Government of India appointed the Committee of the Central Advisory Board of Education (CABE) in September, 2004, on the subject of 'Universalisation of Secondary Education', under the chairmanship of Shri Ghanshyam Tiwari, Education Minister, Rajasthan. Besides the Chairman, it had nine Members. Prof. Krishna Kumar, Director, NCERT, was the Member-Secretary, Prof. Puran Chand, Joint Director (CIET), NCTERT was nominated by Prof. Kumar, to act as Member-Secretary on his behalf. The Committee gave its recommendations in 2005.

Terms of Reference of the Committee

To prepare a blue-print for the universalisation of secondary education consequent upon the attainment of universalisation of elementary education.

Guiding Principles of Universalisation of Secondary Education

The Committee suggested that the following four guiding principles may act as the pillars on which the edifice of Universal Secondary Education should be built.

1. *Universal Access*: Access is to be envisaged in physical, social, cultural and economic terms – all interwoven in a common concept.
2. *Equality and Social Justice*: Six dimensions of equality and social justice for which the school system must strive for are: (a) gender, (b) economic disparity, (c) social, i.e. SCs and STs, (d) cultural (including the issues of religious and linguistic diversity, (e) disability (both physical and mental), (f) rural-urban. All these dimensions need to be reflected with sensitivity in the curriculum such that the self-esteem of each child is built up. This is considered necessary for ensuring that all children are able to complete their secondary education.
3. *Relevance and Development*: No education today can be accepted as being relevant unless it (a) helps in unfolding the full potential of the child and (b) plays the role of linking in the development of the child with the society and its political, productive and socio-cultural dimensions.

Five domains in which the developmental role of education an be envisaged are: (i) Building up citizenship for a country that is striving to become a democratic, egalitarian and secular society.

(ii) Inter-disciplinary approach to knowledge, concept formation (not just piling information) and its application in daily life and attributes such as critical thought and creativity.

(iii) Evolving values in a plural society that is, at the same time stratified and hierarchical.

(iv) Generic competencies that cut across various domains of knowledge as well as skills.

(v) Skill formation in the context of rapidly changing technology which demands formation of mutual skills, transfer of learning and ability to continue to unlearn and learn. The learner should have access to global knowledge and challenges.

4. *Structural and Curricular Aspects*: These aspects are:

(a) productive work must be introduced in the curriculum as a pedagogic medium for acquisition of knowledge, building values and skill formation for pre-primary stage to the +2 stage.

(b) A nation-wide programme of Vocational Education and Training (VET) must be built up in mission mode and be structurally and administratively placed outside the school system including modular courses with lateral and verticle linkages.

5. Physical and Material Norms for Secondary Schools: (See Chapter 13)

Table 9.2: Number of Classrooms and Teachers Required from 2003-04 to 2019-20 (Based on 100% Success of SSA)

Year	*Additional Enrolment (Grades IX-X) (In Million)*			*Additional Classrooms Required*	*Additional Teachers Required*	*Cumulative Additional Teachers Required*
	Boys	*Girls*	*Total*			
1	2	3	4	5	6	7
2003-04	1.81	1.75	3.58	119488	179232	179232
2004-05	0.97	1.11	2.09	69811	104716	283948
2005-06	1.03	1.22	2.27	75573	113359	397307
2006-07	1.10	1.35	2.45	81810	122715	520022
2007-08	1.17	1.48	2.66	88562	132844	652866
2008-09	1.25	1.64	2.88	95872	143808	796674
2009-10	1.33	1.80	3.11	103785	155677	952351
2010-11	1.42	1.99	3.37	112351	168526	1120877
2011-12	1.33	1.07	2.40	79995	119992	1240870
2012-13	1.40	1.13	2.53	84360	126540	1367410
2013-14	1.49	1.18	2.67	88965	133447	1500857
2014-15	1.57	1.24	2.81	93822	140733	1641591
2015-16	1.66	1.31	2.97	98946	148419	1790010
2016-17	1.76	1.37	3.13	104351	156527	1946537
2017-18	1.86	1.44	3.30	110053	165080	2111617
2018-19	1.97	1.51	3.48	116069	174103	2285720
2019-20	2.08	1.59	3.67	122414	183621	2469342

Basis of Computation:

1. Projection of number of classrooms is based on pupil-teacher ratio of 30:1. Since, the

pupil-teacher ratio at the secondary level in 2001-02 is 34:1, the teacher-pupil ratio shall be assumed to be 30:1.

2. **Additional requirement of teachers is based on the consideration of subject specialisation of teachers at the secondary level. Hence, it has been assumed that the secondary schools shall be provided with 1.5 teachers per additional classroom.**

Table 9.3: GER in Secondary Education (Based on 100% Success of SSA)

(in Percentage)

	Male	*Female*	*Total*
2002-03*	51.60	41.75	47.00
2003-04	57.45	48.62	53.38
2004-05	59.76	52.29	56.37
2005-06	62.15	56.24	59.52
2006-07	64.65	60.48	62.84
2007-08	67.24	65.04	66.35
2008-09	69.94	69.95	70.06
2009-10	72.75	75.23	73.98
2010-11	75.66	80.91	78.11
2011-12	78.09	82.88	80.32
2012-13	80.59	84.90	82.60
2013-14	83.17	86.97	84.94
2014-15	85.83	89.08	87.35
2015-16	88.58	91.26	89.83
2016-17	91.41	93.48	92.38
2017-18	94.34	95.76	95.00
2018-19	97.36	98.09	97.70
2019-20	100.48	100.48	100.48

9.3 FINANCIAL PROJECTIONS

Estimating Additional Financial Requirement

The additional financial requirement to meet the demand at secondary level on account of 100 per cent success of SSA, has been estimated based on certain cost norms and assumptions. The additional financial requirement has been estimated considering few important components, viz., teacher cost; other recurring cost; cost of inspection and supervision, capital cost and cost on quality improvement. The cost norms and assumptions are given here:

The additional financial requirement from 2003-04 to 2019-20 is given in Table 9.4.

Table 9.4: Estimation of Financial Requirement for Additional Enrolment from 2003-04 to 2019-20 (Based on 100% Success of SSA)

(Rs. in Millions)

Years	Exp. on Salary	Other Recurring Exp.	Recurring Exp.	Insp. & Sup. Exp.	Total Recurring Exp.	Capital Expenditure	Total Financial Implica-tions
1	2	3	4 = 2+3	5 = 4+2%	6 = 4+5	7	8= 6+7
2003-04	24734	6184	30918	618	31536	17923	49459
2004-05	40889	10222	51111	1022	52133	10472	52605
2005-06	59596	14899	74495	1490	75985	11336	87321
2006-07	81123	20281	101404	2028	103432	12272	115704
2007-08	105764	26441	132205	2644	134849	13284	148134
2008-09	133841	33460	167302	3346	170648	14381	185028
2009-10	165709	41427	207136	4143	211279	15568	226847
2010-11	201758	50439	252197	5044	257241	16853	274094
2011-12	230802	57700	288502	5770	294272	11999	306271
2012-13	262543	65636	328178	6564	334742	12654	347396
2013-14	297170	74292	371462	7429	378891	13345	392236
2014-15	334884	83721	418606	8372	426978	14073	441051
2015-16	375902	93976	469878	9398	479275	14842	494117
2016-17	420452	105113	525565	10511	536076	15653	551729
2017-18	468779	117195	585974	11719	597693	16508	614201
2018-19	521144	130286	651430	13029	664459	17410	681869
2019-20	577826	144456	722282	14446	736728	18362	755090

Basis of Computation:

1. The salary cost of additional teachers has been arrived at by considering the annual gross salary of TGT as per the Fifth Pay Commission, including the annual increments during the projection period (which is the pay scale of teachers in KVS).
2. The additional teacher salaries are not to exceed 80 per cent of the total recurring expenditure in order to allocate 20 per cent of the spending on improving the quality of infrastructure and other developmental expenditures in secondary education.
3. These additional enrolments, classrooms and teachers in the secondary education system will also require additional expenditure on inspection and supervision. Since the current expenditure on inspection and supervision accounts for 0.55 per cent in the total expenditure on secondary education in 2001-02, the additional requirement for inspection and supervision has been estimated as apportioning 2 per cent of the total estimated recurring expenditure on secondary education for each year.
4. The estimated additional recurring expenditure in each year shall include the salary expenditure, other recurring expenditure, and the expenditure on inspection and supervision.
5. The capital cost of construction per classroom has been assumed to be Rs. 1,50,000 as per the SSA norms. This also includes the expenditure on construction of toilets for boys and girls separately wherever necessary.
6. The cost of providing laboratories will be Rs. 1,50,000 per laboratory.

* *Note*:

Capital Expenditure = Cost of construction of additional class-rooms
= No. of additional classrooms in a year x Rs.1,50,000

10

Secondary Education for the Twenty-First Century

10.1 UNESCO INTERNATIONAL EXPERT MEETING (2001)

The Dakar Framework for Action (UNESCO 2000) stated, "Education is a fundamental human right. It is the key to sustainable development and peace and stability within and among countries, and thus an indispensable means for effective participation in the societies and economies of the twenty-first century, which are affected by rapid globalisation".

Earlier Delors Report (1993-1996) or Report of the International Commission on Education for the Twenty-first Century had observed that Secondary education is a "crucial point in the lives of individuals, it is at this stage that young people should be able to decide their own future, in the light of their tastes and aptitudes, and they can acquire the abilities that will make for a successful adult life. The report continued that secondary education "should thus be adapted to take account both of different processes whereby adolescents attain maturity and of economy and social needs".

It is in the above context, that UNESCO International Expert Meeting on "General Secondary Education in the Twenty-first Century: Trends, Challenges and Priorities" was held in Beijing, People's Republic of China, from 21 to 25 May 2001.

The meeting focused on the following three dilemmas of secondary education.

- In respect of mass and selective schooling.
- In respect of general and selective (vocational) education.
- In respect of cognitive and behavioural outcomes.

10.2 EXECUTIVE SUMMARY OF THE CONSENSUS OF THE UNESCO INTERNATIONAL EXPERT MEETING

Mass and Selective Schooling

- Countries should continue to be committed to the goal of mass Secondary Education as a minimum in terms of policy and provision.
- Commitment to universal access to Secondary Education as an aspiration should be maintained with efforts to remove barriers and obstacles as well as build on strengths and opportunities especially for girls.
- Serious attention be given to making adequate provision for those not selected into Secondary Education, those who drop out or leave

before completing the cycle and those denied access to their preferred streams.

- Where there is not full transition from Primary to Secondary and/or from lower Secondary to upper Secondary, efforts must be made to accommodate all those who are eligible through alternative provisions. Where this is not possible, available places should be allocated equitably and transparently.
- Mass access to Secondary Education will require partnership between governments and other providers (private, NGOs, etc.), but governments should seek to safeguard the interests of learners by ensuring that quality standards are maintained by all providers.
- The structure of programmes and streaming practices should be reviewed to offer greater flexibility and choice to learners in the selection process, including the option to return to a preferred stream.
- Future orientation at Secondary Education should be towards greater quality and diversity of what is provided, more flexibility in the organisation of learning and greater responsiveness to the needs and circumstances of learners.

10.3 GENERAL AND SELECTIVE (VOCATIONAL) EDUCATION

- The Secondary Education system should focus on links between academic and vocational subjects and their interdependence in the overall education of adolescent learners of both genders.
- Secondary Education is about preparation for life and should reflect the reality of life in the twenty-first century that encompasses a seamless to-and-fro between continued learning and the world of work.
- The nature of vocational subjects, the way in which they are organised and taught, as well as the recognition given to them, determine their status in the Secondary school curriculum.
- Secondary Education including Vocational Education needs to address not only the human resource needs of the society but also the development needs and aspirations of the individual.
- There is a strong trend in Secondary Education in most countries to include some element of Vocational Education for all learners. Some countries are experimenting with ways of providing such joint education to different population groups, including migrants, isolated rural populations and learners in regular secondary schools.
- Incorporating Vocational Education into Secondary Education can be expensive resulting in poor quality teaching and a lowering of status of these subjects. Innovative and cost-effective strategies to overcome this problem have included contracting out the teaching of subjects to nearby specialist schools and centres or creating different ways of teaching Vocational disciplines that are less demanding in terms of equipment, materials and practically trained instructors.
- As the trend of life-long learning is becoming clear, Secondary Education is adjusting to this reality by developing flexible structures

and varied options in their programmes, as well as having stronger links to the world of work.

10.4 COGNITIVE AND BEHAVIOURAL OUTCOMES

- There is recognition that academically based education does not adequately address students' needs in terms of realising their full potential, especially in the context of rapid economic, cultural and social change and gender based discrimination.
- Given the declining role of other socialising agencies schools should take greater responsibility for helping learners acquire life-skills.
- The emerging role of teachers (notably as facilitators), their status, integrity and commitment are essential for implementing life-skills education successfully. The quality of pre-service and in-service teacher training is critical in this regard.
- Teaching methods, school facilities and services should be developed and adapted to provide life-skills/behavioural education.
- The role of Secondary school principals needs to be consistent with this new reality.
- Education decision-makers need to be sensitised to the consequences of their choices based on evidence of such factors as the links between academic success and personal and community well being.
- A multi-sectoral approach involving government ministries, NGOs local communities, etc. is essential for successful implementation of this kind of education.

10.5 OTHER THEMES IDENTIFIED BY THE MEETING THAT SECONDARY EDUCATION IS, OR WILL BE, FACING IN ACHIEVING ITS NEW OBJECTIVES AND FUNCTIONS INCLUDED:

- Inclusive and compensatory education.
- Eliminating gender disparities.
- Strengthening equity.
- The effective use of information communications technology.

10.6 RESOURCES AND/OR STRATEGIES NEEDED TO RESPOND TO THE NEW OBJECTIVES AND FUNCTIONS OF SECONDARY EDUCATION AND TO MANAGE THE THEMES OR DILEMMAS

- Commencing with the view that students are at the centre of any education reform.
- Understanding that there are three interrelated components to support students' learning—the people, whether educational professionals, parents or community members, the educational policies that offer a framework for what students need to learn, and the infrastructure.

11

Secondary Education Curriculum

11.1 CURRICULUM CONSTRUCTION FRAMEWORK

While discussing curriculum construction, it must be observed that the curriculum implementation is equally important.

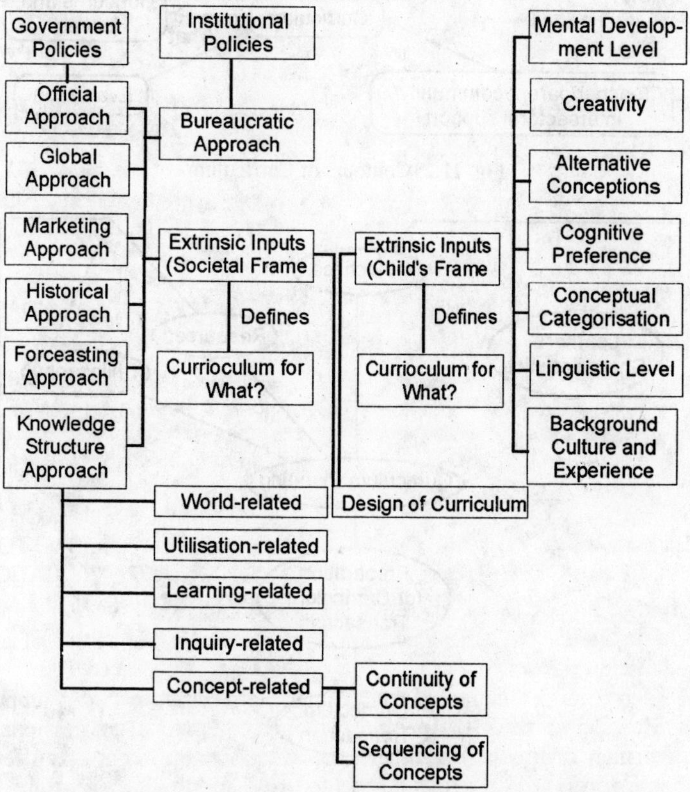

Fig. 11.1: Concept Map of the Inputs for the Design of Curriculum
Source: Prof. J.K. Mahapatra, Journal of Indian Education, November, 1999, NCERT.

Another factor which is important in this regard is that the framework of the society as envisaged in its constitution must be given its due consideration.

Curriculum is always in a state of flux. It changes with the new developments in the society. It cannot be static. It must respond to the challenges posed by thc fast changes occurring on account of information communication technology (ICT) and global concerns.

The following figures throw light on the general curriculum construction framework. These indicate the important concerns in general which the curriculum framers have to keep in view. It may be remembered that there are some fundamentals which are applicable to each stage of education.

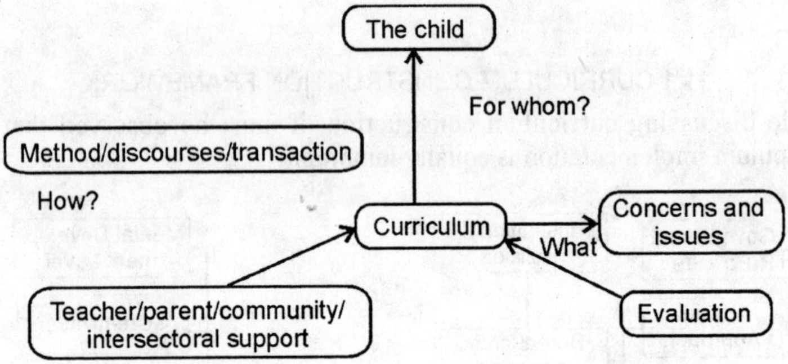

Fig. 11.2: Contours of Curriculum

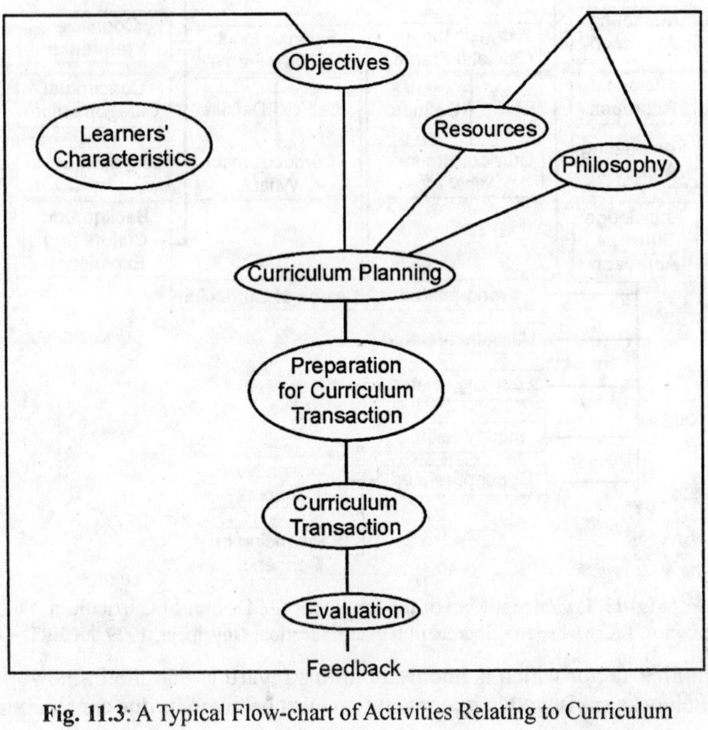

Fig. 11.3: A Typical Flow-chart of Activities Relating to Curriculum

11.2 MECHANISM OF CURRICULUM DEVELOPMENT IN INDIA

All the States and Union Territories have their own mechanism of curriculum development. Curriculum of secondary education (Classes IX and X) and Senior/Higher Secondary Education is developed by the State Boards of Education.

The NCERT, an apex organisation of the Ministry of Human Resource Development, Department of Education, Government of India, prepares the model curriculum which is accepted by the Central Board of Secondary Education, Delhi, with minor modifications. All the schools affiliated to it follow the curriculum. Out of about 1,50,000 high/secondary/senior secondary schools, in the country, only about 6,000 are affiliated with CBSE.

At present, there are 42 Boards/Councils of Higher Secondary Education, besides three Boards at the national level—the CBSE, CISCE (Council for Indian School Certificate Examination) and NIOS (National Institute of Open Schooling).

The Boards in India have the freedom to frame their own curriculum. They may adopt/adapt the NCERT curriculum.

From above it is clear that the NCERT curriculum is not binding on the Boards.

Curriculum is prepared by Curriculum Committees/Boards of Studies Comprising/Academic Councils comprising educators, researchers, teacher educators, university teachers, representatives of industry, etc.

11.3 BRIEF HISTORY OF CURRICULUM REFORMS IN INDIA

See also Chapters 3 and 4

11.4 NATIONAL CURRICULUM FOR ELEMENTARY AND SECONDARY EDUCATION (1988)

The curriculum was prepared in 1988. It took note of the major thrusts and highlights contained in the NPE (1986). Representatives of almost all States/ Union Territories Governments participated in various seminars and meetings held to finalise the curriculum.

Emerging Curricular Concerns

I. *Socio-cultural, Political and Economic Considerations*

1. Equality of Education and Opportunity.
2. Preservation of Cultural Heritage.
3. Constitutional Obligations.
4. Strengthening of National Identity and Unity.
5. Character Building and Inculcation of Values.
6. A Global Perspective.
7. Protection of the Environment and Conservation of Natural Resources.
8. Observance of Small Family Norms.

II. *Pedagogic Concerns*

(i) Education for All-round Development.

(ii) Evolving a Child-Centred Approach to Education.
(iii) Facilitating 'Learning How to Learn'?
(iv) Facilitating Creative Expression.
(v) Inculcation of the Scientific Temper.
(vi) Interface Between Education and the World of Work.
(vii) Continuous and Comprehensive Evaluation.
(viii) Utilisation of Media and Educational Technology.

III. *National System of Education*

(a) Provision of Equal Educational Opportunity to All.
(b) A Common 10+2+3 Structure of Education.
(c) A National Curricular Framework.
(d) Introduction of Norms of Minimum Levels of Learning for Each Stage of Education.
(e) Linkages with the World of Work.
(f) Promoting National Identity and Unity.
(g) Training through Different Modes of Learning.
(h) Continuous Improvement of the Quality of Education.

Table: Different Curricular Areas and Time Allocation Secondary Stage

Curricular Area	*Percentage of Time Allotted*
Language(s)	30
Mathematics	13
Science	13
Social Sciences	13
Art Education	9
Health and Physical Education	9
Total	**100**

General Curriculum Concerns Related in to All Stages of School Education in India

11.5 NCERT 'NATIONAL CURRICULUM FRAMEWORK FOR SCHOOL EDUCATION' (2000)

New Concerns. The curriculum should take into account the following concerns:

A. *National Concerns*

1. Building a cohesive society based on pillars of relevance, equity and excellence.
2. Integrating indigenous knowledge and recognising India's contribution to world civilisation.
3. Nurturing a sense of pride in being an Indian, patriotism and nationalism tempered with the spirit of '*Vasudhaiva Kutumbakam*' (World is one family).
4. Value development at all stages of education.

B. *Global Concerns*

5. Meeting the challenges of information and communication technology (ICT)
6. Meeting the challenges of globalisation.

C. *Psychological Concerns*

7. Reducing the curriculum load.
8. Recognising the interface between cognition, emotion and action.
9. Viewing the learner as a constructor of knowledge.
10. Coordinated decentralisation of the process of curriculum development.

D. *Concerns Relating to Integration of Subjects and Experiences*

11. Integration of environmental education with languages, mathematics and other activities.
12. Integration of science and technology.
13. Bringing mathematics closer to life.
14. Integrating thematic approach to the teaching of social sciences.
15. Sticking to the basic policy of the language formula.

E. *Evaluation Concerns*

16. Reducing the predominance of external examinations.
17. Using different methods of grading scholastic and co-scholastic areas of learning.
18. Using alternative evaluation procedures for learners with special needs.

F. *Specific Concerns for the Secondary Stage (Class IX and X)*

19. Taking into consideration the needs of a large number of students who join 'world of work' and hence the need for a kind of training which would enable them to face the world effectively.
20. Developing basic concepts in each area.
21. Enabling the learners to acquire skills to apply the theoretical knowledge in their day-to-day life and continue to be life-long learners.
22. Developing knowledge, skills and attitudes to pursue further education.

Scheme of Studies at the Secondary Stage

1. Three languages: the Mother Tongue/the Regional Language, Modern Indian Language and English.
2. Mathematics.
3. Science and Technology.
4. Social Sciences.
5. Work Education.
6. Art Education: Fine Arts: Visual and Performing.
7. Health and Physical Education (Including Games and Sports, Yoga, NCC, Scouting and Guiding)

Senior Secondary Stage

Senior Secondary Stage Curriculum: Major Concerns, Areas of Study and Salient Features

1. *Major Concerns*: Students offer a common scheme of studies up to ten years of general education. After this, the Higher Secondary Stage assumes great significance as students for the first time move towards diversification. By this time, students start developing their own thinking. As such, they are better placed to exercise a choice of courses keeping in view their needs, interests, capabilities and aptitude, which would enable them to cope with the challenges of future. They may, therefore, choose either specialised academic courses or job-oriented vocational courses at this stage. For majority of students, the Higher Secondary Stage may be the end of their formal education leading to the world of work. For others, it would be a bridge to the tertiary stage of education—academic or professional courses.

Higher Secondary Stage is the stage of maximum challenge. Whether, after completing twelve years of schooling, the students would be able to get into some job or vocation or pursue future studies of their own choice/preference is the upper-most concern in their minds and in the minds of their parents. It causes anxiety and stress, which may be avoided by careful planning and strategies for designing courses and suited to their future requirements.

Normally, only a small percentage of student population reaches the tertiary stage. Obviously, it is from amongst them that the eventual leadership emerges. The quality of these people depends on the foundation laid in early years especially at the higher secondary stage. It goes without saying that students at this stage must be fully equipped with basic knowledge, skills, aptitude and entrepreneurship so that they can qualify for self-employment as well.

2. *Courses of Study*: Courses at the higher secondary stage will fall into two broad streams—academic and vocational. In each of these, there will be a judicious blending of foundation courses and specialised elective courses. The existing groupings like arts, science, commerce and agriculture should not be treated as sacrosanct components. Students should have freedom within practical limits to choose subject of study according to their needs, interests and aptitude.

Curriculum at this stage in the academic stream will comprise:

(i) Foundation Courses, and

(ii) Elective Courses

(i) *Foundation Courses*: At the higher secondary stage, students opt for academic or vocational courses. However, they all need to have a foundation course. The common component of curriculum thus would consist of: (i) language and literature, (ii) work education, and (iii) health and physical education, games and sports.

(ii) *Elective Courses*: The elective courses will have to cater to the varied and heterogeneous clientele. While quite a few of the students may be preparing for entry into tertiary education, many more would be preparing to enter the world of work.

A student would be required to choose three elective courses out of the subjects prescribed by the Boards. The list of courses may include modern

Indian languages and their literature. Sanskrit and its literature, classical languages and their literature, English (academic and specialised), other foreign languages, physics, chemistry, biology, mathematics, computer science, geology, political science, geography, economics, history, sociology, psychology, philosophy, fine arts, sculpture, instrumental music, vocal music, home science, accountancy, business studies, engineering drawing, etc. The list is not exhaustive. It would be essential to review the list of courses periodically in collaboration with various interest groups, such as, industry, business, universities, employment and manpower specialists and common people represented through parents, artists, social workers and political representatives for effecting meaningful changes in tune with the changing needs of the society and those of the individual.

Evaluation of the Curriculum

Merits of the Curriculum

1. It is based on the ancient heritage of India.
2. It takes note of the developments in Science and Technology.
3. It takes into consideration the integration of information and communication technologies into schooling.
4. It is forward looking.
5. It aims at not on learning but how to learn and acquire skills and attitudes needed for a changing society.
6. It eliminates a lot of dead wood matter.
7. It provides for value education.

Demerits

1. It increases the learning load of the students.
2. It tends to saffronise education.
3. It is unrealistic as it puts heavy demands on teachers.
4. It needs huge finances for its transaction.

11.6 NATIONAL CURRICULUM FRAMEWORK (2005)

Background of the Construction of the Curriculum

The United Progressive Front Government, under the Leadership of the Congress Party came into power in 2004. The Minister of Human Resource Development, Government of India, in a statement said that the National Curriculum Framework for School Education (NCFSE) developed in 2000 during the period of the National Democratic Alliance (NDA) did not meet the requirements of the secular State. It was also observed that it did not redress the issues relating to the teaching burden and stress on the children. Accordingly the Education Secretary, Ministry of Human Resource Development Communicated to the Director NCERT the need to review the NCFSE in the light of the report '*Learning Without Burden*' (1993). In the context of these decisions, a National Steering Committee chaired by Prof. Yash Pal, Former Chairman of the University Grants Commission and 21 National Focus Groups were set up in July 2004. The Curriculum was given a final shape in 2005.

Drawbacks Pointed out in the Curriculum by the National Curriculum Framework (2005)

In India we have traditionally followed a subject-based approach to organising curriculum, drawing on only the disciplines. This approach tends to present knowledge as 'packaged' usually in textbooks, along with associated rituals of examinations to assess, and marks as a way of judging competence in the subject area. This approach has led to several problems in our education system.

First, those areas that do not lend themselves to being organised in textbooks and examined through marks became sidelined and described as 'extra' or 'co-curricular', instead of being an integral part of the curriculum. They rarely receive the attention they deserve in terms of preparation of teachers or school time table. Areas of knowledge such as crafts and sports, which are rich in potential for the development of skills, aesthetics, creativity, resourcefulness and capabilities for team work, also become sidelined. Important areas of knowledge, such as, work, and associated practical intelligences, have been completely neglected, and we still do not have an adequate curriculum theory to support the development of knowledge, skills and attitudes in these areas.

Second, the subject areas tend to become water tight compartments. As a result, knowledge seems fragmented rather than inter-related and integrated. The discipline, rather than the child's way of viewing the world tends to become the starting point and boundaries get constructed between knowledge in the school and knowledge outside.

Third, what is already known gets emphasised subverting children's own ability to construct knowledge and explore novel ways of knowing. Information takes precedence over knowledge, lending itself to producing bulky textbooks, 'quizzing' and mechanical retrieval rather than understanding and problem solving. This tendency of mistaking information for knowledge leads to 'loading' the curriculum with too many facts to be remembered.

Fourth, there is the issue of including 'new subjects'. The need for subjects to address contemporary concerns of society is important. But there has been a misplaced tendency to address these concerns in the school curriculum by 'creating' new subjects, producing related textbooks and devising methods of evaluation for them. These concerns may be far better addressed if they are incorporated in the curriculum through existing subjects and ongoing activities. Needless to say, adding new areas as 'subjects' only increases curriculum load, and perpetuates undesirable compartmentalisation of knowledge.

Finally, the principles for selecting knowledge for inclusion in the curriculum are not well worked out. There is insufficient consideration of developmental appropriateness, logical sequencing and connection between different grades, and overall pacing, with a few or no opportunities to return to earlier concepts. Further, concepts that cut across subject areas, such as, in secondary school mathematics and in physics, are not placed in relation to one another.

New Developments and Concerns to Which Curriculum should Respond

- connecting knowledge to life outside the school,
- ensuring that learning is shifted away from rote methods,

- enriching the curriculum to provide for overall development of children rather than remaining textbook-centric, and
- making examinations more flexible and integrated with classroom life.

Principles Regarding the Approach to Knowledge in the Curriculum

- Acquiring a critical perspective on social reality and the natural environment, through the lenses provided by the subject matter.
- Connecting with the local, and contextualised in order to 'situate' knowledge and realising its 'relevance' and 'meaningfulness', to reaffirm one's experiences outside school; to draw ones learning from observing, interacting with, classifying; categorising, to question, reason and argue in relation to these experiences.
- Making connections across disciplines and bringing out the interrelatedness of knowledge.
- Realising the 'fruitfulness' and 'openness' of enquiry, and the provisional nature of truths.
- Engaging with 'local knowledge/indigenous and practices in the local area, and relating this to school knowledge wherever possible.
- Encouraging questions and leaving space open for the pursuit of new questions.
- Being sensitive to the issues of 'equality' in classroom transaction as well as established stereotypes and discrimination, regarding learnability of the knowledge area by different groups (e.g., girls not given field-based projects, being excluded from the option of learning mathematics, etc.)
- Developing the imagination, and keeping imagination and fantasy alive.

Scheme of Studies or Curricular Areas

The Scheme of Studies includes the following subjects areas:

1. Language/languages
2. Mathematics
3. Science
4. Social Sciences
5. Art Education
6. Health and Physical Education
7. Work and Education
8. Education and Peace
9. Habitat and Learning

11.7 EVALUATION OF THE NATIONAL CURRICULUM FRAMEWORK FOR SCHOOL EDUCATION

Merits

1. It takes note of the rapidly changing environment and the need to incorporate necessary changes in the curriculum.
2. It stresses 'child-centred' education.

3. It points out the need for reforms in the system of examination and evaluation.
4. It very rightly outlines the shortcomings of the present system of education which lays emphasis on knowledge aspect.
5. It suggests that needs of individual students should be given attention while planning school curriculum.
6. Its suggestion of having not more than 30 students in a section is very sound for quality education.
7. Decentralisation of educational planning and administration is the need of the hour.

Demerits

1. The most important drawback of the document on curriculum is that it is theoretical and philosophical in nature.
2. It does not list the subjects which are to be studied at the secondary and higher secondary stages.
3. It requires huge infrastructure to implement it.
4. It puts heavy demands on teachers.
5. Its suggestions of permitting a school to have its own curriculum seems to be 'utopian'.
6. It envisages to have a class of not more than 30 students.
7. It talks of providing autonomy to teachers.

11.8 CBSE SCHEME OF STUDIES

Secondary stage (Classes IX and X)

1. Language I
2. Language II
3. Mathematics
4. Science and Technology
5. Social Science

Senior Secondary Stage: Academic Stream (Classes XI and XII)

I & II Two Languages (Core/Elective) out of

Hindi, English, Assamese, Bengali, Gujarati, Kashmiri, Kannada, Marathi, Malyalam, Manipuri, Oriya, Punjabi, Sindhi, Tamil, Telugu, Urdu, Sanskrit, Arabic, Persian, Limboo, Lepcha, Bhutia, Nepali, Tibetan, French, German, Portuguese, Russian and Spanish.

Notes: 1. Out of the languages, one shall be English or Hindi, both English and Hindi can also be offered simultaneously.

English can be offered at any of the three levels given below:

(i) English Core
(ii) English Elective
(iii) Functional English

2. The languages may be offered either at Core/Elective level. The same language, however, cannot be offered both at the Core level and Elective level.

3. A candidate has the freedom to offer, in lieu of one of the two languages above, any other elective subject provided under III below.

III to V. Three Electives out of the following:

Mathematics, Physics, Chemistry, Biology, Biotechnology, Engineering Drawing, Economics, Political Science, History, Geography, Business Studies, Accountancy, Home Science, Fine Arts, Agriculture, Computer Science/ Informatics Practices, Multimedia and Web Technology, Sociology, Psychology, Philosophy, Physical Education, Music and Dance, Entrepreneurship, Fashion Studies, Environmental Education.

12

Methods of Teaching

12.1 NEED FOR DYNAMIC METHODS OF TEACHING

The Secondary Education Commission 1952-53 has emphasised the need for using right methods of teaching in these words, "Every teacher and educationist of experience knows that even the best curriculum and the most perfect syllabus remain dead unless quickened into life by the right methods of teaching and the right kind of teachers". John Welton has stressed the significance of the good methods of teaching in these words, "No matter how admirably a lesson is planned, there is no really, methodical teaching unless the pupils by their own efforts pass along the road suitable for them. True teaching is nothing but arousing and directing activity".

In the words of Herbard Ward and Frank Rosceor, "While it is true that good method is not merely a collection of artifices of mechanical devices and that every teacher must devise his own method, it is important to remember that good methods can result only from the constant observation of certain broad principles. These include orderly procedure in teaching, an arrangement of the subject-matter which will avoid waste of time and of energy and a distribution of emphasis which will secure the greatest cooperation from the pupils and maintain their active interest".

12.2 MEANING OF TEACHING METHOD

E. Stones and S. Morris have defined teaching method in these words, "Teaching method is a generalised plan for a lesson which includes structure, desired learning behaviour in terms of goals of instruction and an outline of planned tactics necessary to implement the method".

Broudy has stated the definition of teaching method as, "A method refers to the formal structure of the sequence of acts commonly denoted by instruction. It involves the choice of what is to be taught and in which order it is to be presented".

The principle of 'Learning by Doing' has been accepted by all the progressive educators and in all the progressive countries. All educationists recognise that activity is an important instrument of education.

12.3 OBJECTIVES AND CHARACTERISTICS OF GOOD METHODS OF TEACHING

Objectives and characteristics may be listed as under:

1. They should aim at inculcating 'love of work'.

2. They should aim at developing the desire to do work with the highest measure of efficiency of which one is capable.
3. They should provide numerous opportunities of participation in freely accepted projects and activities in which discipline and cooperation are constantly in demand.
4. They should aim at developing the capacity for 'clear thinking' which distinguishes every truly educated person.
5. The methods of teaching should expand the range of students' interest.
6. They should aim at providing opportunities to pupils to apply practically the knowledge that has been acquired by them. They should aim at transforming present bookish schools into 'work schools' or 'activity schools'.
7. They should aim at the quickening of interest and training in efficient techniques of learning and study.
8. They should train the students in the art of study. They should train the students in the use of reference material, such as, the list of contents and index in books, the dictionary, the atlas, and reference books like the encyclopaedia.
9. They should be adapted to suit different levels of intelligence.
10. They should be such as they balance the claim of individual work with cooperative or group effort. The training of emotions, attitudes and social capacities takes place best in the context of projects and units of work undertaken cooperatively.

12.4 CLASSIFICATION OF METHODS OF TEACHING

There are a large number of ways of the classification of methods of teaching. Sometimes they overlap. Sometimes they include some techniques and devices of teaching also. As a matter of fact it is a very difficult task rather an impossible task to draw a line to distinguish these. Classification is also arbitrary.

12.5 BRIEF DESCRIPTION OF METHODS OF TEACHING

1. *Telling Methods*: These include lecture method, debates and discussions, panel discussion, oral quiz, story telling, etc.

2. *Showing Methods*: These comprise using demonstration, charts, diagrams, observation of on-site operations, etc.

3. *Doing Methods*: These consist of assignments, committee work, guided experiences, projects work, written tests, etc.

4. *Large Group Instruction*: This includes descriptive method, lecture method, tele-lecture, etc.

5. *Medium Group Instruction*: This denotes informal lecturing, such as, discussions in medium groups, dialogue, buzz group, brain storming, role playing, demonstration, field trips, etc.

6. *Small Group Instruction*: Seminars and discussions in small groups are the important methods covered in this category.

7. *Independent Study*: Under this, mention may be made of the assignments, use of Dalton Plan, programmed learning, computerised instruction, committee work, work experiences, etc.

8. *Discovery Methods*: These methods are high on all the three dimensions; learner activity, experience and experimentation by the learner, and cognitive understanding. Simulations primarily come under this category. The main emphasis of methods in this category is on problem-solving and providing necessary framework to the learner, so that while solving the problem the learner is also able to learn the rationale and logic of what he has done.

9. *Encounter Methods*: Carl Rogers popularised the term 'Encounter'. Since the emphasis is on providing experience through confrontation or through encounter, and not through cognitive understanding, these methods are effective for change in basic behavioural patterns and developing new ways of looking at things. Role play also involves some amount of encounter.

10. *Expository Methods*: In these methods cognitive emphasis is very high, while emphasis on experience is low. One good example of expository method is the lecture method in which the main emphasis is on imparting cognitive information to the learners.

11. *Individualised Methods*: These methods are quite well known mainly through the popularity of programmed instruction. The main characteristic of these methods is the guided search encouraged by the instructor or the teacher. In addition to programmed instructions, self-study computer-oriented instruction, case method, and prescribed experiments in science are other examples of individualised learning in which the main emphasis is for each learner at his own pace.

12. *Inspirational Methods*: These methods are primarily based on high activity on the part of the instructor or the teacher. Giving a sermon to the students or to any group of learners is a good example of this methodology.

13. *Natural Learning Methods*: The main rationale of these methods is that learning takes place in a natural way and planning for learning is not necessary. Learners are left on their own, with free and unplanned activity. Thus, the emphasis on learning activity is high, whereas it is low on planned experience and on cognitive inputs.

14. *Project Method*: This is discussed in detail separately.

Whether the method is activity-centred, life-centred, pupil-centred, teacher-centred or even subject-centred, there must be the abiding enthusiasm and interest of the teacher which would make teaching-learning efficient, enjoyable and pleasant.

12.6 IMPORTANT METHODS OF TEACHING

Among the important methods, following deserve careful attention. However, it may be stated that these methods overlap in their treatment and it is not always possible to draw a clear-cut line:

1. Audio-Tutorial Method
2. Assignment Method
3. Case Study Method
4. Dalton Method
5. Discovery/Inquiry Method
6. Discussion Method
7. Home Assignment or Home Task
8. Laboratory Method

9. Lecture Method
10. Note Dictation
11. Observation Method
12. Problem Method
13. Project Method
14. Question-Answers Method
15. Quiz Method
16. Review Method
17. Role Playing/Group Dynamics Method
18. Socialised Classroom Recitation Method
19. Source Method
20. Story Method
21. Supervised Study Method
22. Survey Method
23. Textbook Method
24. Transactional Analysis Method

Note: Sometimes some methods of teaching are also called techniques of teaching and vice versa. There is no water-tight compartment between methods and techniques. However, the Dalton Plan, the Problem Method and the Project Method are not used as techniques of teaching.

A teacher is expected not to be wedded to any particular method. He should make use of all these methods where possible.

12.7 RELATIVE MERITS AND LIMITATIONS OF TEACHING METHODS

Sl. No.	*Method*	*Best Suited*	*Limitations/Not Suitable*
1.	Learning	For presenting factual and informational material.	1. For developing skills 2. Very little scope for student participation.
2.	Demonstration	1. For teaching principles. 2. For showing manipulative operations of any equipments. 3. For explaining a process	For presenting factual information especially in humanities and social sciences.
3.	Individual practical work	1. For providing direct experience to students. 2. For enabling students to fully understand principles, phenomena and process by investigation.	1. It requires a lot of preparation. 2. It is a time consuming process.
4.	Individual work in workshop	1. For developing specific skills 2. For teaching operations about machines. 3. For producing articles.	Needs huge funds.

(Contd.)

(*Contd.*)

5. Field trips	1. For providing direct experience in a natural setting. 2. For linking theory with practical knowledge.	1. Likely to turn into a pleasure trip. 2. A costly affair.
6. Projects	1. For making students realise the pragmatic use of knowledge. 2. For providing correlated, direct and purposeful activity in a natural setting. 3. For making learning activity based.	1. It needs very dynamic and experienced teachers to undertake a project. 2. This activity is very time consuming.
7. Discussion	1. For motivating students to think. 2. For reviewing areas already dealt with. 3. For promoting better comprehension. 4. For attending to individual needs in small groups.	1. Discussion is likely to go astray. 2. Dominance of a few students.
8. Conference, Seminar, etc.	1. For proving sharing of experience and knowledge. 2. For encouraging group thinking. 3. For developing understanding.	Conferences and seminars become futile if background material is not supplied well in time.
9. Class and Home assignments	1. For consolidating knowledge. 2. For applying knowledge.	Unchecked and heavy assignments fail to serve any purpose.
10. Tutorial (Individual)	For meeting the needs of students individually.	1. Very time consuming. 2. Students are deprived of getting association.
11. Programmed Instruction	1. For enabling the student to learn at his own pace. 2. For providing scope for self-evaluation.	1. It is not possible to cover the entire course. 2. It is very expensive. 3. Needs expert programmers.
12. Teaching Machines	1. For individual learning. 2. For providing scope for self-correction.	1. Expensive. 2. One-way communication.

12.8 INDUCTIVE AND DEDUCTIVE METHODS OF TEACHING

Inductive Method of Teaching

Meaning and Definition of Inductive Method of Teaching: The inductive method is a method of development. In the inductive method, the child is led to discover truth for himself. The various processes in the inductive method are: (i) Observation of the given material; (ii) Discrimination and analysis noting differences and similarities; (iii) Classification; (iv) Abstraction and generalisation; (v) Application or verification.

In the inductive method, the pupils are led from particular instances to general conclusion. Inductive method is defined by Megrath as "a method that proceeds from own data to a generalisation, such as, a theory or hypothesis that will explain the evidence at hand".

According to Herbart, in the inductive method, the learner synthesises the broad principles from the study of the case.

Functioning of the Inductive Method: Concrete examples are given and with their help students are helped to arrive at certain conclusion of principles. In the teaching of science, mathematics and languages, this method is very helpful. The students, by examining a number of examples in science, conclude that heat expands and cold contracts.

In a geometry lesson the students by measuring the angles of a triangle come to the conclusion that their sum is equal to two right angles.

In a geography lesson, the students by examining the heights of the places located at high place conclude that temperature decreases as height increases. The students may examine the heights and temperatures of places like Simla, Nainital, Dalhousie, Darjeeling, etc.

In an economics lesson the students by examining a number of cases may conclude that agriculturists in India are in debt. The process runs like this. Ram is in debt. Sham is in debt. Krishan is in debt and so on. Ram is an agriculturist. Sham is an agriculturist. Krishan is an agriculturist and so on. From this it will be concluded that all these persons are agriculturists and are in debt.

In a language lesson, the teacher while teaching preposition may give examples like 'Ram is in the room'. 'The cat is under the table'. 'The book is on the table' and may lead the students to find out the definition of 'preposition'.

We find that a crow is black; we find another crow is also black; still another crow is black and so on and say that all crows are black.

This method is more useful in lessons where rules, definitions, generalisations, laws and casual connections between facts are to be established.

Merits of the Inductive Method

1. Knowledge is self-acquired and is soon transformed into 'wisdom'. "General truths in order to be learned must be earned" is a famous saying and the inductive method is true to it.
2. It promotes mental activity on the part of the pupils and make them active participants in the learning-teaching process.
3. It makes the lesson interesting by providing challenging situations to the students.
4. The method affords opportunities to the students to be self-dependent and develop self-confidence.
5. The student's curiosity is well-kept until the end when generalisations are arrived at.

6. This method is very natural because the knowledge in possession of man has been acquired in this way from the practical side of experience.
7. The child learns how to tackle problems. He not only acquires mere facts but also learns the way of acquiring facts, which proves him useful for practical life.
8. The method is based on sound psychological principles. Learning by doing is the basis of this method.

Demerits of Inductive Method

1. There is every possibility that the students may draw conclusions very hastily and these may be based on insufficient data and therefore may be wrong.
2. The method is very slow and lengthy.
3. It is not very helpful in the case of small children.
4. It is not suitable in the teaching of subjects in which there is more stress on the teaching of facts. It is not possible for us to experience facts in history and in so many other subjects.
5. The inductive method is not a complete method in itself. It has been said, "Induction does not prove but only provides the material to prove, it only discovers. When we have discovered a principle, we have to apply it again on some concrete instances for its verification". Therefore, we need deductive method to ensure the value of inductive process.

The Deductive Method of Teaching

This method is the other way round. In the deductive method, rules, generalisations and principles are provided to the students and then they are asked to verify them with the help of particular examples. The students are told that 'metals expand when heated' and then they are asked to verify it by means of experiments. They are told that places situated at high attitudes are cold and then particular examples are taken to prove it. The students are told that the sum of the angles of a triangle is equal to two right angles and then particular examples are taken to prove it. Such examples can be multiplied.

Merits of the Deductive Method

1. The teacher's work is simplified. He gives general principles and the students verify them.
2. This method is very economical. It saves time and energy both of the students and the teachers. Many principles for the discovery of which mankind has taken a lot of pains can be told to the students very easily.
3. It is very suitable for small children who cannot discover truths for themselves. They get ready-made material.
4. There is no danger of arriving at wrong and incomplete conclusions.

Demerits and Limitations of the Deductive Method

1. Knowledge is not self-acquired and, therefore, not assimilated properly.
2. The child is deprived of the pleasure of self-activity and self-effort as ready-made formulas, principles and rules are given to him.

3. It encourages memorisation of facts which are soon forgotten and, therefore, knowledge is rendered useless.
4. This method is unnatural and unpsychological for the students do not possess the ability to appreciate abstract ideas in the absence of concrete examples.
5. It fails to develop motivation and interest in the learning as the truths are not discovered by students themselves and, therefore, they are not of much value to them.
6. It fails to develop self-confidence and initiative in the students.

Combination of Deductive and Inductive Methods

According to I.E. Miller, induction is the making of the tools of thought and deduction is the using of tools. Both supplement each other and are not opposite things. Both are wanted for the discovery of truth as both legs are wanted for walking.

The only method for the teacher is the method by which mind adds to its knowledge.

Induction should be followed by deduction and deduction by induction. Our approach should be inductive-cum deductive.

Deductive and Inductive Methods Compared

	Deductive		*Inductive*
1.	General laws are first stated and particular cases are taken as examples to prove them.	1.	First particular cases are dealt with and then laws are derived from them.
2.	It does not lead to new knowledge.	2.	It leads to new knowledge.
3.	It is a method of verification and explanation and, therefore, it is a method of instruction.	3.	It is a method of discovery and, therefore, it is a method of education.
4.	This method is very quick. The child gets ready-made knowledge and he makes use of knowledge acquired by others.	4.	This method is very slow. The child acquires first-hand information by actual obser-vation of a lot of material.
5.	This method encourages dependence upon others as it is based on borrowing from others.	5.	This method gives training to the child to depend upon himself and develops self-confidence and initiative.
6.	It is a downward movement of thought and leads to a more perfect comprehension of the principle of generalisation.	6.	It is an upward movement of thought and leads to rules, definitions or, principles.

12.9 ANALYTICAL-SYNTHETIC METHOD

In teaching analytical method means the study of different aspects of a subject as well as of a topic, the analysis aspect from an important element of effective and efficient teaching. All effective and successful teachers use this method. They discuss the various elements of the subject after isolating them, the complex subjects can be taught in a systematic way with this method. The process of synthesis also takes place as the process of analysis is followed.

The process of synthesis is just the reverse of the process of analysis. In the synthetic method, the scattered elements of the subject are collected and the classification of these elements is presented. Synthesis makes the learning process somewhat difficult, sometimes we present some subject as a whole in the process of synthesis. The process of analysis is more organised as well as more easy as compared with the process of synthesis.

For a teacher it is preferable to start his teaching work in his class with analysis. His analysis is known as 'from part to whole'. This approach is more useful in the teaching of science and social studies. Analysis makes it easier to present the subject-matter.

William J.I. Gordon's Synthetic Model of Teaching

This model depends upon a number of assumptions regarding the process and development of creativity:

Focus: The focus of this model of teaching is to develop the creativity of the students relating to some academic discipline.

Syntax: The structure of the model comprises two strategies. One is to explore the unfamiliar elements. The other is creating something new.

The first strategy involves the following seven phases:

(i) In the first phase, the teacher provides information about the new topic.
(ii) In the second phase, the teacher suggests direct analogy and asks students to explain the analogy.
(iii) In the third phase, the teacher gets students to understand and master the direct analogy.
(iv) In the fourth stage, the students compare the new and direct analogy.
(v) In the fifth phase, the students explain the difference between the analogies.
(vi) In the sixth phase, the students re-explore the original topic.
(vii) In the last phase, the students can provide their own direct analogy and identify similarities and differences.

The second strategy also includes the seven phases as under:

(a) The teacher gets students' perception of the situation as they perceive.
(b) The teacher defines task.
(c) The students suggest direct analogies, select one and explore it.
(d) The students select personal analogy.
(e) Description is involved.
(f) The students create and select direct analogy based upon the conflicts.
(g) The teacher gets to move back towards original task.

12.10 PROBLEM SOLVING METHOD OF TEACHING

Meaning and Definition of Problem Solving

Problem solving may be defined as a planned attack upon a difficulty or perplexity for the purpose of finding a solution. It is an instructional device whereby the teacher and the pupils attempt in a conscious planned, purposeful effort to arrive at explanation of solution to some educationally significant difficulty. Yoakam and Simpson define it as "a problem occurs in a situation in which a felt difficulty that is clearly present and recognised by the thinker. It may be a purely mental difficulty or it may be physical and may involve the manipulation of data. The distinguishing thing about a problem, however, is that an individual who meets it as needing a solution. He recognises it as a challenge".

Dewey observes, "The problem fixes the end of thought and the end controls the process of thinking".

Gates has defined the problem thus, "A problem exists for an individual when he has a definite goal he cannot reach by the behaviour pattern which he already has available".

Why Problem Solving?

Life is full of problems and the successful man in life is he, who is fully equipped with adequate knowledge and reasoning power to tackle these problems successfully. There are problems and puzzling situations which are a normal feature of a child's everyday life. These problems grow in complexity as he grows older and older. The solution of these problems enables him to have a mastery of the environment. Therefore, if the function of education is to enable the child to prepare him for life, problem solving must be encouraged in school life.

Children are curious by nature. They want to find out answers of many questions which sometimes are puzzling even to the adults; nevertheless they must be helped to satisfy their curiosity, whenever possible, by solving various problems. We must teach the pupils, how to think so that they are able to transfer these techniques to a vast number of varied problem situations.

Steps in Problem-Solving

The steps of problem-solving are given below:

1. *Formation and appreciation of the problem*: The nature of the problem should be made very clearly to the students. They must also feel the necessity of finding out a solution for the problem.

2. *Collection of relevant data and information*: The students should be stimulated to collect data in a systematic manner. Full cooperation of the students should be secured.

3. *Organisation of data*: The students should be asked to sift the relevant material from the superficial one and put it in a scientific way.

4. *Drawing of conclusions*: Discussions should be arranged collectively and individually with each pupil. Panton suggests that the teacher's aim should be to secure that, as far as possible, the essential thinking is done by the pupils themselves and that their educative process produces the particular solution where formulation of generalisation is at stake. "Care should be taken that judgement is made only when sufficient data is collected".

5. *Testing conclusions*: No conclusion should be accepted without being properly verified. The correctness of the conclusion must be proved. The students must be taught to be critical, to examine the "truths" which they

"discover" to see "whether they fit all the known data". We should have our minds free from every bias in the process of problem-solving.

Teacher's Role in Problem-Solving

Valentine Davis quotes Prof. Pasher who suggests the following points in problem-solving:

1. Get them (the students) to define the problem clearly.
2. Aid them to keep the problem in mind.
3. Get them to make many suggestions by encouraging them: (a) to analyse the situation in parts, (b) to recall previously known similar cases and general rules that apply, (c) to guess courageously and formulate guesses clearly.
4. Get them time to evaluate each suggestion carefully by encouraging them: (a) to maintain a state of doubt or suspended conclusion, (b) to criticise the suggestion by appeal to known facts, minister experiments, and scientific treatises.
5. Get them to organise the material by proceeding: (a) to build an outline on the board, (b) to use diagrams and graphs, (c) to formulate concise statement of the net outcome of the discussion.

It has been stated that for the success of the problem-solving teaching technique we need "a teacher who has the ability to see problem clearly, the power to analyse with a keen discernment and the faculty to synthesise and draw conclusions with an uncanny accuracy".

Procedures in Problem-Solving: There are two procedures in problem-solving and they are: (i) the Inductive, and (ii) the Deductive.

Essential features of a problem: Following are the essential features of a problem:

1. The problem should be meaningful, interesting and worthwhile for children.
2. It should have some correlation with life.
3. It should have some correlation with other subjects.
4. It should arise out of the real needs of the students.
5. The children must possess some background of the problem which they are going to discuss.
6. The problem should be clearly defined.
7. The solution of the problem should be found out by the students themselves working under the guidance and supervision of the teacher.
8. The problem must have some educational value.

Merits of Problem-Solving: Following are the merits of problem-solving.

1. It helps in stimulating thinking.
2. It develops reasoning power.
3. It helps to improve knowledge.
4. It helps in developing good study habits.
5. It affords opportunities for participation in social activities. Problems are solved with the joint efforts of many students. The students learn to appreciate the different points of view and thus become tolerant.
6. The students learn to be self-dependent.

7. Discussions help to develop the power of expression of the students.
8. The method provides opportunities to the teachers to know in detail their pupils. They learn which students are shy in nature and which are very active and accordingly they assist the students.
9. Students learn facts which are meaningful and which have been discovered by their own efforts.
10. It helps in the maintenance of discipline. The students remain busy in finding out the answers to their own problem.
11. Knowledge is easily assimilated as it is the result of a purposeful activity.
12. Learning becomes more interesting in place of a dread.
13. It develops the power of critical judgement.
14. It helps to verify an opinion.
15. It satisfies curiosity.
16. It helps to learn how to act in a new situation.

Demerits of Problem-Solving: The demerits are given below:

1. Generally speaking problem-solving involves mental activity only. There is less of bodily activity.
2. A large number of students do not possess sufficient background information and, therefore, do not take interest in problem-solving.
3. There is a paucity of suitable reference source and books in the school library.
4. It involves a lot of expertise on the part of teachers to use this method.
5. The problem-solving involves a lot of time and the teachers find it difficult to complete the prescribed syllabus.

Examples of General Problems

1. Inflation: Rise in prices.
2. Population explosion.
3. Prohibition.
4. Eradication of poverty.
5. Indo-Pak tensions.
6. Limitation of economic policies.
7. Drug addiction.
8. Illiteracy.
9. Women's education.
10. Raising standard of education.
11. Checking pollution.
12. Bringing transparency in public life.

13

Human and Physical Resources

13.1 CONCEPT AND MEANING OF HUMAN AND PHYSICAL RESOURCES

Human Resources of the School

Human resources of the school include all the human groups or individuals associated with secondary education.

Among the most important groups that influence the quality of secondary education are:

(1) Teachers including the Head of the Students, (2) Students, (3) Parents, (4) Community, (5) Members of the Managing Committee/Governing Body, (6) Curriculum Framers, (7) Research Workers, (8) Educational Administrators, (9) Educational Planners, (10) Textbook Writers, (11) Examiners, (12) Professionals, (13) Health Educators.

Physical Resources

The physical resources of the school include the school plant, i.e. school building, laboratories, playground, equipment, furniture, craft material, etc.

13.2 HUMAN RESOURCES

Generally Prescribed Qualifications for Secondary School Staff

(a) *Principal of Senior Secondary School.* Post Graduate in one of the teaching subjects with II Class degree or diploma in teaching for direct recruitment. For promotion, 10 years experience as PGT or 5 years as Vice-Principal/Headmaster or combined experience.

(b) *Headmaster of a Secondary/High School.* Post Graduate with degree or diploma in teaching. As regards promotion, 5 years experience as Post-Graduate Teacher or 10 years as Trained Graduate Teacher or combined.

(c) *Post Graduate Teacher/Lecturer.* Post Graduate Degree in one of the school subjects with degree or diploma in teaching. As regards promotion, 5 years experience as Trained Graduate Teacher.

(d) *Trained Graduate Teacher/Language Teacher/Drawing Teacher.* Bachelor degree (Pass or Hons.) in two schools subjects out of which one should be at elective level with at least 45% marks and diploma or degree in teaching.

13.3 NORMS FOR POST FIXATION

Generally one and a half teacher is allowed per section. In addition, a post of Head of the institution with Librarian, Ministerial and Class IV employees according to the strength. In addition, work-experience teacher and one additional PET is also allowed if the school is co-educational.

Physical Resources. 300 sq. mt. land as per rules for affiliation, framed by CBSE for running a secondary school.

13.4 NORMS FOR HUMAN AND PHYSICAL RESOURCES FOR SECONDARY SCHOOL (CLASSES IX AND X) RECOMMENDED BY CENTRAL ADVISORY BOARD OF EDUCATION COMMITTEE (CABE COMMITTEE), DEPARTMENT OF EDUCATION, MINISTRY OF HUMAN RESOURCE DEVELOPMENT, GOVERNMENT OF INDIA (2004-2005)

A. Norms for Human Resources. One teacher for every 30 students to be steadily moved to 1:20; at least one for every subject area; qualified teachers for sports, games and physical education, music and art.

B. *Norms for Physical Resources*:

Land		*2 to 4 acres*
Constructed area		Not more than 50% of the land area
Facilities	-	One classroom for every 30 students
	-	One integrated junior science lab. (for Classes 6th to 8th)
	-	One Science lab each for physics, chemistry, biology, English language, geography, mathematics for 9th to 12th grades
	-	Disabled-friendly facilities like ramp, special toilets, classroom furniture, etc.
	-	Braille and sign language-related equipment/computer software*
	-	SIT to receive EDUSAT programmes
	-	OHPs, LCD projector
	-	Musical instruments, Gym equipment, sports and games material
	-	Junior computer lab with 30 computers for 6th to 8th graders with internet connectivity*
	-	Senior Computer lab. with 30 computers for 9th to 12th graders with internet connectivity
	-	Separate health/restrooms for boys and girls
	-	Separate cubicles for teachers with computing facilities-one computer for every 4 teachers with internet connectivity
	-	Safe drinking water facilities
	-	School canteen and stores
	-	Separate toilets for girls and boys, and staff
	-	Library with computer facilities and professionally qualified staff

(*Contd.*)

(Contd.)

Land	*2 to 4 acres*
	- Separate offices of Principal and vice-principal with computer facilities
	- Electricity
	- Telephone
	- School office for non-teaching staff with computer facilities
	- Hobby room(s) for developing creativity and life skills including music, art and paintings
	- Playgrounds—soccer, hockey, volleyball, basketball, badminton, tennis, preferably separate for girls
	- Indoor games facilities separately for girls and boys
	- Gymnasium separately for girls and boys
	- Gardens and Social Forestry

* In Chinese schools, the computer centres are usually huge with 150 to 200 computers, VDUs nearly sunk into the desks; all with high band internet connectivity, probably served through a high power server.

The norms listed above already exist in large number of Kendriya Vidyalayas. Many of the reputed private schools have facilities much more than what is laid out in these norms. For large majority of the secondary schools, particularly the government aided institutions in various states, however, the norms would appear to be an Utopia. This mirage of an 'Utopia' is probably because large number of schools do not have these facilities. The State did not reprioritise the national economy to mobilise adequate resources for creating such facilities in the government, local body or aided schools in spite of the commitment made in the 1986 policy that the public outlay on education shall "uniformly exceed 6 per cent of the national income". Yet, it is necessary because without these facilities diversified quality schooling through constructivist paradigm is impossible.

The Committee does not maintain that these facilities can be created here and now. These facilities can be developed over a period of time in a phased manner. It may begin with the minimum provision of additional classrooms and teachers, but must move on to laboratories, libraries, computer lab., sports and games facilities, art and culture facilities, etc. in phases.

The school facilities are used for not more than four to five hours a day. Effort should be made to make better use of the schooling facility by running it in more than one shift wherever feasible. For example, it is quite common among the Delhi Government Schools to use the same building for two shifts.

Significance of Physical Resources of the School

A school cannot work effectively without adequate physical resources. Physical resources have a great bearing on the functioning of the school. Adequate, attractive, well equipped and properly maintained physical infrastructure of the schools serves as a great motivating force in the teaching-learning process. It is very important that the physical infrastructure of the school becomes the 'learning laboratories', directly or indirectly.

Winston Churchill, a former Prime Minister of England expressed the significance of the school plant in these words, "We shape our buildings and ultimately they shape us".

A school is a life-giving and vital environment. Therefore, a concerted effort on the part of all concerned with the school should be made to ensure that it has an artistic appeal. A healthy, beautiful and refreshing environment soothes the eyes and pleases the soul. In such an environment, the intellectual faculties of the students and teachers function at their best. It has been very aptly observed by Yeager William, "Nothing in the whole educational programme is more conducive to cooperative attitude among the pupils and a love of school than an attractive and wholesome environment.

13.5 SCHOOL PLANT

Meaning of the School Plant

The school plant is a comprehensive term which includes building, grounds, school furniture, other equipment and apparatus. The school plant is an integral part of a learning environment. It facilitates effective teaching-learning.

Essentials of a Good School Plant

These may be categorised under five heads:

1. Adequate and suitable site.
2. Structurally suitable building.
3. Proper building services.
4. Adequate equipment.
5. Proper maintenance and repairs.

GENERAL PRINCIPLES OF DESIGNING SCHOOL BUILDING

1. *Principle of Adequacy of Space*: The school plant must provide for all the necessary facilities for curricular and co-curricular activities.

2. *Principle of Safety*: The building must be planned in strict conformity with safety and hygienic considerations. Full attention must be given to site, soil, ventilation, light and other allied problems. The school plant must be able to protect the health of the students and teachers.

3. *Principle of Durability*: As far as possible, the building must be '*pucca*' rather than '*kachcha*'.

4. *Principle of Economy*: The school plant should be economical in original cost, upkeep and operation. Economy can be affected by the adoption of a standard classroom unit.

5. *Principle of Accessibility*: The school should be built at a place which is easily accessible to the students and free from road dangers.

6. *Principle of Mobility*: The question of easy movement, particularly in large schools of more than one storeys is important.

7. *Principle of Flexibility*: There should be no rigidity in the design and use of the plant. Scope must be left for modification in accordance with the needs.

8. *Principle of Coordination*: There must be full coordination among the various parts and their location at particular place must have a purpose. For

instance a workshop will be away from the classroom and staff room very near to principal's room.

9. *Principle of Simplicity*: The design of the building should be simple but artistic.

10. *Principle of Comprehensiveness*: A comprehensive vision is necessary in which function, form and space are so harmonised that the soil from which the synthesis grows will be enriched by such a pattern.

11. *Principle of Utility*: It must give the maximum utility to the students as regards accommodation, protection from weather, maximum light and ventilation, free movement and comfortable stay in rooms for longer hours. It would be an advantage if sound proof adjustable partitions could be provided; and where partition walls are provided they should be left free from carrying loads so that they can be moved if, at some future date, it should be necessary to rearrange the rooms.

12. The plan must provide for a plentiful supply of pure drinking water.

13.6 SELECTION OF SCHOOL SITE OR PLACE

In the selection of school site, important considerations which must be taken into account are given below. It must be stressed that the selection of the site which is the first requisite of a good environment needs careful consideration.

1. *Surroundings*: The site should be located in healthy surroundings. It should be near a road so as to be accessible by bus or other means of transport, yet back from the road. It should be located in a quiet and pleasant environment.
2. *Level*: The level of the area should be little raised so that water logging does not take place. There should be no danger of floods or breach of any canal.
3. *Direction*: The site selected should permit the construction of the rooms in such a way that no corner remains without sunlight.
4. *Shape*: The shape of the site preferably should be rectangular.
5. *Public Service Conveniences*: Various public services like drainage, water-pipe arrangement and lighting arrangement should be easily accessible.
6. *Scope for Future Expansion*: The site for a school should be so selected as to allow normal expansion towards one direction at least.

Situations to be avoided in the Selection of Site/Space for the School

1. Noisy and busy roads.
2. Public places like bus stand, railway station, grain market, etc.
3. Places like cremation grounds and burial grounds.
4. Marshy lands.
5. Uneven and undeveloped lands.
6. Stagnant pools, cattle ponds and other unhealthy surroundings.
7. Places of public entertainment like the cinema houses.

13.7 HIGHER SECONDARY SCHOOL BUILDINGS: AREA REQUIREMENTS FOR DIFFERENT ROOMS/PURPOSES

Area Per Student in the Class: An area of 12 sq. ft. per student shall be provided in a class/section.

Laboratories: Laboratories shall be planned for even number of students subject to a minimum of 20. The area of laboratory shall be worked out at 20 sq. ft. per student seat provided. Store of 80 to 120 sq. ft. area may also be provided.

Library: A library of 600 sq. ft. shall be adequate to meet the present educational needs. In certain cases the area may be increased to 690 sq. ft.

Assembly Hall: Ordinarily Assembly Hall shall be planned in all school designs for future construction only.

Assembly Hal shall be planned for 50 per cent of the total enrols at the rate of 7 sq. ft. per seat capacity. The areas of the hall so arrived at shall be inclusive of internal passage gangways but shall be exclusive of the area of stage.

Scale of Accommodation for Administrative Units: The following scale of accommodation is recommended for administrative units:

(a) Principal's office	200 sq. ft.
(b) Staff common room	For 75 per cent members of the total teaching staff at the rate of 20 sq. ft. per staff member subject to a minimum of 200 sq. ft.

(c) General office, record and 200 sq. ft. files room.
(d) Guidance room 200 sq. ft. which may also be used as visitor's room.
(e) First-aid or doctor's room 150 sq. ft. with attached lavatory.

Built-in Storage Space: Adequate built-in storage space in the shape of cupboard, open shelves, etc. shall be provided in a classroom.

General storage space shall be in the neighbourhood of 5 per cent of the teaching area.

Cafeteria: Cafeteria and students' common room, etc. need not be provided except under special circumstances.

Sanitary Fittings. The following scale of sanitary fittings is recommended:

Latrines or W.C.	1 for every 100 students or part thereof.
Urinals	1 for every 25 students or part thereof.

(In case of girls schools, urinals shall be provided in separate enclosures with foot squatting).

Water taps with troughs	1 for every 50 students or part thereof.

13.8 TYPES OF BUILDING DESIGN OF SCHOOL (GENERALLY APPLICABLE TO A GOVERNMENT SCHOOL)

Important types of design are:

I Type	: This is the simplest form of school building. It consists of a number of classroom in a single row. This can be a temporary arrangement and allows scope for further expansion.
L Type	: This is an improvement of I type. In this pattern I type will have an expansion on one side.
T Type	: This consists of I type with extension on one side both ways.
U Type	: This has two I's joined on one side.
E Type	: In this design I type will have three extensions on the same side of the main block.
H Type	: This consists of two I's joined in the centre with the block of rooms.

Note: Several public schools have air-conditioned buildings, make provision for swimming pools, gymnasium, etc. They provide a number of activities normally not provided in government schools. Thus, they have their own plans for school buildings.

13.9 SECONDARY SCHOOL LABORATORIES

Meaning and Significance of School Laboratory

A school laboratory is a big room in which practical work relating to science is done. It is considered as the 'hub' of science activities. It is a field of experiments. Students learn here by doing.

In a secondary and senior secondary school, separate laboratories for history, chemistry and physics are provided. Teaching of these subjects cannot be imagined without a laboratory.

Main Objectives or Purposes or Need for a Laboratory

1. To develop scientific temper among students.
2. To develop the power of observation of the students.
3. To provide real knowledge of scientific phenomenon.
4. To provide conducive environment for learning.
5. To provide opportunities to verify scientific laws.
6. To provide opportunity to students for training in the use of scientific method.
7. To help students in developing values of cooperation and working together.
8. To help students in developing initiative and self-confidence.
9. To provide opportunities to observe, think, analyse and synthesise facts.
10. To draw conclusions on the basis of cause and effect relationships.

Equipment for Different Types of Laboratories

General Science Laboratory:

(i) Working tables (ordinary) with drawers.
(ii) Demonstration table (8′ × 4′) provided with gas and water points.
(iii) A minimum of two sinks in the corners of the laboratory.
(iv) A black-board.
(v) Stools (in two sizes)
(vi) Almirahs (steel or wooden)

Biology Laboratory:

Biology laboratory should be equipped with the following:

(i) Tables (6′ × 2′ × 2.5′) with water fittings and drawers.
(ii) Two sinks at the corners of the laboratory.
(iii) Almirahs.
(iv) Stools (in two sizes).
(v) Wall board or black-board.
(vi) Small table racks.

(vii) Wall shelves.
(viii) A froggery, where necessary.

Special attention must be paid to lighting arrangement in biology laboratory. It should have glass panes on the northern side and pendent lights over the tables.

Chemistry Laboratory

The equipment for chemistry laboratory is as under:

(i) Almirahs (wooden and steel).
(ii) Wall board or black-board.
(iii) Demonstration table (8′ × 4′) with cupboards, water and gas points.
(iv) Working tables with cupboards, shelves, water and gas points.
(v) Balance room should be attached to the laboratory.
(vi) Sinks on each working table or at least two large sinks at the corners of the laboratory.
(vii) A fume cupboard.
(viii) A wooden box half filled with sand for use as waste material box.
(ix) Acid proof drainage system.
(x) Shelves for reagent bottle on each working table and wall shelves for storage of reagent bottles.

Physics Laboratory

Physics laboratory should have the following equipment:

(i) Working tables (ordinary) with teak wood top.
(ii) At least one table having gas point fitted to it. This may be used for experiments on heat.
(iii) Projected platforms for balances.
(iv) Almirahs.
(v) Demonstration table having drawers, water and gas points.
(vi) Wall board or blackboard.
(vii) Two large sinks at the corners of the laboratory.
(viii) Stools (in two sizes).
(ix) Physics laboratory should have an attached dark room.

13.10 THE PLAYGROUND AS THE UNCOVERED SCHOOL

The playground is said to be the cradle of democracy. Various co-curricular activities and especially games and sports contribute a lot for the development of all the major qualities needed to be an ideal citizen. It is called the 'uncovered' school as it is a place where character and personality develop.

Important Elements of the Playground

(1) Spacious space for different games
(2) Boundary wall
(3) Free from thorns
(4) Shady trees
(5) Regular up keep

Area of Playground

An Ad Hoc Enquiry Committee on games and sports appointed by the Government of India (1958), recommended the following area for playground:

	Type of Institute	*Recommended Area*
1.	College (with a student population of 1,000 to 1,500 students)	10 Acres
2.	A High School of Senior Secondary School (with a student population of 500 to 1000 students)	5-6 Acres
3.	A Middle School (with a student population of 200 to 500 students)	3-5 Acres
4.	A Primary School	1 Acre

Where separate playgrounds cannot be made available for each educational institution, a common pool for a group of institutions should be created.

Quarters for the School Staff

The Secondary Education Commission has greatly stressed the necessity of providing quarters for the school staff as possible. The Commission writes, "We feel that the presence of the headmaster and at least some of the staff in or near a school, particularly if there are hostels attached or where the schools are residential, will be of the greatest benefit to the school going population".

School Building and Health of the School

Following points should be taken note of:

(i) Healthy surroundings of the school.
(ii) Airy and well ventilated rooms.
(iii) Suitable colour of the walls.
(iv) Cleanliness of the school building.
(v) Good seating arrangements.
(vi) Suitable chairs and desks.
(vii) Right type of black-boards and use of right type of chalk.
(viii) Fresh drinking water.
(ix) Sanitation of latrines and urinals.
(x) Spacious playgrounds.

13.11 NATIONAL POLICIES ON EDUCATION (1986, 1992): SCHOOL INFRASTRUCTURE

Sports and physical education are an integral part of the learning process. A nation wise infrastructure for physical education, sports and games will be built into the educational edifice.

The infrastructure will consist of play-fields equipments, coaches and teachers of physical education as part of school improvement programme.

Available open space in urban areas will be reserved for playgrounds if necessary by legislation.

14

Administration of Secondary Education

14.1 VITAL ROLE OF THE STATE GOVERNMENT IN SECONDARY EDUCATION

Although education is a concurrent subject, yet the major and predominant role in secondary education is played by the State Government.

Keeping in view of the National Policy of Education, the State Governments exercise full control over the secondary and higher secondary schools. This excludes a few schools being run by the Central Schools Organisation and other autonomous bodies of the Department of Education, Ministry of Human Resource Development, Government of India.

The State Government undertakes the following types of programmes relating to secondary and higher secondary schools:

1. Undertaking educational reforms.
2. Running State Schools.
3. Controlling Government Aided and Private Schools.
4. Organising Departments of Public Instruction, State Boards, SCERTs, Curriculum Committees and Textbook Bureaus, etc.
5. Enacting Acts and Education Code.
6. Providing equalisation of educational opportunities.
7. Undertaking pilot projects.
8. Appointing Commissions and Committees for suggesting reforms.
9. Functioning as a clearing-house.
10. Establishing liaison.
11. Undertaking Centre-sponsored schemes.
12. Determining Service conditions of teachers.
13. Opening different types of secondary and senior secondary schools.
14. Prescribing medium of instruction.
15. Supervising schools.
16. Giving grant-in-aid to aided schools.

14.2 STATE LEVEL EDUCATIONAL BODIES IN THE FIELD OF SECONDARY AND HIGHER SECONDARY EDUCATION OR RELATING TO SECONDARY AND HIGHER SECONDARY SCHOOLS

1. Department of Education
2. State Board of Education.
3. State Council of Educational Research and Training (SCERT).
4. State Institute of Educational Technology (SIET).

5. State Resource Centre (SRC).
6. Institutes of Advanced Studies in Education (IASE).
7. Colleges of Teacher Education (CTE).
8. District Institutes of Education and Trainings (DIETs) primarily working in the field of elementary education.

14.3 SCHOOL BOARDS OF EDUCATION

The main functions of the Board are to:

1. prescribe courses of instructions for schools;
2. conduct examinations;
3. admit to its examinations—on conditions that may be prescribed by it from time to time—candidates who pursue the prescribed course of instructions; (a) in recognised institutions; and (b) in privately managed institutions;
4. publish the results of such examinations;
5. grant diplomas or certificates to persons who have passed the examinations of the Board;
6. prescribe conditions for recognition of schools and other institutions which send candidates to the examinations conducted by the Board, as well as in terms of teachers' qualifications, school curriculum, equipment, buildings and other educational facilities;
7. demand and receive such fees as may be prescribed by the Board from time to time;
8. cooperate with other authorities in such manner and for such purposes as the Board may determine from time to time; and
9. place before the government the views of the Board on any matter with which it is concerned.

14.4 STATE COUNCIL OF EDUCATIONAL RESEARCH AND TRAINING

The functions of SCERT are as:

1. Promotion of action research in education.
2. Coordination of research in education.
3. Organisation of pre-service and in-service training programmes.
4. Providing guidance and training in educational research to agencies engaged in school-extension services.
5. Acquainting the schools and the functionaries of Education Department with the improved methods, techniques of teaching and innovations in education.
6. Working with Departments of Education and State Universities to accomplish its objectives.
7. Accumulating and disseminating latest information and ideas pertaining to school level education.
8. Counselling State administration and other agencies on matters of raising standards of education.
9. Preparing and publishing essential teaching-learning material.
10. Carrying out programmes of educational research and training assigned by the State Government.

11. Organising and implementing the special education programmes/ projects sponsored by NCERT, UNICEF and other agencies for qualitative improvement of school education and teacher educators.
12. Organising correspondence-cum-contact courses for professional development of teachers, teacher educators and inspecting staff.

14.5 ADMINISTRATION OF THE SCHOOL AND EDUCATION CODE

Generally speaking, schools are administered in accordance with the Education Code which includes Acts and Rules on different dimensions of the administration of the school. It lays down the role of the Department of Education/Department of Public Instruction, Rules of Recognition of Schools, Schemes of Management of the Schools, Recognised Rules of Recruitment, Terms and Conditions of Service of Employees of the Private Schools, Admission Policy, Fees and Other Charges, responsibilities of the Head and the Teachers, Managers and Managing Committees of the School and Inspection and Supervision of Schools. The Code also includes the role of the Panchayati Raj Institutions in Education.

14.6 THE HEAD OF THE SECONDARY SCHOOL

Supreme Position of the Head of the Secondary School

It is generally observed, "As the head, so is the school". "He is said to be the seal and the school as the wax".

An educationist has said, "What the mainspring is to the watch, the flywheel to the machine or the engine to the steamship, the head is to the school".

W.M. Ryburn compares the position of the head in a school to the captain of a ship.

According to Jaswant Singh, "The headmaster or the principal of the school is the hub of the education process".

P.C. Wren describes the role and position of the head in these words, "Schools are good or bad, in a healthy or unhealthy mental, moral and physical condition, flourishing or perishing as the head is capable, energetic and of high ideals and reverse. Schools rise to fame or sink to obscurity as greater or lesser heads have charge of them".

The Secondary Education Commission (1952-53) has stated the role of the Head of the School as "The reputation of the school and the position that it holds in the society depends in a large measure on the influence that he exercises over his colleagues, his pupils and the general public".

"He acts as a liaison between it (the school) and the department and the general local community".

According to S.N. Mukerji, "The Headmaster is a link between internal and external administration of the school".

"The Headmaster is a keystone of the arch of school administration".

It is stated, "He is an organiser, leader, governor, business director, coordinator, superintendent, example, teacher, guide, philosopher and friend".

Multiple Roles, Responsibilities and Relationships of the Head of the School

The functions of Headmaster are very complex. He has to supervise each and every activity in the school. He has to play a very delicate and critical role. He has always to work with four varied interest and groups: pupils, people, teachers and the authorities. He has often to come across and strike a balance in the practical fields among quarrelling and fighting students, complaining parents and exacting departments. He is expected at various times and various interests to play different roles. He must, by nature of his position, be:

1. A *teacher* of teachers.
2. A *supervisor* not only of teachers but of service personnel.
3. A *disciplinarian*, just but effective.
4. A *psychologist*, at least to the extent of being able to detect maladjustments, especially of teachers, which definitely hinder effective instruction and achievement of desired goals.
5. A *financier* in organising the school budget.
6. A *lawyer* at least to the extent of knowing his obligations, rights and legal abilities as well as of those of all school personnel.
7. A *sociologist* to the extent of at least being able to understand the relation of school with social forces.
8. A *technical expert* in educational measurement and evaluation.
9. An *expert in group dynamics* to the extent of working effectively with staff, pupils, public and the authorities.

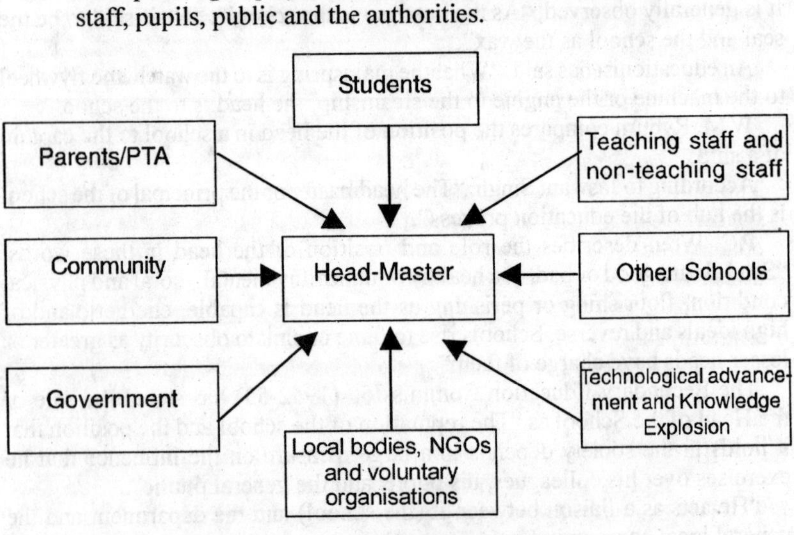

Fig. 14.1: Multiple Roles and Responsibilities and Relationships of the Head of the School

The head is responsible for the smooth running of the school. He is responsible for carrying out the policies and programmes of the Department of Education. He is the coordinator of educational work. He sets the tone of the school. He acts as a 'liaison' between the Education Department and the management or the general of head and heart he possesses.

14.7 IMPORTANT MANAGEMENT ROLES

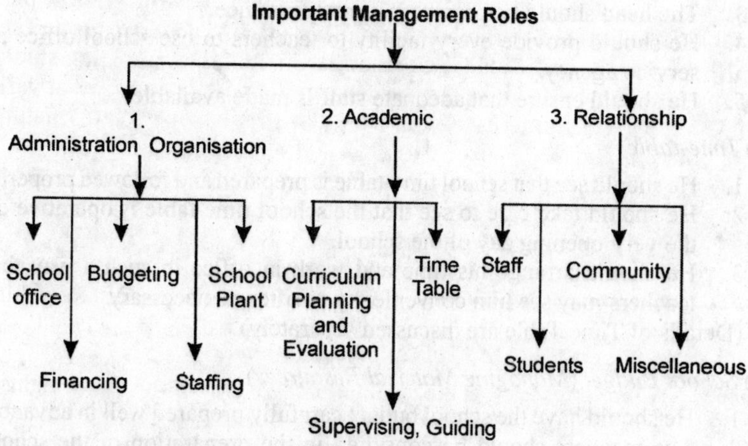

Note: Roles, responsibilities and relationships overlap.

In the words of S. Balakrishna Joshi, "By virtue of his office, he has to be a nexus between the government and the school authorities, the management and the staff, the masters and the pupils, and the parents and teachers—character rather than capacity, tact rather than authority, sympathy rather than severity are his forte".

14.8 DUTIES AND RESPONSIBILITIES OF THE HEAD OF THE SCHOOL

The duties and responsibilities of the head are manifold and in fact he is concerned with each and every activity of the school. In the words of an educationist, "He should be a man who has finger on the pulse of the school, aware of the slightest rise in tempo".

Following are the six major duties and responsibilities of the head of an institution:

I. Duties and responsibilities relating to administrative matters.
II. Duties and responsibilities relating to supervision of teaching-learning programme.
III. Duties and responsibilities relating to educational leadership and human relations. (Managing Human Resources)
IV. Duties and responsibilities relating to students.
V. Duties and responsibilities relating to the community.
VI. Duties and responsibilities relating to the Managing Committee of the School and Department of Education.

I. Duties and Responsibilities Relating to Administrative Matters

(a) *School Office*

1. The head should ensure that the records are properly and systematically maintained and kept up-to-date.

2. The head should go through 'dak' carefully.
3. The head should be prompt in correspondence.
4. He should provide every facility to teachers to use school office as service agency.
5. He should ensure that adequate staff is made available.

(b) *Time-table*

1. He should see that school time-table is prepared and followed properly.
2. He should take care to see that the school time-table is operative on the very opening day of the school.
3. He should arrange his time and work in office in such a way that teachers may see him conveniently as often as necessary.

(Details of Time Table are discussed separately)

(c) *School Budget* (*Managing Material Resources*)

1. He should have the school budget carefully prepared well in advance.
2. The teachers should be consulted in the preparation of the school budget.
3. He should ensure that provision is made is the school budget for all regular and anticipated needs so that the necessity of reallocation and reappropriations may be minimised during the school year.

(d) *School Supplies* (*Managing Material Resources*)

1. He should ensure that educational supplies, viz. paper, pencils, pens, ink, chalk, dusters, black-board, paint and laboratory chemicals, etc. are purchased only from reliable firms in accordance with rules.
2. He should invariably ask the firm to submit specimens of the commodities to be purchased.
3. He should always insist on purchasing materials of good quality for use in the school.

(*e*) *School Plant* (*Managing Physical Resources*)

1. He should make arrangements for checking the cleanliness of classrooms, laboratory, library, and playground regularly.
2. He should see that pupils' desks and seats and other articles of furniture in the school are kept in proper repair.
3. He should see that toilet and lavatory arrangements are suitable and adequate to the needs of the school.
4. He should see that the supply of drinking water is adequate for students and staff and it is maintained in proper sanitary condition.
5. He should see that school building is kept in good condition.
6. He should see that the school campus looks beautiful and attractive with shady trees, ornamental bushes, hedges and ornamental flower plants.

(*f*) *School Library* (*Managing Material Resources*)

(Discussed Separately)

II. Duties Relating to Supervision of 'Teaching-Learning' Programme

1. The principal should regularly pay supervisory visits to the classrooms to acquaint himself with the learning situations provided to pupils.
2. He should not interfere with the regular class work during his supervision visits.
3. He should inspire confidence and friendliness in the teachers by his attitude during the class visit.
4. He should regularly arrange for demonstration lessons for the benefit of the teachers.
5. He should recommend suitable instructional materials and professional books for the use of the teachers and should see that those are provided in time.
6. He should hold teachers' meetings to inspire and stimulate them in their educational thinking.

III. Duties and Responsibilities Relating to Educational Leadership and Human Relations

(Discussed Separately)

IV. Responsibilities Towards Pupils

(*a*) *Health Services and Physical Education*

1. The Principal should see that the provision for regular and thorough medical check-up of the pupils is made.
2. He should plan for a follow-up programme of medical check-up.
3. He should see that equal opportunities are provided to all pupils under the physical education programme.
4. He should see that the energies of the teacher in-charge of games, sports and physical education are directed towards the physical development of all pupils and not only to the production of winning teams or individuals.

(*b*) *Curriculum*

(Discussed Separately)

(*c*) *Co-curricular Activities*

(Discussed Separately)

(*d*) *Discipline*

1. The principal should believe in the concept of 'self' and 'social' discipline. He should encourage constructive solution for solving disciplinary problems of pupils faced by the teachers.
2. He should allow teachers to deal with the disciplinary cases of pupils and should deal himself only with cases of serious nature.
3. He should develop such traditions in the school as will socially shape conduct and behaviour of the pupils.

V. Responsibilities Towards Community

1. The principal should encourage the parents of the pupils to visit the school frequently and treat them cordially.
2. He should encourage the parents to consult the teachers as well as himself on special problems of their wards.
3. He should organise parent study groups from time to time.
4. He should provide adequate facilities for the organisation and proper functioning of the Parent-Teacher Association in the school.
5. He should plan school programme with reference to the needs of the community.
6. He should encourage the use of community resources for vitalising classroom instruction through excursions, field trips, study of local history, etc.
7. He should encourage and organise social service programmes to render public service.
8. He should allow the community to use school facilities and services like school building, library, and dispensary seeing at the same time that the work of the school does not suffer.
9. He should arrange social and cultural activities in the school to interpret the school programme to the community.
10. He should be secular in organising school programmes.
11. He should not allow his political beliefs to influence the administration of school.

VI. Responsibilities Towards Managing Committee of the School and the Department of Education

He should follow all the rules and regulations and instructions of the Managing Committee and the Department of Education.

(See Chapter 23 also)

14.9 DELEGATION OF AUTHORITY/POWER

Meaning of Delegation of Authority

Delegation of authority implies assigning responsibility of work to another person or group of persons, working in the same institution or organisation. The need for delegation of authority arises primarily on account of the following considerations:

1. Democratic functioning of an institution demands that the head should share the responsibility with the staff.
2. The head of an institution, say the headmaster/principal has to look after several activities. It is not, therefore, desirable that he himself should undertake each and every activity.
3. Sharing of responsibility develops the feeling of 'belongingness' or 'oneness' to the institution. 'We feeling' emerges.
4. Delegation of authority enables the head to make the optimum use of the talents and capacities of the staff.

5. Delegation of responsibility is an indication of mutual faith – faith of the Head in the staff and of the staff in the head.
6. Delegation of authority makes easier the work of monitoring and supervision of the head.
7. Delegation of authority introduces an element of accountability on the part of all those who work in an organisation, say the school.

Areas of Delegation of Authority

We have already dealt with the role, functions and responsibility of the Head of the school.

It has been stated that he has to deal with various groups and individuals, associated directly or indirectly with the education of the students. All this demands that he should delegate some responsibility to his co-workers.

Following are the illustrative areas in which delegation of authority may be given:

1. Academic work.
2. Admission work.
3. Co-curricular activities.
4. Community liaison.
5. Cultural programmes.
6. Discipline.
7. Evaluation and examination.
8. Finance.
9. Games and Sports.
10. Guidance and counselling.
11. Library and reading room.
12. Prayer and Assembly.
13. School beautification and cleanliness.
14. School property.
15. School sanitation.

Principles of Delegation of Authority

1. Principle of need and requirement.
2. Principle of seniority.
3. Principle of experience.
4. Principle of aptitude and interest.
5. Principle of willingness.
6. Principle of classification of work to be delegated.
7. Principle of human relations.
8. Principle of sincerity in delegation.
9. Principle of cooperation.
10. Principle of motivation.
11. Principle of coordination.
12. Principle of monitoring.
13. Principle of supervision.
14. Principle of consultation.

14.10 ACCOUNTABILITY IN SCHOOL EDUCATION: IMPORTANCE, NEED AND MEANING

It is an accepted fact that without proper accountability, no organisation or institution can grow. Accountability brings an element of responsibility on the part of all those who work in an organisation. Where there is no accountability, there is little efficiency. Absence of accountability may result in chaos and confusions; without it an organisation would be without any direction.

The word 'accountability' is a concrete and matter-of-fact expression of what the schools owe as duties and responsibilities to their establishing/employing organisation, to the student community and the society at large, with the ultimate aim of doing good by their performance. The idea of accountability should not appear as objectionable or foreign to the institutions and teachers if they could open-mindedly look at their own everyday activities and programmes.

As explained by Prof. Ramesh K. Srivastava (University News, Vol. 38, 2000), "Most of us, as customers, go to the market, have a definite idea of our requirements, select the best item in a particular category to suit our taste and purse, scrutinise our merchandise and then bargain to get the best in the price range. But when the bought item does not come to our expectations, or when we visit a government office, a ration shop, or a court, and on finding that the concerned person is absent or on casual leaves, we tear our hair and our blood boils. In all these cases, we have some expectations, some codes or norms within ourselves and when the things or services don't correspond to them, we are disappointed".

"Unfortunately, no such set codes or norms exist in the academic world. There are no fixed qualitative targets to achieve, no tangible yardsticks against which the academic excellence could be measured. Fixing of accountability is one such step in the right direction".

Meaning and Definition of Accountability

1. *According to Good's Dictionary of Education* (1973), "Educational accountability is the theory that teachers and school systems may be held responsible for actual improvement in public achievement and that such improvement is measurable through tests of teacher effectiveness, constructed by outside agencies".

2. *The International Dictionary of Education* by Terry Page and J.B. Thomas (1987) explains the term accountability as "(i) Educational accountability as the term for the extent to which student performance is attributable to instruction rather than ageing, selective admission, etc. (ii) Extent to which a state, college or university is publicly accountable for its actions and expenditure". The same authors define educational accountability as, "Assumption of responsibility for bringing about specified results in students". Again it describes teacher accountability in these words, "Theory that teachers and school systems should take responsibility for improvement in public achievement and that teacher effectiveness by this criterion should be measured by external agencies".

3. *The International Dictionary of Management* (1980) by Hano Jo Hannse and G. Terry Page (1980) defines accountability as "Accountability for action carried out and performance achieved by others, e.g. by a manager to his superior or by the board of directors to its shareholders. Also used more loosely to describe responsibility".

4. *The Concise Dictionary of Education* (1982) gives the following meaning of accountability, "Educational accountability is a concept in which the school system and especially teachers are held responsible for the learning and academic progress of students".

5. *The Blackwell Encyclopaedic Dictionary of Organisation Behaviour* (1995) edited by Nigel Nicholson explains the term 'accountability' as, "The term denotes responsibility for particular activities, results or outcomes specification of the person(s) or group(s) who hold such responsibility in an organisation".

Dimensions of Accountability

Accountability may be viewed from several aspects.

- *Moral Accountability* to those affected by one's actions; pupils, parents, colleagues.
- *Contractual Accountability* to one's employer, which in the case of teachers may be the school board, the school district, regional or State Government, supervisors and superintendents.
- *Professional Accountability* to the standards one sets oneself and one's professional aims, beliefs and mission.
- *Financial Accountability* to the standards set by appropriate authorities.
- *Social Accountability* to the society/community which has set-up the school.
- *Administrative Accountability* to the administrative standards set-up by persons concerned or authorities.

Methods Used for Assessing Accountability

All the above mentioned forms of school accountability can be assessed by the following methods:

1. *Self-assessment by*

(i) Managers of schools.
(ii) Supervisors of schools.
(iii) School staff, i.e. the head and the teacher.

2. *Assessment by*

(i) Students.
(ii) Teachers.
(iii) Supervisors.
(iv) Management.
(v) Community/Parents.
(vi) Autonomous organisation or independent organisation not connected in the running of the school to be assessed.

(vii) Affiliating and Recognising Authority/Board.
(viii) Legislatures.

Issues Involved in Accountability

Important issues involved in accountability are:

1. Who is accountable to whom in our country?
2. How can an institution be made accountable?
3. How can teachers be made accountable?
4. When different teachers in an institution are involved in teaching and evaluation, how could a particular teacher be held accountable?

These issues raise further issues when we consider accountability in school education.

1 Are other social institutions accountable?
2. School education is conducted by a number of agencies. Are these agencies accountable?
3. How can an institution be made accountable when it has little or no control in the preparation of the curriculum, in the prescription of textbooks, in admission of students, in setting question papers, etc.
4. To what extent each section of personnel engaged in education, i.e. administrators, supervisors, teachers, etc. is accountable?
5. Are students accountable for their performance?
6. Are parents accountable for the performance of their children in studies?

A host of such issues arise. Situation seems to be very complex and does not permit any ready-made answer.

While discussing accountability in school education, the aspect of accountability of the Department of Education which formulates educational policies and also sometimes runs and manages its own institutions grants aids to private schools and recognises schools without grants, is hardly taken into consideration. There seems to be no mechanism to fix its responsibility.

Likewise, the Examination Boards/Affiliating Boards seem to enjoy so much autonomy that their work seldom comes under scrutiny.

It is generally observed that only the heads and the teachers are made accountable for poor results at the Board's examination. Others associated with school education are not held accountable. This is a serious lacuna which needs to be removed urgently if worthwhile improvements on school education are to be brought about.

15

Evaluation

15.1 MEANING OF EVALUATION

Evaluation is a process by means of which changes in the behaviour of students are studied and guided towards goals sought by a school.

In the words of Clara M. Brown, "Evaluation involves measurement which means objective quantitative evidence. But it is broader than measurement and implies that considerations have been given to certain values, standards and that interpretation of the evidence has been made in the light of the particular situation".

H.H. Remmers and N.L. Gage point out, "It is the felt need that has caused the shift from the term 'measurement'—implying mathematically precise measurement of knowledge—to the term 'evaluation' which widens the areas to be studied to include subjective opinions and qualitative changes as well as objective and quantitative changes to include changes in attitudes, appreciations and understandings as well as acquisitions of knowledge and skills".

Lester D. Crow and others state, "Evaluation is a broader term than measurement. Evaluation not only is concerned with the determination of learning results but it also involves value judgement of the desirability of those results. It is a continuous process in which various techniques of testing or measurement can be utilised. Evaluation is a cooperative activity in which the principal, the teacher, the pupils and the parents participate".

15.2 TRIANGLE OF OBJECTIVES, LEARNING EXPERIENCE AND EVALUATION

There is an inter-relatedness between objectives (end), learning experiences (means) and evaluation (evidence). Objectives remain central to both learning experience and evaluation. Evaluation comes in at the primary stage when objectives are identified. Learning experiences are also planned in terms of objectives. At every point of learning evaluation is an attempt to discover the extent of the effectiveness of learning situation in evoking the desired changes in students.

15.3 PURPOSES OF EVALUATION

1. To make provision for guiding the growth of individual pupils.

2. To diagnose the weaknesses and strengths of pupils.
3. To locate areas where remedial measures are needed.
4. To provide a basis for a modification of the curriculum and courses.
5. To provide a basis for the introduction of experiences to meet the needs of individuals and group of pupils.
6. To motivate pupils towards better attainment and growth.
7. To test the efficiency of teachers in providing learning experiences and the effectiveness of instruction and classroom activities.
8. To improve instruction.
9. To bring out the inherent capabilities of a pupil, such as attitudes, habits, appreciation and understanding, manipulative skills in addition to conventional acquisition of knowledge.

Aspects of Educational Evaluation

Schematically the concept of educational evaluation may be presented by showing the relationship among objectives, content (subject-matter), learning activities and evaluation procedures (testing). (Fig. 15.1).

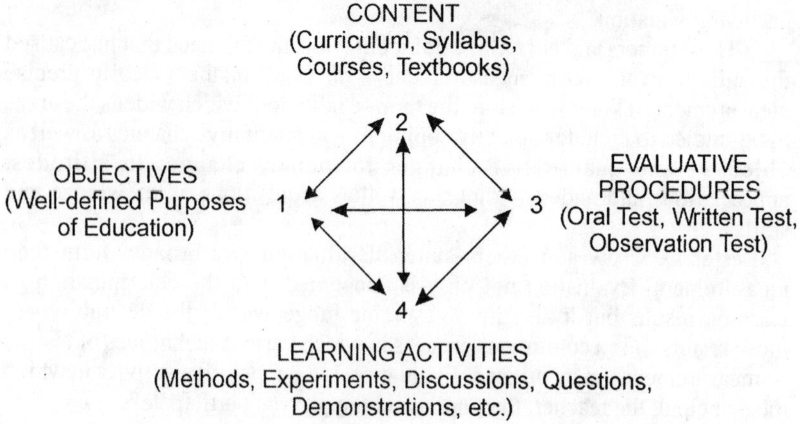

Fig. 15.1: Interrelation of Evaluative Procedures

The interrelationship of these four aspects of evaluation clearly indicates that the process of evaluation is a continuous one and involves continual appraisal of objectives of the teaching-learning process and of the testing procedures used by the classroom teacher.

Fig. 15.2 provides an evaluation design to measure different aspects.

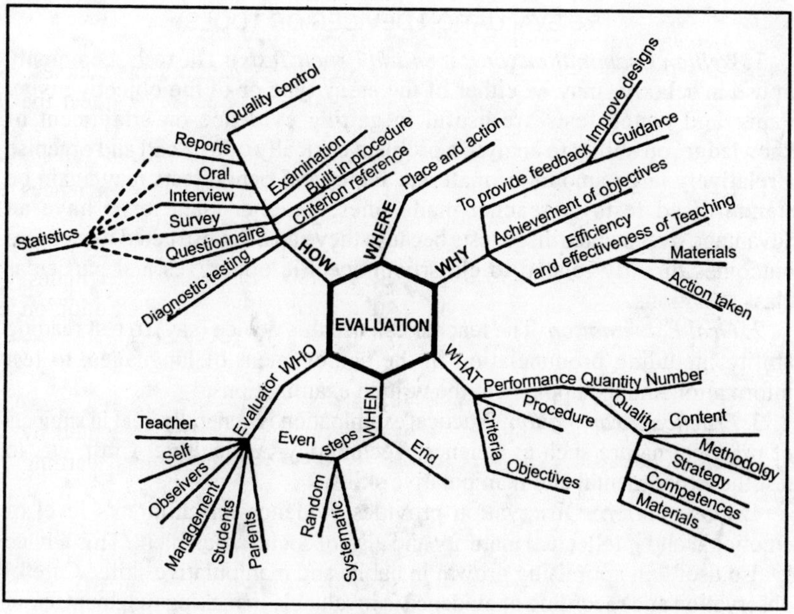

Fig. 15.2: Why, what, who, how, where and when of evaluation?

15.4 TOTAL SCHEME OF COMPREHENSIVE EVALUATION

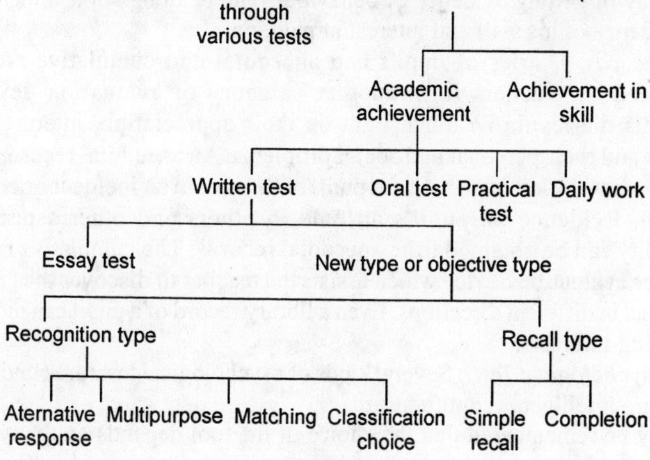

15.5 EVALUATION DEVICES OR TOOLS

1. *Written Examination* (*or Paper and Pencil Tests*): The tests, commonly in use in schools, may be either of the essay type or of the objective type. Paper and pencil tests are useful in getting evidence on attainment of knowledge, on ability to analyse a problem critically or to recall and organise a relatively large amount of material. Paper and pencil tests may again be standardised tests or teacher-made ones. Teacher-made tests have an advantage over standardised tests because they can be constructed to measure outcomes directly related to classroom specific objectives and particular class situations.

2. *Oral Examination*: The teacher can use this device (say) to test reading ability including pronunciation in the achievement of languages, to test information and to supplement the written examinations.

3. *Practical Examination*: Practical examination is generally held in subjects of practical nature such as Science, Technology, Agriculture, Craft, etc. to test the experimental and manipulative skills.

4. *Observation*: Observation provides evidence on children's level of emotional and intellectual maturity and also of social adjustment. This advice is also useful in appraising growth in habits and manipulative skills. Careful observation and recording of evidence is invaluable in making judgment about pupils.

5. *Interviews*: In interviews with students, it is possible for the teacher to secure evidence concerning the growth of interests, change in attitudes, etc.

6. *Questionnaires*: Questionnaires can be used frequently to secure information from pupils. The pupil is made to react to a series of questions in order to collect evidence about growth of interests and attitudes.

7. *Check-list*: This is a variation of the questionnaire in which statements and questions are very specific and incorporate a checking feature.

8. *Pupil Products*: The actual products made by children provide another useful way of getting evidence of behaviour. The paintings of a student can give evidence of his skill and interest in painting.

9. *Records*: Diaries of pupils and anecdotal and cumulative records maintained by teachers form another category of evaluation devices. Children's diaries throw much light on their appreciation, interests and attitudes and their personal and social problems. An anecdotal record is the teacher's description of significant pupil behaviour in an incident or critical situation. Evidence on pupil's attitude to others and other aspects of personality can be obtained from anecdotal records. The cumulative record is another evaluation device which assists the teacher to discover the growth of students in different directions. Even a library record of a pupil can indicate his reading interests.

10. *Psychological Tests*: Several kinds of psychological tests are conducted to measure intelligence, aptitude, etc.

It may be remembered that the choice of the tool depends on the type of evidence or objective.

15.6 CONTINUOUS AND COMPREHENSIVE EVALUATION (CEE)

In CEE student's work in different areas is evaluated constantly. He may not be aware that he is evaluated. Observations are recorded in the cumulative record card.

Following are the main objectives of CEE:

1. To make evaluation an integral part of teaching-learning process.
2. To use evaluation for improvement of students achievement through diagnosis and remediation.
3. To make sound judgment and take timely decisions for learner's growth, learning process and learning environment.
4. To maintain desired standard of attainment.
5. To provide scope for self-evaluation.

15.7 MAIN TYPES OF EVALUATION

Evaluation may be categorised as under:

1. Summative Evaluation.
2. Formative Evaluation.
3. Criterion Referenced Evaluation.
4. Non-Criterion Referenced Evaluation.
5. Diagnostic Evaluation.
6. Prognostic Evaluation.

Evaluation may be:

(a) Internal Evaluation
(b) External Evaluation.
(c) Combined Internal-External Evaluation.

15.8 SUMMATIVE EVALUATION

Meaning of Summative Evaluation

Following definitions throw light on the meaning of summative evaluation.

1. *Gronlund, N.E.* observes, "Summative evaluation typically comes at the end of a course (or unit) of instruction. It is designed to determine the extent to which the instructional objectives have been achieved and is used primarily for assigning course grades or certifying pupil mastery of the intended learning outcomes".

2. *W. Wiersma* and *S.G. Jurs* state, "Summative evaluation is done at the conclusion of instruction and measures the extent to which students have attained the desired outcomes".

Characteristics and Main Features of Summative Evaluation

(i) Summative evaluation is done at the end or completion of a particular instructional programme whose duration may vary from a semester to whole year.

(ii) Summative evaluation checks whether there has been learning or not. If the answer is yes, then what is the quantity and quality of the learning in relation to predetermined objectives?

(iii) The instructional programme should be for the attainment of some objectives.
(iv) It lends to the use of well-defined evaluation designs.
(v) It focuses on analysis.
(vi) It provides descriptive analysis.
(vii) It tends to stress local effects.
(viii) It is concerned with broad range of issues.
(ix) Its instruments are reliable and valid.
(x) For this evaluation, there are external examinations as well as teacher-made tests and rating scales, etc.

15.9 FORMATIVE EVALUATION

Meaning and Definition of Formative Evaluation

According to *N.E. Gronlund*, "Formative evaluation is used to monitor learning progress during instruction and to provide continuous feedback to both pupil and teacher concerning learning successes and failures. Feedback to pupils reinforces successful learning and identifies the learning errors that need correction. Feed-back to the teacher provides information for modifying instruction and prescribing group and individual remedial work".

In the words of *A.J. Nikto*, "Formative evaluation is concerned with judgements made during the design and/or development of a programme which are directed towards modifying, forming or otherwise improving the programme before it is completed".

Characteristics of Formative Evaluation

(i) It is used to monitor the learning experiences of the students during the period of instruction.
(ii) It aims at providing continuous feed-back to both teacher and student concerning learning success or failure during the teaching-learning process.
(iii) Feed-back provides specific learning errors and correction.
(iv) Feed-back to students provides reinforcement.
(v) Feed-back to the teachers provides information as to whether any modifications are necessary in his strategies of teaching.
(vi) Formative evaluation involves assessment of class-work, home-work, oral questions and quizzes, etc.
(vii) Formative evaluation uses mostly teacher-made tests.
(viii) Formative evaluation is used for assessing student learning progress during instruction.
(ix) Results of formative evaluation are not used for assigning course grades.
(x) Formative evaluation is done during an instructional programme.
(xi) The instructional programme aims at the attainment of certain objectives during the implementation of the programme also.

(xii) Formative evaluation is done to monitor learning and modifying the programme if needed before its completion.

(xiii) Its design is exploratory and flexible.

(xiv) It seeks to identify influential variables.

(xv) It requires analysis of instructional material for mapping the hierarchical structure of the learning tasks and actual teaching of the course for a certain period.

Distinction Between Summative and Formative Evaluation

Following are the main differences between these two types of evaluation:

1. Summative evaluation is the terminal assessment of performance at the end of instruction, but formative evaluation is the assessment made during the instructional phase to inform the teacher about progress in learning and what more is to be done.
2. The summative evaluation limits the use of profiles and record of achievement but they are regularly used in formative evaluation.
3. The main consideration in summative evaluation is the determination of the extent to which the examinee has mastered the knowledge and skills associated with a course. On the other hand, the main consideration in formative evaluation is to reveal the processes by which the examinee achieved these outcomes.
4. In summative evaluation, the assessment is done to test learning outcomes against a set of objective criteria without revealing the details of the route to the teacher which the student followed in reaching that point. Formative evaluation takes the form of a dialogue between the student and teacher in which the task is determined by both.
5. Summative evaluation relates to the worthwhileness of the instructional programme which has already been completed. Formative evaluation, on the other hand relates to worthwhileness of the instructional programme which is still going on and can be modified.
6. A formative evaluator is partisan of the instructional sequence and makes all possible efforts to make teaching learning better. A summative evaluator is non-partisan and uncommitted who passes judgment on the teaching-learning endeavour.
7. Formative evaluation is in-house evaluation while summative evaluation is mostly done by outside agencies.
8. Formative evaluation is day-to-day evaluation and is intended to bring about improvement. Public examinations and annual tests and semester tests come under the category of summative evaluation.
9. In a broad sense, all classroom assessments which are not used for grading purpose whether these are home assignments, questioning during teaching, class-room observations of students responses, and informal tools come under the category of formative evaluation. As for judgement (pass/fail) of scoring, summative evaluation is used.

15.10 CRITERION-REFERENCED TEST OR CRITERION REFERENCE EVALUATION

Meaning of Criterion-Referenced Test (CRT)

The CRT aims at measuring the achievement of a learner on a certain domain to find out his level of achievement in that domain. It has little to do with the achievement level of other learners (examinees). Some of the important definitions of CRT are:

Poham, W.J. and Husek, T.R. in their paper, "Implications of Criterion-Referenced Measurement" published in *Journal of Educational Measurement* Vol. VI (1969), define criterion-referenced measures as "Those which are used to ascertain an individual's status with respect to some criterion, i.e. performance standard. It is because the individual is compared with some established criterion, rather than other individuals, that these measures are described as criterion-referenced. The meaning of an individual score is not dependent on comparison with other testees. We want to know what the individual can do, not how much he stands in comparison to others".

Characteristics of Criterion-Referenced Test

1. Its main objective is to measure student's achievement of curriculum-based skills.
2. It is prepared for a particular grade or course level.
3. It has balanced representation of goals and objectives.
4. It is used to evaluate the curriculum plan instruction progress and group student's interaction.
5. It can be administered before and after instruction.
6. It is generally reported in the form of:
   (i) Minimum scores for partial and total mastery of main skill areas.
   (ii) Number of correct items.
   (iii) Per cent of correct items.
   (iv) Derived scores based on correct items and other factors.

Uses of Criterion-Reference Testing

(i) To discover the inadequacies in learner's learning and assist the weaker section of learners to reach the level of other students through a regular programme of remedial instruction.
(ii) To identify the master learners and non-master learners in class.
(iii) To find out the level of attainment of various objectives of instruction.
(iv) To find out the level at which a particular concept has been learnt.
(v) To better placement of concepts at different grade levels.
(vi) To make instructional decisions of what to do with a learner in individually prescribed instructional programme.

Limitations of Criterion-Referenced Testing

1. Criterion-referenced test tells only whether a learner has reached proficiency in a task area but does not show how good or poor is the learner's level of ability.

2. Tasks included in the criterion-referenced test may be highly influenced by a given teacher's interests or biases, leading to general validity problem.
3. Only some areas readily lend themselves for listing specific behavioural objectives around which criterion-referenced test can be built and this may be an obstructing element for teachers.
4. Criterion-referenced tests are important for only a small fraction of important educational achievements. On the contrary, promotion and assessment of various skills is a very important function of the school and it requires norm-referenced testing.

Guidelines for Constructing and Administering Criterion-Referenced Tests

Ronal Hambelton and Daniel Eignor (1978) have suggested the following guidelines.

Determination of Objectives

1. The purposes of the test should be stated clearly and concisely.
2. Objectives should be written in such a way that each item could be identified with one objective.
3. There should be appropriate rationale for the inclusion of each objective in the test.

Construction and Inclusion of Test Items

1. The set of test items should measure an objective for which it has been included in the test.
2. The test items should be valid indicators of the objectives for which they have been prepared.
3. The test items should be in appropriate form to measure the objectives for which they have been selected.
4. The test items should be free from any bias.
5. The test items should be free from technical flaws.

Administration

1. The test administrator should have adequate information relating to the purpose, time limits, answer sheets and scoring of test.
2. The directions of the test should be clear.
3. The test should be easy to score.

15.11 NORM-REFERENCED TEST (NRT) OR NORM-REFERENCED EVALUATION

Meaning of Norm-Referenced Test (NRT)

Norm-Referenced Test is used primarily for comparing achievement of an examinee to that of a large representative group of examinees at the same grade level. The representative group is known as the 'Norm Group'. Norm group may be made up of examinees at the local level, district level, state level or national level. Since the development of norm-referenced tests is expensive and time consuming, they are produced by commercial test publishers.

Bormuth (1970) writes that a norm-referenced test is designed "to measure the growth in a student's attainment and to compare his level of attainment with the levels reached by other students and norm group".

Main Characteristics of a Norm-Referenced Test

1. Its basic objective is to measure student's achievement in curriculum based skills.
2. It is prepared for a particular grade level.
3. It is administered after instruction.
4. It is used for forming homogeneous or heterogeneous class groups.
5. It classifies achievement as above average, average or below average for a given grade.
6. It is generally reported in the form of Percentile Rank, Linear Standard Score, Normalised Standard Score and Grade Equivalent Score.

Uses of Norm-Referenced Testing

N. Vasantha Ram Kumar and *K. N. Lalithamal* (1990), state the following uses of NRT:

1. To make differential prediction in aptitude testing.
2. To get a reliable rank ordering of the pupils with respect to the achievement we are measuring.
3. To identify the pupils who have mastered the essentials of the course more than others.
4. To select the best of the applicants for a particular programme.
5. To find out how effective a programme is in comparison to other possible programmes.

Limitations of Norm-Referenced Testing

According to the above mentioned authors, some of the criticisms raised against these tests are:

1. Test items that are answered correctly by most of the pupils are not included in these tests because of their inadequate contribution to response variance. They will be the items that deal with important concepts of course content.
2. There is lack of congruence between what the test measures and what is stressed in a local curriculum.
3. Norm-referencing promotes unhealthy competition and is injurious to self-concepts of low scoring students.

Process for the Development of NRT

L.M. Carey (1988) has described the following stages for the development of NRT:

1. *Design Stage*: It is done through:
   (i) Curriculum analysis.
   (ii) Selecting objectives to be measured.
   (iii) Analysing objectives for determining prerequisite skills.

(iv) Determining specifications for items.

2. *Development Stage*: This consists of:
   (i) Writing items according to specifications.
   (ii) Developing needed art work and illustrations.
   (iii) Writing response directions and examples.
   (iv) Writing administrative directions.
   (v) Reviewing items, illustrations and directions.
   (vi) Developing test lay-out.
   (vii) Developing simple test.
3. *Conducting Field Test*: At this stage, test is tried out.
4. *Developing Test Norm*: Norms of the test are developed through:
   (i) Describing characteristics of population.
   (ii) Selecting representative norm group.
   (iii) Administering test to norm group.
   (iv) Scoring.
   (v) Converting raw scores to standard scores.
   (vi) Creating norm tables.

CRT and NRT Compared

Similarities between NRT and CRT

1. Achievement domain is measured in both.
2. Same types of items can be used in both.
3. Same rules are followed for writing items in both excepting the item of difficulty.
4. Validity and reliability are needed in both.
5. Sample of test items should be relevant and representative in both.

Differences in NRT and CRT

NRT	*CRT*
1. It stresses discrimination among individuals.	1. It stresses what examinees can do and what they cannot do.
2. NRT covers a large domain of learning task with just a few items measuring each specific task.	2. It focuses on a delimited domain of learning tasks with a relatively large number of items measuring each specific task.
3. It contains items of average difficulty.	3. It contains easy as well as difficult items.
4. A student is tested after each unit (usually large) of the new material presented.	4. A student is tested after each unit for mastery of objectives.
5. A student is assigned the marks or grades to indicate his performance.	5. A student is allowed to proceed to the new material if mastery is obtained.

(Contd.)

(Contd.)

NRT	CRT
6. A student is allowed to go the next unit along with the whole class.	6. A student is given remedial instruction if the material presented is not mastered.
7. A student is presented with the new materials of the next unit.	7. A student is tested again after remedial work to check for mastery of the material.
8. A student is tested for the new material and assigned marks.	8. A student is tested for mastery of objectives.

Summing up: Both, the CRT and NRT are used to measure the attainment of the learner. The fundamental distinction between NRT and CRT is based on the manner in which one interprets the results of the learner's test performance. In the case of NRT one interprets learner's test performance according to the performance of 'others'. In case of CRT, one interprets learner's performance in relation to well defined norms of knowledge, skills, attitudes and the like.

15.12 DIAGNOSTIC EVALUATION

Meaning of Diagnostic Evaluation/Testing

A diagnostic test has been defined by English and English (1958) in these words, "One designed to locate the particular source of a person's difficulties in learning especially in school subjects".

Uses of Diagnostic Tests

(i) Diagnostic tests serve as guides to the attainment of the students.
(ii) Diagnostic tests serve as guides to locate the attainments of difficulties of the students.
(iii) Diagnostic tests help in isolating difficulties of students individually.
(iv) Diagnostic tests help to group students for remedial or special coaching.

Development of Diagnostic Testing: *Essential Points*: Following points should be kept in view by the teacher and the tester while planning diagnostic evaluation:

1. The diagnostic tests should be prepared in accordance with the specific tasks regarding a particular subject or area of a subject, for instance diagnostic tests for comprehension and spelling, etc. would be quite different.
2. There should be a large number of items/questions covering various aspects of the relevant subject matter for which test is designed.
3. Variety of questions like very short type and the multiple type should be included in the diagnostic test.

4. On a particular skill to be evaluated a large number of items should be included in the test.
5. Scoring should be easier and quicker.
6. The nature of the questions should be such as they can be administered.
7. Several equivalent forms of diagnostic tests may be prepared.
8. Different kinds of tests may be made use of on students of different abilities.

Diagnostic Tests and Achievement Tests: A Comparison

Diagnostic Tests	*Achievement Tests*
1. Diagnostic tests are normally meant for below average students.	1. Achievement tests are meant for all students.
2. Diagnostic tests are used to identify difficulties and weaknesses of the students.	2. Achievement tests are used to evaluate the achievement level of the students.
3. Diagnostic tests lead to remedial teaching or special coaching.	3. Achievement tests are used to compare the achievements of students and also for grading.
4. Diagnostic tests concentrate on difficult content areas.	4. Achievement tests relate to the entire unit/course covered.
5. Diagnostic tests are not usually used to evaluate the efficiency of the teachers and the teaching-learning process.	5. Achievement tests, at various occasions, are used to determine the effectiveness of the teachers and the teaching-learning processes.

Broad Areas Related to Diagnostic Evaluation

1. Achievement of the students in specific subjects.
2. Achievement of the students in specific areas of a subject or subjects.
3. General educational achievement.
4. Intelligence.
5. Personality.

15.13 TRADITIONAL SYSTEM OF EXTERNAL AND INTERNAL EXAMINATIONS

Epithets Given to Traditional System of Examinations

(i) A bane of educational system. (ii) A begetter of rivalry and strife. (iii) A blood sucker. (iv) A dead hand of education. (v) An enemy of creative work. (vi) A glorification of memory. (vii) A growing tyranny. (viii) A necessary evil. (ix) A presumptuous attempt to gauge the depth of human ignorance. (x) An enemy of true education. (xi) An incubus. (xii) An obstacle to learning.

Limitations and Shortcomings of the Examinations

Successive Commissions and Committees have pointed out the following limitations and shortcomings of the examinations:

1. Students and teachers tend to lose sight of the real goals of teaching and learning and tend to substitute the attainment in a subject of high marks at the public examinations as the goal.
2. Element of chance decides the fate of a large number of students.
3. Use of unfair means affects the moral standard of different sections of population.
4. Glorification of memory is predominant.
5. Students begin to depend on cheap notes and do not develop serious habits of study and work.
6. Examinations put heavy mental strain on students.
7. Examinations stimulate an unhealthy competitive spirit.
8. An element of subjectivity in marking leads to wide variability in marking. It led Vernon to point out, "The same script might receive a different mark if read after instead of before dinner". Results are greatly affected by the fancies, moods and whims of the examiners.
9. Examinations are very much limited in their scope and do not test several important aspects of pupil's personality development.

15.14 REFORMS IN THE SYSTEM OF EXAMINATIONS

There is no doubt that the examinations are very important in the educational set up. Perhaps they cannot be ended and can only be mended. To mitigate the limitations of the examinations, following measures are suggested. Some action on these lines has already been taken by several examining agencies and institutions.

1. Introduction of objective tests side by side essay tests and short-answer tests.
2. Setting thought provoking and application questions.
3. Appointment of examiners who possess the necessary experience of teaching those classes for which examinations are conducted.
4. Prescribing norms of marking and circulating marking schemes to the examiners.
5. Balanced questions in the question paper.
6. Training examiner and paper setters.
7. No overall options in the questions paper.
8. Training students to take examinations on the pattern of proposed examination system.
9. Provision of weightage in monthly and terminal tests.
10. Maintenance of cumulative records.
11. Reduction in the number of public examinations.
12. Symbolic rather than numerical marking.
13. Multiple sets of question papers.
14. Strict check on the use of unfair means by the students and also by all those who are engaged in various operations like marking, tabulating and declaring results.

15. Weightage to internal assessment.
16. Compartmental examinations.
17. No compulsory public examination and instead a certificate based on the record of every pupil to be issued by the school.

15.15 DESIGN OF THE QUESTION PAPERS (SECONDARY/SENIOR SECONDARY)

1. Weightage to Instructional Objectives/Learning Outcomes

S. No.	*Objectives*	*Marks*	*% of Marks*
1.	Knowledge	30	30%
2.	Understanding	45	45%
3.	Application	15	15%
4.	Skill	10	10%
	Total	100	100

2. Weitage to the Content or the Subject-Matter

This is to determine according to weighage given to units of the content.

3. Weightage to Types/Forms of Questions

S. No.	*Form of Question*	*Marks for Each Question*	*No. of Questions*	*Total Marks*	*%*
1.	L.A.	8	4	32	32%
2.	S.A. I	5	8	40	40%
3.	S.A. II	2	9	18	18%
4.	Map	5	2	10	10%
	Total		23	100	

L.A.	= (Long Answer Type Questions)	4
S.A. I	= (Short Answer I Type Questions)	8
S.A. II	= (Short Answer II Type Questions)	9
Maps		2
Total		23

4. Scheme of Options

1. There will be no overall option in the form of 'Do any ten questions or so'.
2. Internal choice (either/or type) on a very selective basis may be given in long answer questions testing higher mental abilities.
3. The alternate question given by way of choice should be based on the same objective and the same unit. It would have the same anticipated difficulty level and length of answer.

5. Weightage to Difficulty Level of Questions:

S. No.	Estimated Difficulty Level	Percentage
1.	Easy (C)	15%
2.	Average (B)	70%
3.	Difficult (A)	15%

6. Marking Instructions and Marking Scheme

Broad hints regarding points to be covered to be issued to the examiners so that evaluation of answer books should be as objective as possible.

Chief Purposes of a Marking Scheme

1. To bring consistency in judgment.
2. To ensure objectivity in evaluation.
3. To eliminate differences in score.
4. To make results more reliable.
5. To avoid inconsistency in marking.
6. To bring uniformity in marking and to reduce variations in marking—both inter-examiner and intra-examiner.

15.16 GRADING SCHEME OF THE CENTRAL BOARD OF SECONDARY EDUCATION (CBSE, DELHI)

For awarding the grades, all the passed students are put in a rank order and awarded grades as follows:

A-1 Top 1/8th of the passed candidates
A-2 Next 1/8th of the passed candidates
B-1 Next 1/8th of the passed candidates
B-2 Next 1/8th of the passed candidates
C-1 Next 1/8th of the passed candidates
C-2 Next 1/8th of the passed candidates
D-1 Next 1/8th of the passed candidates
D-2 Next 1/8th of the passed candidates
E Failed candidates
(*Source*: CBSE)

15.17 CUMULATIVE RECORD CARD

Meaning and Significance of the Cumulative Record Card

A cumulative record card is that card which contains the salient features of constant and comprehensive evaluation of the student.

In the words of *W.C. Allen*: "The cumulative record is defined as a record of information concerned with appraisal of the individual pupil—usually kept on a card—kept in one place".

"Periodically the significant information gathered on students through the use of various techniques—tests, inventories, questionnaires, observations, interviews, case studies, case conferences and the like—should be assembled in summary form on a cumulative record", writes Jane Warters.

A good record contributes to guidance work in general in the following ways: (a) By providing a sound basis for understanding the individual, (b) By showing the significant experiences of individual, (c) By indicating his readiness for new experiences, (d) By pointing out the routes to new goals, (e) By pointing out his strengths and weaknesses.

Information Contained in the Cumulative Record Card

1. Personal data about the learner.
2. Schools attended.
3. Family history.
4. Attendance.
5. Physical data.
6. Medical report.
7. Psychological data.
8. Scholastic performance data.
9. Performance in co-curricular activities.
10. Position of responsibility held.
11. Personal traits.
12. Vocational information.

Note: The data in the cumulative record card should not be shown to those who are in no way connected with the development of the child. It should not be misused. Its sanctity and secrecy should be maintained.

A Specimen of the Commutative Record Card

1. *Personal Data*

Name of pupil .... Date of Birth ....
Father's Name .... Occupation ....
Guardian's Name .... Occupation ....
Relationship with the child .... Address ....

2. *School Attended*

Sl. No.	Name of the School	Month and Year of Joining	Class of Joining	Month and Year of Leaving	Class from Which Left	Reason for Leaving
1.						
2.						

3. *Family History*

Year	200...	200...	200...
Type of family (whether joint or unitary)			
No. of members in the family			
Economic status of the family			
Child' Position in the family (whether only child, eldest) or youngest child, his number among the siblings)			
Any other significant factor			

4. *Physical Data*

Year	Height	Weight	Chest Measurement			General Condition
			Normal	Expd.	Contrd.	

5. *Medical Report*

		Any Serious illiness
200...		
200...		
200...		

6. *Attendance*

Year	Possible	Actual	Nature of Long absence, if any, with reasons
200...			
200...			
200...			
200...			

7. *Psychological Report if any and Results of Intelligence and Aptitude Tests*

200...		
200...		
200...		

8. *Scholastic Achievement*

Subjects	Class............ Year..............		Class............ Year..............		Class............ Year..............	
	Half Yearly	Annually	Half Yearly	Annually	Half Yearly	Annually
English						
Hindi						
Sanskrit						
Mathematics/Arith and domestic science						
Physics						
Chemistry						
Economics						
History						
Geography						
Commerce						
Drawing						

(*Contd.*)

(*Contd.*)

Art						
Craft						
Physical Education						
Agriculture						
Practicals						
Totals						
Position in the class						
No. of students in the class						

9. *Performance in Co-curricular Activities*

Activities	*Average Grade of the Child for Each performance throughout a year*		
	200……..	*200……..*	*200……..*
Sports and Games			
Personal Hygiene			
Literacy Activities			
Cultural Activities			
Social Service			

10. *Position of Responsibility Held or Merits Obtained, if any*

Activities	*Year……..*	*Year……..*	*Year………*
Studies			
Games			
Bal Sabha			
Scouting			
Social Service			
Any other			

11. *Personality Traits*

Traits	*200……*	*200……*	*200……*
Truthfulness			
Honesty			
Courtesy			
Cooperativeness			
Industry			
Self-confidence			
Emotional stability			
Initiative			

(*Contd.*)

(Contd.)

Traits	*200.....*	*200......*	*200......*
Leadership			
Sociability			
Reliability			
Signature of the class teacher			
Signature of the Head			

15.18 CHARACTERISTICS OF A CUMULATIVE RECORD

1. *Validity*: The facts recorded must be authentic. It is better not to write any information than to give untrue information.

2. *Comprehensiveness*: A cumulative record should contain as complete and comprehensive information as possible.

3. *Accuracy*: The information in the record should be accurately recorded from original sources.

4. *Objectivity*: Personal opinions and judgments should be reduced to the minimum.

5. *Economy of Space*: The criterion of a good cumulative record form is that the maximum possible information is contained in the space available.

6. *Recency*: Any piece of information should be recorded as soon as it is obtained.

7. *Outcomes of a Cooperative Enterprise*: It should be the result of group thinking.

8. *Evaluation*: It should be evaluated every year so as to know how far does it serve the purpose.

Problems in the Maintenance and Uses of Cumulative Record Cards

1. *Who should Maintain the Record*?: The Records may be kept by the class teacher and he should be responsible for getting the necessary entries made. Class teacher's responsibility is greater as he will not only ensure correct and up-to-date entries but also act as a liaison between the pupil and the subject teachers, and between the pupil and the parents.

2. *Where to Keep Them*?: This is a very formidable problem. Arrangements will have to be made so that is easily accessible to the teachers. If possible, it may be kept by the class teacher in the safe custody otherwise it may be kept in the Principle's Office. However, in either case, its contents should remain confidential.

3. *When to Fill-up this Card*?: Entries in the card should be made at the time of a particular event or test. It is advisable that every teacher should have a small notebook to record his observations at the time of the incident about a particular pupil. He may record the significant entries according to his convenience. As a rule, other teachers may not record the entries on the card itself. They would pass on the entries to the class teacher. This would enable the class teacher to maintain the records neatly and scientifically. Too many hands may spoil the beauty and the neatness of the card.

4. *How to Check Maintenance*?: The Principle should check after every

three months that the entries are regularly made and the records kept up-to-date. He may assign this work to one of his colleagues but must sign the record himself.

5. *What should be the Design of Record Card*?: Usually three types of card are being maintained in schools.

(a) Folder type,
(b) File type,
(c) Envelope type.

6. *The Problem of New Admissions and Migrations*: The record should move with the student in case he is transferred from one school to another. It should go with the pupil from class to class and from school to school.

7. *How to help the Teacher in Discharging the Function*?:

(i) Adequate importance should be given to these records in internal assessment.
(ii) The employers may also give due consideration to these records.
(iii) Teachers should be trained in the maintenance of these records.
(iv) The state authorities should get prepared model forms of records for the schools.
(v) This work should be done by the teachers on the last working day of the month. There may not be any teaching work on that day. If we do not give adequate time to the teacher to fill up these cards, they will fill up these mechanically.

16

Vocationalisation of Education at the Secondary Level

16.1 MEANING OF VOCATIONALISATION OF EDUCATION

Frequently the terms vocational education, vocationalisation of education, occupational education, job-oriented education and education for the world of work, etc. are used interchangeably except where special mention is made of a particular type of education in a particular situation or environment.

For understanding the meaning and concept of vocational education we may refer to its important definitions.

1. '*The American Educator's Encyclopaedia*' (1982) defines vocational education as "a part of the school curriculum designed to make the student employable in at least one occupation".
2. Carter V. Good in '*Dictionary of Education*' (1973) has stated, "Vocational education is a programme of education below college grade organised to prepare the learner for entrance into a particular chosen vocation or to upgrade employed workers".
3. '*The Encyclopaedia America*' (1985), defines vocational education in these words, "the preparation of young people and adults for skilled trades and semi-professional careers. It is most frequently offered at the high school or junior college level and does not normally include training for professions such as law and medicine".
4. UNESCO, in its recommendations of 1947 defined it as a "Comprehensive term embracing those aspects of the educational process involving, in addition to general education, the study of technologies and related sciences and the acquisition of practical skills, attitudes, understanding and knowledge relating to occupation in the various sectors of economic and social life".
5. Regarding the concept of vocationalisation, the Kothari Commission (1964-66) stated, "We visualise the future trend of school education to be towards a fruitful mingling of general and vocational education—general education containing some elements of pre-vocational and technical education and vocational education in turn, having an element of general education".
6. In the words of National Review Committee or Adiseshiah Committee (1978), "The vocationalised spectrum of the higher Secondary School is learning of a skill or a range of skills, through study of technologies, related sciences and form for other practical work".

7. The National Working Group (1985) constituted by the Ministry of Education, Government of India under the Chairmanship of V.C. Kulandaiswamy, Vice-Chancellor of Anna University, explained the concept of vocational education as, "Traditionally 'vocational education' has been understood as education designed to prepare skilled personnel at lower levels of qualification for one or more groups of occupations, trade or jobs. Vocational education has been usually provided at upper secondary level".

The last definition quite fits in the present scenario.

16.2 NEED FOR VOCATIONAL EDUCATION AT THE SECONDARY STAGE

'Eat the bread at the sweat of the brow'; thus gocs a Biblical injunction. What better way to follow it could there be than taking recourse to vocational education as well as vocationalisation of education!

The ratio of enrolment in vocational courses at the lower secondary and higher secondary schools in India is very negligible as compared with 20 per cent in China, 24 per cent in France, 29 per cent in Italy, 59 per cent in erstwhile USSR, 65 per cent in U.K. and 80 per cent or more in Denmark, Germany and Switzerland. This explains the reason for low productivity and unemployment in India.

The Education Commission pointed out, "Another programme which can bring education into closer relationship with productivity is to give a strong vocational bias to secondary education and to increase the emphasis on agricultural and technological education at the university stage".

The Adiseshiah Committee 1978 observed that special attention has to be given to the self-employment factor. It recommended 64 courses divided into 8 categories.

The National Policy on Education stressed the importance of Vocational education in these words, "The introduction of systematic, well planned and vigorously implemented programmes of vocational education is crucial in the proposed educational reorganisation".

The Policy pointed out the following merits:

1. *Enhancement of Employability*: Vocationalisation of education enhances employability.
2. *Reduction in Mismatch*: Vocationalisation of education reduces the mismatch between the demand and supply of skilled manpower.
3. *Alternative Courses*: Vocationalisation of education provides an alternative for those pursuing higher education without particular interest or purpose.
4. *Dignity of Labour*: Vocationalisation of education leads to dignity of labour.
5. *Self-Employment*: Vocationalisation of education enables individuals for self-employment.
6. *Increased Productivity*: Vocationalisation of education is related to productivity.
7. *Maximum Utilisation of Resources*: Vocationalisation of education is

helpful in the maximum utilisation of the human and material resources of the country.

16.3 MAJOR STEPS TAKEN IN VOCATIONALISATION OF EDUCATION

1 A Centrally Sponsored Scheme of Vocationalisation of Higher Secondary Education was introduced in February 1988, with the following objectives:
   (a) To enhance individual employability.
   (b) To reduce the mismatch between demand and supply of skilled manpower.
   (c) To provide an alternative for those pursuing higher education without particular interest or purpose.
2. A Joint Council for Vocational Education (JCVE) was set up in April 1990 for policy formulation and coordination at the national level.
3. In 1993, Pandit Sundarlal Sharma Central Institute of Vocational Education (SSCIVE) was set up at Bhopal to provide technical and academic support to the programme in the country.
4. Nearly 60 vocational courses have been notified under the Apprenticeship Act.
5. Collaborative arrangements have been made with the Ministry of Railways, etc.

16.4 TARGETS SET AND ACHIEVED IN NPE, 1986 AND 1992

Target set in NPE, 1986: "It is proposed that vocational courses cover 10 per cent of higher secondary students by 1990 and 25 per cent by 1995. Steps will be taken to see that a substantial majority of the products of vocational courses are employed or self-employed. Review of the courses offered would be regularly undertaken. Government will also review its recruitment policy to encourage diversification at the secondary level".

Target set in NPE, 1992: "It is proposed that vocational courses cover 10 per cent of higher secondary students by 1995 and 25 per cent by 2000. Steps will be taken to see that a substantial majority of the products of vocational courses are employed or become self-employed. Review of the courses offered would be regularly undertaken. Government will also review its recruitment policy to encourage diversification at the secondary level".

Present Position: At present, only 10 per cent of the students are opting out for the vocational courses against a target of 25 per cent by 2005. Thus the situation is of great concern. (See Table 16.1)

16.5 SLOW PROGRESS AND PROBLEMS OF VOCATIONALISATION

1. General indifference to vocational pursuits.
2. Vocational courses as dumping ground.
3. Inadequate content of vocational courses.
4. Lack of equipment.
5. Lack of trained vocational teachers.

6. Non-determination of equivalence of vocational degrees.
7. Limited choice of vocational courses.
8. Inadequate guidance and counselling facilities.
9. Lack of research.
10. Lack of systematic vocational set up.
11. Evaluation difficulties.

16.6 SUGGESTIONS FOR ACCELERATING VOCATIONALISATION OF SECONDARY EDUCATION

1. *Vocational institutions not to be regarded as dumping ground for drop-outs and educationally backward pupils*: It is extremely important that our attitude towards schools should undergo a revolutionary change. We should form right type of attitude towards dropouts, who go in for vocational institutions.

2. *Vocational courses should be terminal in character*: At the end of a course, the students should be prepared for career or independent work. The knowledge imparted should be theoretical as well as practical. The courses should produce semi-skilled and skilled workers for lower level and middle level requirements.

3. *Vocational courses for drop-outs*: In our country it is estimated that out of 100 students who join class I, only 50 reach class VIII and only 16 class XII. It is, therefore, suggested that part-time courses should be organised for these drop-outs. Separate courses should be devised for girls in accordance with their requirements.

4. *Provision for further training and retraining to persons opting for vocational courses*: Provision for further training and retraining to persons opting for vocational courses will have to be assured so that they may have the chance for advance studies and higher specialisation if they have the capacity and will to do it.

5. *Training of village worker for agriculture extension programme*: Short refresher courses to increase food production and to give a new outlook to agriculture should be organised for such workers.

6. *Compulsory introduction of work experience in all primary and secondary schools*: Establishment of school complex consisting of a group of schools to provide work experience to the pupils individually as well as in groups will be very useful. Proper care should be taken to see that it does not meet the fate of basic education.

7. *Preoccupational education and vocational guidance*: There should be provision not only to provide vocational advice but there should also be provision for aptitude and psychological testing wherever possible.

8. *Placement or organised transfer from vocational schools to industries, or enterprises*: A separate state-wise agency should be set up for this purpose.

9. *Part-time vocational courses for self-employed persons*: There is a great need to organise courses for the agriculturist who works on the family farm. A careful study of the local needs should be made before the selection of various courses. A few central places in the district should be selected for such courses.

10. *Provision for on-the-job training*: Provision for on-the-job training should be made with the help of nearby industries or enterprises, both of private and public sector.

11. *Provision of building and equipment*: Adequate building and proper equipment are essential for the implementation of any educational programme and vocational education is no exception to it. A central place in each district should be selected for vocational schools with hostel accommodation.

12. *Training of vocational teachers*: All progressive and industrialised countries attach great importance to this training programme. In India also we have to give due attention to this aspect.

13. *Adequate preparation: more challenging task*: It will be necessary to prepare suitable textbooks and other reading material for various courses to be selected in different vocational schools.

14. *Freeships and stipends to vocational trainees*: In order to encourage more young boys and girls to take up vocational courses, freeships and stipends will be very necessary. The existing Apprenticeship Scheme will have to be strengthened.

15. *Low fees for vocational courses*: Vocational courses of all types should be provided without charging any fees or with only nominal fees at all levels.

16. *Vocational education to become people's movement*: The Government may take the lead but the cooperation of the State Government as well as other non-governmental agencies is very essential.

17. *Study of manpower needs*: It is widely felt that in India the expansion of vocational and technical education should be done with caution and with regard to the development of organised, industries and needs of the society.

18. *District and state vocational committees*: District and state vocational committees having representatives of productive activities and services, trade and commerce, administration, planning and educational institutions would be most useful not only in deciding upon the vocations for which facilities should be provided from year to year, but also in deciding on the content of the vocational courses and more than this, the manner of facilitating training in these vocations by the cooperative participation of the above mentioned agencies.

19. *School industry link*: Through proper legislation, the government could consider involving large public undertakings and workshops, such as those belonging to the railways to take positive steps to adopt higher secondary schools for teaching and training in certain fields so that the costs of vocationalisation do not mount, at least in part, owing to the duplication of facilities. The laboratories and workshops of these institutions should be made available during the vacations and during holidays.

Needless to say that vocational programmes in most cases will have to be run by sharing the facilities of professional institutions also, besides part-time staff. It is in sense a partnership programme between education and other sectors of the economy and the services between the school and the factory or the farm.

20. *Need for systematic supervision and effective administration of vocational education programmes*: A separate department should be established at the State level for the administration and supervision of vocational education.

21. *Problems related to reorientation and training*: The introduction of vocational courses has created enormous problems of training of teachers. As

a matter of fact only bonafide vocational experts can impart vocational education effectively. Ways and means will have to be devised so that such trained vocational experts come forward for working in educational institutions. Proper qualifications will have to be prescribed for teachers teaching vocational subjects.

22. *Problems related to evaluation*: Suitable evaluation tools will have to be developed immediately to assess the performance of the students in the vocational courses. Subjective element will have to be reduced to the minimum.

23. *Redesigning of Teacher Training Courses*: The teachers training colleges and departments are required to recast their curriculum so that it is in accordance with the new requirements.

24. *Problems related to the determination of equivalence of diplomas/ certificates and degrees*: A student will not go in for a vocational course unless he is sure that a particular course will lead him to a specific job. This points to the need of a more centralised system for identifying the courses which are acceptable to the organised sector and whose equivalence is already determined.

Similarly, proper arrangements will have to be made for those students who wish to go in for higher education after completing a two-year vocational course.

25. *Problems related to research*: So far we have been guided by the subjective opinion of a few educational experts who dominate and whose opinions carry considerable weight. Our educational programmes, by and large, have not been based on try-outs and surveys. It is very much surprising that no authentic survey has been conducted to assess the reactions of the students who are directly involved in the new scheme of secondary and higher secondary education. It is very imperative that suitable techniques of educational research are evolved and used to find out the reactions not only of the students who are studying under the new pattern but also of their parents and teachers. This would provide pragmatic guidelines for formulating scheme of educational reforms.

26. *Easy loans*: Adequate provision will have to be made for a system of easy loans so that vocationally trained students are motivated to set up their own business.

27. *Coordination with the finance department*: It has generally been observed that there is no proper coordination between the educational administrators and the officials of the Finance Department of the States with the result that there is undue delay in getting financial sanctions for the requisite staff, equipment, etc. Suitable ways and means will have to be devised so that the officials of the Finance Department appreciate the urgency and significance of educational reform in their real perspective and shed their traditional attitude of putting unnecessary obstacles in clearing schemes of educational reform.

To the above may be added the following recommendations made by the Ramamurti Committee (1990).

28. *Work benches and practice schools*: In order that the process of vocational education is enriched by a meaningful combination of teaching of theory and practice and effective linkages are established with the 'world of work', 'work benches' and 'practice schools' should be identified, accredited and involved. 'Work Benches' and 'Practice Schools' are work situations

selected for the purpose of giving vocational training and direct experience to students within production units or developmental activities of the official agencies. This arrangement offers a more effective educational strategy for providing vocational experiences to students than what can be arranged within the four walls of the 'classroom'.

Table 16.1: Number of Schools, Sections, and Enrolment Capacity in States/UTs under the Scheme of Vocationalisation of Secondary Education (2001-2002)

Sl. No.	*States/UTs*	*No. of Schools*	*No. of Sections*	*Enrolment Capacity*
(1)	(2)	(3)	(4)	(5)
1.	Andhra Pradesh	668	1880	94000
2.	Arunachal Pradesh	4	4	200
3.	Assam	225	510	25500
4.	Bihar	251	752	37600
5.	Chhatisgarh	—	—	—
6.	Delhi	38	93	4650
7.	Goa	43	106	5300
8.	Gujarat	364	1032	51600
9.	Haryana	170	876	43350
10.	Himachal Pradesh	40	82	4100
11.	Jammu & Kashmir	38	38	1900
12.	Jharkhand	—	—	—
13.	Karnataka	564	1427	71350
14.	Kerala	363	1008	50400
15.	Madhya Pradesh	465	1307	65350
16.	Maharashtra	1141	3480	17400
17.	Manipur	19	57	2850
18.	Meghalaya	10	20	1000
19.	Mizoram	17	51	2550
20.	Nagaland	8	16	800
21.	Orissa	231	924	46200
22.	Punjab	282	846	42300
23.	Rajasthan	155	465	23250
24.	Sikkim	7	9	450
25.	Tamil Nadu	700	2140	107000
26.	Tripura	12	12	600
27.	Uttar Pradesh	910	2350	117500
28.	Uttaranchal	—	—	—
29.	West Bengal	39	39	1950
30.	Andaman & Nicobar Islands	3	3	150
31.	Chandigarh	17	58	2900
32.	Dadra & Nagara Haveli	2	2	100
33.	Daman & Diu	2	5	250
34.	Lakshadweep	—	—	—
35.	Pondicherry	12	16	800
	Total	6800	19599	979950

17

Distance Education and Open Learning

17.1 NOMENCLATURE OF DISTANCE EDUCATION AND LEARNING

Distance education is known by different names. On account of a variety of terms used for distant education, Prof. F.R. Jevons (1983) called it a "bewildering nomenclature". Important terms associated with this type of education are as under:

(1) Continuing Education (2) Correspondence Education (3) Correspondence Learning (4) Correspondence Course; (5) Correspondence School; (6) Correspondence Teaching; (7) Distance Education; (8) Distance Learning; (9) Distance Teaching; (10) External Degree Programme; (11) External Studies; (12) Extra-mural System; (13) Home Study; (14) Home Tuition; (15) Independent Learning; (16) Independent Study; (17) Life Long Education; (18) Non-Formal Education; (19) Off-Campus Study; (20) Open Education; (21) Open Learning; (22) Open School; (23) Open Education; (24) Open University; (25) Out of School Education; (26) Postal Courses; (27) Teach Yourself Programme; (28) Tele University; (29) University of the Art; (30) University without Walls.

All the above mentioned terms are associated with non-traditional and non-conventional teaching-learning programme. These terms derive their names from the medium of communication. By and large, they are based on same economic, educational, philosophical and psychological basis.

17.2 MEANING OF DISTANCE EDUCATION

Distance education as the name indicates is a form of education in which there is usually a long distance between the learner and the teacher. (The word 'long' is a relative term and it has no limits.) It is in a sense a remote control system of education wherein the learner and the teacher may not be face to face. They are separated by physical distance. Some of the important definitions of distance education are given below:

1. In the words of Dohmen (1967) "Distance education is a systematically organised form of self-study in which student counselling, the presentation of learning material and the securing and supervising of students success is carried out by a team of teachers, each of whom has responsibilities. It is made possible at a distance by means of media which can cover long distances".

2. Peter (1973) defines distance education as "Distance teaching/education is a method of imparting knowledge, skills and attitudes which is rationalised by the application of division of labour and organisational principles as well as by the extensive use of technical media, especially for the purpose of reproducing high

quality teaching material which makes it possible to instruct great numbers of students at the same time wherever they live. It is an industrialised form of teaching and learning. It is a method of indirect instruction implying geographical and emotional separation of the teacher and the taught. Whereas in the mainstream of education, the relationship between teacher and students in the classroom is based upon social norms, in distance education it is based upon technological norms".

3. In the words of Holmberg (1979) "The term Distance Education covers the various forms of study at all levels which are not under the continuous, immediate supervision of tutors present with their students in lecture rooms or on the same premises, but which, nevertheless, benefit from the planning, guidance and tuition of a tutorial organisation".

4. Moore's (1991) definition is: "The transaction that we call distance education occurs between individuals who are teachers and learners, in an environment that has the separation of one from another, and a consequent set of special teaching and learning behaviours. It is the physical separation that leads to a psychological and communication gap, a space of potential misunderstanding between inputs of instructor and those of the learner, and this is the transactional distance".

5. Mackenzie N., Postgate R. and Scupham (1975) use the term 'Open Learning'. According to them Open Learning Systems are designed to offer opportunities for part-time study, for learning at a distance and for innovations in the curriculum. They are intended to allow access to wider sections of adult population, to enable students to compensate for lost opportunities in the past or to acquire new skills and qualifications for the future. Open Learning systems aim to redress social and educational inequality and to offer opportunities not provided by conventional colleges or universities".

6. Wedemeyer (1971) discusses the concept 'Independent Study' which "consists of various forms of teaching-learning arrangements in which teachers and learners carry out their essential tasks and responsibilities apart from one another, communicating in a variety of ways for the purpose of freeing internal learners from inappropriate class pacing or patterns, of providing external learners with opportunities to continue learning in their own environment, and of developing in all learners the capacity to carry on self-directed learning".

17.3 CORRESPONDENCE EDUCATION, OPEN LEARNING, FORMAL EDUCATION AND DISTANCE EDUCATION

Correspondence Education and Distance Education. The basic difference between the correspondence education and distance education is the use of mode of communication. In correspondence education, postal system is the mode whereas in distance education postal system and multimedia are used.

Distance Education and Open Learning. In distance education there may be minimum educational qualifications prescribed for joining a course but in open learning there may not be any such qualifications required for pursuing a course. Open learning is not limited to geographical boundaries. Open learning is relatively more flexible than distance learning. Distance education is a mode of learning while open learning is the opportunity of learning in the mode of learning. Nevertheless, for all operational purposes, they convey the same meaning.

	Distance Education		Formal Education
1.	It is indirect education, as it is not centred on face-to-face communication.	1.	It is direct education, as it is centred on face-to-face communication.
2.	It is part-time education.	2.	It is usually full-time education.
3.	It concentrates on the needs of the learner.	3.	It puts the institution first.
4.	It is flexible in the sense that a course can usually be completed in a number of years.	4.	A course is to be completed within a given period.
5.	It takes into account the convenience of the learner.	5.	It is teacher centred.
6.	It looks for unorthodox modes and means of educating all those who are willing to be educated.	6.	It depends upon conventional means of education.
7.	Its place of instruction is not fixed.	7.	Its place is usually fixed within four walls of the school or college.
8.	There is separation of the learner from his peer group.	8.	Learners are in close contact.
9.	It lacks a certain kind of vitality which only the presence of a teacher can generate.	9.	It provides vitality with the presence of the teacher.
10.	It uses media like computer, radio and television.	10.	Print word is the most prominent element.
11.	It is flexible with regard to qualifications for entry.	11.	It is rigid.
12.	It may or may not be for a degree or diploma.	12.	It is for a degree or diploma.
13.	It is a system of mass education.	13.	Education is imparted in a group.
14.	It is available even in the areas where there is no school or college.	14.	It is not possible without an educational institution.
15.	It is available even to those with poor health or disadvantageous psychological conditions that inhibit them from undergoing institutionalised education.	15.	It is not available to such groups as they cannot attend educational institutions.

17.4 CHIEF CHARACTERISTICS OF DISTANCE EDUCATION

Chief Characteristics of Distance Education

1. There is physical distance between the teacher and the learner.
2. There is little face-to-face relationship.
3. There is no fixed classroom or lecture room.
4. There is less of oral instruction.
5. There is no immediate supervision by the tutor present with his students.
6. Learning is on an individual basis and not on group basis.
7. There is multi-media use, i.e. use of postal services, radio, TV, etc.
8. Industrial form of production is used.
9. Learning is on part-time basis.
10. Learner is more motivated.
11. It also provides for a two-way communication when contact courses are organised.

17.5 MAIN OBJECTIVES OF DISTANCE EDUCATION

1.To provide a suitable alternative path to wider opportunities in education and especially higher education.

2. To provide an efficient and less expensive system of education.

3. To provide opportunities to students who had to discontinue their formal education on account of various circumstances—pecuniary, etc.

4. To cater to the educational needs to people residing in geographically remote areas.

5. To provide for educational opportunities to students who had to discontinue studies because of lack of aptitude and motivation but who may later on become motivated.

6. To provide opportunities for citizens who are willing to improve their standard of knowledge and learning through continuing education while in business.

7. To provide opportunities to students who cannot find a seat or do not wish to join a regular college or university department although they possess the necessary qualifications to pursue higher education.

8. To provide opportunities to persons engaged in different professions to get higher degrees or certificates which may enable them to get higher jobs or promotions or better emoluments.

9. To cater to the needs of citizens who look upon education as a life-long pursuit and may like to refresh their knowledge and skill or to acquire knowledge and skills in new areas.

10. To provide opportunities for promoting aesthetic, citizenship and cultural values.

11. To provide courses according to the specific needs of individuals.

12. To provide opportunities for in-service training to teachers.

13. To provide opportunities for pre-service training to teachers.

14. To enable the students to learn while they earn.

15. To enable the students to earn while they learn.

16. To provide opportunities for getting education, vocational and personal guidance.

17. To help socio-economically backward students receive education.

18. To make the educational institution go to the students, rather than the students coming to the university.

19. To provide opportunities to the educated citizens study further while remaining at the places of their work.

20. To train in-service personnel in different fields to make them more efficient in their work.

21. To provide instruction in technical and vocational courses.

22. To impart basic knowledge to the farmers regarding modern ways of farming.

23. To enhance the technical knowledge of the farmers to such a level that they would take full advantage of printed literature dealing with agricultural sciences.

24. To enable farmers to pass on the acquired knowledge to others.

25. To assist elderly people, people in armed forces, dependents of embassies abroad, and others in improving their qualifications.

26. To solve the problem of increasing pressure on formal education.

27. To minimise the gap in the academic standard of the regular and private students through planned and regular postal education.

28. To ease the problem of financial constraints on the part of the government to start new educational institutions.

17.6 MERITS AND LIMITATIONS OF DISTANCE EDUCATION

Merits and Salient Features of Distance Education

1. It fulfils the needs of various categories of persons who are unable to make use of the formal system of education.

2. It is a very flexible educational system which is not limited by time and place restrictions.

3. Under this system a learner can progress at his own speed.

4. Distance education makes higher education accessible to all sections of society.

5. The courses cater to all segments of society.

6. There is no need to spend on buildings and other equipment.

7. In-service personnel, housewives, disabled persons, under-privileged people, people residing in remote areas, school drop-outs, etc. can all avail of the courses offered.

8. The inherent flexibility of distance education system is conducive to a greater variety of subjects of study.

9. It leads to self-learning.

10. It can reach remote areas through postal service or radio or TV.

11. It is an economical method of teaching-learning as compared to the regular formal system.

12. Teaching-learning can be made more efficient and powerful through the media like radio and TV.

13. It can supplement the studies of regular students.

14. It can be used at various levels.

15. Learners can take advantage of the lectures of the most efficient teachers which is not always possible in all conventional educational institutions.

16. Contact courses provide opportunities for face-to-face learning also.

17. Limited full-time academic staff is needed. Part-time teachers can deliver the goods.

18. Students are not concentrated in the campuses and there is little chance of student unrest.

19. Number of students in an open university system may be unlimited.

20. The Indira Gandhi National Open University has its jurisdiction over whole of the country.

21. The likely higher quality of the self-instructional package produced by multidisciplinary team of experts for use in distance education seems likely to enhance the learning experience of distance students.

22. It suits all age groups.

23. It is very flexible. It even arranges courses as demanded by specific groups.

24. It provides equality of opportunity irrespective of income and status of individuals.

Limitations of Distance Education

1. The system of distance education has very limited scope for making people aware of cultural change and social development.

2. The courses become stereotyped in due course.

3. The scope for practical experience is very negligible.

4. Usually the provision for study-centres and book banks is very meagre.

5. The experts do not have the adequate means to ensure whether the students are entirely satisfied with the material given.

6. Normally suggestions are not invited from the students about the utility of the material.

7. The students are given extensive written material through post but the same is not suitably supplemented by discussion on radio or TV.

8. Periodic review of the courses is not frequent.

9. The students hardly get opportunities for different types of co-curricular activities during contact programmes except listening to lectures.

10. Opportunities of learning through social contact among students are very limited.

11. Generally speaking, same importance or weightage is not given to distance education degrees as is given to the degrees and diplomas obtained through formal education. By and large, it is considered an inferior type of education.

17.7 BRIEF HISTORY OF DISTANCE EDUCATION IN INDIA

University of Delhi was the first University to start correspondence course in higher education in 1962.

Andhra Pradesh was the first Open University to be opened in the country in 1982.

The National Policy on Education – 1986 (revised in 1992) states:

"The open learning system has been initiated in order to augment opportunities for higher education, as an instrument of democratising education and to make it a lifelong process. The flexibility and innovativeness of the open learning system are particularly suited to the diverse requirements of the citizens of our country, including those who had joined the vocational stream.

The Indira Gandhi National Open University, established in 1985 in fulfilment of these objectives, will be strengthened. It would also provide support to establishment of Open Universities in the States".

17.8 DISTANCE SYSTEM OF EDUCATION AT WORK

(Ref. Fig. 17.1 on page 170)

17.9 NATIONAL INSTITUTE OF OPEN SCHOOLING (NIOS), B-31B, KAILASH COLONY, NEW DELHI-110 048, INDIA

The National Institute of Open Schooling (NIOS) was established in November, 1989, with an objective to impart education among these interested learners through courses and programmes of general education. It commenced as an autonomous organisation in pursuance of the National Policy on Education, 1986 by the Ministry of Human Resource Development, Government of India. Open Schooling was originally experimented upon since 1978 as a project of the CBSE and was later amalgamated with the NIOS, otherwise known as National Institute of Open Schooling.

Mission

- Education for all
- Greater Equity and Justice in Society; and
- Evolution of a Learning Society

17.10 OBJECTIVES

- To provide opportunities for continuing and developmental education to interested learners through courses and programmes of general education, life enrichment modules and vocational courses at the school stage.
- To provide consultancy services and to engage in model building in close collaboration with the States and a variety of other agencies or institutions.
- To serve as an agency for effective dissemination of information related to Distance Education and Open Learning.
- To identify and promote standards of learning in distance education systems and open schools which may be set up in different parts of the country through research and evaluation and to maintain standards of equivalence with the Formal System, while keeping its own distinct character.

17.11 COURSES OFFERED

Academic Courses

Foundation Course: This course is offered to those who have completed four to five years of primary education but have left studies. This is equivalent to

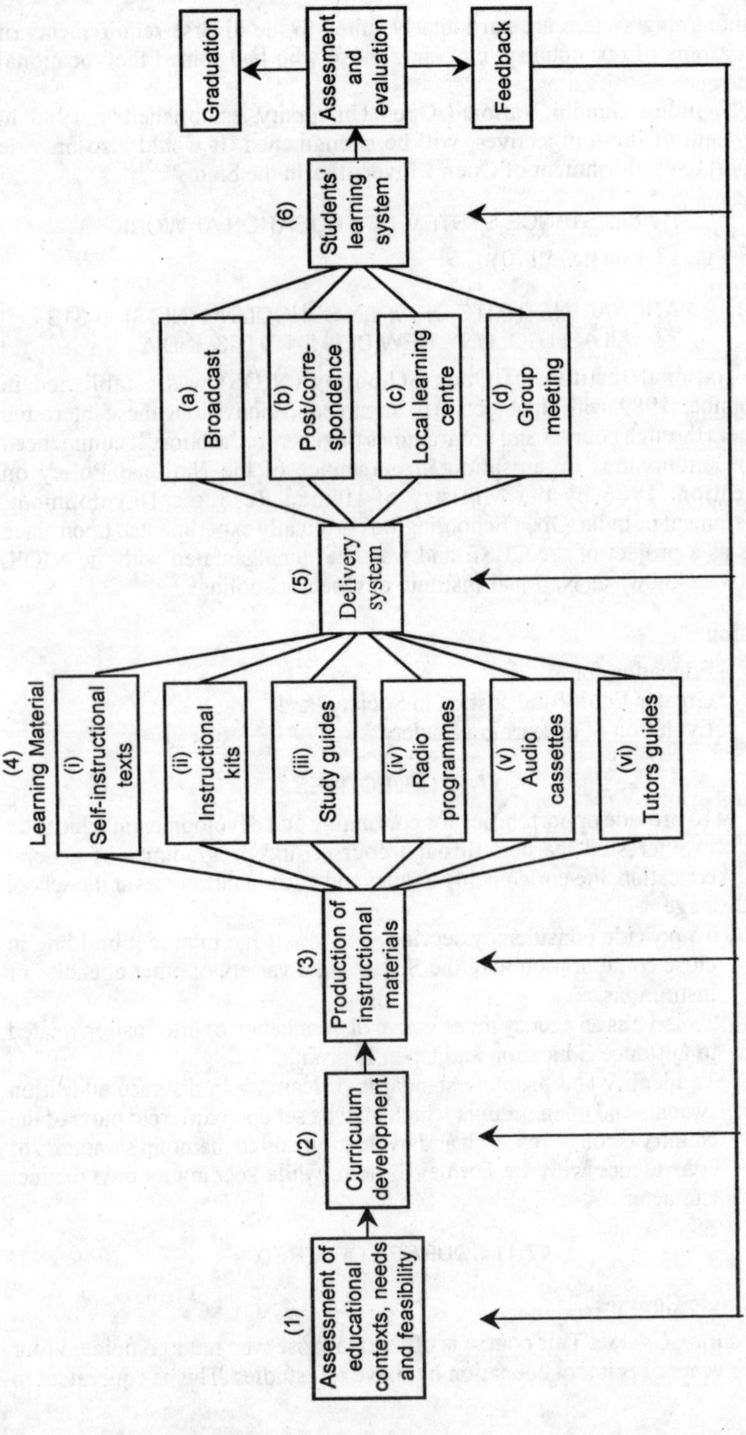

Fig. 17.1: The Operational Model of Distance Education

Eighth standard. It serves as a bridge course for joining the secondary level programmes in the NIOS. No Public Examination is conducted and no Mark Statements/Certificates are awarded.

Secondary Education Course: This is offered to those who are desirous of completing 10th standard education leading to Secondary School Certificate.

Senior Secondary Education Course: This is designed for those who have passed 10th standard or equivalent and would like to continue their education for 12th standard. This leads to the Senior Secondary School Certificate.

Open Basic Education: The NIOS has started the open basic education programme with the collaboration of National Literacy Mission for neo-literates. The materials have already been developed in Hindi and English medium. These are available for the States, which are interested to introduce Basic Education programme.

Open Elementary Education: The NIOS proposes to introduce open elementary education programme for non-school going children.

Courses Offered Under Vocational Education Programme

- Agriculture
- Business & Commerce
- Technology
- Health
- Home Science
- Life Enrichment Courses

Stand-Alone Vocational Courses

Secondary Level

1. Typewriting (Hindi)
2. Typewriting (English)
3. Word Processing (English)
4. Jute Production Technology
5. Carpentry
6. Solar Energy Technician
7. Biogas Energy Technician
8. Laundry Services
9. Bakery and Confectionary

Senior Secondary Level

1. Typewriting (Hindi)
2. Typewriting (English)
3. Stenography (Hindi)
4. Stenography (English)
5. Secretarial Practice
6. Word Processing (English)
7. Plant Protection (Part I & Part II)

8. Water Management for Crop Production
9. Oyster Mushroom Production Technology
10. Furniture and Cabinet Making
11. Electroplating
12. House Keeping
13. Catering Management
14. Food Processing
15. Play Centre Management
16. Hotel Front Office Operations
17. Poultry Farming
18. Soil and Fertiliser Management
19. Understanding the Child
20. Early Childhood Care and Education—Principles and Process. Organising and Managing an Early Childhood Care and Education Centre

17.12 EXAMINATION SYSTEM

The NIOS is a National Board for Secondary and Senior Secondary Examinations similar to the Central Board of Secondary Education (CBSE) and the Council for the Indian School Certificate Examinations (CISCE).

The NIOS conducts examinations twice a year during the month of March-May and September-November. Candidates are allowed to appear in one, two or more subjects and credits are accumulated till the certification criteria are fulfilled. A candidate can avail as many as nine chances to appear in public examinations.

17.13 PUBLIC EXAMINATION/SCHEME OF EXAMINATION

The Public examinations are held twice a year in the month of March-May and September-November on dates fixed by the NIOS. In 2005-06, the number of candidates who appeared for examinations was 267026.

Table 17.1: Gender-wise Enrolment for Last 5 Years (2001-2005)

Year	*Male*	*Female*	*Total*
2005-06	182440	84586	267026
2004-05	162351	75718	238069
2003-04	220103	100907	321010
2002-03	164550	113684	278234
2001-02	152286	62296	214582

Table 17.2: Course-wise/Gender-wise Enrolment 2005-06

Gender	*Secondary*	*Senior Secondary*	*Total*	*%*	*Vocational*	*%*
Boys	102562	79878	182440	68%	11693	51%
Girls	49271	35315	84586	32%	11186	49%
Total	151833	115193	267026		22879	

Table 17.3: Category-wise Enrolment 2005-06

Category	*Academic*	*%*	*Vocational*
General	214667	80.39%	20803
SC	30679	11.49%	1590
ST	19933	7.46%	379
Ex-Servicemen	304	0.11%	24
Handicapped	1443	0.54%	83
Total	267026		22879

18

Teacher Education at Secondary Level

Pre-Service and In-Service

18.1 MEANING OF TEACHER EDUCATION

Good is Dictionary of Education (1973) defines teacher education as "All formal and informal activities and experiences that help to qualify a person to assume the responsibility as a member of the educational profession and to discharge his responsibility most effectively".

In *Encyclopaedia of Educational Research* (1941), Walter S. Monroe defines teacher education as, "The total education experiences which contribute to the preparation of a person but the term is completely employed to designate the programme for courses and other experiences offered by an educational institute for the announced purposes of preparing persons for teaching and other educational service and for contribution to their growth in competency for such service. Such teacher education programmes are offered in teacher colleges, normal schools and colleges and universities".

18.2 NEED AND SIGNIFICANCE OF TEACHER EDUCATION

The contention that teachers are born, not made, can be true only in a few cases. It is also not contended that training by itself is sure to make a good teacher. But it is generally observed that a teacher with training becomes more mature and confident to perform his task more efficiently. Proper training and education enables the teacher to have a knowledge of how children grow, develop and learn, how they can be taught best and how their innate capacities can be brought out and developed. Teacher education is needed for kindling the initiative of the teacher, for keeping it alive, for removing the evils of 'hit and miss' process, for according a professional status to the teaching profession and above all for making the optimum use of time and energy of the teacher and the taught.

It has been aptly remarked, "If you educate a boy, you educate one individual. If you educate a girl you educate the whole family and if you educate a teacher, you educate the whole community".

The Education Commission (1964-66) said, "A sound programme of professional education of teachers is essential for the qualitative improvement of education. Investment in teacher education can yield very rich dividends because the financial resources required are small when measures against the resulting improvements in the education of millions".

Teacher education is needed for:

1. Having better understanding of the students.
2. Building Confidence in the teacher.
3. Familiarising with the technology of teaching.
4. Building a favourable attitude for the teaching profession.
5. Familiarising with school organisation.
6. Creating social insight.
7. Training for democracy.
8. Improving quality of education.
9. Training in the use of teaching aids.
10. Developing communication skill.

18.3 OBJECTIVES OF SECONDARY TEACHER EDUCATION AND HIGHER SECONDARY TEACHER EDUCATION

A. General Objectives of Secondary Teacher Education and Higher Secondary Teacher Education

The general objectives of secondary teacher education may include the following:

- Making student teachers understand not only the subject but also the unity of knowledge among different subjects.
- Developing among student teachers an integrated and holistic approach in the teaching of social sciences and science and technology.
- Empowering student teachers to know how learners construct knowledge and to facilitate the process.
- Developing among student teachers the skills of communication and language proficiency.
- Helping student teachers to acquire a repertoire of strategies, competencies and skills for transaction and evaluation.
- Developing among student teachers the competencies in the use of locally available educational resources.
- Developing among student teachers the skills of ICT and making use of internet for enrichment of knowledge content.
- Appreciating the impact of various changes taking place in the society, i.e. liberalisation, privatisation and globalisation (LPG), etc. on different aspects of life and their imperatives.
- Enabling student teachers to promote self-learning/mutual learning in and outside the classroom in order to eventually become independent learners.
- Developing among student teachers skills of life-long learning for their professional development.
- Inculcating among student teachers social, cultural, aesthetic, moral and spiritual values and scientific approach and their skill of integrating and transacting these.
- Developing among student teachers competencies to deal learners with special educational needs leading to inclusive education.
- Making student teachers appreciate India's unity in diversity.

- Making student teachers appreciate the contribution of India to world's civilisation and *vice-versa* in various walks of life.
- Enabling student teachers to establish rapport with parents and the community to ensure reciprocity for the development of both.
- Enabling student teachers to acquire skills for guidance and counselling.
- Developing among student teachers the competencies of conducting action research for total quality improvement.
- Enabling student teachers to integrate values in all subjects/activities;
- Developing among student teachers awareness and sensitivity towards environment concern and promoting skills for meeting environmental challenges;
- Enabling student teachers to develop competencies for an error-free, responsive and transparent evaluation.

B. General Objectives of Higher Secondary Teacher Education

The general objective of higher secondary teacher education (academic stream) may include the following:

- Developing among student teachers the capacity to understand the place of academic stream and developing a correct perspective of its nature, purpose and philosophy.
- Familiarising student teachers with effective techniques of transaction and evaluation, especially in the context of learners reaching the final phase of adolescence.
- Empowering student teachers to develop strategies to promote discipline-wise learning as well as to appreciate linkages among different subjects.
- Making student teachers capable of using need-based ICT.
- Empowering student teachers to guide learners for self-study, reference skills, group work/mutual learning, critical thinking, abstract conceptualisation and application of knowledge by adopting various methods such as project work and tutorials.
- Enabling student teachers to integrate values in all subjects/activities in the classroom and outside the classroom.
- Developing among student teachers awareness and sensitivity towards environment concern and promoting skills for meeting environmental challenges.
- Enabling student teachers to acquire skills for guidance and counselling.
- Developing among student teachers the competencies of conducting action research for total quality improvement.

Objectives of Higher Secondary Teacher Education: Vocational Stream

The general objectives of higher secondary teacher education (vocational stream) may include the following:

- Developing among student teachers a proper perspective towards work ethics.

- Making student teachers understand nature, purpose, philosophy, perspectives and problems of vocational education.
- Enabling student teachers to understand the emerging vocational needs of the society.
- Enabling student teachers to combine world of work and learning.
- Developing among student teachers the capacity to establish proper linkages between school, society, industry, agriculture and environment.
- Empowering student teachers to acquire with competencies, commitment and performance skills for effective management of vocational education.
- Developing among student teachers right attitudes and skills of entrepreneurship.
- Enabling student teachers to undertake community survey for assessing new vocational needs and establishing coordination with relevant agencies and voluntary organisations.
- Sharing experiences and ideas with the teachers in order to obtain necessary feedback for further improvement in the educational system.
- Familiarising the teachers comprehensively with planning and administration related aspects in respect of school/educational set up.
- Enabling teachers to integrate values in all subjects and activities.
- Enabling teachers to understand the nature and extent of learners with special educational needs.
- Enabling teachers to be sensitive to gender and environment-related issues.

('*Curriculum Framework for Teacher Education*', NCERT, 2004)

18.4 TYPES OF TEACHER EDUCATION AND INSTITUTIONS

Types of Teacher Education and Institution

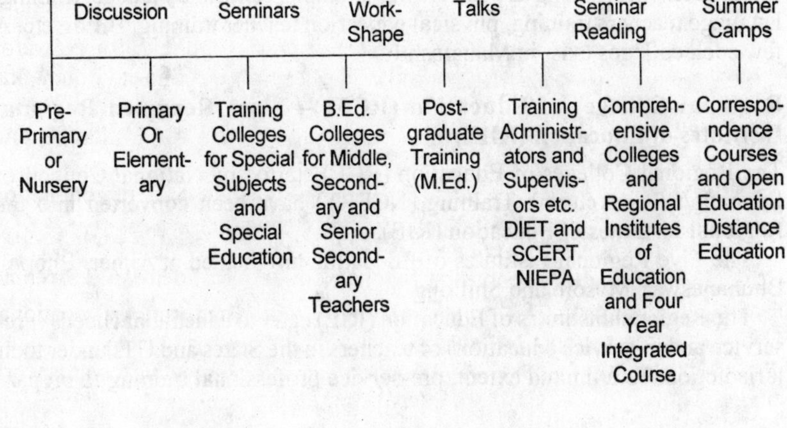

1. *Pre-primary or nursery teacher education institutions*: Catering to the needs of teachers for Kindergarten, Montessori, Bal Vihars, etc. Minimum qualifications for admission to this course is secondary, higher secondary and the duration of the course is one year. Many institutions impart training for two years.

2. *Training schools for elementary teachers*: In general the course lasts for two years and the minimum qualifications for entrance is Secondary. The present trend is to prescribe higher secondary as the minimum qualification for entrance. The duration of the course is 2 years.

The Delhi University has started an integrated teachers' training course for three years in some colleges. The Degree imparted is B.Ed. Elementary Education.

3. *Secondary training schools*: These schools provide teachers for the middle and junior secondary schools. However these training schools are gradually disappearing.

4. *Training colleges or colleges of education for secondary and senior secondary or higher secondary teachers*: The minimum qualification for entrance is graduation with usually 45 per cent marks. The duration of the course is one year. Degrees awarded are B.T. or L.T. or B.Ed. These colleges provide teachers for secondary and senior secondary schools.

5. *Institutes of advanced studies in education*: These provide opportunities to take up Master of Education and Ph.D. Courses.

6. *Training colleges for special subjects*: These are separate colleges for preparing teachers in certain subjects like physical education, home science, craft, languages, etc.

7. *Training colleges for special education*: These colleges prepare teachers for teaching students with various types of handicaps—the deaf and the dumb, etc.

Comprehensive College of Education

The idea was suggested by the Indian Education Commission (1964-66) and the objective of a comprehensive college of education is to break the isolation of teacher education. A comprehensive college of educational runs as many levels of teacher training as possible, for example, elementary teacher training, language teachers training, physical education teacher training, B.Ed., etc. A few such colleges exist in Maharashtra.

Regional Colleges of Education (RCEs)—Since Renamed Regional Institutes of Education (RIEs)

The Regional Colleges of Education (RCE) started by National Council of Education Research and Training (NCERT) have been converted into the Regional Institutes of Education (RIE).

The Five Regional Institutes of Education are located at Ajmer, Bhopal, Bhubaneswar, Mysore and Shillong.

The Regional Institutes of Education (RIE) cater to educational needs (pre-service and in-service education) of teachers in the States and UTs under their jurisdiction. To a limited extent, pre-service professional training to prepare school teachers for teaching Science and Mathematics and to teacher educators of elementary Teacher Training Institutions is also offered by the RIE. They act as Regional Resource Institutions for school education and teacher education, extend required assistance in implementing the policies of the States/ UTs and assist in implementation, monitoring and evaluation of the Centrally Sponsored Schemes.

Colleges of Teacher Education (CTE) and Institutes of Advanced Studies in Education (IASE): As envisaged in the NPE and Programme of Action (1986), the Centrally Sponsored Scheme of Restructuring and Reorganisation of Teacher Education was taken up in 1987 to create a viable institutional structure, academic and technical resource base for orientation, training and continuous upgrading of knowledge, competence and pedagogical skills for school teachers in the country. Under the scheme Eighty Six CTE have been set up by upgrading existing Secondary Teacher Education (STEIs) offering B.Ed. courses and 38 IASE by upgrading Colleges and University Departments of Education offering M.Ed. Courses.

Table 18.1: Number of Teachers Training Institutes (Elementary) and Teacher Training/Education Colleges (Secondary) Since 1950-51

Year	*Teacher Training Schools*	*Teacher Training Colleges*
1951	182	128
1961	317	272
1971	427	469
1981	480	627
1991	833	872
2001	1023	1089
2004	1150	1300

18.5 STATE OF TEACHER EDUCATION IN INDIA: SHORTCOMINGS

From time to time, a great concern has been expressed regarding the quality of teacher education in India. Some efforts have also been made to improve the quality but result has not been quite rewarding.

In '*New Era in Teacher Education*' (1966), Dr. G. Chaurasia drew a very dim picture of teacher education in India. He stated, "Teachers colleges are merrily existing in a dream world. They dream any intellectual contact with other university disciplines; their theory is pedantic and a poor imitation of foreign concepts and beliefs. They have scant respect for schools; their familiarity with educational practices is pedestrian. The sheet weight of deadwood and routine performances drain away all the energy of staff and students in the training colleges".

The NCERT document entitled '*Teacher Education—A Curriculum*' (1978) has made an important observation regarding improvement in all aspects of teacher education that "a fundamental change be effected in all aspects of teacher education, i.e. objectives, structures, staffing pattern, administrative machinery and control of teacher education in the country".

Prof. R.P. Singh has struck a very pessimistic note in *'The Teacher in India'* (1984) when he observed, "No matter what the Education Commission may have to say about improving their quality of produce, they, I think, will go on with their ageless practices unmindful of the 'revolutionary changes' in school and society". He further observed, "To conclude, the training colleges, at various levels, are operating on the periphery of the problems Indian education faces today and hardly, if ever, touch upon the major issues that constitute the hard-core of our education.... Numerous studies have shown that teachers themselves are the bitterest critics of teacher education programmes. They call them irrelevant, lacking in vision and meaningful substance".

Prof. Uday Shanker has observed in *Education of Indian Teachers* (1984) that "in such a short time how could one expect to inculcate in the trainee a 'teacher personality' with proper outlook, attitude, teaching skills and faith in the profession".

The Challenge of Education (1985) described the deteriorating situation of teacher education as "....but unfortunately, the process of updating the curricula of teacher education has been very slow. Much of teacher education is irrelevant even to contemporary requirements, leave alone those of the future".

The National Commission on School Teachers (1983-85) lamented: "What obtains now in the majority of our Teachers Colleges and Training Institutions are woefully inadequate in the context of the changing needs of India today". The situation is no better at present.

Major Drawbacks and Problems of the Present System of Teacher Education

1. Faulty methods of selection because of political, social and personal influences.
2. Inadequacy of one-year B.Ed. Course. (Divided opinion on increasing the duration)
3. Lop-sided curriculum.
4. Obsolete and irrelevant methodology of teaching.
5. Neglect of study of education as a discipline.
6. Inadequate training in practical skills.
7. Insufficient time and attention paid to actual practice teaching.
8. Isolation between the Colleges of Education and the schools.
9. Insufficient training in the art of communicating with the community.
10. Meagre training in the art of organising co-curricular activities.
11. Ineffective supervision of the teaching practice by the supervisors.
12. Faulty methods of assessment of trainee's work.
13. Less qualified teacher educators.
14. Lack of physical facilities.
15. Shorter working hours.
16. Dearth of new technology of teaching.

18.6 REVITALISING AND MODERNISATION OF PRE-SERVICE TEACHER EDUCATION

The National Commission on School Teachers (1983-85) suggested the following measures:

1. Recruitment before training where possible.
2. Effective Selection Procedures.
3. Four-year Integrated Course.
4. Restructuring the Curriculum.
5. Study of Education as a Discipline.
6. Due emphasis on Practical Skills.
7. Systematic Internship or Practice of Teaching.
8. Comprehensive Content-*cum*-Methodology.
9. Use of Technology in the Training of Teachers.
10. Adequate Physical Facilities.
11. Appointment of competent Teacher Educators.
12. Increased Working Hours.

Suggestive Programme for Revitalising Pre-Service Teacher Education in India

The NCERT Working Group for preparing a scheme for Revitalising and Modernisation of Pre-Service Education (1986) made the following important recommendations:

1. The national accrediting agency should appoint expert committees to inspect teacher training institutions and on the basis of their reports decide about the recognition of the institution.
2. The candidates passing from an institution or a course not recognised by the national accrediting agency should not be appointed as teachers at the primary or secondary level.
3. After completing the course of studies at a recognised teacher training institution, a candidate will be required to undergo internship in teaching for a period of six months under a trained registered teacher at a recognised secondary/primary school. On satisfactory completion of the internship, he will be granted a teacher's licence and registered as a teacher.
4. No person should be employed as a teacher unless he possesses a valid teacher's licence. A teacher's licence may be invalidated if at any time teacher is found guilty of gross misconduct, corrupt practices, criminal offences or serious neglect of his duties as teacher.
5. The Central and State Governments should make studies to determine the requirement of teachers subject wise and level wise during each five year plan period. The number of teachers to be trained in each State during the five year period should be fixed on the basis of manpower study.
6. Admission to the teacher training institutions in a State should be made on the basis of results of a common entrance test given by a State agency. The entrance test should be quite comprehensive.
7. The teacher-pupil ratio in a teacher training institution should be 1:10, subject to minimum of 10 teacher educators. There should be at least one teacher educator in each school subject and at least three in pedagogical subjects. There shall be at least two teacher educators

in Science Methodology; one in Physical Science and one in Biological Science.

8. Every teacher training institution should have a good library with at least 5000 books in all subject areas. It should have adequate reading room space where at least one-fourth of the student strength can study at a time. It should also subscribe to a minimum of five professional journals.
9. Every teacher training institution should have a good Science Methods Laboratory with necessary equipment and apparatus for conducting all experiments in sciences up to higher secondary level. Necessary tools and materials should be available to prepare models and teaching aids in science.
10. There should be a separate laboratory for educational technology where trainees can do practical work for resource material development for teaching different school subjects.
11. Every teacher training institution should have adequate hardware and software in educational technology and trainees should be provided practical work in the use of educational technology under micro and mini-teaching sessions.
12. Every teacher training institution should have facilities for practical work in art, music and other aspects of culture. Every student should do some practical work in art and culture.
13. Every teacher training institution should provide practical work in games and physical education in groups for at least two hours a week for each group.
14. Every teacher training institution should have facility for organising practical work in some locally relevant socially useful productive work.
15. The State government should provide full financial support to all teacher training institutions in the State so as to provide the minimum facilities as outlined above.
16. The four-year integrated programme of teacher education is a better model of teacher education. Such institutions can be started by amalgamating the facilities of an arts and science college and one-year B.Ed. college existing in the same town.
17. The minimum qualifications for a teacher educator in a teacher training college or university department of education in the methodology subject should be Master's degree in the concerned subject together with Master's degree in Philosophy, Psychology or Sociology together with Master's degree in Education. In addition, he should have M.Phil./Ph.D. in Education.
18. The minimum instruction time in one-year B.Ed. course should be 36 weeks after the last date for admission. Out of 36 weeks instruction at the college, not more than 4 weeks should be spent in teaching practice. No candidate should be allowed to appear at the B.Ed. degree examination unless he has completed 36 weeks instructions at college.
19. The teacher training institution should be regarded as non-vocational departments so that the services of the staff should be utilised for conducting entrance tests and annual examinations.

18.7 IN-SERVICE EDUCATION OF TEACHERS

Importance and Need of In-Service Teacher Education

Gurudev Rabindra Nath Tagore has very aptly stated: "The teacher can never truly teach, unless he is still learning himself. A lamp can never light another lamp unless it continues to burn its own flame".

The Report of University Education Commission (1948-49) appointed by the Government of India contains the following passage: "It is extraordinary that our school teachers learn all of whatever subject they teach before reaching the age of twenty-four or twenty-five and then all their further education is left to experience which in most cases is another name for stagnation. We must realise that experience needs to be supplemented by experiment before reaching its fullness and that a teacher, to keep alive and fresh, should become a learner from time to time. Constant out-pouring needs constant in-taking; practice must be reinforced by theory and the old must be constantly tested by the new".

The teacher must catch the spirit of Thomas Arnold, an eminent teacher at Rugby who said, "I prefer that my students should drink from a running stream rather than a stagnant pool".

NCTE has stressed the importance of in-service education of teachers on account of the following considerations:

(1) The in-service teacher education programmes are essential in view of obsolescence as well as explosion of knowledge and are necessitated to acquire and execute new and different roles. Advances in the fields of curriculum, evaluation, audio-visual aids, telecommunication, etc. demand updating and orientation of teachers. An innovation at a macro level would invariably fail if teachers are not equipped and properly oriented to implement that innovation. In the Indian context, the developments, such as, the 10+2+3 scheme, the making of science compulsory up to the class 10 standard, new practices in evaluation the internal assessment, question banks, continuous and comprehensive evaluation and grading, introduction of new topics like environmental education, population education, computer education, etc. demand continuous in-service training of teachers.

(2) The National Commission on Teachers recommended that promotion (upward mobility) of teachers would also depend upon the completion of certain number of in-service programmes. This stipulation itself demands regular in-service programmes of teachers.

(3) In-service programmes need to be built around 'transformational objectives', i.e. increasing motivational level, enriching self-concept, developing climate of enquiry and making teachers reflective practitioners. The thrust of transformational objectives is to develop such qualities in teachers as would enable them to become receptive, innovative and dynamic.

(4) Due to advances in tele-communication and open market policies the world is gradually becoming a global village. Globalisation and liberalisation are becoming key words. Teachers and teacher educators, therefore, would be required to be conversant with international trends and develop competencies in internationalism, multi-culturalism and multi-racialism.

The Department of Education in England has stated the significance of in-service teacher education as follows: "The hall-mark of a good teacher is that he is himself always learning and always developing his knowledge and understanding of children and young people. In short a teacher should be a person who because of his attitude of knowledge, to ideas, to his fellows and to life generally is better educated today, than he was yesterday and will be tomorrow better educated than he is today".

Meaning of In-Service Teacher Education

The term is self-explanatory. It refers to the education a teacher receives after he has entered the teaching profession and after he has had his education in a teachers' college. It includes all the programmes, educational, social or others, in which the teacher takes a vital part, all the extra education which he receives at different institutions by way of refresher and other professional courses, and all the travel and visits which he undertakes. All these things enlarge his experiences and vision.

The Commission on Teacher Education in USA explained this clearly as: "The continued education of teachers means much more than making up in preparation. It means continuous growth in the capacity to teach. It means broadened understanding of human development and human living. And now more than at any previous periods in school history it means growth in one's capacity to work with others, with classroom teachers and principals in a variety of activities with the administration, with the parents and community leaders and with children of different age groups".

Aims of In-Service Teacher Education and Training of Teachers (INSET)

1. To maintain the knowledge and skills of teachers.
2. To give teachers the opportunity to enlarge and improve their knowledge and educational capacities in all fields of their work.
3. To make teachers ready and able to understand and face in time new situations coming up in society and to prepare their students for the new economic, social or cultural challenges.
4. To enable teachers to gain additional qualifications and to develop their special talents and dispositions.
5. To raise the cultural and professional standard of the teaching force as a whole and strengthen its innovative vigour and creativity.

Institutions for In-Service Education

1. State Institutes of Education and District Institutes of Education.
2. State Institutes of Science.
3. State Institutes of English.
4. Extension Services Departments.
5. State Directorates of Education.
6. Voluntary Organisations.
7. NCERT (National Council of Educational Research and Training).
8. NCTE (National Council for Teacher Education).
9. UGC (University Grants Commission).

10. NIEPA (National Institute of Educational Planning and Administration now known as National University of Educational Planning and Administration).
11. Professional Organisations of Teachers.
12. International Educational Organisations.
13. Indira Gandhi National Open University.
14. State Boards of Education

Programmes for In-Service Education

Programmes for in-service teacher education are: (1) Seminars, (2) Extension Lectures, (3) Refresher Courses, (4) Workshops, (5) Study Groups, (6) Conferences, (7) Experimenting, (8) Professional Writings, (9) Discussions and Debates, and (10) Educational Tours and Exchange Programmes.

Shortcoming and Inadequacies of In-Service Education Programmes

The Working Group on In-Service Education of Teachers 1986 (NCERT) pointed out the following shortcomings of the in-service teacher education (INSET):

(a) *Inadequate understanding of the importance of in-service teacher education*: INSET not only helps to update the teacher continuously but also remedies inadequacies of the existing pre-service education. In the process of providing in-service education, teacher educators gain experience relevant to pre-service education of teachers.

(b) *Absence of a national system of in-service education*: This has resulted in inadequate and unsystematised service to teachers.

(c) *Lack of attention to methodology of in-service education*: In the absence of specific infrastructure including manpower for in-service education, suitable methodologies for communication with small groups have not evolved.

(d) *Unsystematic selection of participants and resource persons*: Lack of advance planning and communication regarding content and objectives affect the deputation of suitable participants from various institutions. It can also affect the quality of resource input.

(e) *Ineffective follow-up*: Contact with teacher participants of in-service programmes is usually not maintained. Institutions and groups do not follow up the functioning of their trainees.

(f) *Poor coordination and monitoring of in-service education programmes*: Agencies are not identified at the State/Central level to monitor the total efforts in the area. There is adhocism both in planning and implementation.

(g) *Limited opportunities for training of in-service education personnel*: Opportunities for renewal and interaction with colleges are equally important for those who are responsible for planning and implementing in-service education.

(h) *Absence of research base for making in-service education more effective*: It is the result of poor recognition given in the area which in turn impinges upon its development along suitable lines.

(i) *Inadequate infrastructures for INSET at the State and national levels*: To make the programme of in-service teacher education really effective, these shortcomings need to be rectified. In-service education needs of a large number of teachers cannot be met without a well developed appropriate infrastructure.

The National Commission on School Teachers 1983-85 pointed out the following inadequacies:

1. There is today an absence of clear-cut policies and priorities for in-service education.
2. There has been no systematic identification of needs.
3. The content and quality of programmes offered are generally poor.
4. Strategies for training are vague and half-hearted.
5. Not much emphasis appears to have been placed on solving the practical problems of teachers or meeting their educational needs.
6. In-service courses rarely result in the development of a crop of instructional material that can be used by participants and other teachers.
7. Hardly any use is made of new media and technologies.
8. Administrative support for innovations is lacking as headmasters, and supervisors are not often involved in programmes where teachers are being trained in the use of new methodologies.
9. The phenomenon of routine transfers finds trained personnel not placed in positions where they should use their training maximally.

Suggestions for Improving In-Service Education

1. *Identification of Needs*. The need for in-service teacher education must be identified by the teachers working in schools and not decided by other agencies.
2. *Workshops*. During the in-service education programme, more emphasis should be on class-oriented work.
3. *Need for Expanding Facilities*. It has been observed that so far thousands of teachers especially those belonging to private institutions have not been actively involved in the Extension Services Programmes because of inadequate facilities. There is therefore, a great need for expanding the programme of in-service education.
4. *Cooperation of Various Agencies*. The various agencies like the Extension Services Department, State Institutes of Education, State Department of Education, and State Boards of School Education need to co-ordinate their activities so that there is no overlapping.
5. *Role of Inspectors*. It is the duty of the heads of institutions to encourage their staff to take part in the programmes of in-service education. The education officers like-wise should also encourage this participation and should ensure that all teachers attend these programmes.
6. *Well-planned Programmes*. The programmes of in-service education should be very well planned and organised properly.
7. *Resource Persons*. Well-qualified teachers should act as resource persons. They should be drawn from the staff of the Colleges of

Education and the State Departments of Education. They must have something new to give to the teachers. The purpose of in-service programmes is not mere repetition of pre-service courses, but it is to break new ground in content, organisation, teaching and evaluation processes.

8. *Follow-up Programmes*. One important weakness of the present day extension service programme is that follow-up work is completely missing. Thus it is not known how far the participants benefit from the programme. Some way should be found out to ensure proper follow-up.
9. *Research*. These programmes should be backed by the findings of research. School teachers should be encouraged to take small research projects and to report their findings to others.
10. *Incentive to Teachers*. There is need for providing some incentive to teachers who attend the courses of longer duration and during the holidays. Attendance at these longer courses should entitle them to some credit towards their professional degree such as B.Ed. or M.Ed., which they want to take up at a later stage. This practice is followed in U.S.A.
11. *Subject Teachers' Associations*. As suggested by the Kothari Commission, Subject Teachers' Associations should be formed at the city, district, state and all-India level on the different school subjects. This will stimulate initiative and experimentation and assist in the revision and upgrading of curricula through the provision of better teaching materials and the use of improved techniques of teaching and evaluation. The State Education Department should assist the subject teachers associations to hold periodical seminars and conferences and to conduct journals of their own.
12. *Subject Experts*. In order to provide guidance to teachers in the techniques of teaching various subjects, subject experts should be appointed at the district level.

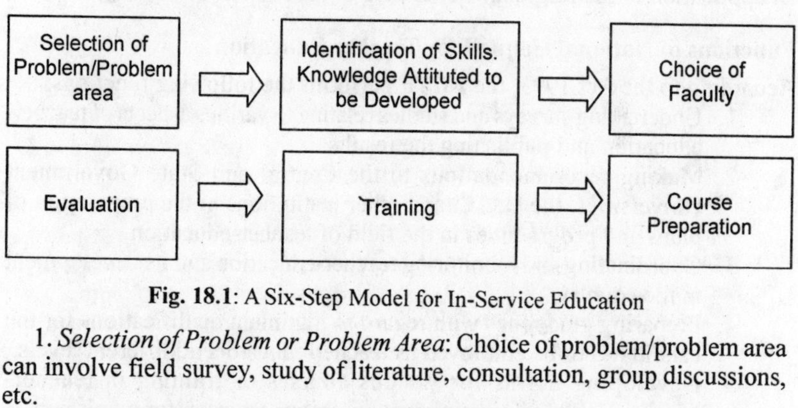

Fig. 18.1: A Six-Step Model for In-Service Education

1. *Selection of Problem or Problem Area*: Choice of problem/problem area can involve field survey, study of literature, consultation, group discussions, etc.

2. *Identification of Skills*: It is necessary for evaluation.

3. *Choice of Faculty*: Success of the programme will depend greatly on the suitability of the course faculty.

4. *Evaluation*: This will involve among other things include:

(i) Definition of goals/objectives related to serial number 2;
(ii) Definition of tasks/activities to be arranged; and
(iii) Choice of methodology including preparation of instruction materials.

5. *Training*: This will involve the preparation of the course programme and daily time table.

6. *Course Preparation*: It can involve the use of questionnaires and other tools relevant to assessing the relevance and effectiveness of this course.

18.8 NATIONAL COUNCIL FOR TEACHER EDUCATION (NCTE)

The National Council for Teacher Education (NCTE) which had been in existence for the last more than two decades was given a statutory recognition by a gazette notification issued on August 17, 1995 (Notification No. 484) by the Ministry of Human Resource Development (Department of Education). This was done in pursuance of the National Council for Teacher Education Act, 1993 (No. 73 of 1993). This Act has been enacted with a view to achieving planned and coordinated development of the Teacher Education system throughout the country, the regulation and proper maintenance of norms and standards in the teacher education system and for matters connected therewith. According to the Act "Teacher Education" includes programmes of education, research or training of persons for equipping them to teach at pre-primary, primary, secondary and senior secondary stages in schools, and includes non-formal education, part-time education, adult education and correspondence education. It is further provided in the Act that every institution offering or intending to offer a course or training in Teacher Education on or after 17th August 1995 is to seek recognition in accordance with this Act by making an application to the respective Regional Committee of the NCTE. Further, any institution which has been recognised under the Act has to seek permission to start any new course or training in Teacher Education by making an application to the Regional Committee of the NCTE.

Functions of National Council for Teacher Education

According to the Act 1993, the NCTE performs the following functions:

1. Undertaking surveys and studies relating to various aspects of teacher-education and publishing the results.
2. Making recommendations to the Central and State Government Universities, the U.G.C. and other institutions in the preparation of plans and programmes in the field of teacher-education.
3. Coordinating and monitoring teacher-education and its development in the country.
4. Preparing guidelines with regard to minimum qualifications for the candidates to be employed as teacher-educators at different levels.
5. Developing norms for various courses or training in teacher-education, including minimum eligibility criterion for admission.
6. Preparing guidelines and specified requirements for starting new courses and programmes under teacher-education.
7. Developing guidelines for general teacher-education programme.

8. Promoting innovations and research studies.
9. Supervising the teacher-education programmes and providing financial assistance.
10. Enforcing accountability of teacher-development programmes in the country.
11. Preventing commercialisation in teacher-education and maintaining quality and standard of teacher-education.
12. Preparing programmes for in service teacher-education for orienting teachers for latest developments.
13. Establishing international relations in the area of teacher-education.
14. Preventing B.Ed. correspondence courses which are lowering the standard and quality of teacher-education and commercialising the teacher-education.
15. Preparing Code of professional ethics for teachers.
16. Developing curriculum of teacher-education.
17. Developing methodology of teaching and techniques of evaluation procedures, continuing and non-formal education.
18. Improving role of teacher in social and vocational areas.

Need for Vigilance

It is true that NCTE has taken several steps to revitalise teacher education. However, it has not been quite effective in checking the mushroom growth of teacher education institutions with very meagre infrastructure. It is also a matter of great concern that teacher education programmes, in general, lack pragmatic and operational approach. Teaching practice programme remains ineffective. There is very little quality control vigorous efforts and stringent measures are needed in this direction.

UNIT III : SPECIFIC ISSUES AT THE SECONDARY LEVEL

19

Moral Education

19.1 INTRODUCTION

Moral education is ingrained in our culture and philosophy. Yet it is a matter of great regret that gradually we tend to lose moral values and our country is rated quite high in this context in the global scenario. Even our role models are under suspect. This trend must be asserted. It is true that a good deal of responsibility rests in our leaders in different walks of life. Nevertheless, educational institutions that are especially catering to the secondary education can play a significant role in the promotion of moral values.

The Essence of Moral Values

The essence of moral values lives in the promotion of welfare of the society. This idea is very beautifully expressed in one of our ancient prayers:

सर्वे भवन्तु सुखिनः, सर्वे सन्तु निरामयः।
सर्वे भद्राणि पश्यन्तुः, मा कश्चिद् दुख भाग भवेत्।

"Let us all be happy and free from disease. Let men see well of another, let be no sorrow or unhappiness in the world".

Moral values are important at every point of life. In the Vedic period, when a '*Shishya*' completed his education in the '*Ashram*', at the feet of his *Guru*, he was exhorted by his '*Guru*' to follow certain values throughout his life.

सत्यंवद। धर्मम् चर। स्वाध्यायान्मा प्रमद

"Speak truth, fulfil your duties, never lax in self-study".

19.2 NEED FOR MORAL EDUCATION

Following are some of the important reasons which necessitate the development of moral values.

1. The progress in science and technology without simultaneous development of moral values have serious repercussions in almost all dimensions of life. It is very important that moral awareness is developed and promoted among the students to orient the progress in science and technology towards the well-being of mankind.
2. With the general decline of traditional values, some common values must be followed to unite human beings.
3. There is an increasing moral complexity in the contemporary world

and the learners are expected to face even more complicated decision-making situations about issues involving values. They should be guided in developing the ability to make proper choices based on moral values in such situations.

4. It cannot be ignored that the rate of juvenile delinquency has been increasing of late. It is a clear symptom of a crisis which today's youth undergoes in the process of his personal growth. In such a situation, moral education assumes a special significance.
5. Schools are set up by the society to prepare children to assume their role of an enlightened and responsible citizen of a democratic state. A true democrat must imbibe moral and social values and the educational institutions must play their role effectively.

Einstein, one of the greatest scientists of the world, has observed, "A positive aspiration and effort for an ethical and moral configuration of our common life is of overriding importance. Here, no science can save us… This, I believe has directly led to the importance of ethical values".

The University Education Commission (1948-49) observed, "If we wish to bring about a savage upheaval in our society, a '*Rakshash Raj*', all that we need to do is to give vocational and technical education to starve the spirit. We will have a number of scientists without conscience, technicians without taste, who find a void within themselves, a moral vacuum and a desperate need to substitute something, anything for their last endeavour and purpose".

Gandhiji observed, "All our learning or recitation of the *Vedas*, correct knowledge of Sanskrit, Latin, Greek and what not will avail us nothing if they do not enable us to cultivate absolute purity of heart".

Ramount states, "The teacher's ultimate concern is to cultivate, not wealth of muscle, nor fullness of knowledge, nor refinement of feeling but strength and purity of character".

Swami Vivekananda has said, "The end of all education, all training should be character development".

19.3 DEFINITION AND MEANING OF MORAL VALUES

I. *The Committee on Moral and Religious Education* (1959) constituted by the Ministry of Education, Government of India defined moral value as, "Anything that helps us to behave properly towards others is of moral value". It further observed, "Good manners are a very important part of moral education".

   While deliberating upon moral values, we may keep in mind that cultural, ethical, moral, religious, social and spiritual values are interlinked.

II. *Stanford Encyclopaedia of Philosophy*:

   The term "morality" can be used either

   1. descriptively to refer to a code of conduct put forward by a society, or
      (a) some other group, such as a religion, or
      (b) accepted by an individual for her own behaviour.
   2. normatively to refer to a code of conduct that, given specified conditions, would be put forward by all rational persons.

III. *Wikipedia, The Free Encyclopaedia*
Morality refers to the concept of human ethics which pertains to matters of good and evil—also referred to as "right or wrong", used within three contexts: individual conscience; systems of principles and judgments – sometimes called moral values – shared within a cultural, religious, secular, humanist or philosophical community; and codes of behaviour or conduct. Personal morality defines and distinguishes among right and wrong intentions, motivations or actions, as these have been learned, engendered, or otherwise developed within each individual.

IV. *Swami Vivekananda* has laid stress on the following values:
1. Cultivation of heart.
2. Fearfulness.
3. Non-injury
4. Purity, not only personal purity but social purity also
5. Self-sacrifice
6. Service to others

Regarding service to others, Swami Vivekananda said, "I call him a Mahatma (a great soul) who feels for the poor. Service to mankind is the highest service!"

V. *Gandhiji* mentions the following eleven values:
1. *Ahimsa* (Non-violence)
2. *Satya* (Truth)
3. *Astayam* (Non-thriving)
4. *Brahmacharya* (Purity)
5. *Aparigraha* (Non-acquisitiveness)
6. *Sharishrama* (Physical work)
8. *Aswada* (Control of palate)
9. *Sarva Dharma Sambhava* (Looking at all religions equally – toleration)
10. *Swadeshi* (Patriotism – love of one's country)
11. *Sparsha Bhavna* (Abolition of untouchability)

VI. *The NCERT* in a book , *Documents on Social, Moral and Spiritual Values in Education* (1979) has listed 82 values. Out of these we may include the following moral values:

1. Consideration for others
2. Compassion
3. Cooperation
4. Cleanliness
5. Common good
6. Courtesy
7. Duty
8. Discipline
9. Equality
10. Good manners
11. Gratitude
12. Integrity
13. Honesty
14. Helpfulness
15. Justice
16. Kindness
17. Non-violence
18. Obedience
19. Punctuality
20. Purity
21. Regularity
22. Respect for elders
23. Self-discipline
24. Sincerity
25. Sympathy
26. Tolerance
27. Truthfulness

VII. *Psychology of the Child and Curriculum*, published by NCERT (1983) has listed the following important moral qualities which need to be developed in the students:

1. Compassion
2. Duty consciousness
3. Honesty in words and deeds
4. Respect for others
5. Righteousness
6. Self-control
7. Self-respect
8. Truthfulness

19.4 DEVELOPMENT OF MORAL VALUES

Secondary Education Commission (1952-53) on the Development of Moral Values in Students

The Commission considered that healthy trends in regard to moral behaviour spring from three sources:

1. The influence of the home which is the dominant factor;
2. The influence of the school through the conduct and behaviour of the teachers themselves and life in the school community as a whole;
3. Influence exercised by the public of the locality and the extent to which public opinion prevails in all matters pertaining to moral codes of conduct.

The Commission observed, "No amount of instruction can supersede or supplant these three essential factors. Such instruction can be supplemented to a limited extent by properly organised instruction given in the schools. One of the methods adopted in some schools is to hold an assembly at the commencement of the day's session with all teachers and pupils present, when a general non-denominational prayer is offered. Moral instruction in the sense of inspiring talks given by suitable persons selected by the headmaster and dwelling on the lives of great personages of all times and of all climes will help to drive home the lessons of morality".

The Committee on Religious and Moral Education (1959)

The Committee recommended the following programme at the secondary stage of education:

(a) The morning assembly should observe two minutes' silence followed by readings from the scriptures or great literature of the world or an appropriate address. Community singing should also be encouraged.

(b) The essential teachings of the great world religions should be studied as part of the curriculum pertaining to social studies and history. Simple texts and stories concerning different religions may be included in the teaching of languages and general reading.

(c) One hour a week should be assigned to moral instruction. The teacher should encourage the habit of discussion in the class. Apart from this regular class instruction, suitable speakers may be invited to address the students on moral and spiritual values. Joint celebrations may be organised on the occasion of important festivals of all religions.

Knowledge and appreciation of religions other than one's own and respect for their founders should be compulsory and physical education, including sex hygiene, should be a normal part of school programme.

(d) Qualities of character and behaviour of students should form an essential part of the overall assessment of a student's performance at school.

Education Commission (1964-66) on the Development of Moral Values: Moral Education: Indirect as Well as Direct Methods

"This education, we believe, should be provided, both by direct and indirect methods, by suggestion as well as by discussion and teaching". The Commission attaches great importance to the role of indirect influence in building up good character. The school atmosphere, the personality and behaviour of the teachers, the facilities provided in the school, will have a large say in developing a sense of values. The Commission emphasises that the consciousness of values must permeate the whole curriculum and the programme of activities in the school. It is not only the teachers in-charge of moral instruction who are responsible for building character. Every teacher, whatever be the subject he teaches, must necessarily accept this responsibility. He must ensure that in the teaching of his particular subject and in his dealings with his pupils, fundamental values such as integrity and social responsibility are brought out. A sense of purpose should inspire all school activities and must be reflected in the life, tone and atmosphere of the school. The school assembly, the curricular and co-curricular activities, the celebration of religious festivals of all religions, work-experience, team games and sports, subject clubs, social service programmes—all these can help in inculcating the values of cooperation and mutual regard, honesty and integrity, discipline and social responsibility. These values have a special significances in Indian society today, when young men and women are passing through a crisis of character.

Direct Instruction of Moral Values

In addition to this indirect approach for inculcating moral and spiritual values, the Commission notes that specific provision for direct moral instruction in the school programmes is highly desirable. One or two periods a week should be set aside in the school time-table for instruction in moral and spiritual values. At the secondary stage, there may be frequent discussions between the teacher and the pupils on the values sought to be inculcated. Whatever be the method of teaching, it should not lead to moral instruction being divorced from the rest of the curriculum or being confined to a single period. If the values are to become a part of the student's character, an all-embracing treatment of the moral way of life is needed.

Relation between Moral Values and Religion

The Commission observes there will be natural points of correlation between the moral values sought to be inculcated and the teachings of the great religions. Stories drawn from the great religions of the world will be most appropriate in a discussion of moral values and of problems in life. All religions stress certain fundamental qualities of character, such as honesty and truthfulness, consideration for others, reverence for old age, kindness to animals, and compassion for the needy and the suffering. In the literature of every religion, the story of parable figures prominently as a means of impressing an ethical value on the followers. The narration of such stories by the teachers at the right moment in the programme of moral education would be most effective, particularly in the lower Classes of the school.

At a later stage, accounts of the lives of great religious and spiritual leaders will find a natural place. Some of these may be included in the study of social studies or literature, but it is essential that all important religions are represented properly in the programme. Similarly, the celebration of the festivals of different religions will afford opportunities for the narration of incidents from the life history of the leaders of these religions. In the last two years of the secondary school, a place should be found for the study of the essential teachings of the great religions.

National Policy on Education (1986 and 1992) on Value Education (Moral Education)

In PART VIII, the NPE has laid less on value education in paragraphs 8.4, 8.5 and 8.6.

Para 8.4: The growing concern over the erosion oi essential values and an increasing cynicism in society has brought to focus the need for readjustments in the curriculum in order to make education a forceful tool for the cultivation of social and moral values.

Para 8.5: In our culturally plural society education should foster universal and eternal values, oriented towards the unity and integrity of our people. Such value education should help eliminate obscurantism, religious fanaticism, violence, superstition and fatalism.

Para 8.6: Apart from this combative role, value education has a profound positive contact, based on our heritage, national goals and universal perceptions. It should lay primary emphasis on this aspect.

19.5 MORAL-ORIENTED THOUGHTS FROM RELIGIOUS SCRIPTURES

Hindu Scriptures

'Yajurveda'

- Do good to humanity.
- Earn wealth in a righteous way.
- Perform noble needs.
- Purify your mind.

'Manu'

- Cultivate the spirit of forgiveness under all circumstances.
- Do not be dishonest by taking a thing without the permission of its owner.
- Free yourself from hatred.
- Be just.

'Ram Charitmanas'

1. There is no virtue like benevolence.

2. There is no meanness like oppressing others.

'Christianity'

1. You should not steal.
2. You should not covet your neighbour's goods.

'Islam'

1. Be honest in exchange of things.
2. Do not acquire another's goods wrongfully.

'Sikkhism"

1. Truth is higher, but higher still is truthful living.
2. God's eye of mercy falls on those who take care of the lowest.

'Buddhism'

1. Earn livelihood rightly.
2. Do right action.

'Jainism'

1. Have right conduct.
2. Do right action.

19.6 ILLUSTRATIVE LIST OF PROGRAMMES AND INCULCATION OF MORAL VALUES

	Programme	*Value/Values to be Inculcated*
1.	Morning Assembly	Orderliness. Punctuality. Good manners.
2.	Flag Hoisting	Discipline.
3.	Bhajans and Chorus Singing	Devotion. Team Spirit. Penance. Humility.
4.	Cultural Programmes	Good Manners. Cooperation.
5.	Group Games and Sports	Cooperation. Love for Rules. Consideration of others.
6.	School Cleanliness	Dignity of Labour. Love for Cleanliness. Selfless Service.
7.	Social Service Camps	Spirit of Service to Others. Dignity of Labour.
8.	Social Service in Fairs and Other Occasions	Spirit of Service. Companions.
9.	Scouting, Girl Guide and NCC	Spirit of Service. Discipline
10.	Visit to Hospitals.	Spirit of Service.
11.	Honesty Campaigns	Honesty
12.	Courtesy	Courtesy
13.	Lectures on Morality	Clarity of Thought. Moral Awakening.
14.	Community Survey	Social Service. Love for Community.
15.	Adult Education Programme	Service of Others.

19.7 ROLE OF THE TEACHER IN THE PROMOTION OF MORAL VALUES AMONG STUDENTS

Traditionally, teachers have been regarded as the best promoters of moral values among the students. It was once said that their way of living, dress, speech, etc. had great impact on the minds of the students. They were regarded as role models before the students. They were supposed to be symbols of moral values – honesty, truth, simplicity, etc. On account of their high moral values, they have enjoyed a great esteem in the society. But gradually, their status has been diminishing. At the secondary and senior secondary stages of education, their influence on the young minds has greatly declined. However, all is not lost. They still influence the students. The most important aspect is that they should set good examples of conduct and behaviour which the students may imbibe in themselves. They should not discriminate between the rich and the poor students. They should be fair and just. They should follow the prescribed code. They should reach the class in time, prepare their lessons and put their heart and soul into the work. All these values are bound to exercise a healthy influence on the students.

Having said all this, it must be accepted that the major responsibility of creating a suitable moral environment rests upon the leaders working in different fields. They are expected to rise equal to the occasion.

19.8 SUMMING UP

India is on the move again with the promise of new renaissance in the making. The most powerful tool in this process of renaissance and modernisation is education based on moral values on the one hand and on the other science and technology (representing materialism). In this context we cannot do better than to quote Pandit Jawaharlal Nehru, "Can we combine the progress of science and technology with the progress of mind and spirit also? Let us then pursue our path to industrial progress with our strength and vigour and at the same time remember that material riches without toleration, compassion and wisdom may well turn to dust and ashes".

20

Women's Education

20.1 IMPORTANCE OF WOMEN'S EDUCATION

Women play a prominent role in the cultural, economic, political, religious and social life of a country. The ancient people of India fully realised this fact and accorded a reasonable status to women and encouraged their education. According to Vedas, women should have opportunity to attain knowledge of the Vedas from all four courses (Rig Veda 14.9.64). More than 400 verses in the Vedas are ascribed to 24 women seers. In the Vedas, women have been called '*Updeshtri*' of knowledge and this indicates women working as teachers (Rig Veda 1.3.11).

Swami Vivekananda has emphasised, "If you do not raise the women who are living embodiment of the divine mother, don't think that you have any other way to rise".

Gandhiji stated the importance of women education in these words, "I am strongly of the opinion that women should have the same facilities as men and even special facilities where necessary".

Jawaharlal Nehru very rightly observed, "Education of a boy is the education of one person, but education of a girl is the education of entire family".

In view of the importance of women education in national development, the University Education Commission 1948-49 remarked, "There can't be an educated people without education of women. If general education had to be limited to men or to women, then opportunity should be given to women, from them it would more surely be passed to the next generation".

Similarly, the Kothari Commission 1964-66, stated, "For full development of human resources, the improvement of human beings and for moulding the character of children during the most impressionable years of infancy, the education of women is of greater importance than that of men".

20.2 PROGRESS OF WOMEN'S EDUCATION IN INDIA

Table 20.1: Progress of Women's Education: Literacy Rates (1951 to 2001)

Census Year	*Persons (Total)*	*Males*	*Females*	*Male-Female Gap in Literacy Rates*
1951	18.33	27.16	8.86	18.30
1961	28.30	40.40	15.75	25.05
1971	34.45	45.96	21.98	23.98
1981	43.37	56.38	29.76	26.62
1991	52.21	64.13	39.29	24.84
2001	65.38	75.85	54.16	21.69

Source: Census 2001

Table 20.2: Percentage of Girls Enrolment to Total Enrolment by Stages since 1950-51

Year	*Primary I-V*	*Middle VI-VIII*	*Sec./Hr.Sec./ 10+2/Inter*	*Hr. Education (Degree & above level)*
1950-51	28.1	16.1	13.3	10.0
1960-61	32.6	23.9	20.5	16.0
1970-71	37.4	29.3	25.0	20.0
1980-81	38.6	32.9	29.6	26.7
1990-91	41.5	36.7	32.9	33.3
2000-2001	43.7	40.9	38.6	36.9
2001-2002	44.1	41.8	39.5	39.9

Table 20.3: Sex-wise Enrolment by Stages/Classes Since 1951 (in Million)

Year	*Primary*			*Middle/Upper Primary*			*High/Hr. Secondary*		
	Boys	*Girls*	*Total*	*Boys*	*Girls*	*Total*	*Boys*	*Girls*	*Total*
1950-51	13.8	5.4	19.2	2.6	0.5	3.1	1.3	0.2	1.5
1960-61	23.6	11.4	35.0	5.1	1.6	6.7	2.7	0.7	3.4
1970-71	35.7	21.3	57.0	9.4	3.9	13.3	5.7	1.9	7.6
1980-81	45.3	28.5	73.8	13.9	6.8	20.7	7.6	3.4	11.0
1990-91	57.0	40.4	97.4	21.5	12.5	34.0	12.8	6.3	19.1
2000-2001	64.0	49.8	113.8	25.3	17.5	42.8	16.9	16.7	27.6
2003-2004	68.4	59.9	128.3	27.3	21.4	48.7	20.6	14.3	34.9

Table 20.4: Women Student Enrolment Per Hundred Men Student

Enrolment (Hr. Education)

Year	*Total Women Enrolment (000s)*	*Enrolment for Hundred Men*
1950-51	40	14
2004-2005	4234	68

Table 20.5: No. of Women Colleges

Year	*No. of Women Colleges*
1986-87	780
1996-97	1195
2000-2001	1578
2001-2002	1625
2002-2003	1650
2003-2004	1798
2004-2005	1950

Table 20.6: Total Women Student Enrolment in Higher Education and Per centage of Women (2004-2005)

Total Enroment	*Women Enrolment*	*% of Women*
10481042	4234340	40.40

Table 20.7: Literacy Rates of Women and Men (1951-2001)

Census Year	*Total (Person)*	*Women*	*Men*
1951	18.33	8.86	27.16
1961	28.30	15.35	40.40
1971	34.45	21.97	45.96
1981	43.57	29.76	56.38
1991	52.21	39.29	64.13
2001	64.84	53.67	75.26

Table 20.8: Women /Total Literacy Rate (2004)

Total	*61%*
Men	73
Women	48

20.3 WIDE GAP BETWEEN GIRLS' EDUCATION AND BOYS' EDUCATION

From the figures given above, it is quite clear that there has been phenomenal progress in education since Independence but still there is a wide gap between boys' education and girls' education.

Usually following causes of slow progress are mentioned:

(i) Lack of proper social attitudes in the rural and backward areas for the education of girls.
(ii) Lack of educational facilities in rural areas.
(iii) Economic backwardness of the rural community.
(iv) Conservative nature and co-educational aspects.
(v) Lack of suitable curriculum.
(vi) Lack of proper incentives to parents and children.
(vii) Lack of women teachers.
(viii) Lack of proper supervision and guidance due to inadequate women personnel in the Inspectorate.
(ix) Uneducated adult women and lack of social education.
(x) Social ills.
(xi) Inadequate systematic publicity.
(xii) Indifference of Panchayats.

20.4 MEASURES FOR THE PROMOTION OF GIRLS' AND WOMEN EDUCATION

Following measures are suggested:

I. *Creating Proper Social attitude in the Rural and Backward Areas for the Education of Girls*: Following measures may be taken:

Vocational Courses

(i) Immediate steps should be taken to expand the provision of vocational courses for girls.

(ii) The possibilities of employing women on a large scale on a part-time basis in as many vocations as possible should be explored.

20.7 CO-EDUCATION AT THE SECONDARY STAGE

Meaning of Co-education

Co-education is the education of boys and girls together in the same class on equal footing. It does not mean just the admission of girls into boys' school merely for the purpose of teaching or *vice versa*. It also implies freedom of association of both the sexes in co-curricular programmes of the school.

Merits of Co-education

1. *Economic considerations*: Co-education is economical. When the number of students is small, separate institutions for boys and girls need more investment.
2. *Psychological considerations*: Greater contact between boys and girls results in better understanding of the various issues concerning both the sexes. In this context Hayword wrote, "Future mothers should not have to confess with tears that they do not understood boys".
3. *Humanising influence*: Co-education tends to make boys more refined and makes the girls less suspicious of boys and more receptive.
4. *Positive impact on disciplinary problems*: Discipline becomes easier to maintain because boys want recognition of the girls and *vice versa*.
5. *Modification in personality traits*: On account of co-education, boys may learn values of perseverance, conscientiousness and industriousness from girls and the latter learn values of independence, self-reliance and resourcefulness from boys.
6. *Increase in modesty*: It is felt that boys become more modest. There is less under current excitement and more excitement of a natural and obvious kind.
7. *Intellectual benefits*: There is no doubt that attendance in the classes becomes almost cent per cent.
8. *Homely atmosphere*: Co-education enables us to have a polished homely environment.
9. *Better domestic life*: Addison once said, "Female friendship is necessary for intellectual development".
10. *Reduction in Mental Illness*: Dr. Freud was of the view that co-education alone could keep young people free from diseases of mind.

Limitations of Co-education

1. *Free mixing up leading to troubles*: Dr. Stanley Hall writes, "During the early years of adolescence when the body is rapidly changing and a sense of awkwardness and reticence is felt, the two sexes should not

intrude upon each other". Since in our tropical country sex consciousness develops at an early age, free mixing is fraught with danger.

2. *Less attention to girls*: Girls usually suffer. It is generally seen that in co-educational institutions adequate facilities are not provided for girls.
3. *No thorough cleansing of the mental make-up*: Co-education is a farce in many cases as we have not taken to this business in the right spirit. There must be a sane attitude and healthy outlook.
4. *Separate needs of men and women*: Dr. Joad has remarked, "Girls tend to be more interested in their immediate surroundings, in what is pretty and ornamental, boys in what is more remote from them, in what is useful, in what is general and what is abstract. Boys seek expression in investigation, exploring and constructing while girls through artistic and emotional undertaking channels.

Rousseau wrote, "A man seeks to serve, woman seeks to please. The one needs knowledge, the other taste". To be pleasing in his sight, to win his respect and love, to train him in childhood, to tend him in motherhood, to counsel and to console, to make his life pleasant and happy, these are the duties for all time".

5. *Physiological Factors*: A uniform programme of physical and mental activities for boys and girls may adversely affect the adolescent girls.
6. *Undue emphasis on dress*: Both boys and girls tend to wear glamorous dress. This leads to the possibility of stealthy eying and shy glances.
7. *Separate code of discipline*: The two sexes need separate codes of discipline.
8. *Sex complications*: In the absence of adequate sex guidance, adolescent boys and girls tend to develop unhealthy sex values.

Suggestions for Making Co-education Successful

1. Co-education should be adopted as the general policy at the primary level.
2. At the middle and secondary stage separate schools should be provided in areas where there is a demand for them. But the effort to pursue co-education, as a general policy at these stages should continue side by side.
3. At the university level, co-education should be the general policy and opening of new colleges exclusively for girls should be discouraged.
4. There should be no bar on admission of girls to boys' institutions.
5. Whenever separate schools/colleges for girls are provided, it has to be ensured that they maintain required standards in regard to the quality of the staff, provision of facilities, relevant courses and co-curricular services.
6. Acceptance of principle of mixed staff should be made a condition of recognition for mixed schools.
7. Where there are mixed schools separate toilet facilities and retiring rooms for girls should be provided.

8. The lady teachers as well as male chers must be appointed in these schools.
9. There should be adequate provisi for those subjects which are usually preferred by girls, i.e. Mc, Home Craft, Drawing and Painting, etc.
10. Separate rooms, playfields and itary conveniences should be provided for girls.
11. There should be at least one woml teacher in a rural school even if the number of girls students is vy less.
12. Special co-curricular activities sed to the girls like Home Nursing, Needle Work and Girls Guidinghould be introduced.
13. The women representatives shld be taken on the management so that they could plead for proving necessary facilities for girls.

20.8 EMPOWERMENT OF WOMN: EQUALITY AND EDUCATION

Recently special schemes have been lanched for the economic, educational, political and social empowerment of omen. The reservation of seats in local institutions, globalisation and liberasation, etc. have led to great awakening among the females. Now there is grat demand for education at all levels by them.

In some states, girls' educatiomis free at all levels. In a large number of States it is free up to the secondar stage.

Hostel facilities for girls are povided at various places.

20.9 NPE AND EDUCATION OF GIRLS

The NPE 1986 stipulates, "Education will be used as an agent of basic change in the status of women. In oder to neutralise the accumulated distortion of the past, there will be a wellconceived edge". For achieving this the national education system will play apositive, interventionist role in the empowerment of women".

The NPE's programme includes the following:

1. Redesigning the courses to develop new values.
2. Redesigning textbooks for eliminating sex bias.
3. Orientation of teachers for developing sensitiveness to women's issues.
4. Orientation of decision makers and administrators to women's issues.
5. Increasing participation of women in vocational, technical and professional education at all levels.
6. Providing more facilities to girls and women in educational institutions.
7. Expanding literacy programmes for girls.

UGC and Empowerment and Education of Women

The UGC has taken the following measures for promoting higher education among women:

1. Special scheme for construction of women hostels.
2. Establishment of Women Study Centres.
3. Past time research associateship for women.
4. Infrastructure for women students and teachers.

Mahila Samakhya Progmme (Education for Women's Equality): The Mahila Samakhya Programe was started in 1989 for the education and empowerment of women in ra areas, particularly of women from socially and economically marginalise goups. It is being implemented in more than 14,000 villages in 60 districts of ine states.

A group of two or more womecalled 'Sakhi' or 'Sahayaki' are trained to work as catalysts who facilitate formation as well as discussions in the Sangha. The funds are earmarkefor this puppose. Both formal and non-formal education programmes are ganised by the Mahila Sanghas.

Kasturba Gandhi Balika Vidlayas: The programme includes 750 residential schools in different areas ith free boarding facilities at elementary level for girls belonging particularlyo the SC, ST, OBC and miorities.

21

Study of Secondary Education System in USA, UK, Germany and Japan

21.1 SECONDARY EDUCATION SYSTEM IN USA

Education in USA – A Local Matter

The United States does not have a national school system. From Hawaii to Delaware, from Alaska to Louisiana, each of the 50 states in the United States of America, has its own laws regarding education.

Education is compulsory, beginning at age 5 in seven states, at age 6 in twenty-two states, at age 7 in nineteen states, and at age 8 in two states (information was not available). Usually a person is required to attend school until age 16. Since 1989 there is a trend toward more states with mandatory school until age 18. In the year 2000, students were required to be enrolled in school to age 16 in twenty-eight states to age 17 in seven states, and to age 18 in fifteen states. Schooling is free, through completion of secondary school (Grade XII) for those fifteen states who attend public schools.

21.2 SECONDARY SCHOOL AS THE KEY STONE

Organisation of Secondary Education

In the words of President L.B. Johnson, "The secondary school is the keystone of American education; for millions of our young people it lies on the threshold of higher learning; for millions more it is the pathway …adult life and useful citizenship".

The first secondary school in USA was established by the Puritan sect. of Christians in the year 1635 in the city of Boston. No uniform system of classes could be evolved in USA for adoption by all the schools. Two types of arrangements are usually found in secondary schools. In one arrangement secondary stage consists of four classes, i.e. from 9th to 12th. In the reorganised system of education the educational structure is divided into 6, 3, 3 and 2 years. The first six years constitute elementary stage, three years each for junior secondary and higher secondary and two years for junior college stage.

20.3 OBJECTIVES OF SECONDARY EDUCATION

The Commission on Life Adjustment Education appointed in 1947 by the Federal Government to go into the details of the requirements of secondary education, laid down the following objectives of secondary education:

1. Education for successful citizenship.
2. Education for training the young men in the day-to-day life requirements.
3. Education for making worthy members of the family.
4. Education for enabling him understand the basic rules of learning.
5. Education for preparing an individual for a vocation.
6. Education for enabling to make a worthy use of leisure.
7. Education for developing the spirit of appreciation of beauty.
8. Education for understanding the significance and method of science.
9. Education for the development of mental health and physical fitness.
10. Education for moral and ethical development.

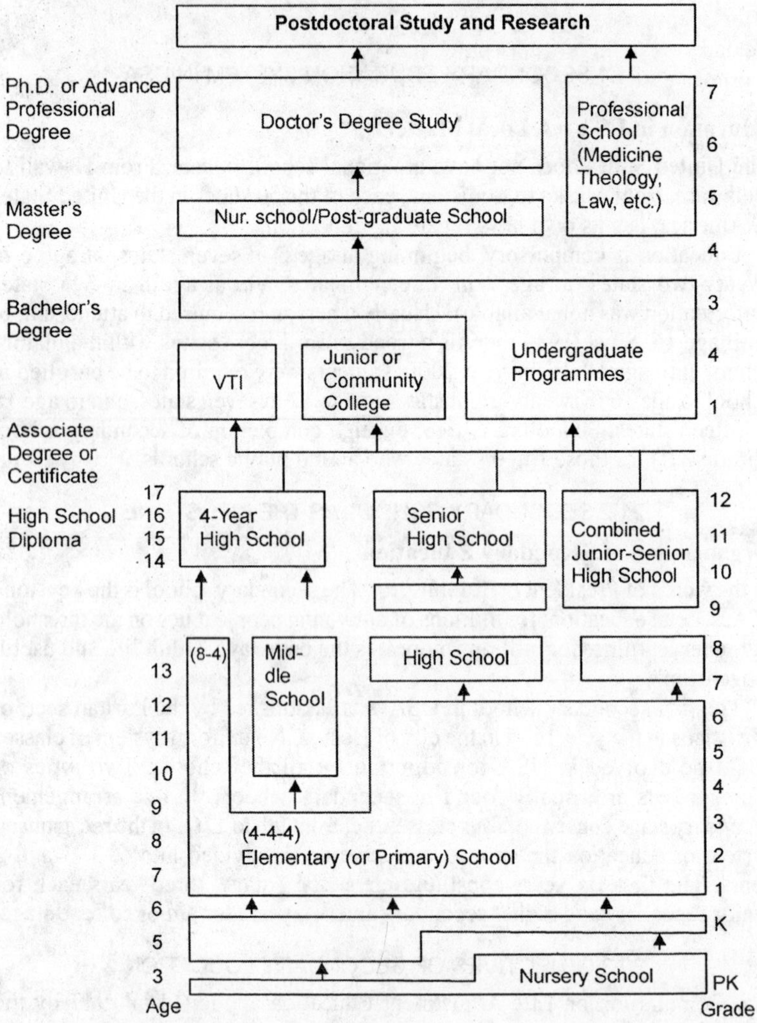

Fig. 21.1: The Structure of Education in the United States

Types of Secondary Schools

1. Junior High Schools.
2. High Schools or Higher Secondary Schools.
3. Comprehensive High Schools.
4. Specialised Schools.
5. Vocational and Industrial Schools.
6. Part time schools.
7. Junior Colleges.

Junior High Schools: These schools have been formed by taking away the last two classes, i.e. classes 7th and 8th of the primary stage and class 9th of the secondary stage. These schools were created with a view to imparting education to adolescents in the first two years, i.e. from 12 to 14 years for a proper utilisation of educational potentialities. The Classes differ from the traditional 7th and 8th Classes of a primary school and the 9th Class of a secondary school in respect of their courses. They are mostly housed in independent buildings.

High Schools or Higher Secondary Schools: High school is the common term used in USA for a higher secondary school. Generally the higher secondary Classes consist of 10th, 11th and 12th Classes.

Comprehensive High Schools: These schools include four classes, i.e. from 9th to 12th which start at the end of 8 year course of the primary stage. A comprehensive high school is supposed to be well equipped. Provision is made in imparting education in a variety of subjects. There are even such schools where as many as two hundred subjects are taught.

Main Features of Comprehensive Schools

1. There is no distinction of colour, sex, class, etc. in getting admission in these schools. These schools are open to all.
2. These schools provide for the teaching of several subjects.
3. They are based on a democratic spirit.
4. Comprehensive schools have proved more economical.
5. Education in different subjects, i.e. arts, profession, commerce, agriculture, etc. is being given in these schools according to local needs under one administration.

Specialised Schools: Most of these schools are technical, commercial, art, agricultural and business schools. These schools provide introductory vocational training.

Vocational and Industrial Schools: Schools of these types have been established mostly in big industrial cities of the country. These too are included in the category of specialised schools.

Part-time Schools: These are of two types: (i) Continuation schools which provide education for 144 hours during a year, i.e. 3 to 4 hours a week, (ii) Evening Adult Schools which run their classes daily in the evening.

Junior Colleges: Junior colleges compromise the first two classes of the college stage, i.e. 13th and 14th. These colleges are helpful to those students who do not want to go to distant places for college education.

21.4 SALIENT FEATURES OF SECONDARY EDUCATION

(a) *Secondary Education for All*: Today 90 per cent of those between the ages of 14 and 17 are enrolled in high schools. A secondary school education for every American youth – boy and girl—is the goal of education in the United States.

(b) *Varied Courses*: Students are given opportunities to select those subjects in which they are most interested, or which further the career they plan to follow. Some of the larger urban schools offer as many as 100 courses. The choice for the students is unlimited.

(c) *Outside Activities*: In addition to classroom work each student is encouraged to take part in one more outside activity.

(d) *Students' Self-Government*: A democratic form of student self-government is to be found in most of the large high schools.

(e) *Gymnasium*: Almost every school has a gymnasium for indoor sports and play fields for outdoor athletics.

(f) *Grading in Attitudes*: Students are graded not only in subjects but also in their attitudes.

(g) *Comprehensive Type of Schools*: The secondary schools in America have come to be known as comprehensive high schools, because they offer many different subjects under one roof preparing for different careers and accommodating both right and not so bright students. James B. Conant, former President of Harvard University wrote, "The comprehensive high school is characteristic of our society. It offers in one spot secondary education for almost all the high school-age children of our town or neighbourhood. It educates the boy who will be an atomic scientist and the girl who will marry at 18; the prospective captain of a ship and future captain of industry".

(h) *Specialised Schools:* Although the comprehensive high school is most common, there are some specialised high schools, chiefly in the large eastern cities. They emphasise science, or music and art, commercial and industrial courses or pre-college academic subjects.

21.5 CURRICULUM

School Curriculum Regulations: The responsibility for setting graduation requirements and curriculum regulations lies with the State legislature, the State Board of Education and the State Department of Education. In general, few curriculum requirements are State legislative mandates.

They are, instead, standards set up by the State Department of Education or regulated by the State Board. They are designed to enable the secondary schools to maintain standards recognised by colleges and universities as suitable for admission. This is important, especially for students who plan to enter college. But most State legislatures and Boards, even if they specify requirements, leave much latitude to the local School Boards to create their own programmes of required subjects and to add to them if they desire. Approximately 160,000 local School Board members throughout the country, serving usually without pay, give time and thought to these matters with reference to their community needs.

Study of English, Mathematics, Science, Social Studies: When State legislatures become involved, they usually are concerned with prescribing how and to what degree the teaching shall be devoted to American and State history, government and physical education. Although different States have varying requirements, large city school systems usually require four years of English, one year of mathematics, one year of science, two to three years of social studies (that is government, history, political science and the like), and four years of health study and physical education.

Foreign Languages, Psychology, Fine Arts, etc.: The required subjects form about half of the usual course of study, the remaining subjects are chosen by the student. He may choose such subjects as foreign languages, psychology, fine arts, shorthand and typing, and in some schools automobile driving.

Broadened Curriculum: The trend today is to increase the number of required units in science, mathematics and social studies. More emphasis also is being placed on foreign-language study. In many schools the curriculum is being broadened in keeping with the times.

The National Science Foundation has developed, and is developing, new programmes in science and mathematics designed to broaden and deepen the teaching of these vital subjects. Efforts to improve the curricula of the nation's schools are being made by the Office of Education of the Department of Health, Education and Welfare through various projects such as one in English and one in social studies.

21.6 BEYOND THE CURRICULUM

Student Council. In both the junior and senior secondary schools, work of the student council is an important and rewarding activity. This type of student government forms a strong link between students and faculty and helps to create an environment in which they can work effectively together for the well being of the whole student body and the general benefit of the school. But the main work of the council, work to which about half its time is devoted, involves the social programme of the school. As part of this it sponsors such social events as picnics, dances, carnivals and parties—social events that bring the students together for recreation away from the classroom.

Sports: Sports, of course, have an important place in most secondary schools. The school authorities require that those skilful enough to get on the various school teams also measure up to the school's academic standards.

Club Activities: In almost any American secondary school, club groups link students with special interests. Most club activities are held after school hours, usually under the supervision of a teacher. The clubs may be centred on art, dramatics, literature, science, foreign languages, poetry—almost any field of interest. They offer creative outlets and broaden students' knowledge. Often, too, they help to crystallise student's choice of a career.

Most schools have orchestras and various kinds of singing groups. They provide the musically inclined both training and expression.

School Magazine: Journalistic activities depend a great deal upon the size of the school. The larger school often has a school newspaper and some kind of literary magazine and a yearbook made up of contributions by students.

21.7 VOCATIONAL EDUCATION

Vocational education is an integral part of the secondary education in the U.S.A. The primary object of vocational education is to provide a suitable background to students in order to increase their vocational skill. The Federal Government gives matching assistance to different community agencies and educational institutions.

The secondary schools include it as a subject and teach it like other subjects.

General Vocational Education Programme in Secondary Schools

The programme may be divided under the following four main categories:

1. Industrial Education
2. Business and Commerce Education
3. Agricultural Education
4. Home Economics Education.

Industrial Education: This programme includes training in machines, like motor engine, railway engine, aeroplanes, radio, electricity, mining, painting, metal work, etc.

The students during the training period are trained and taught in different uses of general subjects such as arithmetic, art, science, etc. which are frequently applied in the industrial sphere. Provisions are made for the employment of specially trained teachers and using instruments of the latest design.

Business and Commerce Education: The primary object of providing courses of this nature is to make available facilities of service or jobs to young men and women and also enable them to do their work with better skill and efficiency. Besides typing and shorthand, this programme includes training in hotel running, merchantship, storage, etc. This system of education exists mostly at the secondary stage. Arrangements have also been made for higher education and research work.

Agricultural Education: Agricultural education in U.S.A. has become very progressive now-a-days and has an important and nation-wide programme. The system of training includes both classroom study and outside work in fields with farmers, and young men are given training in the various activities of farm and farm shops, e.g. preparation of fields, production, sale and consumption of products, etc. The schools have their own independent buildings and farms for carrying on the agricultural education. The schools are provided with the latest implements.

Home Economic Education: This education aims at training young boys and girls in matters relating to family life so that they are prepared to become worthy members of the family. The educational programmes include training in home furnishing, cooking, dressing, care of health, child care, family adjustment, family budget and inter-relationships.

21.8 PROBLEMS AT THE SECONDARY STAGE OF EDUCATION IN THE USA

Following are the major problems which pose serious challenge to educational administrators and reforms at the secondary level of education:

1. Students dress.

2. Teenage pregnancy.
3. Violence and vandalism.
4. Drug addiction.
5. Sex education

21.9 SECONDARY EDUCATION SYSTEM IN THE UK

Introduction

The UK is made up of 4 different countries – England, Scotland, Wales and Northern Ireland. The education system in Scotland differs at school and undergraduate level to the other countries who follow a similar system.

Education in the UK is compulsory for everyone between the ages of five and sixteen, and is provided by two kinds of schools: independent (fee-charging) schools and state-funded schools.

21.10 SECONDARY EDUCATION IN ENGLAND AND WALES: CHIEF FEATURES

1. *Duration*: In England and Wales, secondary school usually admits pupils aged 11 years, but in areas where three-tier systems exist, pupils may transfer from middle schools at 12 or 13 years or from junior high schools at 14 years. Schools may be organised in a number of ways, including those that the full secondary school age ranges from 11 to 18; middle schools whose pupils move on to senior comprehensive schools at 12, 13 or 14, leaving at 16 or 18; and schools with an age range of 11 or 12 to 16 combined with a sixth form a tertiary college for pupils over 16.

2. *Comprehensive schools*: In England, over 90 per cent of secondary pupils attend comprehensive schools, which admit pupils without reference to ability or aptitude, and provide a wide range of secondary education for all or most of the children of a district.

3. *Grammar Schools and Secondary Modern Schools*: Most other children receive secondary education in grammar or secondary modern schools, to which they are allocated on the basis of their performance in selection tests, taken at the age of 11:

(i) *Grammar schools* provide a mainly academic course for selected pupils from the age of 11 to 18 or 19,

(ii) *Secondary modern schools* provide a general education up to the minimum school leaving age of 16, although their pupils can stay on beyond that age and are tending to do so in increasing numbers.

4. *CTCs and CTCAs*: In addition the Education Reform Act 1988 provided for the setting up of *City Technology Colleges (CTCs)* and *City Technology Colleges of the Arts (CTCAs)*, in order to extend choice of school locally, and to pioneer new approaches to delivery of the curriculum. They are required to offer free education to pupils of all abilities accepted within their catchment areas. They are funded by central government directly and by industrial sponsors. These new schools have to teach all the core and foundation subjects of the national curriculum to all pupils. CTCs, however, put considerable emphasis on science and technology across the curriculum, while CTCAs

will specialise in arts, technology, film, video and a range of technical skills related to the arts world.

5. *Miscellaneous*: Young people over the age of 16 have a number of education and training options open to them. They may stay on in sixth form of their school or they may transfer to a *Sixth-form college, a tertiary college or a further education college*, depending on take system operated in the area they live in. (The three latter types of establishment offer a range of academic and vocational course for young people over the age of 16. There are differences in the range and number of courses available and in the regulations which govern them. *Sixth-form colleges* are part of the schools' system, while *tertiary colleges* are part of the further education system. Young people may choose to join the Government-backed *Youth Training Scheme*.

21.11 GRAMMAR SCHOOLS

A grammar school means a secondary school providing an academic course, usually for pupils aged 11 to 18 or 19. It has the following main characteristics:

1. It has a high standard of scholarship.
2. It is selective in nature.
3. It is independent by birth or existence.
4. Its traditional role is to enable its students to secure university place.
5. It secures most of the children of the professional and executive classes.

School for the Brightest Children

The grammar schools tend to recruit from brightest children from the primary schools. Since success even at that early stages is associated with home background, it becomes possible for the grammar schools to secure most of the children of the professional and executive classes. One of the important reasons for its esteem and attraction is its socially selective character. There is a certain measure of assurance in the minds of most parents that their children will not have to mix with children from neglectful homes and will not come in contact with standards of speech, behaviour and dress markedly inferior to their own. Thus, much is expected of a boy entering a grammar school. This is well expressed in the remarks of a certain headmaster:

"If you want him to be a success at the grammar school, it will mean the child breaking with his present friends, the home, not switching on television till 8 o'clock, having a seater in a separate room for his homework, keeping him from joining civic youth clubs, and being prepared to keep him at home for several more years. Don't choose a grammar school unless you are prepared to do this".

Curriculum

Beside this socially selective character, there are other factors which help to enhance the esteem of grammar schools. The intellectual training that they seek to provide and the coveted occupations to which success in their examinations leads are no significant attractions. The curriculum is not prescribed by regulations. It is determined by several factors. The most important is the values attached to various subjects by the universities, the teacher training colleges, the technical colleges and professional bodies. Until the age of 15 or 16, it is normal to study one or more classical or foreign languages, mathematics, history, geography and one or more sciences. Around this 'academic' core, physical education and religious instruction have their place. Many schools also have music, art, domestic science (for girls) and wood-work (for boys). The course leads to the 'Ordinary' level of General Certificate of Education. After this stage, those who remain at school in the sixth form until the age of 18 or 19 have to specialise intensively in three (or at the most four) subjects for taking the 'Advanced' level examinations. Generally, the subjects taken by the students are English, History and Languages in Arts or Mathematics, Physics, Chemistry, Biology in Science.

Contribution of Grammar Schools

In the main, they have two great contributions. First, towards the end of the last century and at the beginning of the present they spread an awareness of the value of higher academic education to the British population at large. Secondly, they provided it.

21.12 SECONDARY EDUCATION IN GERMANY

Compusory Schooling

It begins for all children at the age of six and usually lasts nine years of full time schooling (ten years in Berlin). In India it lasts eights years i.e. 6 to 14 years.

Secondary Education

It breaks down into the following two years:

(i) *Lower Secondary Level* I: It comprises grades 5 to 10 or 7 to 10. It usually covers the age group 10-16 years.

(ii) *Upper Secondary Level* II: It includes all the courses of education that build on the foundation laid in lower secondary. It includes the age group 16 to 19 years.

In India high school or lower secondary cover the age group 14 to 16 and Senior Secondary or higher secondary 16 to 18 years.

Length of School Year

At the lower secondary level, schools have 28 weekly periods in compulsory and optional subjects in grades 5 and 6 of all types of schools and 30 periods in grades 7 to 10. At upper secondary level also, there are around 30 periods of which 20 periods are spent on compulsory subjects and 10 on optional subjects.

Curriculum

The types of schools and educational courses at secondary level I (grades 5 and 6) are based on the idea of providing all pupils with a basic general education combined with an element of individual specialisation in line with support and advancement of the pupil according to his interests and performance. From grade 7 onwards, the types of schools and educational paths increasingly differ in terms of subjects after, their requirements with regard to individual specialisation and the leaving qualifications they aim at. There are some core subjects to be taught in schools in every lander (State or Province). These core subjects are: German, Mathematics, one foreign language, natural and social scineces. Music, art and sports have to be among the compulsory or elective subects offered.

An introduction to the professional and working world is a compulsory component of every course.

Regious education is subject to the respective regulations in each province.

The development of syllabi for secondary education is the responsibility of the Ministries of Education and Cultural Affairs in the provinces.

The education and training institutions for 16 and 19 years olds at upper Secondary Level include general education schools, full time vocational schools training companies and part time vocational schools.

21.13 SECONDARY EDUCATION IN JAPAN

Lower Secondary Education

The lower secondary school aims to provide children between the ages of 12 and 15 years with general secondary education suited to the level of their mental and physical development, based on the education given in the elementary school.

Curriculum at the Secondary Stage

The following table presents the subjects to be taught in lower secondary schools, as well as the national standard number of yearly school hours to be devoted to each subject, as specified in the current Courses of Study, which was put into effect in the school year 1993.

Standard Number of Yearly School Hours in Lower Secondary Schools(1)

Subjects	*Ist Year*	*2nd Year*	*3rd Year*
Japanese Language	175	140	140
Social Studies	140	140	70/105
Mathematics	105	140	140
Science	105	105	105/140
Music	70	35/70	35
Fine Arts	70	35/70	35
Health and Physical Education	105	105	105/140
Industrial Arts and Homemaking	70	70	70/105
Moral Education(2)	35	35	35
Special Activities(3)	35/70	35/70	35/70
Elective subjects, etc.(4)	105/140	105/210	140/280
Total	**1,050**	**1,050**	**1,050**

(1) One school hour is defined as a class period of fifty minutes.

(2) In private lower secondary school, a part or all of the school hours for moral education may be replaced by religious education.

(3) 'Special Activities' include 'classs activities' (including guidance on school lunch), pupils' councils, club activities and 'school events'. In this table, however, the number of hours for special activities includes that for 'class activities' (other than guidance on school lunch) and club activities only.

(4) The number of school hours for elective subjects shall be allotted to elective subjects and may be allotted to additional hours of Special Activities. Regarding elective subjects, the standard school hours of Foreign Language shall be 105 to 140 in each year, and the standard school hours of other subjects are as prescribed in the Course of Study.

Upper Secondary Schools

Upper Secondary Schools include grades 10 and 12 and the age group 16 to 18 years. About 97 per cent of students completing 9 years of primary education enter upper secondary Schools and Colleges of technology. The duration of the upper Secondary stage is three years.

Curriculum

Upper secondary schools may offer a number of elective subjects at their discretion, so that the curriculum in each school may be adapted to the aim of the courses offered in the school and to differing abilities, aptitudes and future prospects of individuals, and so that students may choose appropriate subjects suited to their own abilities, aptitudes and future prospects. About 75 per cent of upper secondary school students are enrolled in general academic courses, and the rest in vocational and other specialised courses.

The Course of Study specifies the subjects both in general education and in specialised education, as well as the objectives and the standard content of teaching in each subject. In addition, it lays down the standard number of credits to be acquired for most of the general education subjects.

General Education Subjects in Upper Secondary Schools

1. Japanese Language
2. Geography and History
3. Civics
4. Mathematics
5. Science
6. Health and Physical Education
7. Art
8. Foreign Languages (Not compulsory)
9. Home Economics

List of Specialised Subjects in Secondary Schools

1. Home Economics, 2. Agriculture, 3. Industry (Including Information), 4. Business, 5. Fisheries, 6. Nursing, 7. Mathematical Sciences, 8. Physical Education, 9. Music, 10. Art, 11. English, 12. Foreign Languages.

Freedom in School Curriculum

Each school organises its own curriculum in accordance with the provisions of the relevant statutes and courses of Study, taking into account the actual circumstances of the locality in which the school operates. The curriculum is also determined according to the characteristics of the children enrolled and the stage of their mental and physical development.

Evaluation and Examination

There is no external examination certificates are issued on the basis of internal assessment by the individual school principal.

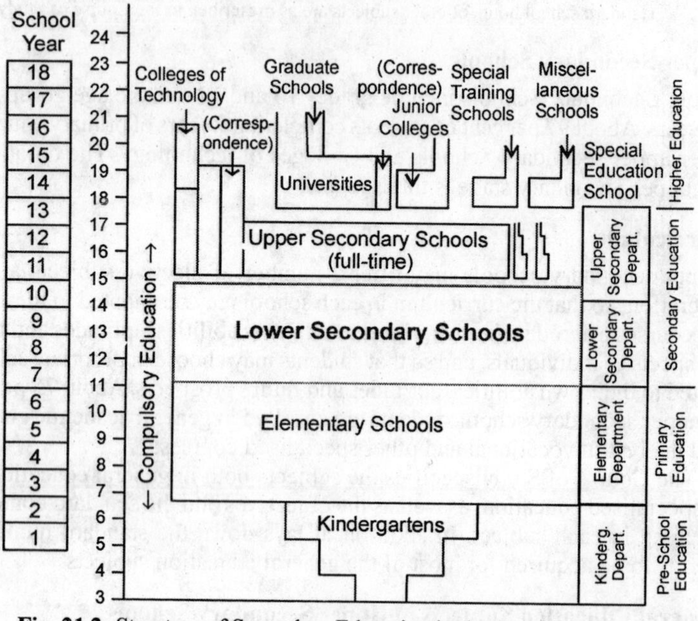

Fig. 21.2: Structure of Secondary Education in the Overall Structure of Eduation in Japan

21.14 COMPREHENSIVE SCHOOLS

A comprehensive school takes children of all types and all grades of ability from the age of 11. The population of such a school includes about 20 per cent of children of grammar school ability.

The Ministry of Education in Circular No. 144, 16th June 1947, defined a comprehensive school as "one which is intended to cater for all the secondary education of all the children in a given area without an organisation in three sides". At present about nine-tenths of state secondary pupils in UK go to comprehensive schools.

The term 'comprehensive' implies a common school not rigidly structured into different 'sides' (grammar, technical and modern) but having a flexible inner organisation which offers its pupils a wide variety of courses. In these schools the pupils generally follow a common curriculum between the ages 11 and 14 (sometimes 13) after which students choose different paths as a result of careful guidance at the age of 14.

Chief Characteristics of a Comprehensive School

1. A comprehensive school completely does away with the necessity of competitive selection at eleven-plus.
2. Children are not 'labelled' at an arbitrary early age in a comprehensive school.
3. Comprehensive school allows a fairly large time to the teachers to see students from various aspects of school work and grade them accordingly.
4. Transfer of a child from one stream to another becomes easy and it is possible to manipulate the syllabus approximately as closely as possible to the abilities and interests of the children.
5. Since a comprehensive school caters to a cross-section of all levels of ability and all backgrounds of class and status in the community, it affords many opportunities to the students to cooperate amicably and responsibly and appreciate the viewpoints and limitations of others.
6. A comprehensive school encourages leadership not only in academic directions but also with reference to all kinds of ability. Every child has something to contribute to the life of the school.
7. A comprehensive school seems to be more economical as there will be only one secondary school in the neighbourhood which could afford to provide best equipment and staff.
8. The range offered for the selection of subjects and activities is very wide in such a school.

21.15 PUBLIC SCHOOLS

Meaning of a Public School. A public school in England is usually defined as a fee-paying boarding school of more than local standing, catering for boys and girls up to the age of 18 or 19 and independent of sate or local funds. There are at present nearly 800 public schools including independent schools out of about 3,500 secondary schools.

Characteristics of Public Schools

All are controlled by their own boards of governors. Most public schools are boarding schools. The usual age of entry to the independent public schools for boys is 13 and the leaving age about 18. There are some girls' public schools modelled to a certain extent on the public schools for boys. Public schools have emphasised the importance of character-building, and have developed the perfect system, whereby day-to-day discipline is largely maintained by the pupils themselves, and the house system, in which a school is divided into groups of about 50, each under the care of a housemaster. The public school is also characterised by a high staffing ratio and a high proportion of pupils doing advanced work often leading to university.

UNIT IV : SCHOOL MANAGEMENT

22

Concept of School Management

Characteristics and Scope

22.1 MEANING OF THE CONCEPT SCHOOL MANAGEMENT

School Management is the dynamic side of educational enterprise. Educational philosophy sets the objectives of education; educational psychology explains the principles, and school management is the operational side of the principles for the realisation of the objectives.

A Cyclopaedia of Education (1913) by Paul Monre states the meaning of school management in these words, "School management, as a body of educational doctrine comprises a number of principles and precepts relating primarily to the techniques of classroom procedure, and derived largely from the practice of successful teachers. The writers in the field have interpreted these principles and precepts in various ways usually by reference of larger and more fundamental principles of psychology, sociology and ethics". This concept of school management hardly fits in the modern times when far-reaching changes have taken place in various disciplines especially with the explosion of information and communication technology (ICT). Management has emerged as a distinct discipline. Accordingly, the concepts of educational management and school management are increasingly being used.

In the present context, school management may be defined as an art and science in coordinating human and material resources of the school in such a way as to attain the objectives to optimal level of satisfaction of those served and with a high degree of morale and sense of attainment on the part of those rendering the service.

School management is to forecast, to plan, to organise, to command, to coordinate, to motivate and complement school.

Until the beginning of the 20th century, the term 'management' was not in common use in educational literature, although it had figured as far back as 1872 when the title of a publication by Harding was *Practical Handbook of School Management by Teachers.*

The development of school management as a field of study began in United States in early part of the 20th century. Development in the United Kingdom came as late as the 1960s.

An article entitled *Some General Principles of Management Applied to the Problems of School Systems* was published in 1913 by Franklin Bobbit of the University of Chicago.

In India, the concept of school management hardly existed before 1980.

This is borne out of the fact that *in Encyclopaedic Dictionary and Directory of Education* (with special reference to India), Volume II (1990), A. Biswas and J.C. Aggarwal, while listing the books relating to school organisation, mention only one book *School Management* by R.C. Sharma (1983). The concept of school management became popular only in the last decade of the 20th century.

22.2 CHARACTERISTICS OF SCHOOL MANAGEMENT

Following are the chief characteristics of school management:

1. *School Management as an Organised Structure to Fulfil Certain Objectives*: School management implies the practical and pragmatic measures which the school takes to ensure that the system of work which it uses will be of the greatest possible assistance in fulfilling its objectives and of the greatest possible value to the students in their all-round development.

Management may be functionally defined as an organised body or system or structure or arrangement or framework which is used for ensuring unity of effort, efficiency, goodwill, harmonious relations and appropriate use of resources.

2. *School Management as an Embodiment of Ideals*: School management is the embodiment of an ideal and of a spirit. It must enable different limbs of the school organism to function harmoniously in happy coordination, blending themselves into a composite personality like a collage of different colours and shapes which attracts persons of all shades and provides a soothing environments.

3. *School Management as a Lens*: School management may be compared to a lens that brings everything about the school system as well as educational system into focus — faculty (staff), students and the community. If it is a poor lens, the image is fussy and obscure and no one in the school system or the community gets a clear picture of what the educational system or the school system is trying to do. If it is a good lens, the school system becomes a clear-cut and vivid projection of the ideals, ideas and values that have been envisaged to bring into being in the school system.

4. *School Management as the Coordination of Various Elements of the School*: This is illustrated in Fig. (22.1).

5. *School Management is Dynamic*: School management changes with the concept of changing times. Its objectives undergo changes in the light of philosophy of the education as reflected in the constitution of a country. Its processes are influenced by philosophy as well as changes in information and community technology (ICT).

22.3 OBJECTIVES OF SCHOOL MANAGEMENT

The objectives of school management must be in accordance with the objectives of the school for the fulfilment of which it is set up. In a simple language, the objectives of the school are to educate the students in such a way as they become aesthetically rich, culturally refined, emotionally stable, mentally alert, morally sound, physically strong, socially efficient, spiritually enlightened and vocationally oriented. Naturally, therefore, the school management must be geared to these objectives.

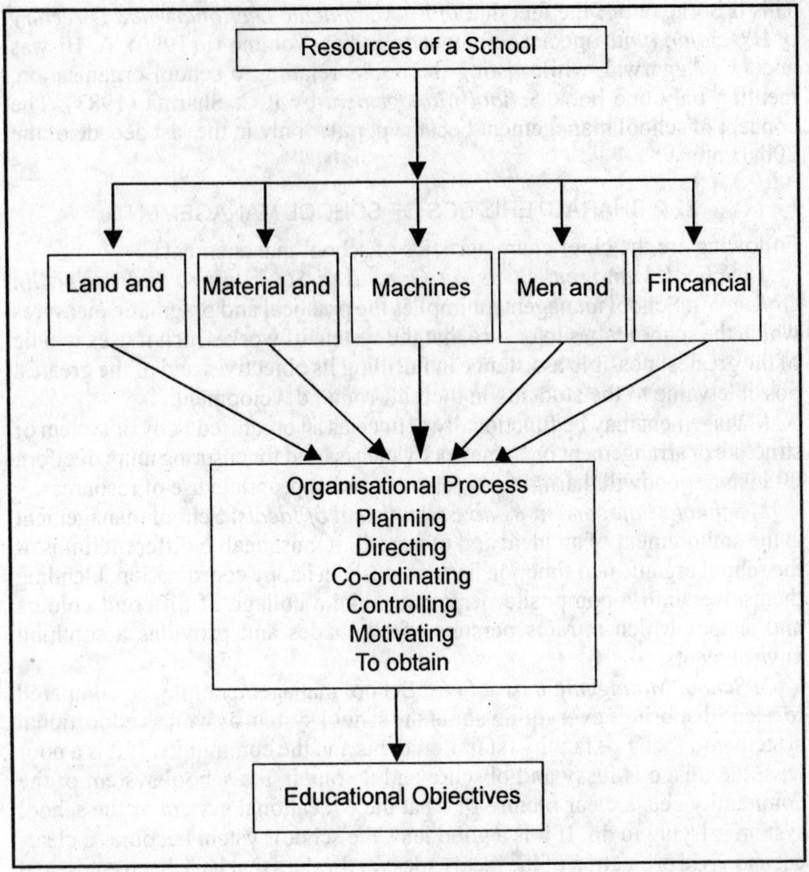

Fig. 22.1: School Management as Coordination of Various Elements of the School

Broadly speaking, the objectives of school management may be considered from two points of view which are complementary and supplementary and certainly not competitive.

A. Objective of School Management from the Point of View of the Society

The objectives of school management from the point of view of the society are:

1. Consolidating the spiritual strength of the society.
2. Maintaining the historical continuity of the society.
3. Securing the past achievements of the society.
4. Guaranteeing the future progress of the society.

B. Objectives of School Management in Relation to the Development of the Students

A school should be organised to:

(i) train the faculties of the students.
(ii) widen their outlook.

(iii) cultivate their minds.
(iv) form and strengthen their character.
(v) develop and cultivate their aesthetic faculty.
(vi) build up their bodies and enable them to acquire health and strength.
(vii) teach them their duties to themselves, the community and the State.
(viii) enable them to be emotionally well balanced.
(ix) prepare them to be spiritually well balanced.
(x) enable them to adjust themselves with the society.

22.4 MAIN FUNCTION OF SCHOOL MANAGEMENT

The main function of school management is to make the optimum use of the human elements and material elements of the school system for the optimum fulfilment of the objectives of the school as stated above.

The human resources include: (i) Students, (ii) Staff, (iii) Parents, (iv) Community, (v) Board of Education, (vi) Department of Education, (vii) Managing Committee of the School and the Governing Body, (viii) In-service and pre-service training institutes like DIETs, etc.

Material resources include: (i) Finances, (ii) School plant, (iii) Instructional supplies and equipment.

22.5 SCOPE OF SCHOOL MANAGEMENT: 5 M's

School management includes five elements which may be expressed as 5 Ms, i.e. Men, Money, Materials, Machines and Methods.

Elements	*Inputs*	*Process*	*Outputs*
1. Men	Cooperation of students, teachers, parents, community managing committee, Department of Education	1. Planning 2. Organising 3. Staffing 4. Directing 5. Coordinating 6. Reporting 7. Budgeting 8. Monitoring	(i) Aesthetic Development of Students (ii) Cultural Development of Students (iii) Ethical Development of Students (iv) Intellectual Development of Students
2. Money	Use of school funds		(v) Moral Development of Students
3. Material	Use of furniture, stationery, raw material, etc.		(vi) Physical Development of Students
4. Machines	School workshops, Laboratory Apparatus, etc.		(vii) Recreational Development of Students
5. Methods	Appropriate - Teaching, Learning - Classroom Management - Evaluation - Supervision		(viii) Social Development of Students (ix) Spiritual Development of Students (x) Vocational Development of Students

(*Contd.*)

Scope of school management is very vast. As a matter of fact, anything and everything having to do something with the education of the child through the agency of the school comes under the purview of school management.

Following may be listed as necessary components of school management. These are the outcomes of the management of 5 Ms (Men, Money, Materials, Machines and Methods) as listed above:

1. Providing and organising the human material—teaching staff, non-teaching staff and the students.
2. Providing and organising the material equipment such as school building, furniture, farms, laboratories, library etc.
3. Preparing the curriculum for different classes.
4. Preparing the time-table.
5. Management of co-curricular activities.
6. Maintaining discipline.
7. Organisation of student-government.
8. Organisation of health and physical education.
9. Organisation of educational and vocational services.
10. Organisation of mid-day meals.
11. Organisation of various ancillary services like drinking facilities.
12. Organisation of labour and social service weeks.
13. Organisation of home-work time-table.
14. Organisation of evaluation machinery.
15. Maintenance of school records.
16. Financing and budgeting.
17. Making purchases of different kinds.
18. Following department rules and regulations.
19. Organising admissions.
20. Organising transport for students.
21. Establishing liaison with several organisations and institutions including parents.

22.6 SCHOOL MANAGEMENT PROCESS

Planning	*Organizing*	*Motivating*	*Controlling*	*Monitoring*
Forecasting and fixing goals	Doing division of work	Providing effective leadership	Laying down standards	Checking Process from time-to- time
Collecting and comparing data	Assigning tasks	Communicating effectively	Evaluating performance	
Selecting best alternative and decision-making	Delegating authority and responsibility	Providing incentives	Finding out reasons for deviation	
Formulating policies, procedures and programmes	Fixing accountability	Humanising organizational process	Taking corrective measures	

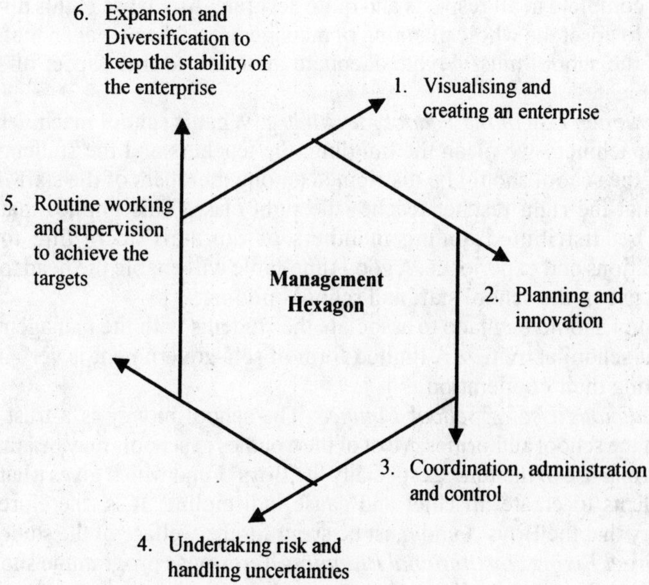

Fig. 22.2: School Managerial Hexagon

22.7 PRINCIPLES OF EFFICIENT SCHOOL MANAGEMENT

Important principles are:

1. Principles of democratic management.
2. Scientific collection of the data.
3. Systematic and optimum use of the school machinery.
4. Judicious use of school finance.
5. Target fixing.
6. Monitoring.
7. Periodic checking or evaluation.
8. Flexibility.

1. *Principle of Democratic Management*: An efficient management must be based on the following principles:

(i) Principle of harmonious human relations.
(ii) Principle of sharing responsibility.
(iii) Principle of equality.
(iv) Principle of freedom.
(v) Principle of cooperation.
(vi) Principle of justice.
(vii) Principle of recognising individual worth.
(viii) Principle of leadership.
(ix) Principle of coordination.

2. *Systematic and Scientific Collection of the Data*: This implies that the school records must be maintained in a proper manner. They must be kept up-

to-date, complete in all respects and quite accurate. Any lapse in this direction is likely to upset the whole planning of management. The manager, that is, the head of the school must devote adequate attention to this aspect of school management.

3. *Optimum Use of the School Machinery*: What is school machinery? By school machinery we mean the building, the teachers and the students. The work of the school should be distributed among members of the staff in such a way that the right teacher teaches the right class. This implies that work should be distributed among members of the staff according to their qualifications and experience. A good time-table will enable the head to make the best use of the school staff and school building.

Attempt should be made to associate the students with the management of different school activities. A limited form of self-government is very helpful in enlisting their cooperation.

4. *Judicious Use of School Finance*: The school money is a trust in the hands of the school authorities. Most of the troubles in schools may be attributed to the wrong use of the funds, especially the Boys' Fund which gives a handle to the students to create mischief and cause indiscipline. It is, therefore, very necessary that the Boys' Fund must be spent for the welfare of the students.

5. *Target Fixing: Institutional Planning*: Term-wise programme should be chalked out. The entire syllabus to be covered during the academic year should be divided into four terms. Programme of all activities must be carefully planned so as to make the best use of school and community resources.

6. *Monitoring*: Monitoring implies establishing a suitable mechanism for the identification of milestones of achievement, collecting and analysing data and establish information flows among different levels.

7. *Periodic Checking*: Terminal and monthly tests should be conducted to judge the progress of the students as well as of teachers.

8. *Flexibility*: It must be stressed that management is a means and not an end. It must not dominate the end. The end is the many-sided development of the personality of the child. The curriculum, the methods of teaching, the evaluation the time-table and in fact every aspect of school management is devoted to this end. Therefore, it is but proper that the management should be kept flexible.

22.8 FLEXIBILITY AND NOT RIGIDITY IN SCHOOL MANAGEMENT: MANAGEMENT GOOD SERVANT BUT A BAD MASTER

In view of rapid changes, new developments and new situations encounter with while implementing educational programmes, it is essential that we should have an open mind. Planning as visualised may not remain a realistic one with a change in situation. One plan for a particular school system or a class system or teacher may not be suitable for the other. After all school organisation is a means and not an end. The means should not be allowed to dominate school organisation which is for the pupils and its effectiveness and efficiency must be measured to the extent to which it contributes to teaching and learning. No doubt there must be planning but there should be no absolute rigidity in it.

H.G. Stead has rightly said that management should be 'fluid'. In the words of Mort Paul, "Adaptability, stability and flexibility are really facets of the same thing. A school must have these three characteristics if it is to achieve its purpose and at the same time give due regard to all persons immediately or remotely concerned. It must hold fast to the good, change what requires change and be fertile in considering individual differences and in all personalities involved". A fluid system believes in evolution rather than revolution.

Freedom should be given to the teachers to use their own methods of teaching. Similarly, students should not be forced to obey a multiplicity of rules and regulations. Self-discipline cannot be achieved through rod and punishment. It can only be realised through love and sympathy.

Similarly, monthly tests should not be treated all in all. They are a means to the end as enumerated above. All the aspects of school management and management itself are the servants of the students, the teachers and the head and as such it must not be given the place of a master. It should be dynamic and not static and should change according to the circumstances.

22.9 CHANGING CONCEPT, FUNCTIONS AND SCOPE OF SCHOOL MANAGEMENT: FACTORS AFFECTING SCHOOL MANAGEMENT

In view of the new challenges, the roles of the present day school have been radically changed and accordingly the concept of school management change is the order of the day and the school management must reflect a positive note in this regard. The old principles and practices of school management are now fading into insignificance in the dazzling light of the new ones.

Organisation of the Traditional School (Organisation was the earlier term)

A traditional school was considered to be a place where knowledge was manufactured and this used to be bookish, mechanical and stereotyped. Education being uniform; no importance was attached to the individual needs of children. Rote memory and memorisation played the dominant role. Children were regarded just like dumb driven cattle. Examination dominated the entire system of education. Rod was the chief weapon to educate the educand. 'The fear atmosphere' prevailed in the school. The teacher was called a policeman and drill sergeant. Co-curricular activities were almost unknown. No attempts were made to enlist the cooperation of the parents. Technology of teaching-learning was very simple.

Management of the Present-Day Schools

1. *Ideals and Values of Democratic India*: The functions of the present-day schools have undergone a great transformation in India since the advent of Independence. Our country is wedded to the ideals of democracy. Democracy imposes many responsibilities on the citizens of a country. It is based upon love, cooperation, tolerance, open-mindedness, truthfulness and fellow-feelings. If democracy is to survive, education must develop certain qualities needed for its survival. It must enable an individual to take part effectively and freely in the affairs of the group to which he belongs. Education is not worth the name, if it does not help an individual to live harmoniously and cooperatively in the society.

2. *Ideals of Socialism and Secularism*: Besides democracy, we have accepted socialism and secularism as our ideals. Our educational institutions, therefore, must serve these ends and produce individuals imbued with the ideals and attitudes of secularism and socialism.

3. *New Concept of Education*: Education in terms of traditional 3 Rs has been replaced by the present 7 Rs, i.e. Reading, Writing, Arithmetic, Recreation, Rights, Responsibility and Relationship.

4. *Guidance and Counselling*: Individual differences of children must be taken into account and diversified courses provided. A well organised system of guidance and counselling is therefore needed.

5. *Activity Methods*: New activity methods such as Dalton Plan, the Project Method, the Heuristic Method, the Montessori Method, etc. have brought about far-reaching changes in our methods of instruction.

6. *Impact of New Technology*: New technology has affected the old system of school management. Information and CommunicationTechnology (ICT) has placed new processes and equipments at the disposal of school organiser which must be made use of profitably.

7. *Impact of the New Pattern of Education, i.e.* 10+2: School curriculum and methods of teaching-learning have undergone important changes with the introduction of the new pattern of school education in 1975. This has important implications for principles and practices of school management.

8. *Introduction of Vocational Courses and Socially Useful Productive Work*: These two elements have greatly influenced the philosophy and practices of school management.

9. *Multifarious Co-curricular Activities*: At present day school is expected to provide for a number of co-curricular activities which need an altogether a new concept of school management.

10. *Increase in the School-Going Population*: People are becoming increasingly education conscious. Today we find a large number of students attending the school. They differ in tastes, needs, aptitudes and in various other ways. Family and social background of the students also vary. This has made the problem of educational management very complex.

11. *Multifarious Functions of the School*: The school of today is not only concerned with the intellectual development of the child but is also to train him in the 'art of living together' which in itself is a complicated affair.

12. *Role of the School in Fostering Values of Emotional Integration and National Unity*: There is a growing recognition of these new demands upon management and the necessity of an imaginative response in transforming the principal's job. Schools are expected to help in achieving national unity and as such the importance of its impact on educational management can hardly be ignored.

22.10 AUTOCRATIC AND DEMOCRATIC SCHOOL MANAGEMENT

Why Democratic School Management?: We are wedded to a democratic philosophy and a democratic way of life and as such it must prevail in all our institutions and organisations including educational. If this point is lost sight of, the very purpose of school management goes into oblivion. As observed by the Secondary Education Commission. "The educational system must make its contribution to the development of habits, attitudes and qualities of character which will enable its citizens to bear worthily the responsibilities of democratic citizenship". The school is an important social agency which provides numerous opportunities to the students to imbibe democratic values and train them in the 'art of living together'.

Characteristics of Democratic School Management	Characteristics of Autocratic School Management
1. An environment of mutual trust exists.	An environment of mutual distrust exists.
2. Cooperative planning is done by the entire staff.	Planning is done by the management.
3. 'We feelings prevails' in the school environment.	'I' feelings are predominant. Ego of one individual prevails.
4. The committees are chosen to do the work.	The head of management chooses committees and dominates them.
5. Managers discuss problems with teachers and accept suggestions.	Management tells teachers what to do.
6. The organisers and the Head respect teacher's personality and plan cooperatively with him.	The Management/the Head sometimes embarrasses teachers before children.
7. The Head gives co-workers credit for success.	Management/Principal takes credit for all success.
8. The Head encourages faculty to make use of human resources in the community.	Management/Principal gives no recognition to parents and leaders.
9. Managers, administrators and principals are educational leaders as well as administrative persons.	Managers, administrators and heads are concerned only with the details of management and administration.
10. The managers, administrators and heads make possible an active in-service programme for teachers.	The managers, administrators and principals take the attitude of 'get it yourself'.
11. Teachers plan with the supervisors in special fields for work to be done.	Special supervisors outline course for teachers to follow in teaching special subjects.
12. The management allows teachers to make flexible programmes which best suit the interests and needs of children.	Management requires a set type of common programme.
13. Faculty meetings are cooperatively planned by the entire staff.	Faculty meetings are planned only by the head.

(*Contd.*)

(*Contd.*)

	Characteristics of Democratic School Management	Characteristics of Autocratic School Management
14.	The teachers can adopt an exploratory attitude.	The teachers give directions in a firm manner.
15.	Teachers are encouraged to use cumulative records.	Cumulative records are only for the use of principal.
16.	Teachers participate in selection of text-books.	Text-books are selected by the management.
17.	Audio-visual materials are made easily available to the teachers.	Audio-visual programme is operated on a rigid time schedule, prepared by the management.
18.	The staff and students are allowed to plan social gatherings after school time.	Such occasions are very rare.
19.	Students are teacher-guided.	Students are teacher-dominated.
20.	The students are guided by the teachers in the choice of many activities.	The teacher plans activities without conferring with the pupils.
21.	The budget is prepared cooperatively, with teacher's participation.	The budget is prepared by the managerial and administrative staff.
22.	The teachers are sympathetic.	The teachers spring awe and fear.
23.	Students committees also assume responsibility for selecting equipment and supplies needed.	Teacher or the principal assumes responsibility for selecting and purchasing equipment.
24.	The teachers try to understand the child.	The teachers works according to set procedure.
25.	The daily programme is flexible and can be changed as the group decides.	Daily programme is rigid.
26.	Students are encouraged to correct their mistakes.	The teacher directs pupil activities.
27.	Students are encouraged by the teacher to make suggestions concerning their work.	The teacher ignores suggestions of the pupils.
28.	The students share with the teacher the responsibility of appraising their work.	The students are not conferred with in appraising their growth.
29.	The pupils share with teachers establishing standards of achievement.	The teachers set-up standards of achievement without conferring with the pupils.
30.	The students assist in planning the academic work, make suggestions and proposals.	The students answer questions asked by the teacher.

22.11 CHIEF CHARACTERISTICS OF A WELL MANAGED SCHOOL

The pen-picture of a well managed school has been aptly described by S. Bala Krishna Joshi in the words, "A school is not a mere brick and mortar structure housing a miscellany of pupils and teachers; a school is not a market place where a heterogeneous crowd gathers with diverse objects; a school is not a rigorous reformatory where juvenile suspects are kept under vigilant watch. A school is a spiritual organism with distinctive personality of its own; a school is a vibrant community centre, radiating life and energy all-round; a school is a wonderful edifice, resting on the foundation of goodwill—goodwill of the public, goodwill of the parents, goodwill of the pupils. In a word, a well conducted school is a happy home, a sacred shrine, a social centre, a state in miniature bewitching Brindavan, all beautifully blended into a synthetic structure".

According to the Secondary Education Commission 1952-53, "The secondary school must make itself responsible for equipping its students adequately with civic as well as vocational efficiency—and the qualities of character that go with it—so that they may be able to play their part worthily and competently in the improvement of national life. They should no longer emerge as helpless, shiftless individuals who do not know what to do themselves". The school is one of the most important formal agencies of education. It plays a major role in moulding the ideas, habits and attitudes of the children with a view to producing well balanced personalities, culturally sound, emotionally stable, mentally alert, morally upright, physically strong, socially efficient, vocationally self-sufficient and internationally liberal. Informal agencies of education such as the church and the home fail to satisfy the increasing educational requirements of a complex society and thus are losing their hold on the people. The school is a social institution set up by the society to serve its ends. It is a place where men of tomorrow are trained and disciplined in certain forms of activities.

It is not without reason that the Education Commission 1964-66 wrote, "The destiny of India is now being shaped in her class-rooms. This, we believe, is no mere rhetoric". In a world based on science and technology, it is education that determines the level of prosperity, welfare, and security of the people. On the quality and number of persons coming out of schools and colleges will depend our success in the great adventure of national reconstruction whose objectives are to raise substantially the standard of living of our people and to create a new social order based on the human values of the dignity of the individual, freedom, equality and justice.

The most important and urgent reform needed in education is to transform it, to endeavour to relate it to the life, needs and aspirations of the people and thereby make it a powerful instrument of social, economic and cultural transformation necessary for realisation of the national goals. For this purpose, education should be so developed as to increase productivity, achieve social and national integration, strengthen democracy, accelerate the process of modernisation and cultivate social, moral and spiritual values."

Chief characteristics of a well managed school may be listed as under:

1. Provision of a stimulating environment.
2. Transformation into an activity school.
3. Provision for experimentation.
4. Training students in the art of living together.
5. Opportunities for developing self-discipline.
6. Making library as the hub of school activities.
7. Providing work experience and socially useful productive work.
8. Use of progressive methods of evaluation of students' performance.
9. Organising self-government in some select areas of school work.
10. Making school as a centre of community service.
11. Ensuring goodwill and cooperation of all sections associated with the school.
12. Making the optimum use of physical, material and human resources.

23

Management of Human and Material Resources

Role of the Head of the School

23.1 THE AUTHORITARIAN MANAGER AND THE DEMOCRATIC MANAGER

"The boss drives his men; *the leader coaches them.*
The boss depends on authority; *the leader on goodwill.*
The boss inspires fear; *the leader inspires enthusiasm.*
The boss assigns the task; *the leader sets pace.*
The boss says, "Get here on time"; *the leader gets there ahead of time.*
The boss fixes the blame for the breakdown; *the leader fixes the breakdown.*
The boss makes works a drudgery; *the leader makes it a game".*

23.2 CONCEPT OF HUMAN-ORIENTED MANAGEMENT AND LEADERSHIP

Since education is tool for social transformation, it must explicitly inculcate and generate a sense of identification, a sense of fellow being. This can only happen if we completely change or bring about a radical change in the pattern of educational management, administration and style of leadership. J.M. Hughes observes in *Human Relations in Educational Organisation* that "every educational personnel is characterised by a system closely interlocking roles". The school programme involves the participation of the head of the school, the teachers, the students, the parents, the community leaders, government officials and the managing committee and its success depends upon the competency of the educational administrator to make all efforts to maintain good human relationships. The head of the institution as the educational administrator and manager of the school must make all efforts to create goodwill, understanding and will to cooperate between himself and each category of the participants and among the participants themselves. It must be remembered that in an educational organisation like the school, it is the quality of personnel relations which exists among its members that has a direct relation to the achievements of the school. Sustained cooperation is a fundamental requirement of efficient working of a school.

In *Administering Community Education,* Ernest O. Melby has described the importance of human relations as "If a school system has a good general administration of education, with good human relationships, regardless of race, colour or creed or race, difficulties are not likely to occur. Similarly, if the human relations in a particular school administration are less than satisfactory, the incident of conflict will be higher".

Prof. S.N. Mukerji thinks that "Education administration is concerned with the management of things as well as with human relationships, i.e. the better working together of people. In fact, it is more concerned with human beings and less with inanimate things. It is, therefore, primarily a social enterprise".

K.G. Saiyidain states, "The educational administrator must learn that his concern is not only—or even mainly—with files, procedures and techniques or even the tackling of human relations. He should endeavour to become a living bridge between ideas and tested scientific knowledge, on the one hand, and practical problems and situation, on the other. Practice without enlightened theory is apt to become dull and lifeless and theory without practice runs the risk of losing social significance. We must all combine in the attempt to radiate our school practices with the display of creative ideas that would meet the new situations as they arise".

According to Dr. Sampurnanand: "educational administration should be such that it makes the teacher believe in his work, brings out the best of which he is capable, stimulates him to bigger and better efforts, comes to his rescue when his courage begins to falter."

23.3 THE HEAD OF THE SCHOOL AND HUMAN RELATIONS INCLUDING RELATIONS WITH THE STAFF

General Principles of Developing Human Relations

The success of the head of the school depends on the extent to which he brings out the best of the staff, students and their parents and the community and develops wholesome relationships. Following are the important practices which the head should adopt to develop human relations with all the groups he comes into contact:

1. *Principle of Sharing Ideas*: The Head should be ever ready to consider new ideas on education coming from others and should be willing to try out those which seem to be useful.
2. *Principle of Progressive Views*: He should consistently hold progressive views in educational matters.
3. *Principle of Pragmatism*: He should try to apply such new methods as are suitable to Indian conditions.
4. *Principle of Experimentation*: He should encourage teachers to experiment with new procedures and techniques of education.
5. *Principle of Modernisation*: He should keep in touch with the latest development in the field of education.
6. *Principle of Democracy*: He should be democratic in his relations with teachers.
7. *Principle of Steadfastness*: He should prove by his actions that he always means what he says.
8. *Principle of Justice*: He should not favour any of the teachers unduly.
9. *Principle of Faith*: He should show by his actions that he has confidence in his teachers.
10. *Principle of Appreciation*: He should give proper recognition to the good work done by the teachers.

11. *Principle of Sociability*: He should not keep himself aloof from other members of the staff.

12. *Principle of Appreciation*: He should show in his dealings a real respect for the opinion of others.

13. *Principle of Acceptability*: He should not attempt to dominate his teachers by the force of his position.

14. *Principle of Humanness*: He should have due regard for the feelings of others.

15. *Principle of Fair Play*: He should never play one teacher against another in order to maintain his official superiority.

16. *Principle of Reconciliation*: He should try to mutually reconcile differences if they arise among teachers, between teachers and parents, and between teachers and the employers.

17. *Principle of Sharing Responsibility*: He should be ready to share with his co-workers the responsibility for any deficiency or weakness in the school programme.

18. *Principle of Delegation of Powers*: He should share his work with and delegate responsibilities to staff members and committees.

19. *Principle of Guidance*: He should provide all possible assistance to new teachers.

20. *Principle of In-service Education*: He should encourage and provide opportunities for in-service education of teachers.

21. *Principle of Accountability*: Delegation of responsibility should be followed by accountability.

22. *Principle of Using the Term Colleague*: The head should use the word 'colleague' in place of 'subordinate'.

23. *Principle of the Use of the Word 'We' and Not 'I'*: While taking credit for any achievement of the school, the head should say, 'we' have done it and not 'I' have done it.

24. *Principle of Constructive Criticism*: Constructive criticism of the work of the colleagues pays dividends. The role of a policeman or military officer does more harm than good.

25. *Principle of Friendly Supervision*: The head should not interrupt classes. He should not create an environment of 'fear'. He should make the teachers feel at home when he visits their classes.

23.4 STAFF MEETINGS

Importance

Efficient running of the school demands that members of the staff should occasionally meet for sharing ideas responsibilities and experiences. These meetings should be presided over by the Head of the school and be convened from time-to-time.

Briggs found that teachers expected the following things in a staff meeting:

(i) Help in their problems.
(ii) A wider outlook on education.
(iii) Meeting to be happy and wholesome.

(iv) Meeting based on appreciation of effort and accomplishment rather than shortcomings and faults.

Planning of Staff Meetings

The teachers should be informed in advance of the problems to be discussed in the meetings. It is very important for the head to listen to every teacher with attention and care. Minutes of staff meetings should be kept if possible.

A limit must be put to staff meetings and the best appears to be once a month. Of course, there need not be any rigidity in observing this principle. Occasional meetings for some particular purposes may have to be called. Sometimes it may become necessary for the head to convene a staff meeting to clarify certain points of written order issued by him. An atmosphere of cheerfulness should prevail in all such meetings.

The head of the institution should take note of the teachers' problems and accordingly give his suggestions for the solution of the problems concerned. His attempt should be to help the teachers as much as possible.

Staff meetings should not be too long. Usually not more than one and half-hour should be spent upon 'a meeting'.

Characteristics of Staff Meetings

1. All discussions should be above personal level.
2. They should be economical in time.
3. Discussion should not go off the track.
4. They should start in time.
5. They should result in concrete suggestions.

Staff Club

The formation of Staff Club will facilitate intimate contacts between the head and the members of the staff and also among members of the staff themselves. One member of the staff should serve as a secretary who should be elected every year so that most of the members get a chance of leading others.

The functions of the club would be recreational-*cum*-educational. It may arrange tea during recess for the staff members. Its another function would be to arrange welcome and farewell parties. Its third function will be to arrange excursions and picnics on holidays. Its fourth function will be to arrange discussions on important school problems.

The Head should not look upon this club with suspicion. He should occasionally attend meetings of the club. Through such informal meetings, he will learn about the members of the staff and this will also help in cementing the bonds of friendship, goodwill and mutual understanding.

23.5 MANAGING HUMAN RELATIONS WITH STUDENTS PARENTS AND THE COMMUNITY

The Head's Human Relations with Students

Often it is seen that the Headmaster makes the error of not coming into direct contact with the pupils. He should not forget that he can directly influence them to a considerable extent and as such he must avail himself of every opportunity of addressing them and attending various functions organised in the school. Regarding his work and relations with the students, we may quote Dr. V.S. Jha: "A good Headmaster or Principal is not merely a scholar, he is a man of sound character, deep sympathy and understanding and considerable tact and experience dealing with pupils. He should be profoundly sensitive to the physical, mental, moral and spiritual needs of the pupils and should know how to minister them".

The head must view the educational programme as a whole and assist students directly in having a balanced experience in terms of individual needs. To accomplish this he should:

- Show by action and in discussion that besides academic achievement, he gives importance to positive attitudes, citizenship skills, aesthetic appreciation, individual initiative, cooperative tendencies, etc.
- Give leadership to planning student activities, clubs and projects which will supplement and complement the academic class.
- Approach individual student's problems from a guidance point of view, and help teachers to recognise individual differences in teaching and in dealing with students' problems.
- Make it a practice to get to know students personally, showing friendship to them and expressing interest in what they are doing.
- Involve students in real responsibility for the operation of significant aspects of the school, through student governments, the house system and other techniques.

The great heads have always been great friends of their pupils. The head should possess the following skills:

1. Loves them intensely.
2. Shows interest in student activities.
3. Shows due regard to their personality.
4. Shows friendliness towards individual students.
5. Shows a spirit of 'oneness' and 'belongingness' with them.
6. Gives due regard to student opinion.
7. Takes a keen interest in the welfare of the students.
8. Spares time for conferences.
9. Shows keen interest in solving their problems.
10. Shares responsibility with them.

Head's Human Relations with Parents

Educators, managers and administrators are now fast realising that effective and cordial relations with parents are very necessary for the efficient organisation and management of school work and activities. The head of an institution must find out ways and means for establishing happy contact with students' parents and guardians.

His treatment with the parents should be very courteous. As Ryburn puts it, "He should always treat parents with scrupulous courtesy when they come to the school".

Schools serving the public in a democracy should be responsive to the wishes of parents regarding the school programme. Also, the school programme should be related to the community. Towards these ends the headmaster should:

- Arrange a variety of activities and programmes for keeping the public informed about the school programme, new projects, progress in achieving objectives.
- Encourage parents to make constructive suggestions regarding ways of improving the school, providing avenues through which parents' ideas are reported and discussed.
- Assist the school staff in knowing the community and in teaching students different ways through which they can contribute to community development.
- Make the school facilities available for use by appropriate community groups for meetings, recreation and adult education.
- Organise ways in which parents and community groups can help the school, through fund-raising for specific activities, making community educational resources more readily available to the school, and assisting teachers and students in studying the community.
- Organise parent-teacher meets from time-to-time.
- Make the school a centre of community service.

The Head and Development of Human Relations with the Community

1. The Head should encourage the parents of the pupils to visit the school frequently.
2. He should see that parents are cordially received when they visit the school.
3. He should regularly inform the parents of the progress of their wards.
4. He should encourage the parents to consult the teachers as well as himself on special problems of their wards.
5. He should visit the homes of the pupils in special situations and suggest to the teachers also to do the same.
6. He should organise parents-study-groups from time-to-time.
7. He should provide adequate facilities for the organisation and proper functioning of the Parent-Teacher Association in the school.
8. He should plan school programme with reference to the needs of the community.
9. He should encourage the use of community resources for vitalising classroom instruction through excursions, field trips, study of local history, etc.
10. He should encourage and organise social service programmes to render public service.
11. He should allow the community to use school facilities and services like school building, library, and dispensary ensuring at the same time that the work of the school does not suffer.
12. He should organise social and cultural activities in the school to interpret the school programme to the community.
13. He should actively participate in the social and cultural functions of the community.

14. He should be above politics and religion in organising school programmes.
15. He should not allow the school to become a tool in the hands of any pressure group.

23.6 SIGNIFICANCE OF EACH LETTER OF THE WORD 'HEADMASTER': QUALITIES OF THE HEAD OF THE SCHOOL

H stand for
(i) Hard work.
(ii) Helping attitude
(iii) Honesty
(iv) Humility
(v) Humorous nature

E stands for
(i) Enthusiasm
(ii) Efficiency
(iii) Ethics of the profession

A stands for
(i) Accuracy
(ii) Adaptability
(iii) Alertness
(iv) Amicability
(v) Attentiveness
(vi) Attractive manners

D stands for
(i) Definiteness
(ii) Dependability
(iii) Desire for self-improvement
(iv) Devotion to the democratic ideal
(v) Devotion to the profession

M stands for
(i) Mastery of the subject matter
(ii) Maturity
(iii) Mental alertness
(iv) Morality

S stands for
(i) Scientific attitude
(ii) Self-discipline
(iii) Self-reliance
(iv) Sincerity
(v) Sociability
(vi) Steadfastness

T stands for
(i) Tact
(ii) Truthfulness
(iii) Teaching skill
(iv) Training

E stands for
(i) Ethics of the teaching profession
(ii) Experimental attitude

R stands for
(i) Readiness to serve others
(ii) Reasoning ability
(iii) Regularity
(iv) Relationships
(v) Resourcefulness

23.7 MANAGING MATERIAL RESOURCES

23.8 MEANING OF PHYSICAL RESOURCES

Physical resources include resources other than human resources.

Material resources of an educational institution include the following resources:

1. Building and its fittings.
2. Equipments like furniture and stationary, etc.
3. Playgrounds and their equipment.
4. Hostel building and equipment.
5. Agricultural land and its implements, etc.
6. Gardens and its products, if any.
7. School farm and its products.
8. School workshop and its equipment.
9. School library, books and equipment.
10. Instructional aids like Television, Computers, etc.

Building: It includes:

(i) Principal's Office
(ii) School Office
(iii) Staff Room
(iv) Reading Room
(v) Library Room
(vi) Assembly Hall
(vii) Auditorium
(viii) Museum Room
(ix) Workshop Room
(x) Laboratories
(xi) Sanitary Blocks.
(xii) Classrooms

23.9 PRINCIPLES OF MANAGING MATERIAL RESOURCES

1. Principles of determining the needs of various physical resources.
2. Principles of acquiring material resources.
3. Principles of utilising material resources.
4. Principles of maintaining and keeping material resources in order.
5. Principle of keeping records of material resources.
6. Principle of determining accountability criteria in handling material resources.
7. Principle of developing indigenous material aids.
8. Principle of mobilising community resources.

Principles of Acquiring and Using Equipment

(a) Principle of standardised equipment.
(b) Principle of durability.
(c) Principle of serviceability.
(d) Principle of economy.

(e) Principle of adaptability.
(f) Principle of simplicity.
(g) Principle of aesthetic sense.
(h) Principle of maintenance and timely repairs.
(i) Principle of keeping inventories.
(j) Principle of keeping records.
(k) Principle of observing financial and technical rules.

Maintenance of School Plant

Adequate attention should be paid to the upkeep and repair of the school building. The cleanliness of the school building is equally important. It should be annually washed and daily cleaned. At intervals it is necessary that it should be disinfected through spray of disinfectants.

Material Resources and Health of the Students

Following points to be attended to:

1. Healthy surrounding of the school.
2. Airy and well ventilated rooms.
3. Suitable colour of the walls.
4. Cleanliness of the school building.
5. Good seating arrangements.
6. Suitable desks.
7. Right type of blackboards.
8. Fresh drinking water.
9. Hygienic urinals and latrines.
10. Playing fields free from stones and dust, etc.
11. Mid-day meals.
12. Good postures.
13. Medical inspection.
14. Daily inspection of the personal cleanliness of the hands, feet, nails, teeth, hair, clothing, etc.
15. Sufficient exercise.
16. Health instruction.
17. Games.
18. The teacher as an example before the students.
19. Examination in physical activities.
20. Sex instruction.

23.10 MANAGEMENT OF SCHOOL FINANCES

Proper Management of Finances

The most optimum utilisation of the financial resources of the school is one of the major tasks of the head of the school. It is generally observed that quite a large number of school problems arise on account of the improper maintenance of financial resources. There are specific rules governing financial transactions which must be strictly followed by the head of the institution so that he has a clear image. Transparency is the key word in financial matters.

Sources of School Finances

A. *Grants from different sources*

(i) Government grants in case of private aided schools in accordance with grants-in-aid rules.
(ii) Grants from the Trust/Managing Committee.
(iii) Income from the sale of craft work, etc.
(iv) Income from fees.
(v) Grants for specific educational plans/experiments from the NCERT, SCERT, etc.
(vi) Disbursement of various kinds of scholarships.

B. *Non-Government Funds*

(i) Pupil's fund.
(ii) Donations from the public.
(iii) Transport charges.
(iv) School bookshop and stationery.
(v) School uniform.
(vi) School canteen.
(vii) Hostel funds.
(viii) Miscellaneous sources like fete.
(ix) Community help in form and kind in rural areas.

Major Tasks Relating to Financial Management

1. Preparing budgets.
2. Maintaining cash book/books for recording daily receipts and expenditure of various types.
3. Maintaining following types of registers:
   (i) Remittance register; (ii) Staff pay register; (iii) Voucher files, (iv) Issuing financial receipts, and (v) Provident register.
4. Authorising expenditure.
5. Inviting tenders/quotations.
6. Making entries in all registers.
7. Preparing list of approved suppliers.
8. Making timely deposits/funds in the treasury/banks/post offices, etc.

Principles of Managing Financial Transactions

1. Principle of observance of departmental rules.
2. Principle of transparency.
3. Principle of utility.
4. Principle of delegation of powers.
5. Principle of accountability.
6. Principle of keeping cash book and other records up-to-date.

23.11 MAJOR CHARACTERISTICS OR QUALITIES OF THE HEAD OF THE SCHOOL FOR THE MANAGEMENT OF HUMAN RESOURCES AND MATERIAL RESOURCES

1. *Considers the Administrative Machinery as an Instrument of Social Service*: "An educational administrator is more than an official punctilious about administrative routine; he is a leader guiding and directing a sacred undertaking. The official apparatus that is at his disposal, the education department that is under his control, is more than a bureaucratic machine. It is an instrument of social service". —*Chitra Naik*

2. *Co-operative Attitude*: "The leader of the school can be successful only when he secures willing cooperation from his co-workers; when he makes those co-workers feel that the problems of the school are theirs and not his own". —*Mohi-ud-din*

"Dignity does not consist in aloofness and in maintaining an air of superiority; it rather consists in being helpful and doing the right thing". —*Mohi-ud-din*

3. *Democratic Attitude*: "A democratic administrator should look upon the personnel as socially equal to himself; he should not take decisions by himself, but with his colleagues; he should make them feel responsible and share in administration; he should have a code of set rules of administration which he and his colleagues should follow rigidly, making no discrimination in their application; and lastly, he should want no special privilege". —*R.R. Kamria*

4. *Educational Statesman*: In the words of E.P. Cubberly, "He must learn to lead by reason, by his larger knowledge and courageous enthusiasm rather than to drive by reason of his superior power. ...He must reach up out of the routine of school supervision and execute duties in to the higher level of educational statesmanship".

5. *Expert in Human Psychology*: An ideal head always remembers that all people cannot be equally intelligent and hard working. A trouble shooter needs to be handled firmly in the very beginning. Praise and appreciation sometimes help even if a person does not deserve it. Sometimes sympathetic hearing is all that is needed to blow off the steam of emotions. Sometimes valuable suggestions help in easing the tension.

6. *Faith in Human Nature*: "It is essential, therefore, that be a man of faith, faith in his vocation, faith in his pupils, faith in human nature and faith in himself". —*W.M. Ryburn*

"He must unlimited faith in himself and his creator". —*Jaswant Singh*

7. *Recognition to Good Work Done*: Ryburn writes, "Nothing will more encourage a man or a woman, a boy or a girl, to greater effort, than an encouraging recognition of good work done, of sincere effort made or good qualities shown. If those in-charge of institutions, and those carrying on the administrative work of department wish to enable those working with them to do their best, they should always realise the value of ungrudging recognition of all that merits such recognition".

8. *Judicious Decision-Making*: (i) Decides cases promptly. (ii) Gives judgements only after weighing and considering relevant evidence.

(iii) Perceives true nature of cases. (iv) Decides cases on the basis of principles rather than expediency. (v) Makes decisions without bias and prejudice.

9. *Headmaster not by Appointment but by Superior Ability*: "It must not be known by his staff and scholars that he is their headmaster by appointment but felt that he is their master by superior ability, energy and character".

—*P.C. Wren*

"He is the organiser, leader, governor, business director, coordinator, superintendent, teacher, guide, philosopher and friend".

10. *Health*: "A person with indifferent health and poor stamina will not be able to discharge the multifarious and heavy responsibilities of his office".

—*Jaswant Singh*

11. *Life one of Immolation*: In the words of S. Balakrishna Joshi, "The progress of the school community is his thought by day and dream by night, and his aching passion is to wear himself out in the service of the shrine in which he feels spiritually wedded. It is his conviction that while the life of a teacher is one of consecration that of the headmaster should be one of immolation".

12. *Leader by Courage and Reason and not by Power*: "He must learn to lead by reason, by his larger knowledge and courageous enthusiasm rather than to drive by reason of his superior power.... He must reach up out of the routine of school supervision and execute duties into the higher level of educational statesman". —*E.P. Cubberly*

"The successful administrator gets people to work with him, not primarily because he has power over them and can order them but because he is the kind of leader for whom they want to do their best". —*Pagors and Myers*

13. *Man of Integrity*: He fights all temptations to pad his purse with money to which he is not entitled. To quote S. Balakrishna Joshi, "He does not try to exploit school influence for private gains because he realises that if he does it, he signs his moral death-warrant. The result is that no amount of pressure can wean him from the path of duty and justice. Authority, cannot coerce him, nor can temptation reduce him into any course of conduct, not conducive to the highest interests of the school".

14. *Optimistic Outlook*: He has an unlimited faith in himself. He does not accept defeat. He always thinks of success all the time. Ryburn stresses, "It is essential, therefore, that he be not only a man of high character but also that he be a man of faith; faith in his vocation, faith in his pupils, faith in human nature, and faith in his staff".

15. *Patience*: "Patience is a virtue that will pay very generous dividends to assists, not to control the educative process". —Reaves

"Go slow the first day, the first week, the first month, and even the first year, make changes slowly and always with the cooperation of the faculty".

—*William T. Melchor*

16. *Philosophy of Education*: "A good Headmaster needs to have a sound philosophy of education". —*Jaswant Singh*

17. *Planning Expert*: "If a principal is not careful, he will find himself spending much of the time in answering telephone, running errands for teachers, signing excuses, making repairs to the buildings, handling money,

raising campaigns, and performing other minor duties than budget his time accordingly". —*Margaret Grag*

18. *Professional Devotion*: "He should derive the same satisfaction from working for institution as the artist or the sculptor derives when working late hours over his handiwork, fully attentive to the smallest details, never tiring". —*Jaswant Singh*

19. *Progressive Outlook*: "It is reasonable to expect that a headmaster should be progressive in his outlook". —*Mohi-ud-din*

20. *Resourcefulness*: "He rises equal to any occasion, and by his resourcefulness and readiness to render service, solves knotty problems. To him it is not beneath his dignity to strike the gong in time if the peon is engaged otherwise, or to lead a band of devoted volunteers to flush the latrine if scavenger is absent. Again he is prepared to 'referee' a match if the umpire has not turned up or step into a class and teach any subject if a teacher is called suddenly. Thus his willingness and ability to do any piece of work pertaining to the school, wrest for him the confidence and regard of all concerned".

21. *Scientific Attitude*: An ideal head is particularly careful in making judgement about persons for whom he cherishes a positive like or dislike. He observes correctly without letting personal feeling, prejudices, and wishes to influence him, draws valid conclusions from given facts and makes sound generalisations as the facts warrant. He does not see things through coloured spectacles. He is able to detach his personal likes and dislikes from the performance of others. He is conscious of the fact that monopoly of truth is not held by anyone.

22. *Sense of Humour*: Dr. Jaswant Singh writes about this quality, "It will enable him to get over an impasse with the help of a smile, a light hearted chuckle, or a jocular remark which will ease the tense atmosphere. The sense of humour will help break resistance, overcome opposition by injecting a spirit of camaraderie into the situation. Many a difficult situation can be resolved by a witty remark".

23. *Sensitive to the Needs of the Community*: "In whatever community the principal finds himself, he should study the characteristic social conditions and needs of his pupils and endeavour in appropriate ways to secure increased cooperation between the school and the community in meeting these needs". —*W. Johnson Frank*

24. *Sensitive to the Needs of the Students*: A good Headmaster should be profoundly sensitive to the physical, mental, moral, intellectual and spiritual needs of his pupils and should know how to minister to them". —*V.S. Jha*

25. *Sensitive to the Needs of Teachers*: "The principal should not interrupt classes, unless invited to do so". —*Jacobson and Others*

"If the principal stays to the end of the class period, he should observe good manners by expressing in a sentence or two his pleasure on visiting the class". —*Jacobson and Others*

26. *Sensitive to the Needs of the Parents*: "He should always treat parents with scrupulous courtesy". —*W.M. Ryburn*

27. *Source of Inspiration*: The members of staff should look to him for

guidance, help and inspiration. "Under any authoritarian regime, where basis of relationship is fear of one sort or another, it is often possible to get certain routine done efficiently. But under such conditions, it is impossible to bring into rapport the best elements in the personality of the teacher—thus education loses its formative influence".

"He gives up the time-old tradition of checking his teachers, frightening his teachers, weakening his teachers and examining them; but manipulates things so as to train his teachers, inspire his teachers, encourage his teachers and trust them".

—D.I. Lall

28. *Thinking Capacity*: "Experience is an indispensable qualification for a head master. This is certainly true. But experience alone without the capacity to think out and plan out new progressive programmes is inadequate".

—Mohi-ud-din

29. *Vision and Imagination*:

(a) Makes decisions which later events show to be sound and reliable.
(b) Searches new practices and techniques.
(c) Seizes opportunities to develop new patterns of action.

30. *Not an Awful Man*: "In a school worth its name the Head will neither sit in his room like a large spider waiting for a chance to pounce on his prey nor be like an awe inspiring God on the Olympian Heights who visits the earth once in a way to thunder disapproval or to subjugate the people by his presence".

—A.M.D. Razario

Personality of the Headmaster

To justify his place as the inspiring leader and guide, the Headmaster must have a strong personality. R.A. Lamb remarks, "To make the perfect head of the school, there is needed, in addition to all these, a quality which is undefinable—and which resides in the personality of the individual. It is not possible to analyse this quality any more than it is possible by dissecting a man's brain to find wherein resides the soul or the spirit of life. But that it exists is beyond question".

24

School Time-Table

24.1 CONCEPT OF SCHOOL TIME-TABLE

The school time-table is a chart which indicates all the activities undertaken by each member of the staff and the student in each class or on farm or workshop at a particular time of the day when the school is functioning. It is the school mirror which reflects the school programme. It is called the 'Second Clock' of the school on the face of which is shown the daily schedule of the school. In the words of H.G. Stead, "It is the time-table that supplies the framework within which the work of the school proceeds."

Time-table is an outline of the day's work in a school which indicates:

1. Time of the beginning and ending of the school day.
2. Time of beginning and ending of each class period and the activity of the class.
3. Subjects and activities being undertaken by students in each class, in each period and by each teacher.
4. Days on which every subject is taught.
5. Name of the teacher teaching a particular subject in a particular period and in a particular room.
6. Room or place where each activity is going on.
7. Recess break or interval time.

24.2 SIGNIFICANCE OF THE SCHOOL TIME-TABLE: SPARK PLUG OF THE SCHOOL

The time-table reflects the essence of the words of wisdom said by Pitman, "Well arranged time is the surest mark of a well arranged mind".

Dr. Jaswant Singh regards the time-table of the school as the "spark plug of the school which sets into motion its various activities and programme". Some educators regard it as the 'mirror' that reflects the entire daily schedule of the school.

Time-table is an indispensable document of the school. The main points of the significance and value of time-table are discussed below.

1. *Brings System in the School Life*: Without the time-table, there will be chaos and confusion all-round in the school. In the absence of the time-table, the school life will come to a standstill and become a free for all affairs.
2. *Eliminates Wastage of Time and Energy*: Undoubtedly all planned programmes eliminate wastage of time and energy and it is equally

true in the case of a school time-table. The entire school work is, by and large, equitably distributed among the members of the staff. It directs the teacher's and student's energy and attention to one thing at a time by placing proper persons at their proper places at the proper time and in the proper manner.

3. *Ensures Due Attention to Every Subject or Activity*: In framing the time-table, due attention is given to every subject. Periods are allotted to different subjects according to their importance and their fatiguing nature.
4. *Develops Moral Values*: It helps to develop qualities like punctuality and regularity both in the teachers and the students by placing before them a set programme of activities.
5. *Ensures Regular and Even Progress*: Regular and even progress is ensured because time-table prevents laxity and shortages.
6. *Provides a Psychological Environment*: It has got a psychological value leading to the removal of fatigue which may occur due to prolonged hours of teaching and learning. It brings new motivation and stimulation to teachers and students.
7. *Ensures Equitable Distribution of Time to Different Subjects and Activities*: Time-table helps in avoiding the allotment of too much or too less work to any teacher.
8. *Develops Good Habits*: It helps in developing regular habits of work in students as well as teachers.
9. *Facilitates Advance Planning by the Teachers and Students*: Time-table helps in chalking out plans in a systematic manner.
10. *Ensures Efficiency*: There will be no looseness, duplication of effort and repetition of items and activities. Everybody in the school system knows what to do at a particular time.
11. *Helps in Maintaining Discipline*: Since the students are kept gainfully busy in desirable activities, they have little excuse to loiter about. When they are busy, they do not think and act in wrong directions.
12. *Facilitates Supervision*: The head finds it convenient to supervise the work of the teachers and students and offer appropriate guidance to them. He can have individual consultation with the teachers when they are not busy with their classes.
13. *Leads to Even and Regular Process*: It avoids imbalances and leads to even and regular process in all areas of school curriculum.

24.3 TYPES OR FORMS OF A SCHOOL TIME-TABLE

The form of a time-table depends upon the nature of activities carried on in a school. The more the number and variety of activities, the more types of time-tables. In an ordinary school four forms of time-table, i.e. consolidated time-table of the school, class time-table, teachers' vacant period time-table and teachers' time-table will serve the purpose. Time-table for co-curricular activities is coming into vogue in view of their importance in the field of education. Similarly in schools where games are properly organised, the need for games' time-table can hardly be stressed. The progressive schools maintain special room time-table. Time-table for homework is also maintained by some schools.

Ideally speaking there should be seven kinds of time-table:

1. Master time-table indicating the entire programme of the school.
2. Class time-table.
3. Teachers' time-table.
4. Vacant period time-table.
5. Games time-table.
6. Co-curricular activities time-table.
7. Home work time-table.

One copy of class time-table should be kept in the class-room concerned. A copy of the teachers' time-tables should be put in the staff room. One copy of each of the time-table should be kept in the Head's office so that he may know at a glance what work a particular class or teacher is doing at a given time.

24.4 PRINCIPLES OF SCHOOL TIME-TABLE CONSTRUCTION

The construction of time-table makes heavy demands on the ingenuity and skill of the Head. Framing of a time-table is a time absorbing task. Usually the head assigns this job to an experienced and senior member of the staff. Some of the chief factors which determine the construction of a time-table are:

1. Principle of following departmental regulations.
2. Principle of considering the type of school.
3. Principle of amount of time available.
4. Principle of relative importance of a subject.
5. Principle of incidence of fatigue.
6. Principle of justice.
7. Principle of variety.
8. Principle of free period for teachers.
9. Principle of play and recreation.
10. Principle of optimum utilisation.
11. Principle of local variation.
12. Principle of initiation.
13. Principle of elasticity.

1. *Principle of Following Departmental Regulations*: Generally, the State Department of Education issues directions regarding the number of working hours of a school, examination and evaluation schedule and holidays to be observed, etc. It is obligatory for the schools to obey these regulations.

2. *Principle of Considering the Type of School*: The type of school, i.e. a boys' school or girls' school, urban or rural, infant school or school for girls, public or ordinary, will determine the nature of activities of the school and accordingly time-table will be framed. The double shift will call for shortening the duration of the school hours. Similarly, co-educational school will necessitate numerous changes so as to meet the specific needs of both the boys and the girls. In the higher grades of schools the duration of the periods will be longer than in the lower grades of schools.

3. *Principle of the Amount of Time Available*: The amount of time to be given to each subject or activity is determined by the total amount of time available at school. Generally speaking, the higher the grade of the school, the longer the school day. There are certain departmental regulations concerning school timings which have got to be obeyed. According to the Punjab Education Code, the hours for opening and closing Government schools shall be fixed by the Inspector, and for other recognised schools by the Local Bodies or Managers concerned, after consideration of the season, locality and Class of pupils and subjects to the restriction that the total weekly period of instruction (excluding the time allotted to drill and recess) does not exceed the following limits:

Class I	16 Hours
Class II and III	19 Hours
Class IV	24 Hours
Secondary Classes	30 Hours

Recommendations of the Education Commission (1964-66): The Commission made the following recommendations:

(A) The working hours per day should vary from four hours at the pre-primary stage to about six hours at the higher secondary stage.
(B) The total period does not include the time for co-curricular activities
(C) The period includes the time for library period or the guided studies.
(D) At the lower primary stage the hours of instruction should be about 900 and at the higher primary and secondary stages they should be not less than 1,000 and preferably raised to 1,100 or even 1,200 if conditions are favourable.

4. *Principle of Relative Importance and Difficulty of Subjects*: There are certain social and economic considerations that determine the importance of a subject in the school curriculum and accordingly time is allotted to each subject in the school time-table. Subjects like English and Mathematics which are considered to be important and difficult are allotted more time.

5. *Principle of Incidence of Fatigue*: The element of fatigue influences the construction of the school time-table in a number of ways. Subjects requiring more brain-work are placed on the time-table when the brains of the students are quite fresh and when they are capable of doing hard and difficult work. Each part of the morning is considered better than the corresponding part of the afternoon. In other words, the middle or the morning is better than the middle of the afternoon although the middle of the afternoon is better than the end of the morning and the end of the morning is better than the end of the afternoon. It is a common feeling that mental freshness is the greatest in the morning. It gradually increases until it reaches its maximum about the middle of the morning. That is the case after recess. Mental freshness is greater not just after recess but in the second period after recess. The best periods for fatiguing subjects are, therefore, the second, and third periods in the morning and second period after recess. The order of subjects causing fatigue is as follows: Mathematics, English, Indian Languages, Science, Nature Study, Science Practical, Drawing, Crafts, Music, etc. The second and the third periods in the morning and the second in the afternoon are considered to be

the best periods for the fatiguing subjects. English and Mathematics should, therefore, be placed as far as possible in these periods. The worst period is the last period in the afternoon and it may be given to manual work, science practical, physical exercises, etc.

The 'fatigue principle' is true of the days of the week also. Tuesday and Wednesday are considered to be the best days in which maximum work could be done. The end of the week is like the end of the day and fatigue is the greatest.

The younger are quickly fatigued, and therefore, the duration of the period in the lower classes should not exceed thirty minutes and in the higher classes it should not exceed forty minutes. In the summer season, the duration of the period should be reduced.

6. *Principle of Justice*: Work among the members of the staff should be equitably distributed. Unequal distribution of work causes frustration among them and hampers progress. Similarly, time should be allotted for different activities according to their importance in the school curriculum.

Likewise teachers are not given four periods continuously to teach.

7. *Principle of Variety*: It should always be remembered that to keep the children sitting the whole day long at the same place is in no way a wise procedure. As often as possible and convenient, the classes should change place. It has been stated "Change of room, of seat, of posture is an antidote against weariness". Change of occupation is one of the best forms of rest. This applies to both students and teachers. The children should not be kept at the same subject or type of subjects or at subjects which have high fatigue element. Variety can be introduced in the following manner:

(a) No subject except in case of science practical should be kept for two consecutive periods as it is likely to cause monotony in the class.
(b) Variation in the subject should be aimed at in order to avoid boredom, e.g. Ancient History should not be followed by Medieval History.
(c) The same class should not, as far as possible, sit in the same room for the whole day.
(d) The same teacher should not have consecutive periods in the same class, as far as possible, except in the primary classes.
(e) If a subject is taught only two or three times a week, the periods should follow at intervals.
(f) The drill period, science practical and craft work, all provide for a change of the nature just referred to above.

8. *Principle of Free Periods for Teachers*: Free periods for the teachers should be provided so as to increase their efficiency and also for correction work. The free periods of the teachers should be scattered all over the week as far as possible. The language teachers should be given more free periods as they have to do a lot of correction work. In the period immediately preceding the science and other practical periods, the teachers concerned should be kept free to enable them to make the necessary preparation for the work to be undertaken in the coming period. On an average, teachers should be allowed two vacant periods per day.

9. *Principles of Play and Recreation*: Attention is to be given to provide for rest and recreation. The children should not be deprived of play. It affords

them a good opportunity for enjoying fresh air outside and mixing freely with each other besides giving them time to have something for replenishing their energy. The recess period provides for rest and recreation and its duration should not be less than half an hour.

Provision for Radio and Television Broadcasts should also exist wherever possible.

Provision for various co-curricular activities should also be made in the time-table.

10. *Principle of Optimum Utilisation of School Building and Equipment*: The number of students in a school, the number of teachers for various subjects the number of rooms, laboratory (arrangement and furniture etc.) also affect the framing of the school time-table. The time-table of a single teacher school will be quite different from that of other schools having many teachers. Sometimes, due to paucity of rooms, two classes are held in the same room. Time-table should in such cases be arranged in a manner that when one class is busy at writing work, the other should be doing reading work and the like.

11. *Principle of Local Variations*: The hours of work and the duration of recess may be marginally adjusted to suit local conditions, i.e. distance of the school especially in rural areas, train timings, rainy days, etc.

12. *Principle of Motivation*: Interesting programmes in the beginning of the day provide motivation to work enthusiastically.

13. *Principle of Elasticity*: The time-table should not be kept rigid but flexible and fluid. In view of the various difficulties that are likely to crop up, a fluid time-table is always desirable. Sometimes specific needs of many children have got to be met and it becomes inevitable to make some variations. The transfer of teachers also necessitates to bring about variation in the time-table. It is not necessary that the time-table should show the time allowed for the sub-branches of a subject. If we allot 12-periods to English per week, it should be left to the teacher to decide how many periods he shall give to grammar, translation and composition and how many to text.

We should always remember that the time-table is a tool and not the master and as such it should never be allowed to dictate procedures and methods.

24.5 PROBLEMS IN THE CONSTRUCTION OF THE TIME-TABLE

The construction of school time-table is a very challenging and delicate task. There are several compelling, competing and conflicting interests which are to be reconciled and solved amicably to the maximum extent.

Following are the major practical problems which are usually faced in the construction of the time-table.

1. Adherence to departmental regulations.
2. Different types of schools having variety of activities.
3. Lack of the sanctioned staff.
4. Amount of time available for various activities.
5. Incidence of fatigue.
6. Equal distribution of work among the staff.
7. Allotment of number of periods to different subjects.
8. Free or vacant periods for teachers.

9. Periods for correction work.
10. Periods for individual contacts with teachers and students.
11. Limitations of the availability class-rooms.
12. Reconciliation of periods allocated to different subjects.
13. Late coming of staff.
14. Unforeseen absence of some staff members.
15. Adjustment of time-table according to local variation.
16. Lack of play facilities.
17. Lack of library facilities.
18. Shortage of furniture.
19. Shortage of instructional material.

24.6 TYRANNY OF THE SCHOOL TIME-TABLE AND MODERN PROTESTS: FLEXIBILITY OF TIME-TABLE

Many modern psychologists and educationists think of the curriculum in terms of activities instead of subjects. They advocate the abolition of the time-table and want to liberate the child from its limitations.

According to modern psychology, each individual is unique in certain respects. Each child has his own nature, his own preferences and his own rate and speed of working. When he is left to himself, he continues what he starts. He leaves it only when he loses interest or feels fatigued. If he is interested in his work, he is alert and active. This interest gives him psychological satisfaction. But when work is regulated by a rigid time-table, a child might have to stop at the time when he has begun to take interest in a subject due to ringing of the bell or the other way that is to feel fatigued with the subject before the period is over. Since the period is meant for a particular subject, he has to continue even though he is disgusted. It is for this reason that some educational reformers would like to abolish time-table altogether. According to them if a child is left to himself, he would give more time to those subjects in which he is interested and give up those in which he is not interested to come back at a more favourable time.

Several modern educationists do not prescribe any collective time-table as they think that education must cater to the individual needs of the students. The very fact that no two individuals are alike, necessitates that to meet the specific needs of many children, different methods will have to be devised and accordingly a new concept of time-table will serve the required purpose.

Usually the modern protest is due to the following defects in the rigid time-table:

1. The co-curricular programme hardly finds any mention in the time-table.
2. By dividing the school day into uniform chunks of 35 to 45 minutes, allocating certain hours per week to the study of individual subjects, the time-table places pupils and teachers in a kind of lock-up.
3. A rigid time-table militates against the integration of various experiences.
4. A rigid time-table is a great hindrance in the total growth of the pupil's learning experiences.

5. In the conventional time-table, there is hardly any coordination of the efforts of teachers.
6. The conventional time-table does not provide time for teacher-pupil conferences.

The present emphasis is on methods like the Dalton Plan, the Project Method and the like which are a great departure from the time-honoured time-table. 'Contract' is the important feature of the Dalton Plan. Class as a unit of organisation remains but as a unit of instruction vanishes. Child promises to do the given work in a specific period which is usually a fortnight and works according to his intellectual attainments. No collective time-tables are formed in such methods of education. During this time, the child is free to work in whatever subjects he wishes, when he wishes and as long as he wishes. The only condition is that he must complete all the work in his various subjects before another contract can be undertaken. In this way, each child can progress in the school at his own rate.

Many programmes have been evolved in progressive schools which provide flexibility and the common features are:

First, the instructional material is organised into larger meaningful units built round the needs and interests of the students.

Secondly, there is provision for some long periods for practical activities.

Thirdly, there are certain "unassigned" periods in which the students may engage themselves in some worthwhile hobby.

Finally, there is no rigidity and the teachers are at liberty to alter the daily programme according to the special circumstances connected with the needs and interests of the students. Of course this has to be pre-planned and in consultation with other teachers so that they may accordingly modify their programmes.

Summing Up

The task of a time-table framer is very delicate and challenging. It involves the interlocking or weaving of different subjects, activities teachers and classes into the school fabric.

The time-table maker should be a man of vision and must be open-minded. He should take into consideration the human factor. He should not try to 'boss' over other teachers. A good time-table maker makes the optimum use of men and materials. The head of the school is expected to take a keen personal interest in this work.

25

Classroom Management

Role of the Teacher

25.1 MEANING AND CONCEPT OF CLASSROOM MANAGEMENT

Classroom management is a very broad concept. It includes all the activities of the teacher that he undertakes for the creation of such an environment that allows the best display of student's abilities in the teaching-learning process. The environment should involve the maximum involvement of the students in the classroom activities. The ideal environment is based on mutual goodwill and trust. The teacher gives due regard to the individuality of the students and the students in turn show spontaneous regard for the teacher. The teacher in the true sense is the friend, philosopher and guide to the students.

Management is needed in every activity and everywhere. Class-room is no exception. It brings order and system in the work. Appropriate class-room management means providing motivation to the learners. It means to ensure that the learners take full interest in the teaching-learning process. It implies creating democratic classroom climate so that the three types of behaviour, i.e. cognitive, conative and psychomotor of the students is developed to the maximum. It means that discipline should take the form of 'self-discipline' and 'social discipline'.

25.2 SIGNIFICANCE OF CLASSROOM MANAGEMENT

Classroom management is one of the most important elements of the school programme. It is not without reason that the Education Commission observed, "The destiny of India is being shaped in her classrooms. This, we believe, is no more rhetoric". The Commission has given so much importance to this element that the report begins with these remarks.

The students spends most of their time in the classroom and likewise most of the work a school undertakes is done in the classrooms. The environment of classrooms has a great influence on the many sided development of the personality of the student. The better the classroom management, the better the performance of the students. There is no doubt that the standard of management of the classrooms determine the standard of the school.

25.3 IMPORTANCE OF THE CLASSROOM AS A SOCIAL GROUP

It has been observed by Kuppuswami that classroom as an instructional group helps its members to satisfy their needs and achieve goals. Classroom group has a special significance in the school programme on account of the following functions:

1. Improvement in the behaviour of the students.
2. Development of mental process through intellectual activities.
3. Development of feeling of service.
4. Preparation for social life—present as well as future social life.
5. Exciting sympathy of members.
6. Developing qualities of leadership.
7. Acquiring more knowledge.
8. Development of the feeling of cooperation.

25.4 FOUR-FOLD PROCESS OF CLASS-ROOM MANAGEMENT

K. Davis has given the four-fold process of class-room management.

1. Planning
2. Organising
3. Leading and motivating
4. Controlling

Planning: Before taking up the classwork, the teacher analyses the content or topic in terms of various elements and arranges these in logical as well as psychological consequences. He then formulates his teaching objectives in behavioural terms. Thereafter he selects the appropriate strategies.

Organising: This is the second step of managing teaching-learning process. The teacher organises the learning resources for the achievement of his objectives efficiently, speedily and successfully. The teacher creates a suitable learning environment in the class. He decides about the teaching-learning strategies to be adopted.

Leading and motivating: The primary task of the teacher is to motivate the students. The key-note of this step is to enable the student to learn how to learn through his own efforts. The teacher encourages the students to participate actively in the teaching-learning process. He provides maximum opportunities to the students in the participation of the classroom activities.

The teacher makes use of his creativity, experiences and constructive imagination in providing appropriate activities relating to learning.

Controlling: This involves three major activities namely (1) Observing the learning system, (2) Evaluating the teaching learning system, and (3) Modifying the teaching-learning system.

25.5 PRINCIPLES OF CLASSROOM MANAGEMENT

1. Principle of professional competence of the teacher.
2. Principle of involvement of the students.
3. Principle of social discipline.
4. Principle of effective classroom routine.
5. Principle of effective psychological environment.
6. Principle of healthy social environment.
7. Principle of healthy physical environment.
8. Principle of motivation of the learners.
9. Principle of overall effective environment.

25.6 INFLUENCING FACTORS OF CLASSROOM MANAGEMENT

The primary responsibility of classroom management rests with the teachers. However, some of the elements of effective classroom management do depend on the provision of various types of physical facilities which are provided by the management. The overall management skills and efficiency of the head of the school also have a bearing on the classroom management.

Here we are basically concerned with the role of the teacher in managing the actual classroom teaching and the allied issues.

Important influencing factors are as under:

1. Overall environment of the school.
2. Psychological environment of the classroom.
3. Physical environment of the classroom. This includes:
   (i) Proper classroom size.
   (ii) Provision of appropriate seating arrangement.
   (iii) Appropriate furniture.
   (iv) Sufficient light and air.
   (v) Necessary facilities for the teacher, i.e. teacher's table, chair, blackboard, etc.
   (vi) Cleanliness of the classroom.
   (vii) Arrangement of the time-table.
4. Personality of the teacher.
5. Teaching-learning process.
6. Teacher's behaviour towards students.
7. Classroom routine, i.e. taking roll-call etc.
8. Disciplinary standard, code of behaviour.
9. Involvement of the students in the lesson.
10. Behaviour of the teacher towards students.
11. Reinforcing attending behaviour of the students, i.e. ensuring students' attention in the class-work.
12. Reinforcing accepting student behaviour of the students – mode of students' entering the class, standing while questioning and answering, observation of proper etiquette.
13. Social environment of the classroom.
14. Appropriate standard of group behaviour.
15. Personality traits of the teacher.

25.7 IMPORTANT ELEMENTS IN THE CLASSROOM MANAGEMENT

- Management of Normal Classroom Routine
- Teaching Methods, Techniques and Skills
- Teaching Skills
- Class-room Discipline Appropriate Student Behaviour
- Effective Group Dynamics
- Teacher's own Motivation
- Personality of the Teacher
- Desirable Teacher Behaviour in the Classroom

25.8 TECHNIQUES OF CLASSROOM MANAGEMENT

Classroom Routine Management: Hints for the Teacher

1. Learn the names of the students quickly.

2. Learn carefully the seating plan of students.
3. Keep the classroom neat and tidy.
4. Keep classroom well ventilated and lighted.
5. Take the roll-call and enquire about the absentees.
6. Insist on correct postures.
7. Be always punctual.
8. Stand throughout the great part of the class period.
9. Impress upon the students the importance of respect for school property.
10. Have a definite system for collecting and distributing material to avoid confusion.

Teaching Procedures and Methods

1. Keep everything ready to start class-work.
2. Be sure you get the attention of every member of the class.
3. Use a variety of teaching aids.
4. Make assignments definite and clear.
5. Word questions clearly so that the students know what you are expecting from them.
6. Teach the whole class and not a few students sitting on the front benches.
7. Distribute questions evenly.
8. Put questions to inattentive students also.
9. Do not often repeat your questions.
10. Do not put questions hurriedly.
11. Allow reasonable time to the students to answer your questions.
12. Encourage students to answer questions rather than doing all the talking yourself.
13. Encourage students to report on anything of current interest to them in the class which pertains to the course.
14. Provide opportunities for all students to participate in the lesson.
15. Avoid being side tracked.
16. Stop trying to teach students something which they cannot learn.
17. Check the written work of the students carefully.
18. Make necessary explanations about corrected assignments.
19. Avoid difficult assignments in the beginning.
20. Allow supervised study time.
21. Vary methods of teaching and learning; use dramas, panel discussion, debate, etc.
22. Make your blackboard writing legible.
23. Keep the students always busy in doing some worthwhile work.
24. Make every pupil feel that he is essential to the success of the lesson.
25. Do not leave anything in disorder when you leave the class.
26. Rub off the blackboard when you leave the classroom.
27. Prepare plan of your daily work systematically.
28. Train your students to keep themselves busy when you are not in the classroom.

29. Do not embarrass pupils before the other pupils.
30. Show consideration for bashful pupils.

25.9 CLASS DISCIPLINE: CODE OF BEHAVIOUR

1. Base your discipline on do's rather than don'ts.
2. Insist on good conduct or manners and high standards of work.
3. Be sympathetic and understanding in your dealings with students.
4. Be firm and consistent in your dealing with students.
5. Do not allow students to wander around.
6. Maintain a certain reserve and be friendly rather than 'chummy'.
7. Try to adopt this philosophy, "I like you even though I do not like what you do".
8. Be just and fair.
9. Avoid telling the class to keep order.
10. Do not use abusive anger.
11. Avoid sarcastic remarks.
12. Avoid threats.
13. Attend to minor problems before they become major ones.
14. Encourage honesty.
15. Make every effort to solve your own disciplinary problems and seldom approach the head for the purpose.
16. Do not discuss your family problems in the classroom.
17. Do not discuss matters relating to your colleagues with the students.
18. Do not narrate of our experiences too often in the class.

25.10 INSTRUCTIONAL INPUT

Broadly speaking an effective instructional input includes:

1. Curriculum Development and Implementation.
2. Adjustment to Individual Differences and Development.
3. Dynamic Techniques of Instruction.
4. Use of Technology of Teaching.
5. Evaluating and Discussing Pupils' Performance.

Curriculum Development and Implementation

This implies:

1. Participation in grade level or subject-matter study of existing curricula and in the development of improved expanded curricula.
2. Determining the object, scope and methods of the grade and subjects to be taught.
3. Devising assignments, when necessary, in order to enrich the teaching programme for the pupils.
4. Correlating his subject-matter curriculum, with the curriculum of other subjects.

Adjusting to Individual Differences and Development Levels

This calls for:

1. Drawing upon and applying basic knowledge of the psychology of the child in order to establish readiness for learning.

2. Making an effort to know as much as possible about the background and out of school environment of each child, in order to improve the teaching-learning process.
3. Developing in each pupil a sense of personal growth and value.
4. Maintaining discipline by being consistently friendly, fair and firm.
5. Handling behaviour problems in a controlled manner.

Dynamic Techniques of Teaching (Effective teaching-learning)

This includes:

1. Selecting materials, teaching aids and methods which will facilitate the learning process and stimulate the desire for further learning.
2. Meeting the needs, backgrounds and capacities of the children being taught.
3. Teaching by using a suitable variety of lectures, discussions, demonstrations, visual and oral presentations, recitation, directed group effort, experimentation, special projects and field trips.
4. Analysing and evaluating the effectiveness of various teaching techniques in order to improve the learning process.
5. Endeavouring to obtain and maintain pupil interest and attention so that teaching is done in a receptive atmosphere.
6. Endeavouring to assure that material taught is applied in such a manner as to develop a pattern of understanding for future use in other areas.
7. Encouraging and guiding critical thinking by pupils.
8. Developing desirable work and study skills and habits.
9. English pupil participation in the lesson planning process.
10. Developing broad outlines and objectives to be attained within prescribed limits, for a subject or skill area based upon the needs and interests of a specific group of pupils.
11. Making suitable lesson plans.

Use of Techniques of Teaching

This relates to:

1. Use of blackboard.
2. Use of charts, models, graphs, etc.
3. Use of new technology, i.e. computer, radio and T.V.

Evaluating and Discussing Pupils Performance

This comprises:

1. Devising and administering appropriate tests to measure the level and quality of pupil learning.
2. Interpreting test results and related findings to pupil progress in order to improve the teaching-learning process.
3. Reporting pupil achievement and progress to parents by means of progress reports.
4. Discussing pupil achievement with the parents individually, in groups and conference.

5. Cooperating and enlisting the cooperation of school specialist in the process of evaluation.

25.11 INSTRUCTIONAL INPUT AND TEACHING SKILLS

While talking of teaching skills, it must be remembered that there is no water-tight compartment as regards skills at different stages. These are classified for the sake of convenience, otherwise they are interrelated. A particular skill cannot be confined to one teaching stage only.

1. Teaching Skills at the Planning Stage

(i) Writing instructional objectives
(ii) Selecting the content
(iii) Organising the content
(iv) Selection of audio-visual aids and their procurement

2. Introductory Stage Skills

(i) Creating set induction—preparing the minds of the students
(ii) Introducing the lessons

3. Presentation Stage Skills

(*i*) *Questioning Skills*

(a) Structuring classroom questions
(b) Fluency in asking questions
(c) Probing question
(d) Question delivery and distribution
(e) Higher order questions
(f) Divergent questions
(g) Management of students' answers

(*ii*) *Presentation of Content/Subject Matter Skills*

(a) Pacing of the lesson
(b) Lecturing
(c) Illustrating with examples
(d) Demonstrating
(e) Explaining
(f) Discussing

(*iii*) *Audio-Visual Aids Skills*

(a) Selecting and using aids
(b) Stimulus variation
(c) Silence and non-verbal cues
(d) Reinforcement

(*iv*) *Managerial Skills*

(a) Pupil involvement and participation
(b) Recognising attending behaviour
(c) Classroom management

4. Closing Stage Teaching Skills

(i) Planned recapitulation
(ii) Evaluating pupil progress
(iii) Diagnosing learning difficulties of the students and taking remedial measures
(iv) Giving assignments.

25.12 DISCIPLINE (SCHOOL DISCIPLINE AND CLASS DISCIPLINE)

School Discipline: Traditional and Modern Concept

There has been a sea change in the concept of school discipline which has passed through the following stages:

Stage 1. Flogging theory.
Stage 2. Impression rather than repression theory.
Stage 3. Laissez Faire Theory.
Stage 4. Self-discipline and social discipline theory.

To quote the Secondary Education Commission, "Discipline is the fruit, the valuable by product of cooperative work willingly and efficiently undertaken".

Discipline according to modern concept is a cooperative mental attitude in which each member of the class freely gives his best because he feels himself a member of corporate body whose aims are recognised as worthy. The aim of such discipline is to produce self-controlled students who will work without supervision.

Discipline from without is always temporisation.

Constructive discipline, like religion cannot be taught but only can be caught and practised. It is the outcome of activities and experiences that inculcate in the students virtues of self-control based on reason and not on force. It is the outcome of persuasion and not compulsion.

Discipline in the school should not be a matter of arbitrary rules and regulations enforced through the authority of the teachers, helped by the lures of rewards or the fear of punishment. The students should be given considerable freedom to organise functions, to conduct most of the school activities through their own committees and even to deal with certain types of small disciplinary cases. Disciplines, thus should be maintained through the influence of the social group and gradually lead to the development of self-discipline.

Old Concept and New Concept of Discipline

	Old Concept of Discipline	*New or Modern Concept of Discipline*
1. *Aim*	Making the child obey.	Enabling the child to appreciate the necessity of obeying.
2. *School Environment*	1. Fearful 2. Repulsive	1. Full of cheerfulness 2. Receptive and attractive
3. *Role of the teacher*	(i) Teacher as a fearful person.	Teacher as a friend, guide and philosopher.

(Contd.)

(Contd.)

	Old Concept of Discipline	New or Modern Concept of Discipline
	(ii) Teacher as an autocrat.	
4. *Methods of control*	(i) 'Do not move' (ii) Do not talk (iii) Scolding (iv) Punishment	(i) Freedom to work. (ii) No physical punishment. (iii) Social control
5. *Curriculum*	Rigid	Flexible
6. *Co-curricular Activities*	(i) Activities mostly confined to the classroom (ii) Very few	(i) Variety of activities. (ii) Several indoor and outdoor activities.
7. *Students' Participation*	No scope or very little or negligible scope	Involvement of students in sharing responsibility self-government
8. *Place of the child*	(i) Passive listener (ii) Like a bird in an egg	(i) Active being (ii) Full of life in free environment

Methods of Achieving Self-Discipline and Social Discipline

Following measures are considered to be of great significance in achieving the goal of self-discipline and social discipline.

1. Overall cooperative and vibrant environment of the school.
2. Philosophy of human relations as the guiding force under the humanistic leadership of the head of the school.
3. Enlightened and sympathetic attitude of the teachers.
4. Students' involvement in running some affairs of the schools i.e. self-government.
5. Provision of rich and varied co-curricular activities.
6. Flexible school curriculum.
7. Dynamic and progressive methods of teaching.
8. Cooperation among the members of the staff.
9. Suitable material conditions of work.
10. Provision for social service activities.

Summing Up

The Secondary Education Commission very rightly has observed, "Discipline, they say, should be a responsibility of parents, teachers, the general public and the authorities concerned".

The problem of discipline is not an isolated one. Many-sided attempts will, therefore, have to be made. If we are to revive a spirit of idealism among students a favourable social environment based on higher values of life will have to be created. Leaders of all shades must set high ideals before the students. Nevertheless, there is much a school can do for raising the tone of discipline among the students and the school staff must play a constructive role to achieve this end.

25.13 MANIFOLD ROLES OF THE TEACHER

The teacher is expected to play the following roles:

1. *Provider* of effective instructional output.
2. *Manager* of teaching-learning process.
3. *Counsellor* of students.
4. *Parent Surrogate* (*parent substitute*): A teacher is expected to act as a parent of the students and treat them with affection and care.
5. *Ego-supporter*: He is expected to build up and maintain a healthy and strong 'ego' and 'self-concept' among children.
6. *Helper*: The teacher is expected to be a helper to students by way of providing them academic and personal guidance.
7. *Resource person*: He is expected to play the role of a resource person who possesses knowledge of the subject-matter and skills better than the pupils.
8. *Detective*: He acts as a detective in detecting offences and rule breakers.
9. *Facilitator of learning*: He is expected to promote significant learning among his students.
10. *Limiter or reducer of anxiety*: He is expected to assist students to control their impulses and reduce anxiety about conduct and performance in different problematic situations.
11. *Referee*: He is expected to settle disputes among students in an objective and fair manner.
12. *Group leader*: He is expected to act as a leader in developing suitable climate and cohesion in the class as a social group.
13. *Inspirer and exemplar*: He is expected to behave in a manner whereby the traits exemplified by him may be emulated by the students.
14. *Judge*: He is expected to evaluate the academic and other performance of the students in an impartial manner.
15. *Confidant*: He is expected to win and share the confidence of the students.
16. *Friend and Philosopher*: He is expected to play the role of a friend, philosopher and guide to the students.
17. *Upholder of the norms and values*: He is expected to uphold the norms and values of the society.
18. *Moral educator*: He is expected to inculcate the attitudes and moral values cherished by the society among the students.
19. *Democrat*: He is expected to play the role of a democrat.
20. *Rationalist*: He is expected to play the role of a rationalist by basing his actions on reason.
21. *Secularist*: He is expected to play the role of a secularist by having an open mind on the beliefs of all religions.
22. *Initiator*: He is expected to play the role of an initiator by exploiting the new technology to the best advantage of the students and the purposes of

education. He should play the roles of a planned organiser of curricular innovator of educational ideas, practices and systems, writer of Radio and TV lessons and programmes, user of video-tapes and computers, etc.

23. *Reformer*: In a country like India, where conservatism and superstitions prevail, a teacher is expected to play the role of a social reformer.

24. *Equaliser*: He should act as equaliser by working for minimising inequalities in the educative process and by building up an egalitarian, secular and socialist society.

Note: All the roles overlap.

Teacher's Role Towards Parents

Close cooperation between the parent who is the first teacher and the teacher, who is the second parent, is the very foundation on which rests the fruitfulness of the training imparted in our institutions.

Following are the important roles of the teachers towards parents:

1. Participating in parent-teacher associations and similar activities.
2. Participating in community affairs.
3. Making himself available to parents at scheduled times to discuss pupil progress and behaviour.
4. Evincing a sympathetic, helpful and understanding attitude towards parents and their children's schooling problems.
5. Reporting and discussing with parents, pupil's progress, problems and needs.
6. Assuring through personal behaviour in the community that the school staff-image in the community is favourable.
7. The teacher should encourage the parents of the pupils to visit the school frequently.
8. He should see that parents are cordially received when they visit the school.
9. He should regularly inform the parents of the progress of their wards.
10. He should encourage the parents to consult the teachers as well as him on special problems of their wards.
11. He should visit the homes of the pupils and should suggest to the teachers also to do the same.
12. He should organise parents-study-groups from time-to-time.
13. He should provide adequate facilities for the organisation and proper functioning of the Parent-Teacher Association in the school.

Teacher's Role Towards Community

1. The teacher should plan school programme with reference to the needs of the community.
2. He should encourage the use of community resources for vitalising classroom instruction through excursions, field trips, study of local history, etc.
3. He should encourage and organise social service programmes to render public service.
4. He should allow the community to use school facilities and services

like school building, library, and dispensary ensuring at the same time that the work of the school does not suffer.
5. He should organise social and cultural activities in the school to interpret the school programme to the community.
6. He should actively participate in the social and cultural functions of the community.
7. He should be above politics and religion in organising school programmes.
8. He should not allow the school to become a tool in the hands of any pressure group.
9. He should not allow his political beliefs to influence his administration of school.

25.14 CHARACTERISTICS AND QUALITIES OF AN EFFECTIVE TEACHER

To play his role effectively and fully, a teacher is expected to possess the qualities in a great measure as given here.

1. *Character and Personality*: Character and personality of the pupils cannot be developed if the teacher who is the model to be followed lacks character and personality. 'Example is better than precept' is an old saying and is absolutely true in the teaching profession. No amount of sermons from the teacher can make much headway. A teacher teaches not only by 'what he says and does' but very largely by 'what he is'.

Montessori stresses that every teachers worth his salt must destroy these sins: pride, anger, sloth, sensuality, gluttony and envy. The teacher should be partly a scientist, partly a doctor and completely religious. He must acquire a moral alertness; mingling of patience, love and humility. He should always be frank, sincere and honest. Raymount urges that the teacher must avoid everything that is petty and mean.

Gandhiji observes, "Woe to the teacher who teaches one thing with the lips and carries another in the heart".

Arthur B. Moehlman states, "The teacher and the principle are always on exhibition, observed by hundreds of eyes. The position involves the strain of producing effect upon others not only through the use of specific methodologies, but also through the extension of teacher personality".

In the words of Dr. Rajendra Prasad, "The teacher's own character should be such that there is no difference between what they say and do. When we act upon this ideal then alone we can be sure of a bright future for our own country".

The Secondary Education Commission observes, "The teacher has always to realise that all his actions are being watched by his pupils".

2. *Love for the Profession*: A person who wants to join this profession must feel the call for it. "If a teacher has not an ideal aim, he had better to take to shop-keeping at once, he will there doubtless find an ideal within his capacity", says Laurie.

In the words of the Secondary Education Commission, "They will not look upon their work as an unpalatable means of earning a scanty living but as an avenue through which they are rendering significant social service as well as finding some measure of self-fulfillment and self-expression".

3. *Love for Children*: It has been said that if a teacher does not actually like boys and girls, he should give up teaching. He must enjoy company in groups. A good teacher feels that some sort of energy is constantly supplied by the young. "Love the child and the child will love you; hate the child and the child will hate you," is a famous maxim. One who does not love children should not stay in teaching.

4. *Respect for the Individuality of the Child*: Emerson states, "The secret of education lies in respecting the pupil. A child wants to be heard. His opinion should not be brushed aside merely because he is a child".

5. *Knowledge of Psychology*: Knowledge of psychology goes a long way in providing that basic orientation towards problems of education and child development without which there would be a considerable waste of time, energy and human resources. With a knowledge of child psychology, a teacher will be in a better position to understand and appreciate the individual differences of children, their nature, temperaments, habits and manners.

6. *Intimate Knowledge of the Child*: Children are not miniature adults. Their peculiar patterns of thoughts and emotions must be studied. Their names must be learnt and faces recognised. They must not be made to feel that the teacher is indifferent to them. Every source should be tapped to know about them to the fullest possible extent.

7. *Emotional Stability of the Teacher*: It is said in *The Education and Training of Teacher* published by UNESCO, "Various researches show clearly that the emotional stability of teachers affects that of pupils. Unhappy, frustrated, dissatisfied teachers cannot help their pupils to become happy, well adjusted young people". The teachers should try to find out their own shortcomings and try to remove them so that the students may be saved from the adverse influence of their unbalanced personality.

K.G. Saiyidain has observed, "You cannot pour out of a vessel except that you have put into it and, if a teacher is poor and shallow from within, if there is no sparkling wire in him, he cannot quicken the mind or humanise the emotions of his children—if he is not a lighted candle himself, he will never be able to light up the flame in others".

8. *Grasp Over the Method*: The Secondary Education Commission states, "Any method good or bad links up the teachers and his pupils into an organic relationship with constant mutual interaction, it reacts not only on the minds of the students but on their entire personality, their standard of work and judgment, their intellectual and emotional equipment, their attitudes and values. Good methods which are psychologically and socially sound may raise the whole quality, bad methods may debase it".

9. *Mastery of the Subject Matter*: According to the University Education Commission, 1948-49, "No teacher who is not a maser of the field, who is not in touch with the latest development in his subject and who does not bring to bear upon his duties a free and untrammelled mind will ever succeed in inspiring youth with the love of truth which is the principal object of all higher education".

10. *Daily Preparation*: Bagley emphasises the importance of daily

preparation in these words, "However able and experienced the teacher, he could do never without his preliminary preparation".

11. *Democratic Attitude*: A teacher cannot afford to be an autocrat. Present day education lays much stress on the inculcation of democratic ideals in the students. A teacher who is to show the way of democracy to the students must develop in himself a democratic attitude. His role is of a friend, philosopher and guide and not of a policeman.

12. *Skill in Questioning*: The success of a class teacher in the class also depends on the art of questioning. One who questions faultlessly, teaches effectively. With the help of right type of questions a wise teacher can lead the students from dark and unknown regions to known and bright ones.

13. *Use of Material Aids*: Various teaching aids bring clarity and vividness. It is a great asset to the teacher to narrate stories and anecdotes which appeal to children at different age and attainment levels. Abstract words and phrases can be made clear by illustrations.

14. *Good Vitality*: In the opinion of Arthur B. Moehlman, "Good vitality is essential to successful teaching, not only in its reflex influence upon the children but also in making possible continuity of work with the fewest possible interruptions from illness because of general fatigue".

15. *Good Memory*: A teacher with a poor memory is ridiculous. It becomes easier for a teacher having good memory to correlate many things. A good creative memory is one of the qualities that differentiates the good teacher from the mediocre.

16. *Good Voice*: The voice of a teacher should be clear, moderately pitched and well modulated. In the words of Mohi-ud-din, "The best voice for the classroom is one which is clear, pleasantly toned, fairly even in its general pitch and yet capable of modulation in order to express different shades of meaning and emphasis. A monotonous voice tires the pupils very soon and is not impressive".

17. *Optimistic Outlook*: Dr. E.A. Pires thinks that the teacher who can infuse happiness into the work of his pupils because he himself enjoys his work is sure to be a successful and popular teacher.

According to S. Balakrishna Joshi, "A teacher whose soul is wrinkled and whose heart is atrophied, who is devoid of energy and enthusiasm, capacity and character and who simply marks time, his eyes fixed on the calendar, is a disgrace to the profession and a curse on society". "The great teacher lives and breathes the spirit of creativity and adventure", writes Dr. E.A. Pires.

18. *Laughter*: A tactful teacher never hesitates to laugh, when there is an occasion for it. Laughter done in an unhealthy spirit defeats its own purpose. A teacher should never make the mistake of laughing at the pupils. He should laugh with them and should also see that they laugh with him and not at him.

19. *Humour*: Humour keeps the pupils attentive. A very wise teacher once remarked, "I consider a day's teaching is wasted if we do not at all have a hearty laugh". Sarcasm is to be avoided.

20. *Thirst for Knowledge*: "A teacher can never truly teach unless he is still learning himself", remarks Rabindra Nath Tagore. A teacher should not feel shy to learn from others. There is no end to knowledge and his attitude

should be like that of Newton: "I am only a child, playing in the sand by the sea-shore, picking up a pebble here and there with a vast ocean of truth lying undiscovered before me".

21. *Judicious Use of Praise and Blame*: Praise and blame are the two important weapons in the armoury of the teacher and these should be used very judiciously. "Praise like gold and diamond owes its value to scarcity", writes Robinson Johnson.

A word of praise or commendation will easily enhance the pupils' interest in any course of action. Praise, rightly employed, is a forceful incentive at the disposal of the teacher.

22. *Justice and Impartiality*: The teacher should not show undue favour to some. All should be equal in his eyes. Undue favour to some students will lead to frustration among others.

23. *Patience*: He has to deal with a large number of students having low and high power of understanding. He may have to repeat his lessons many a time for the sake of the less intelligent and he should not be irritated in doing so. Some students, by nature, pick up lessons very slowly and a teacher should possess the required patience to make them understand gradually. Good habits are not formed overnight. It requires time and patience to inculcate virtues in the students.

24. *True to his Commands*: Less commands should be given to the students and when given, they must be stuck to, otherwise they lose their effectiveness.

25. *Free from Religious Fanaticism*: The minds of the young should not be poisoned through narrow-mindedness and bigotry. The partition of the country has shown what wrong fanaticism can do.

26. *Free from Political Bias*: The students should not be exploited for political purposes. The programmes of the various political parties must be placed before them in their true perspective.

27. *Sense of Patriotism*: If a teacher does not possess a sense of patriotism, he would not be successful in his attempts to develop love for the country in the students. However, the slogan 'my country wrong or right' should be avoided.

28. *Interest in Curriculum Activities*: It is needless to stress the importance of co-curricular activities in the present system of education. They are perhaps more important than the traditional subject. And as such a teacher can hardly afford to be indifferent to this aspect of school life.

29. *Missionary*: S. Balakrishna Joshi feels, "Without a band of devoted teachers who are inspired by a holy zeal, an institution with the paraphernalia of modern convenience will be like a beautiful corpse without spark of life, a carcass without soul". According to same author teaching is a divinely ordained mission.

30. *Teacher as a Guide*: Child being the 'Hero in the drama of education' must be allowed to play an active role in the process of education. "The teacher is a guide, a director, he steers the boat but the energy that propels it must come from those who are learning," remarks Dewey. Similarly, Shri Aurobindo writes, "The first principle of true teaching is that nothing can be taught. The teacher is not an instructor or a task master, he is a helper and a guide. His

business is to suggest and not to impose. He does not actually train the pupil's mind, he shows him how to perfect his instruments of knowledge and helps and encourages him in the process. He does not impart knowledge to him; he shows him how to acquire knowledge for himself. He does not call forth the knowledge that is within; he only shows him where it lies and how it can be habituated to rise to the surface".

31. *Man of Confidence*: The teachers must have an unlimited confidence and faith in himself. It is essential that a teacher should be not only a man of high character but also that he be a man of confidence; confidence in his vocation, confidence in his pupils, confidence in human nature and confidence in his colleagues.

25.17 SUMMING UP THE CHARACTERISTICS OF AN EFFECTIVE TEACHER

Significance of Each Letter of the Word 'Teacher'

T stands for	—	Tact, Tolerance, Truth, Training, Technology
E stands for	—	Efficiency, Enthusiasm, Ethics, Etiquette, Energy
A stands for	—	Accuracy, Adaptability, Affection, Alertness, Appearance
C stands for	—	Character, Clarity, Cooperation, Constructiveness, Creativity, Concern for others
H stands for	—	Hard work, Humility, Honesty, Humour, Human Relations
E stands for	—	Eagerness, Efficiency, Emotional Stability, Expressiveness
R stands for	—	Rationality, Relationship, Resourcefulness, Reliability

25.18 'A' TO 'Z' OF EFFECTIVE TEACHER AND EFFECTIVE CLASSROOM MANAGEMENT AND INSTRUCTION

A 'A' is for alertness on the part of the teacher to the multifarious needs of the learners. Alertness is very helpful in taking appropriate decisions and timely corrective measures.

B 'B' is for business like attitude. It is to be ensured that every learner in the class, remains busy in realising the goals set.

'B' is for balanced behaviour.

C 'C' stands for cooperative teaching-learning. The learners must be made active partners.

'C' is for clarity of purpose. The teacher and the learners must be clear about the goals for the achievements of which they are working.

'C' is for clarity of the subject-matter taught. A teacher must make all possible efforts to make his lesson clear. Difficulties of the learners must be appreciated and clarified.

D 'D' stands for democratic classroom environment.

'D' is for discovery. Children should be guided to find out new facts, ideas and principles. It helps children in becoming independent and resourceful learners.

'D' stands for democratic discipline.

E 'E' stands for expectancies. Each learner should be expected to learn. No learner should be considered without any potential.
'E' stands for enthusiasm. The teacher himself must demonstrate enthusiasm for his work.

F 'F' is for feedback. Feedback helps the teacher and the learners to take timely corrective measures for the completion of the task.
'F' stands for faith of the teacher in himself.

G 'G' is for goal-setting. Appropriate goals should be set for the learners. They should also be made clear about the suitability of goals. Efforts may be made to associate the learners with the setting of goals.

H 'H' is for hard work on the part of the students as well as teachers.
'H' is for humour. Humour on the part of the teacher releases fatigue and tension.
'H' stands for human touch.

I 'I' stands for involvement of all the learners in classroom activities and experiences.
'I' stands for impartial attitude.
'I' stands for inspirational teaching-learning.

J 'J' stands for just attitude.
'J' stands for judicious rewards and punishments.

K 'K' stands for knowing children's abilities, aptitudes and interests.
'K' stands for the knowledge of the sub-matter.

L 'L' stands for linking present, past and future knowledge.
'L' stands for leadership qualities.

M 'M' stands for motivation.
'M' stands for management of the class.

N 'N' stands for needs of the learners and their satisfaction.

O 'O' stands for open-mindedness.
'O' stands for out-of-class activities.
'O' stands for objectivity in approach.

P 'P' stands for praise. Verbal and non-verbal praise of children can motivate them to hard work.
'P' stands for personal contact with every learner.

Q 'Q' is for quiz. From time-to-time, quiz competitions may be arranged in the class.
'Q' stands for quality teaching.
'Q' stands for question-answers.

R 'R' stands for review of the lesson.
'R' stands for relationship.
'R' stands for resourcefulness.

S 'S' stands for success and experience. Success motivates the learner to achieve more.
'S' stands for scientific temper.
'S' stands for self-analysis and self-control.

T 'T' stands for technology of teaching.
'T' stands for tutoring which involves removing difficulties individually or in small groups.

U 'U' stands for undivided attention to teaching.
'U' stands for unbiased attitude to the treatment of controversial issues.

V 'V' stands for visual aids.
'V' stands for variety of experiences.
'V' stands for voice-modulation.
'V' stands for variation in the presentation.

W 'W' stands for welcoming attitude.
'W' stands for warmth towards students.

X 'X' stands for X-ray of the teaching process. It implies finding out of the difficulties and potentials of the students.

Y 'Y' stands for yardstick, i.e. same standard basis of making a judgment on the performance of the students.
'Y' stands for you, implying that you (student) are the most important element in the teaching-learning process.

Z 'Z' stands for zeal and zest for work.
'Z' stands for zenith or excellence.

25.19 SOCIAL MANAGEMENT AND CLASSROOM MANAGEMENT

School management is a very broad concept. Broadly speaking, the primary responsibility of the school management is that of the head of the school. Of course, school management is also the concern of the governing body/school Managing Committee. Its for an internal school management is concerned, the entire responsibility is that of the head. He is responsible for the efficient and smooth management of the human and material resources of the school (Discussed in detail in Chapters 22 and 23).

Class management is concerned with the teacher who teaches the Class. This related primarily to the instructional strategies and behavior modification of the students. It depends upon a number of factors relating to the personality of the teacher, his methodology of teaching, knowledge of group dynamics and disciplinary concept (All these aspects are discussed in this chapter). In the ultimate analysis, the head is responsible for both school management and class management.

26

Maintenance of School Records

26.1 INDISPENSABILITY OF SCHOOL RECORDS

Proper maintenance, accuracy and effective use of records go a long way in the efficient working of any institution or organisation and school is no exception. There is no doubt that the success of a school in each of its elements and its totality depends to a large measure on the scientific and systematic manner in which records are kept. On account of the importance of school records and its indispensability, the school office is often called the 'king-pin of the enterprise"

26.2 NEED OF SCHOOL RECORDS

Records are needed for the following purposes:

1. *Legal Requirements*: School records and reports are used to satisfy the legal requirements of the State Education Department, Examination Board, etc.
2. *Relationships with Home and the Community*: School is a social institution answerable to the parents, the managing committee, the department and the public in general and the records kept by the school help to understand the problems and limitations of the school.
3. *Records Essential for the All-round Growth of the Child*: School is entrusted with the task of all-round development of the personality of each child and to discharge this function it is absolutely essential to keep a record of his day-to-day growth and development.
4. *Financial Requirements of the School*: The school has to supply a variety of data to justify its financial needs. Financial grants are sanctioned for equipment, library books and furniture, etc. by the Education Department, Local Bodies and School Management Committee as the case may be.
5. *Records and Grants-in-Aid*: Sometimes certain conditions are laid down by the department for the payment of grants-in-aid to schools. This requires the supply of certain facts and statistics.
6. *Educational Reform*: Educational reforms can be undertaken only when the school records provide comprehensive data to those who are asked to shoulder the responsibility of educational reform.
7. *Assessment of an Institution*: School records are helpful to assess the progress and needs of particular locality.
8. *Cooperation of Parents*: To make the parents interested in school work and in their wards, schools send progress reports from time-to-time. This helps in establishing closer contacts between the home and the school.

9. *Examination and Evaluation Needs*. Promotions of students are made on their performance which is reflected through the records of tests and examinations.

10. *Guidance and Counselling*: Records of performance of students on psychological tests and measurement prove very helpful in the counselling process.

11. *Future Reference*: It is only through records that the history of the school can be written. Past records may also help in improving the tone of the school and its performance.

26.3 NEED OF SCHOOL RECORDS FOR THE SCHOOL MANAGEMENT, CLASSROOM TEACHERS AND PUPILS

L.M. Camberlain and L.W. Kidred give the following advantages of the school records:

Need of Records for the School

1. To locate each pupil quickly.
2. To make available the significant facts about each pupil.
3. To explain and remove undesirable conditions.
4. To find if all legal requirements are met.
5. To determine if any administrative or other changes are desirable.
6. To make important investigations and case studies possible.
7. To find if school funds are adequate and wisely expended.
8. To reduce retardation and failure to a minimum.

Need of Records for the Classroom Teachers

1. To determine what work a pupil is capable of doing.
2. To provide learning activities suitable to each pupil.
3. To formulate a basis for the intelligent guidance of pupils.
4. To explain the behaviour characteristics or unhappy conditions of any pupil.
5. To make possible the development of unusual capacities or exceptional talents.
6. To identify and make proper provision for the mentally slow children.
7. To make assignments to committee work.
8. To make periodic reports correctly and in time.
9. To be properly informed when conferring with parents and others about a pupil.
10. To make entries in the cumulative record card.

Need of Records for the Pupil

1. To receive fair consideration in his classification.
2. To do his best in making a good record.
3. To make progress in accordance with his ability.
4. To secure development of his natural capabilities.
5. To secure transfer of correct information to other schools when desired.
6. To receive proper adjustment and guidance.

25.4 MAINTENANCE AND ESSENTIAL REQUISITES OF SCHOOL RECORDS

1. *Accuracy*: All information contained in the school records should be accurate, well organised, pertinent and justified solely on grounds of the contribution it can make either directly or indirectly to the welfare of the students.

2. *Completeness*: Data about a child should be gathered continuously, should be kept up-to-date and include information that reveals his true condition at any given time. In the case of his transfer from one school to another, his records should follow hi...

3. *Utility*: Record system should provide for collecting and recording information that ... relevant and useful in working with children.

4. *Comp...ensiveness*: In view of the emphasis on the harmonious develop...t of the child, different kinds of records will have to be kept. All memb... of the staff have a responsibility for keeping records peculiar to the... eld of activity.

... *Easy Maintenance*: The records and reports should be easily maintained ...d should require a minimum of time and energy for making entries.

6. *Systematic Maintenance*: School records should be maintained and located where they will be used to the greatest advantage by staff personnel. Separate files or note-books should be kept for each separate record o... report.

7. *Availability*: School records should always be available in th... ...hool premises and school not be removed from the school premises fo... purpose of scrutiny.

A record system then should be designed carefully, ke... ...iciently, located strategically and should contain all informatio... ...at is essential to the achievement of the aim for which it was est...ished.

26.5 MODE OF K...PING RECORDS

1. Prepare a stock list of r...ters maintained in the school.
2. Write distinctly th... ...llowing particulars on the outer cover of each register.
   (a) The ...e of the school.
   (b) T... serial number of the register.
   (... The name of the register.
   (d) The number of volume.
   (e) The number of pages of the volume.
   (f) The opening and closing dates.
3. Number the pages consecutively either in the red ink or with a number machine when a register is opened.
4. Keep the register tidy. Avoid overwriting.
5. Make all the entries in ink.
6. Get each cutting attested by the Head.
7. Do not open a new volume of a register every year, if the previous volume contains some blank pages.

8. Fill up every column provided in a prescribed register and do not leave any blank space between entries.

School Office: As a general rule every higher secondary or senior secondary school must have one separate room for office. The office-in-charge must be a person trained for the type of work to be done in schools. The head must be relieved of the mechanical details of the officer routine if he is to make the best use of his abilities and to discharge his functions of guidance and counselling and supervising. The school office should be spacious and well ventilated.

26.6 BROAD CLASSIFICATION OR TYPE OF SCHOOL RECORDS

1. Accounts
2. Correspondence
3. Educational
4. Equipment
5. Financial
6. General or Miscellaneous
7. Service
8. Vocational or Productive

1. *Accounts Register:* (i) Cashbook for daily receipts and expend. (ii) General Ledger or Classified Abstract of the monthly totals, (iii) Regis of pay bill, and (iv) Remittance register.

2. *Correspondence*: (i) 'From' and 'To' Registers, (ii) Peon Book, (iii) Memo Book, (iv) File of Departmental Orders and Circulars, and (v) Register of Casual Leave Granted.

3. *Educational*: (i) Pupil's Attendance Register, (ii) Teachers' Attendance Register, (iii) Time-tables' Records, (iv) Examinations' Results Record, (v) Monthly Progress Register, (vi) Private Tuition Register, (vii) Public Examination Register, (viii) Register of Corporal Punishment, (ix) Teacher's Diaries, (x) Cumulative Records, (xi) Staff participation in Orientational Courses, and (xii) Honours Roll.

4. *Equipment*: (i) Stock Book of Furniture and School Appliances, (ii) Library Catalogue, (iii) Accession Register, (iv) Issue Book, (v) Register of Newspapers and Magazines received, (vi) Stock and Issue Register of Sports Materials.

5. *Financial*: (i) Contingent Register, (ii) Acquittance Roll, (iii) Contingent Order Book, (iv) Fee Collection Register, (v) Abstract Register of Fees, (vi) Bill Register, (vii) Register of Donations, (viii) Register of Scholarship, and (ix) Boys' Fund Registers.

6. *General Records*: (i) School Calendar, (ii) Log Book, (iii) Visitor's Book, (iv) Service Registers, (v) Admission and Withdrawal Register, (vi) Transfer Certificate Book, (vii) General Order Book, (viii) Casual Leave Register, and (ix) Staff Meeting.

7. *Service Matters*: (i) Personal Files and (ii) Service condition rules, etc.

8. *Vocational/Production/Related to Socially Useful Productive Work*: (i) Craft Work, (ii) Farm Work, (iii) Producer's Register (iv) Art Work Record etc.

Note: The list is no way a comprehensive and complete one. It includes only those registers which are commonly used. Additions will have to be made to suit the needs and requirements of individual schools. A few of the important school records, relating mainly to the educational aspect of school administration are described below.

26.7 DESCRIPTION OF SOME IMPORTANT RECORDS

Teachers' Attendance Register. This register shows the daily attendance of the teachers in a school, their time of arrival and departure, leave taken by then, holidays and their nature. It is generally placed in the Head Office. Every teacher must sign this register everyday when he comes into the school in the morning and leave at the termination of the school day.

Pupils' Attendance Register. Each class has its own register showing the names of the pupils on the rolls of a class. As far as possible, only one attendance register should be kept by any one teacher. Attendance should be marked both for the beginning of the school day in the morning and its end towards the evening. Ink or ball pen should be used for marking attendance. No blanks should be left. It is also not a good practice to put dots. The students are to be marked as 'leave' or 'sick' only when their leave applications are sanctioned by the competent authority. Holidays should be indicated in red ink. The name of a student may be struck off the rolls by the head of the school on account of (a) Non-payment of fees and other dues for 20 days after the last day for payment. This is not applicable in case of students of Class VIII and below, studying in government or aided schools or in schools run or aided by the appropriate authority except where such students have attained the age of fourteen years; (b) Continued absence without leave for six consecutive days by a student who has attained the age of fourteen years; (c) In the case of absence of any student, who has not attained the age of fourteen years, from a school without leave for six consecutive days, the head of the school shall intimate such absence to the parents or guardian of such student.

Notes: 1. The above mentioned rules are contained in Delhi School Education Act and Rules.

2. There may be different rules in States.

The reason for this action should be given in the remarks column against the name of the boy or girl and the necessary information should be given to the school clerk. The entries thus made should be got signed by the Head simultaneously both in the attendance register and withdrawal register. On the last working day of each month, the summary at the end of each page in the register should be carefully prepared and the register got checked by the teacher deputed for this purpose and then got countersigned by the Head. All amounts received by way of fees and funds must be entered in the register immediately on their receipt.

Truant students should be noted particularly and their cases reported to the Head and the parents concerned.

Leave application for long sick periods should be supported by medical certificates.

Admission and Withdrawal Register

This is one of the most important school registers. The head of the institution is personally responsible for its sanctity. According to departmental rules, it is to be kept permanently, and therefore, it should be specially got bound and arrangements made for its safe custody. Entries should be made as soon as a pupil is admitted or at any rate before the close of the day. Every admission or readmission made in any part of the year should be entered in it. Successive numbers should be given to the pupils on admission. Each child should retain this number as long as he remains in the school. A new entry should be made if a pupil leaves a school and rejoins it with a leaving certificate issued by another school. This register contains the following information: (a) The number of the child in the register. (b) Date of admission or readmission. (c) Name of the child in full. (d) The exact date of birth of the child. (e) Name and address of the parent or guardian. (f) The class to which admitted. (g) The date of leaving and the class in which the child was at that time.

Special care is to be taken in recording the date of birth of every child. The entry once made should not be altered unless authorised by competent authority and that too in writing. The entries are to be made both in words as well as in figures. The exact day of birth is very important as it is also required as evidence in important matters.

Stock of Non-consumable Articles

All items of a more or less permanent nature bought and received in the school are entered in the property register. It contains the name of the article, its price and the ordering authority for its purchase.

The Head should get the stock of equipment checked once a year. Room-wise property list facilitates the work of checking. Proper checking of the equipment has a very good advantage. It helps the Head to know which article of equipment or furniture stands in needs of repairs or is missing.

Nothing should be struck off the register without the permission of the Head who is generally competent to do so.

Ledger: It is a necessary complement the cash-book. All entries made in the cash-book are carried to the ledger in their respective accounts. It facilitates the preparation of monthly and annual accounts. It is also helpful in controlling future financial commitments.

Contingency Register: Every Head is generally provided with a contingency advance money for day-to-day expenses on petty items such as purchase of office stationery, postage, repairs to building and furniture, etc. Details of such expenditure are entered in the contingency register. All entries in this register are supported by proper receipts which are placed in a separate file.

Boys' Fund Register: The Head of an institution is the sole in-charge of the boys' funds. He is responsible for keeping a regular account of the same and rendering it to the departmental auditors and the inspecting staff.

All income and expenditure pertaining to boys' fund should be entered regularly in the Boys' Fund Register.

It will not be out of place to mention that most of the problems in our educational institutions owe their origin to the use of these funds. Undue funds charged from the students lead to indiscipline. Wrong use of funds leads them to suspect the integrity of the authorities. Unfortunately the present trend is to use funds for all sundry purposes. A wise head will make a very judicious use of these funds. He will take his students into confidence and spend these funds through their committees working under the guidance of teachers.

Accounts and Financial Records

Cash-book: It contains a record of all money transactions that are being carried through from day-to-day in the school. The credit side of the cash-book shows all the monies received by the school from different sources, e.g. donations, grants-in-aid, fees, boys' funds, etc. and its debit side indicates all the payments made, e.g. salaries paid, deposits made in the post office or bank, contingent expenditure incurred, etc.

Cash-book should be well bound and the pages should be carefully numbered in print.

Cash-book should be written up daily. The entry relating to each item of receipt and expenditure should be made immediately at the time of transaction.

As far as possible, the cash balance should be immediately deposited in the post office or bank. Daily balancing of the cash-book avoids chances of errors.

Miscellaneous Records

Service Register: The register contains the record of the official life of every employee working in the institution. On the basis of this record matters concerning promotions, leave, superannuation, etc. are determined. It is, therefore, very important to make correct and complete entries in it. The entries in the service register should tally with other records. The date and the number of the appointment order should be noted in the case of the first appointment and in the case of transfers. No change in the date of birth is permissible except with the permission of the competent authority. All cases of suspension, or other punishment should be noted along with the reasons and the authority awarding the punishment. All questions relating to previous service should be settled immediately. Service registers should not be handed over to the persons concerned on their transfer from one school to another but should be sent to the officer responsible for the custody of the registers. Every Head should make it a point to ensure that the registers are free from faults of omission and erroneous insertion.

School Calendar: The school calendar is very conducive to the better and more systematic organisation of school activities. It is drawn up at the beginning of each school session. If possible all schools in the same area should have a uniform school year so that the migrating children are not handicapped and put to troubles. It should contain the following items of information:

(i) All types of holidays.

(ii) Dates for the submission of monthly, quarterly, half-yearly and annual reports and returns.

(iii) Dates of public and school examinations.
(iv) Dates of Meeting of School Committees, Teachers' Associations, Local Excursions, School Tournament, etc.
(v) Schedule of monthly tests.

The Log Book: In our schools it is devoted to the remarks of the inspecting staff in relation to the school and the members of the school staff.

Teacher's Diary

Meaning of a Teacher's Diary: By a teacher's diary, we mean the diary in which a teacher maintains the broad outline of the teaching-learning records of a year.

Contents of a Teacher's Diary: In general, following types of information is included in a teacher's diary.

1. Details of the syllabi of the subjects the teacher teaches in different classes.
2. Methodology of the teaching-learning adopted in each lesson he teaches daily.
3. Daily lesson notes or main points.
4. Students' names and their addresses.
5. Significant details about children under his charge.
6. Names of the gifted children and their specific achievements and problems.
7. Particulars of weak students and steps taken to improve them.
8. Particulars of problem children.
9. Parents contacted.
10. Anything special.

Importance of Teacher's Diary

1. It is helpful to the teacher in planning his daily work.
2. It assists the teacher in bringing order in work.
3. It develops motivation in work.
4. It is helpful in making lesson effective.
5. It is a constant reminder to the teacher that the syllabus must be covered according to schedule.
6. It enable him to prepare aids before the lesson is taken up in the class.
7. It provides an opportunity to the head to provide guidance to the teacher after going through the diary.

The head can evaluate the day-to-day work of the teacher on this bases.

26.8 SPECIMEN OF SCHOOL RECORDS

1. Specimen of Simple Progress Report

Name of the School ....

Month ....

Student's Progress Records for the Term

Students name.. Class...

Admission name .... Date of birth...............................

Father's Name .... Address of Parent/Guardian ....

Academic

Subject	*Max Marks*	*Marks obtained or Grade*	*Position*	*Subject Teacher's Remarks*
Regional Language				
Second Language				
English				
Elementary Maths				
General Science				
Social Studies				
Art/Domestic Science				
Craft Training				
Work Experience				
Diversified Courses				
1.				
2.				
3.				
4.				
5.				
tal				

Co-curricular Activities and Citizenship

Games a *Practical Activities*	*Remarks*
Social Behav	
Cleanliness	
Attendance	
Conduct	
Hand-Writing	
Home Work	
Health	

C ass Teacher's Signature

Guar ian/Parent's Signature

(*Note:* Type of progress report de ... on the nature of activities

Signature

2. ADMISSION AND WITHDRAWAL REGISTER

Date of Admission	Admission No.	Name of the Students	Father's/ Guardians Name	Mother's Name	Date of Birth (In Words and Figures)	Enrolment No./ Registration No.	Occupation	Present Residential Address	Tele-phone No.	Tribe or Caste	Class to Which Admitted	Grade or Tuition Fee	Caution Money Taken	Class of Withdrawal	Date of Withdrawal	Remarks

3. DAILY CLASS ATTENDANCE REGISTER

Sl. No.	Admission No.	Class ……………. Section…………… Name of Scholar	DAYS OF THE MONTH																											
			1		2		3		4		5		6		7		8		9		10		11		12		13		…		31	
			M 1	A 2	M 1	A 2	M 1	A 2	M 1	A 2	M 1	A 2	M 1	A 2	M 1	A 2	M 1	A 2	M 1	A 2	M 1	A 2	M 1	A 2	M 1	A 2	M 1	A 2	… …	… …	M 1	A 2

No. of Scholars at the beginning of the month ……………
No. of Scholars at the close of the month ……………
No. of Scholars struck of the rolls ……………
New Admissions ……………
No. of School Meetings during the month ……………
No. of School Meetings from 1st April ……………
Total No. of attendances during the month ……………
Average daily attendances during the month ……………

Total No. of Students on roll ……………

Sch. Cast……… OBC ……… Others …………

.... School FOR THE MONTH OF ....

4. TEACHERS ATTENDACE REGISTER

NAME																								
DESIGNA - TION																								
DATE	ARR.	SIGNA.		DEP.	SIGNA.		ARR.	SIGNA.		DEP.	SIGNA.		ARR.	SIGNA.		DEP.	SIGNA.		ARR.	SIGNA.		DEP.	SIGNA.	

LEAVES TAKEN

	Sick	Casu.	Priv.	Ear. L	H/P. L.	Total	Sick	Casu.	Priv.	Ear. L	H/P.L.	Total	Sick	Casu.	Priv.	Ear. L	H/P.L.	Total	Sick	Casu.	Priv.	Ear. L	H/P. L.	Total
This Mon.																								
Previous																								
TOTAL																								
Balance																								
TOTAL																								
Tea's.Ini.																								
Special L.																								
Principal's Remarks																								

5. TEACHER DIARY REGISTER

Week Date	Forecast	Amount Taught	Class & Subject	Notes & Observation by the Teacher	Remarks by Principal or Inspector
Date	Home Task for the Week				

6. STOCK REGISTER (FOR CONSUMABLE ARTICLES)

Name of the Institution .... Page No. ....

Name of the Article ....

Date of Receipt	Quantity of Number	Value. (Rs.)	Progressive Total	Quantity Consumer	How Consumed	Signature of the receiving authority	Balance	Signature of the Head of Institution	Remarks

7. STOCK REGISTER
Non-Consumable

Name of the Institution .... Page No. ....

Name of the Article ....

S. No.	Date of Receipt	Quantity Received	Description of Articles inclu. specification and make	Condition old or new	Value (Rs.)	Progressive Total	No. Disposed	Manner of Disposal	Amount realised (Rs.)	Balance Qty.	Signature of Head of Institu.	Remarks

8. DESPATCH REGISTER

Name of the Institution .... Page No. ....

S. No.	Date	Name & Address	Place	Subject	File Head./No.	Stamps Received (Rs.)	Stamps Affixed (Rs.)	Stamps Balance (Rs.)	Remarks

9. CASH BOOK

For the month of ____

RECEIPTS | PAYMENTS

Date	Particulars	Ledger Folio	Cash (Rs.)	Bank (Rs.)		Date	Particulars	Ledger Folio	Cash (Rs.)	Bank (Rs.)

10. LEDGER

Date	Particulars	C.B. Folio	Debit Rs.	Credit Rs.	Dr. or Cr.	Balance Rs.

....School

11. AQUITTANCE ROLL/PAY BILL

for the Month of ....

S. No.	Name	Designation	Monthly Pay		No. of Days	Basic Pay		Stagnating Pay/Personal Pay		D.A.		H.R.A.		C.C.A.		Interim Relief		Teaching Allowance		Medical	
			Rs.	P.		Rs.	P.	Rs.	P.	Rs.	P.	Rs.	P.	Rs.	P.	Rs.	P.	Rs.	P.	Rs.	P.

Washing Allowance		Total		DEDUCTIONS										Total Deductions		Balance Paid		Cheque No.	Payee's Signature with date	Remarks
				I. Tax		G.P.F.		T.B.S.		L.I.C./G.I.C.		Loan								
Rs.	P.	Rs.	P.	Rs.	P.	Rs.	P.	Rs.	P.	Rs.	P.	Rs.	P.	Rs.	P.	Rs.	P.			

27

Organising School Library

27.1 IMPORTANCE OF THE SCHOOL LIBRARY: LIBRARY AS THE HUB AND CENTRE OF SCHOOL LIFE

The Secondary Education Commission has very beautifully described the significance of the school library. "The library will be the hub and the centre of the intellectual and literary life of the recognised school and play the same part vis-a-vis all the other subjects as the laboratory plays for science subjects and the workshop for technical subjects".

In the words of K.G. Saiyidain, "No School or University without a library, adequate for its needs and size should be recognised as a worthy centre of education".

According to Bacon, "Libraries are the shelves where all the relics of saints full of virtue and that without delusion and importance are reposed".

The modern philosophy of education stresses more on the child's learning through experience than on anything else. "Individual work, the pursuit of group projects, many academic hobbies and co-curricular activities postulate the existence of a good, efficiently managed library", wrote the Secondary Education Commission. So library—a good library—is one of the essentials of a school. Oliver Lodge writes, "Part of education should consist in familiarity and practice with the looking up of details with the use of books in general, not only of books of reference".

The dynamic role and the educational possibilities of the school library have long been realised in all progressive countries. In countries like the United States and Great Britain, the school libraries are usually well equipped and are used very profitably in the education of children.

27.2 IMPORTANT FUNCTIONS OF A SCHOOL LIBRARY

Edmonson has described the functions of a school library as, "The modern school library is conceived as a service unit. It supplies materials for developing and expanding interests through the reference tools, indexes, bibliographies and catalogues, the realm of knowledge may be explored. The library cooperates with other agencies of instruction in helping students learn to use books and libraries, to find information, and to study. By its bulletin exhibits, posters and atmosphere, the library teaches informally. By its introduction to books, it suggests the life-time use of reading to further any interest".

A properly organised school library serves the following functions:

1. *Self-Study Opportunities*: It provides opportunities for self-study and self-education. It supplements class work by increasing students' vocabulary. There is no doubt that it is not possible for a single student to afford to purchase all the books that he needs. The school library helps him to read a large number of books.

2. *Broadening of Interest*: It broadens the outlook of the students by placing before them a vast store of useful information that has accumulated through the ages.

3. *Helpful Participation in Co-curricular Programme*: It assists the students to prepare themselves for taking part in the various co-curricular activities like debates, declamation contests and writing for the school magazine for a lot of literature is available.

4. *Source of Inspirational Books*: A good library service helps the students to turn to inspirational books which may enable their lives.

5. *Widening of General Knowledge*: It tends to develop habits of the students to derive pleasure and information from recreational and informative books.

6. *Leisure Time Hobby*: Library reading is a good leisure time hobby and it provides an opportunity for the right use of one's leisure time and thus conserves the time and energy otherwise to be used in card-games, etc.

7. *Training in the Proper Use of Books*: The library imparts training to the student in the proper use of books. The library rules demand that the books should be well kept and thus the students develop in them the habit of keeping books neat and tidy. H.C. Dent observes, "With a good school library widely used, it is possible to teach children how to use books efficiently—a lesson all of us must learn if we are to get the most out of them. It is a lesson not too easily learnt, and far too rarely taught".

8. *Development of Study Habits*: The library develops the habits of silent reading. Reading, borrowing and returning are the watch-words of a library room.

9. *Constructive Discipline*: It lessens the chance of indiscipline in the school by providing an opportunity to the students to make the best use of leisure time.

10. *Moral Training*: The library imparts training in punctuality by impressing upon the students the necessity of borrowing and returning books in time.

11. *Use of Dynamic and Progressive Methods of Teaching-Learning*: A well developed library is a must for the use of methods like Dalton and the Project.

Summing Up: The functions of the school library may be summed up in the words of the Joint Committee of the School Library Association in Britain, We seek in the library to make children familiar with the sight and use of a collection of books and to help them to grow to love and care for them, to provide material for child's own recreational reading and explorations, to supply additional reading material illustrating the subjects taught in class, to give opportunities for elementary instruction in the use of books and for carrying out group and individual projects, to give scope for the exercising of simple responsibilities and finally to prepare the way for the use of larger libraries including public library, in adult life".

27.3 STATE OF SCHOOL LIBRARIES IN INDIA

The Secondary Education Commission lamented on the sad state of affairs of our school libraries. It observed that our libraries are not worth the name and, therefore, do not inspire students to cultivate the love for knowledge. Our schools do not seem to have been influenced by the new trends in education and especially in the matter school library organisation.

The Secondary Education Commission listed the main defects of the existing libraries. Though several decades have passed since the observations were made, the conditions, by and large, remain the same. Important defects are as under:

First, the books are usually old, outdated, unsuitable, selected without reference to the students' tastes and interests.

Secondly, there is a lack of suitable books for children.

Thirdly, books are stocked in a few book-shelves.

Fourthly, generally speaking there are no trained librarians in schools and library work is entrusted to teachers who are very busy in their teaching work and show little interest in library work.

Fifthly, school library is generally housed in an inadequate and unattractive room.

Sixthly, the general tendency of the school authorities is not to encourage students to read extra books.

Seventhly, the books are beyond the comprehension of students.

Eighthly, the books do not meet the needs of the students. Teachers generally stuff the library with those books which they need for some examination or some other purpose.

Factors Responsible for the Poor Condition of School Libraries

These are:

1. Domination of examinations.
2. Defective curriculum.
3. Undue emphasis on prescribed text-books.
4. Over emphasis on textual knowledge.
5. Very little use of progressive methods.
6. Failure to appreciate the value of school library.

27.4 MAIN CHARACTERISTICS OF A WELL MANAGED SCHOOL LIBRARY

Rabindra Nath Tagore has given a very good description of a good library in these words, "My idea of a small library is one that keeps books on every subject, but only select books, not one of which is there merely as an offering of worship to number, but each one of which stands on its own merit; where the librarian is a true devotee, devoid of ulterior seeking, free from pride in the mere loading of shelves, capable of discriminate rejection. A library, in short, which makes just enough provision that can be placed before its guests for their delectation, with a librarian who has the qualities of a host, not a storekeeper".

Organisation of a Good Library

The organisation of a good library may be discussed under the following heads:

1. The librarian
2. Books
3. Cataloguing
4. Library rules
5. Library room and equipment

I. *The Librarian*

The Secondary Education Commission observed that "if the library is to be hub of the academic and intellectual life of the school, if it is not only to meet but also to guide the reading interests of the students, if it is to work as a centre of free and supervised study as well as group work on projects undertaken by them—if it is to do all these things, the librarian will surely have to be wide awake and remain active."

Arnold Benett states that "if libraries spend less on books and more on educated staff, far better results would be obtained." A librarian should possess the following qualifications:

(i) General education.
(ii) Professional, i.e. indexing and cataloguing.
(iii) Pedagogical, i.e. adept in child psychology, familiar with the present trends in the educational field, sympathetic nature, etc.

A librarian is expected to perform the following functions:

1. Preparing and displaying library rules and regulations.
2. Preparing catalogues.
3. Classifying books.
4. Numbering books.
5. Stocking books properly.
6. Training students in the art of looking up reference and other material.
7. Instructing students to keep books neat and tidy.
8. Taking annual stock of books.
9. Making plans for the purchase of books of different types.
10. Attaining skills in the use of modern technological aids like computers etc.
11. Making an environment of perfect silence and conducive to self-study.
12. Displaying cuttings and foldings on the new books and journals etc. on the library notice board.

II. *Books*

According to Secondary Education Commission, the guiding principle in selection should not be the teachers' own idea of what books the students must read but their natural and psychological interests. The contents of a library may be classified as:

1. *Books for Younger Children*: Well illustrated and attractive books giving information on fairy tales and fables, etc.

2. *Books for Older Children*:
   (i) Books depicting stories of travels, explorations, adventures. Discoveries and inventions.
   (ii) Biographies of great men and women.
   (iii) Suitable works of fiction, fun and hobbies.
   (iv) Parallel text-book.
   (v) Books on different subjects.

3. *Reference Books*:
   (a) Source books.
   (b) Dictionaries.
   (c) Encyclopaedias.

4. *Books for Teachers*: A faculty committee including representative of each department should be appointed with the librarian as the convener. The committee should determine policies for the development of the library, draw up rules, governing its use and use funds in such a way as each department of the school work is provided for equitably.

5. *Books for Adults*: To serve as a centre of community service, the school library should contain books for adults also.

III. *Cataloguing*

Views of Tagore are worth noting when he writes, "The usual thing is for a library to say: Here is my catalogue, come and select for yourself. But in the usual catalogue there is no introduction, no invitation, no spirit of welcome. The library alone can be called hospitable, which shows an eagerness to invite readers to the feast at its disposal. It is such hospitality that makes a library big, not its size. That the readers make the library is not the whole truth, the library likewise makes the readers".

IV. *Library Rules*

Among other rules, the following must be included:
   (i) Library periods may be allotted.
   (ii) For the changing and distribution of books, a certain time may be fixed.
   (iii) Each student may be asked to keep a diary wherein name of the books read with date and comments be entered.

V. *Library Room and Equipment*

Regarding this, S.R. Ranganathan observes, "It should be equipped with plenty of attractive, well built, well printed, well illustrated, with comfortable furniture, open shelves, charming pictures, flowers, hangings and bright and cheerful outlook, with a librarian who loves children as well as books".

Reading, lending, borrowing and returning should be the watchwords of a library room. Spitting, smoking, noise making, sleeping, and quarrelling should be prohibited.

27.5 ENCOURAGING STUDENTS TO MAKE THE BEST USE OF SCHOOL LIBRARY

Usually it is observed that the students do not take adequate interest in the use of school library. Only a very negligible number of students make the profitable use of library material. Concerted efforts are needed to develop their interest in this regard. Following measures may be adopted towards the end:

1. The library should be made the most attractive place in the school so that it may attract the students in large numbers.
2. The cooperation of the students should be sought in decorating the library in order to give them the feeling that the library belongs to them.
3. The librarian should behave very sympathetically with the students.
4. Books suiting different tastes and interests should be provided in large numbers.
5. The teachers should give occasional talks to pupils on the importance of extra-reading.
6. The librarian should give thorough instructions to the students in not only how to find out books and other material in the library but also how to make the best use of the material which the library contains.
7. Library periods should be provided for each class in the time-table.
8. As far as possible the open shelf system should be introduced so that the students may have free access to books.
9. Students should be asked to maintain a diary in which they should enter date-wise the names of all the books they have read. They may also be asked to write brief quotations or extracts from the books that may appeal to them. They may also write short reviews and appreciation of these books.
10. Marks may be allotted for extra-reading and entered in the monthly progress report.
11. Book competitions should be arranged from time-to-time and questions on titles, authors and subject-matter may be set.
12. The school library should be kept open during the vacation and long holidays.
13. The beautiful picture-cuttings from newspapers and illustrations from current events and topics should be displayed on the library Bulletin Boards.
14. The furniture should be according to the needs of the students.
15. A catalogue of library books should be available in the library for ready reference.
16. Library Day may be organised once a year to popularise the school library.

We may sum up the discussion with a quotation from Tagore, "In order to bring a library into the fullest use, it is necessary that its contents should be clearly and specifically brought to notice, otherwise it is difficult for the ordinary man to find his way about them, and the library is left as a city of vast accommodation that lacks sufficient means of communication. Those who frequently visit libraries on some special quest of their own may manage to make a track for themselves by dint of the urgency of their particular pursuit. But the library itself should recognise its share of responsibility in the matter. Because it has the books, it is incumbent on the library to get them read, for then alone it is justified. It is not enough that it passively permits visitors; its invitation should be active. For, as the Sanskrit proverb tells us *tannashtam yannadiyate*, that which is not given is wasted".

27.6 CENTRAL OR CLASS LIBRARY

Both of these have got a definite place in the school. By classroom library we mean library in the room of each class. It contains well selected books suited to the needs of the class. Class library is not competitive to central library. It should supplement the work of the central library. "The class library is an important and essential adjunct to the central school library," writes the Secondary Education Commission. It has great educational potentialities.

Classroom library is easier to administer. It does not require an elaborate method of recording.

Its organisation can very easily be entrusted in the hands of the students thus giving them an opportunity to manage their own affairs.

Classroom library affords opportunities to the teachers to see how much reading each pupil is doing and can thus encourage the keen students and stimulate the slow goers. The teachers can also test whether the pupils are reading carefully and intelligently.

As a class teacher spends much of his time with the students, he is in a better position to suggest suitable books to the students according to their tastes and aptitudes.

Subject Libraries

The Secondary Education Commission recommends that besides the class library in every high school, there should be subject-libraries under the charge of subject teachers. In addition to text-books, there should be advanced works, reference books, books on related subjects and allied fields. Such collections will help the teachers in enriching their teaching greatly. The students also will get a wide view of the subject in all its bearings.

27.7 ROLE OF THE TEACHERS IN ENCOURAGING STUDENTS TO USE LIBRARY

Teachers and librarians must make concerted attempts to break down the old barriers that completely separate library and classroom. They must join together so that students make the optimum use of school library.

The teacher should acquaint themselves with the contents and interesting aspects of books and other reading material within the school library and inform students accordingly.

In the day-to-day classroom teaching, they should make pointed reference to important books and other reading materials available in the school library.

They should guide the students as to the type of books they should read.

The teachers may give assignments and project work which the students may complete independently by self-study.

They may maintain records of books read by the students.

They may give extra credit to the students when they read supplementary books.

28

Organisation of Co-Curricular Activities

28.1 CONCEPT OF CO-CURRICULAR ACTIVITIES

Co-curricular activities are those activities, which are undertaken side by side the curricular activities, i.e. instruction of various subjects They supplement curricular activities and prepare the students in the 'Art of Living and Working Together'.

In the past, co-curricular activities were mainly organised after school hours and, therefore, were called extra-curricular. But now they are treated as integral part of the activities of the school as its curricular work and their proper organisation needs just as much care and forethought. The Secondary Education Commission remarks, "Given a clean, pleasant and well maintained school building, we would like the school to see if it can provide a richly varied, pattern of activities to cater to the development of their children's entire personality. It has to formulate a scheme of hobbies, occupations and projects that will appeal to, and draw out the powers of children of varying temperaments and aptitudes".

These activities are as old as education itself though their scope was not so vast as it is today. Monitor system was one of the important institutions of the ancient Indian system of education. The Gurukulas of old were residential institutions providing opportunities of social contacts on a large scale.

In Athens and Sparta, student participation in organising activities like athletics and music was very common.

28.2 TYPES OF CO-CURRICULAR ACTIVITIES

Broadly speaking co-curricular activities may be categorised under thirteen heads, although there are no water-tight compartments as the activities overlap.

Chart Showing Types of Co-Curricular Activities

(1) Academic Development Activities
(2) Aesthetic Development Activities
(3) Cultural Development Activities
(4) Emotional Development Activities
(5) Leisure Utilisation Activities
(6) Literary Development Activities
(7) Moral Development Activities
(8) Physical Development Activities
(9) Productive Activities
(10) Social Development Activities
(11) Scientific Temperament Development Activities
(12) Spiritual Development Activities
(13) Vocational Oriented Activities

Academic Development Activities

- Preparation of Charts, Models, etc.
- Subject Clubs, e.g., Economics Clubs, Geographical Clubs
- Projects
- Symposiums
- Surveys
- Quiz

Aesthetic Development Activities

- Sculpture
- Dramatics
- Drawing
- Exhibitions
- Fancy Dress
- Music
- Painting
- School Decoration

Citizenship Training Activities

- Visit to Assembly and Parliament
- Cooperative Store
- Students Council
- Youth Parliament
- Social Service

Cultural Development Activities

- Dancing
- Drawing and Painting
- Celebration of Festivals
- Visits to Cultural Places

Emotional and Integration Development Activities

- Camps
- Celebration of National and International Days
- Educational Tours
- Speeches

Leisure Time Activities

- Album Making
- Coin Collecting
- Photography
- Stamp Collecting

Literary Development Activities

- Brain trusts
- Declamation contests
- Debates
- Recitation
- Library work
- Public speaking

Moral Development Activities

- Celebration of birth-days of great men
- Lectures
- Morning assembly
- Social service

Productive Activities

- Card board work
- Clay work
- Embroidery
- Craft work
- Leather work
- Kitchen gardening
- Soap making
- Toy making

Physical Development Activities

- Athletics
- Cycling
- Mass drill
- NCC
- Swimming
- Yogic
- Indoor and Outdoor

Social Value Development Activities

- Girl guiding
- Scouting
- Labour week
- First Aid
- Red Cross
- Community Service

Scientific Temper Development Activities

- Science clubs
- Science quizs
- Science fairs
- Visits to places of scientific importance
- Science models

Multipurpose Activities and Projects

- Beautification & cleanliness of school campus
- Social service
- Social surveys
- Tree plantation
- Adult education
- Community service and awareness

28.3 IMPORTANCE OF CO-CURRICULAR ACTIVITIES

The remarks of the Secondary Education Commission (1952-53) on the role of the co-curricular activities are worth noting: "The school is not merely a place of formal learning whose main concern is to communicate a certain prescribed quantum of knowledge but rather as a living and organic community which is primarily interested in training its pupils in what we have called the 'gracious art of living'. Knowledge and learning are undoubtedly of value, but they must be acquired as a by-product of interested activity because it is only then that they can become a vital part of the student's mind and personality and influence his behaviour. 'Art of living' is much more comprehensive concept than the acquisition of knowledge, however intelligently planned. It includes training in the habit and graces of social life and the capacity for cooperative group work. It calls for patience, good temper, sincerity, fellow-feeling and discipline. These objectives can only be cultivated in the context of the social life and the many co-curricular activities must find a recognised place in any schools".

The Indian Education Commission (1964-66) stressed the importance of co-curricular activities in these words, "We conceive of the school curriculum as the totality of the learning experience that the school provides for the pupils through all the manifold activities, in the school or outside, that are carried on under its supervision. From the point of view, the distinction between curricular and extra-curricular work ceases to exist, and a school camp and games are curricular or rather co-curricular activities".

Important Values of Co-curricular Activities

The educational values of co-curricular activities are many as well as varied. Some of the important values derived from these are detailed here.

1. *Academic Development and Growth*: The teaching of civics, composition, history, geography, etc. can be greatly supplemented. Election to the students council would give them a picture of Central and State elections. Excursions to historical, geographical and industrial places enrich the experience of the students. Writing for the school magazine supplements the teaching of languages. Similarly there are many practical activities which afford opportunities to supplement classroom work.

2. *Development of Aesthetic Values*: It is common knowledge that aesthetic sensibility cannot be taught but it is caught and developed through real programmes. Participation in dances, dramatics, fancy dresses, flower shows, etc. by the students provide them opportunities to appreciate and develop aesthetic values.

3. *Civic Training*: The school should be a training ground for democracy. It should be organised and administered on democratic lines. The introduction of self-government provides experience of the life of a democratic society. In this, pupils determine the policies and the programmes. They plan and present assembly programmes. The individual pupil learns how to conduct a meeting in an approved parliamentary style. It gives him an opportunity to exercise his vote. While working together, the students learn that rights involve responsibilities. They get valuable lessons in cooperation which can be learnt by practice. In order to retain his position as a member in a Students Council, Athletic team, etc. a student has to learn to cooperate.

4. *Community Relations*: Social service activities bring closer the school and the society. Students also earn appreciation of the society for the good work done by them.

5. *Cultural Values*: Activities like visits, celebrations of community festivals, dance, drama etc. enable the students to appreciate cultural heritage and develop cultural values.

6. *Dignity of Labour*: In activities like camps and social service, students develop the value of dignity of labour.

7. *Disciplinary Values*: Discipline becomes self-discipline. The students remain busy and different kinds of activities develop their talents in different directions. They make laws for the various societies and come to realise the need for showing respect to other school laws.

8. *Followership Qualities*: By participating in student government, students learn that followership and leadership go hand in hand. Both are complementary and supplementary.

9. *Guidance and Counselling*: Students get opportunities to know their assets and liabilities. The teachers and especially the school counsellor come to know them better and accordingly suggest programmes for their development.

10. *Pleasurable Instruction*: Pleasure and interest combined with instruction and guidance sugarcane the pill of learning and experience.

11. *Leadership Qualities*: Many programmes have to be organised. Many situations have to be faced in the running of various societies. All these inculcate in the students the virtues of initiative, clear thinking, originality, resourcefulness, good judging power, tolerance, patience, enthusiasm, self-confidence and reliance which are very essential in a leader.

12. *Learning and Earning*: Many activities provide opportunities to the students to earn also.

13. *Loyalty*: The more the students run the school affairs, the more they feel that the school belongs to them and they belong to the school. The labour week, i.e. cleanliness of the school by the students themselves develops the ideas: 'This is my school because I have made it with the sweat of my brow'. Tournaments and activities like school functions also foster this sentiment.

14. *Moral Training*: Students get opportunities of social contact. They also get opportunities of doing social service. This teaches them the lesson of morality. They acquire the virtues of honesty, sympathy and good etiquettes.

15. *Physical Development*: Games, N.C.C., Physical Drill, etc. contribute to the physical development of the individual.

16. *Self-Expression*: Someone has a talent for writing, another for speaking, a third for music and so on. These activities bring out these qualities and develop them. This self-discovery and self-knowledge will tell them in what direction they should turn their ability and talent to advantage and help them to make wise vocational choice.

17. *Recreational Interests*: Education for leisure is as important as education for work. If recreational interests are developed during school life, they prove to be very beneficial in the leisure hours of adult life and make life fuller and richer.

18. *Psychological Values*: Co-curricular activities provide the children a psychological compensation from the usual dull, routine like and monotonous classroom environment in the following manner:

(a) The co-curricular activities provide much needed channels or outlets for sublimation.
(b) These activities play a significant role in training the emotions of students.
(c) They cater to the various aptitudes and interests of the students.
(d) They are a potent means of developing and ensuring mental health.

19. *Social Training*: Co-curricular activities are very useful in giving training in 'Art of Living'. According to the Secondary Education Commission, the 'Art of Living is a more comprehensive concept than the acquisition of knowledge if however, intelligently planned. It includes training in the habits and graces of social life and the capacity for cooperative group work. It calls for patience, good temper, sincerity, fellow-feeling and discipline. These can only be cultivated in the context of the social life and the many curricular and co-curricular activities that must find a recognised place in every good school. By participation in co-curricular activities pupils learn valuable lessons in practical cooperation and the habits of team work. They realise the relation of the society to the individual and of the individual to the society.

Mohi-ud-din states that these activities have a social appeal. "By reason of the social appeal of extra-curricular activities, their cooperative method, their spontaneity and their intrinsic interest, they are a significant social medium for the civic training of the young".

To be a good member one must sacrifice one's immediate interests if need be, for the welfare of the group. It is well known that boys and girls in the process of maturity, move from sheer individualism to social awareness.

20. *Sublimation of Instincts*: Gregarious instinct in the adolescent is very predominant. This tendency expresses the desire of the growing boys to behave socially. If no opportunities are provided to them, they will form their own groups. This grouping may be harmful to them and the society also and may take the shape of gangs, etc. Their energies will be misdirected and they will indulge in anti-social acts. Without proper guidance, they are likely to develop wrong scales of social values that will be harmful and even disastrous to them and to society at large. Various co-curricular activities, e.g. self-government, social service league, scouting, etc. will be very conducive to sublimate this instinct by providing them a field for doing something socially worthwhile through group activities. Similarly, their other instincts of self-assertion, sex and self-abasement will be sublimated.

21. *Team Spirit*: In the beginning every player wishes to carry the ball himself and does not realise that he must depend upon others to realise the goal. But with the passage of time an individual discovers that one must play in a team if one is to win anything worthwhile. Thus a team spirit develops in him. Spirit of 'give-and-take' takes the place of selfishness.

22. *Vocational Development*: Through participation in several co-curricular activities like craft work, dramatics, dance, music, gardening, photography, etc. students develop vocational interests which greatly help in career planning.

28.4 PRINCIPLES OF ORGANISING CO-CURRICULAR ACTIVITIES

1. *Principle of Variety of Activities*: A wide variety of activities should be planned in order to meet the different needs of a large number of students.

2. *Principle of Organising Activities During School Hours*: As far as possible, activities should be organised in school time.

3. *Principle of Equal Opportunity to Students*. All the students should have equal opportunity to be a member of school club.

4. *Principle of Gradual Growth of the Programme*: Activities should be started in a small way and developed gradually.

5. *Principle of Careful Consideration*: Every careful consideration should be given when a new society is to be started. Normally, when once an activity is organised and scheduled, it should not be allowed to die.

6. *Principle of Framing Activity Time-table*: An activity time-table and a calendar for activities may be prepared.

7. *Principle of Guidance by Teachers*: The co-curricular programme should be organised under the guidance of teachers.

8. *Principle of Considering Teacher as an Adviser*: The teacher should not play the role of a dominator but that of an adviser.

9. *Principle of Providing Facilities to Teachers*: Some credit either in the form of less teaching periods or in the form of extra-payment to teachers should be given.

10. *Principle of Participation of a Large Number of Teachers*: As far as possible, each member may remain in-charge of a particular activity of his interest.

11. *Principle of Maintaining Records*: Record of the various activities must be kept by every society.

12. *Principle of Reasonable Expenditure*: Activity should be less expensive as far as possible.

13. *Principle of Provision for Funds*: Sufficient funds to meet the expenditure involved on various activities should be raised by the society concerned.

14. *Principle of Balanced Stress*: Funds should not be spent on a few stars (a few players or debaters, etc.)

15. *Principle of Allotting Regular Time*: Regular time should be devoted to these activities.

16. *Principle of Evaluation*: Provision should be made for periodic appraisal of the services and value of these activities.

17. *Principle of No Show Work*: These activities may not be started merely for 'show work'.

18. *Principle of Publicity*: Publicity should be given to the activities of these societies and the community should be well informed.

19. *Principle of Means not Ends*: Co-curricular programme must be organised and considered as a means to the educative process.

20. *Principle of Appointing Activity Director or Coordinator*: To make the activity programme effective, the head would do well to appoint a teacher as

an activity director or coordinator. His teaching load must be so that he may give sufficient time to the planning and execution of various activities in the school. His duties would be:

(i) To plan the schedule of the year's activities; to set dates of special activities, such as concerts, parents day, school dances, etc.
(ii) To secure a list of clubs that the teachers desire to offer.
(iii) To take care of special discipline cases during club periods.
(iv) To coordinate with transport service to take students to various places.
(v) To issue bulletins of club activities.
(vi) To select only those activities which are by and large related to the school curriculum and community needs.
(vii) To make the programme as inexpensive as possible.
(viii) To ensure that each student of the school participates in one activity at least once according to his interest.

28.5 ROLE OF A TEACHER IN CO-CURRICULAR ACTIVITIES

Teachers should take an active interest in organising co-curricular activities as an integral part of the school programme. They should participate enthusiastically in this programme.

In the teaching of subjects, they get innumerable opportunities to suggest a variety of activities. The scope of activities is very fast.

The language teachers can organise essay competitions, handwriting competitions and debates, spelling competitions, etc.

Social studies teachers can take up projects on the lives of great historical figures. Several types of maps could be prepared. Excursions to places of historical importance may be organised. Social surveys could be undertaken.

The science teachers can take up activities as mentioned in the beginning of this chapter.

As a matter of fact, scope of organising co-curricular activities is unlimited.

28.6 CAUSES OF LACK OF DUE INTEREST AMONG THE STUDENTS IN THE CO-CURRICULAR PROGRAMME

1. Interference with studies.
2. Inconvenient hours of activities.
3. No credit in the examinations.
4. Inadequate provisions regarding these activities.
5. Lack of suitable play-grounds in the crowded cities.
6. More emphasis on intellectual development of the child and very little emphasis on his other developments, e.g. physical, moral, aesthetic, social etc.
7. Poor economic conditions of a number of students compelling them to work in their homes after school hours and thus leaving very little time at their disposal for participating in the activities which are organised after school hours.
8. Indifference of parents causes discouragement sometimes.

28.7 CAUSES OF THE LACK OF INTEREST AMONG TEACHERS IN ORGANISING CO-CURRICULAR ACTIVITIES

1. No extra pay or credit is usually given to them for organising such activities.
2. Teacher's teaching hours are not reduced.
3. A majority of the teachers do not possess the proper training for organising such activities.
4. Some of the teachers do not see any good coming out of these activities as they do not fully realise that they should aim at the all-round development of the personality of the student.
5. Due to the rigid outlook of the teachers and the Heads, the idea of the self-government is not allowed to creep into the minds of the students of the school. They feel that the students are not sufficiently mature and may misuse power invested in them.
6. The vain idea of superiority among the teachers checks them from allowing the students to share responsibility with them.

28.8 LIMITATIONS OF A CO-CURRICULAR PROGRAMME

1. *Disregard of Institutional Conditions*: Many schools undertake activities simply because other schools have started these. They do not take into consideration their assets and limitations.

2. *Lack of Accommodation*: Some schools do not have playgrounds; no space for indoor games; no space for mass drill.

3. *Lack of Funds*: Some schools lack finances for purchasing equipment for sports, craft work, hobbies, workshop material, etc.

4. *Lack of Variety*: Some schools organise a few activities only with the result that students with diverse interests do not get opportunity to participate.

5. *Lack of Adequate Staff*: The number of teachers who can provide effective guidance to student in this field is limited.

6. *Conservative Attitude of Authorities*: Many heads and teachers do not find any good coming out of a co-curricular programme and they are rather indifferent to it.

7. *Over-emphasis on Academic Work*: Generally speaking no regular time is allotted to the organisation of these activities and undue stress is laid on academic achievements.

8. *Overemphasis on Co-curricular Activities*: Some schools follow the extreme course. They over-stress this programme.

9. *Heavy Load on Teachers*: These activities put a heavy load on the teachers and they feel over-burdened.

10. *No Credit in the Annual Examination*: Usually very little consideration is shown to students' performance in these activities while promoting them.

Concluding Observations

Harry C. Mckown has very aptly observed, "A school with only extra-curricular activities (co-curricular activities) would be as absurd as a school without them". In other words an ideal balance to be struck between the curricular and co-curricular programme.

27.9 DESCRIPTION OF VARIOUS CO-CURRICULAR ACTIVITIES

I. Clubs in the School or School Clubs

Clubs may be constituted for undertaking different co-curricular activities in the schools. Every club must have its constitution. Its specific aim must be clear. It must meet the needs of the students. Johnson and Faunce give the following objectives of the school clubs:

1. They provide opportunities to the students for learning experiences based on their interests. Students are attracted to a club because of their enthusiasm for the programme it offers.
2. They supplement the curricular work. Visits to places of historical or scientific importance, etc. can be organised by these clubs.
3. They provide opportunities for the development of pupil abilities.
4. Clubs are very helpful in making the constructive use of leisure time.
5. Clubs may help in the exploration of occupational interest of the students.
6. Clubs provide opportunities for the practice of group planning and decision.

Leadership of the Sponsors or the Teachers-in-Charge of the Club

Leaders or sponsors must possess the following qualities:

1. They should be able to enlist the cooperation of the students.
2. They must be able to offer constructive suggestions for activities of the club.
3. They must be able to guide without dictation.
4. They must have the ability to plan systematically.
5. They must be willing to give time and thought in making the work of the club a success.
6. They must be democratic in spirit.
7. They must possess a sense of humour.
8. They must have the necessary talent and skill so that their performance is higher and better than their pupils and they look upon them as a model.
9. They should help the clubs and societies to make a wise choice of office bearers indicating what qualifications are necessary in an office bearer but should do nothing to force their choice in favour of any individual student.
10. They should make as careful a preparation for participation in co-curricular activities as they do for their teaching work.

Clubs may be organised for a variety of activities and school subjects.

II. Educational Excursions and Tours

Meaning of Educational Excursions: Educational excursions imply small journeys which are undertaken to agricultural, cultural, geographical, historical and industrial places which are not very far off from the educational institution. However educational tours may also be for far off places.

Significance of an Educational Excursion and Tour: W.M. Gregory evaluates school excursion in these words, "Education has been too far removed from the basic experiences of modern life. Many students are quite deficient in opportunities for some perceptive exploration and raw experiences. They need fewer words and more activities with things, situations, conditions and relations. For useful learning, pupils require experiences with the raw materials of life. A garden, a shop, a live animal collection, a trip to a farm, a mill, a store, a park, a museum—all must have a place in the modern school". Following are some of the main advantages of excursions:

(i) *They supplement class-work*: Visits to museums, forts, temples, caves, mountains, valleys, canals and fields help in supplementing the teaching of social studies by providing first-hand information. Industrial establishments and laboratories, etc. are very useful places to the students of science. Excursions to these places bring reality, clarity and vividness to the 'dead matter' of various subjects, and provide for valuable correlation of subjects.

(ii) *They introduce variety in the school programme*: These excursions infuse a new life and vigour in the children and give them some relief from the dull and monotonous life of the classroom.

(iii) *They develop qualities of leadership*: Excursions help in developing qualities of initiative and leadership in the students by affording them opportunities to make necessary arrangements. These also encourage a spirit of cooperation among the students.

(iv) *They acquaint the pupils with the environment*: Excursions enable the students to know intimately their environment by putting them in direct touch with the things, persons, organisations and institutions.

(v) *They develop self-activity among the students*: Excursions make pupils active agents rather than passive recipients. Students get opportunities to plan various programmes connected with excursions. Besides they get opportunities to develop keenness and accuracy of observation. All their senses are at work and they experience the joy of discovery.

(vi) *They develop the aesthetic sense of the students*: Excursions to natural settings and places of beauty create love for nature and develop aesthetic sense.

(vii) *They foster ideals of emotional and national integration*: The students come into contact with people of different races, regions and States. This enables them to apperciate the unity in diversity.

Proper Planning of Excursions: To derive the maximum benefit from excursions, it is essential that these should be properly planned. The teachers and the students may work out the plan of the excursion jointly. An excursion must be wisely conceived, properly planned and well conducted. It must be a result of careful thinking. The organisers would do well to obtain sufficient information beforehand regarding the importance of places to be visited so that they may be able to give suitable replies to the various queries of the students.

The fact that the excursions are arranged for educational-*cum*-recreational purposes should not be lost sight of and therefore, if possible, student singers, titbit tellers and photographers should find a place in the party so that learning and laughing should go hand in hand.

The appointment of group leaders facilitates work to a considerable extent. The group leaders should preferably be those students who have some knowledge of the locality or who know the technique of explaining things in a clear way.

The importance of maintaining discipline in an excursion can hardly be ignored and a sympathetic and resourceful teacher shall not find it difficult to do so.

III. Labour Week/Community Service/School Cleanliness

Regarding this type of work, K.G. Saiyidain writes, "I feel strongly that not only in this country, but in the whole world, we have to make an earnest and concentrated effort to give a new orientation to the social ideology of our children and youth particularly in the direction of inculcating a sense of the dignity of labour and cultivating the capacity to work together for constructive and socially worthy causes. I cannot think of any better method of doing so than by bringing all school children together into a fellowship of work and service where the meanest work will be undertaken in a spirit of adventure and comradeship because it is useful and provides healthy outlet for their energies and talents".

Following types of work may be done during a labour week:

(a) Cleaning and white-washing the school building.
(b) Decorating the rooms.
(c) Removing stones, iron nails, waste paper, etc. from the school compound, playground, lanes and streets.
(d) Filling pits in the streets and lanes, and cleaning roads.
(e) Organising first-aid centres for the public.
(f) Teaching adults.
(g) Improving drainage of selected localities and drying marshy land created by open drains.
(h) Turfing school compound.
(i) Impressing upon the public regarding the importance of personal cleanliness and social sanitation in order to ward off common diseases.

To make this programme a success, the teachers themselves should take an active part in activities as stated above. This will give incentive and encouragement to the students.

IV. Morning Assembly/School Assembly

Meaning: Flora T. Cook describes the morning assembly as "The morning assembly is a common meeting ground to which each brings his offerings, the fruit of his observation and studies or music, literature, and art that delight him, a place where all cooperate for the pleasure and well being of the whole".

Prof. Fretwell calls the assembly as "Town meeting of the school".

In the words of W.R. Smith, "School assembly can serve as a focusing centre of all form of extra-curricular life".

Nature of Activities in the Assembly: Common activities of an assembly are:

(i) School prayer.

(ii) Singing of national anthem.
(iii) Singing of devotional song.
(iv) Roll call.
(v) Checking of cleanliness.
(vi) Checking of school uniform.
(vii) Short speech or some moral aspect by the head or the teacher or the student or the guest speaker.
(viii) Announcements.
(ix) Commendations.
(x) Mass drill.
(xi) Daily news.

Objectives, Purposes and Values of the School Assembly

(i) *To provide a solemn occasion*: The singing of morning prayer and devotional songs provides a very solemn and elevating occasion and makes it good beginning for school work.

(ii) *To develop devotion to God and Spirituality*: It can be used to create in the students an urge for prayer and meditation which also helps in emotional stability.

(iii) *To develop spirit of patriotism*: Singing of some patriotic song or narration of some patriotic event inculcates the sentiment of patriotism and love for the country.

(iv) *To celebrate festivals and days*: Some of the important national days and religious festivals can be celebrated.

(v) *To unify the school*: An assembly is very helpful in developing a community spirit among the students. They get occasions to see, feel and know the school as an organised group. An average student remaining in his class does not appreciate his relationship to the school as a whole.

(vi) *To serve as clearing house*: The school assembly serves as a clearing house for all school activities both curricular and co-curricular.

(vii) *To familiarise the students with the common rules and ideals of the school*: Every child must become a full-fledged citizen of the school. In a school assembly, the students should be told about the traditions, rules and ideals of the school.

(viii) *To develop correct audience habits*: To be socially efficient, every child must know how to behave in a gathering. Social etiquette demands that children must listen to the speakers with courtesy and patience. When and how to applaud is another quality that must be developed. The school assembly trains the students in this art.

(ix) *To give due recognition to worthwhile achievements publicly*: Prizes to the students for outstanding accomplishments of nature, curricular or co-curricular should be given before the entire school. This action will motivate other students to perform outstanding accomplishments.

(x) *To give opportunities to students to face the audience*: It gives training to a large number of students in effective appearance and expression before a critical audience. Students advanced in different spheres present their programmes and give stimulus to others to emulate their example.

(xi) *To widen interest*: Assembly experience deepens and widens student interest.

(xii) *To develop good habits*: Habits of punctuality and regularity are developed.

(xiii) *To motivate students*: Announcement and public recognition to outstanding performance of some students in academic and co-curricular programmes motivate other students to work hard.

(xiv) *To make general announcements*: Changes in the school schedule, preparation of any special programme can be announced in the morning assembly.

Edmonson and others expect the assembly to discharge the following functions:

1. To develop school unity.
2. To encourage school spirit.
3. To motivate curricular functions.
4. To stimulate extra-curricular activities.
5. To motivate expression and overcome self-consciousness.
6. To develop proper habits and attitudes in audience.
7. To share information.
8. To influence public opinion.
9. To develop aesthetic sense.

Essentials for Ideal Assembly Programmes

1. All programmes should be carefully planned and executed.
2. Sufficient care should be exercised to ensure that the students observe disciplinary etiquettes.
3. The assembly should not be made a forum for saying unpleasant things.
4. One of the worst things a Head would do in an assembly is to find fault openly with some staff member or to criticise the entire student population of the school. This unpleasant element should be avoided.

V. School Magazine

Significance and Values of School Magazine: A school magazine is the embodiment of the corporate life of an institution and affords suitable opportunities to the students for giving expression to their thought and ambitions.

In the words of Jacobson, "The school magazine offers great opportunities for those who participate in it. It is not uncommon to find that pupils and their parents consider the editorship of the school paper the most valuable experience which has come to a pupil, particularly when directed by a wise sponsor who make it a very purposive educative experience. All pupils who serve on the magazine secure some experience in creative writing, usually the form of their writing improves because a powerful incentive for correct form exists when the material is to be printed or mimeographed for public examination".

It serves as a link between the school and the parents as it reaches them through the students.

A school magazine supplements class work to some extent. The students learn to write their thoughts in an effective, clear and concise manner. Study habits are developed as the students consult some books or journals to write for their school magazine and make the best use of their leisure time.

Spears and Lawshe list the following functions of the school paper as an aid to the school:

1. To educate the community about the work of the school.
2. To publish school news.
3. To create and express school opinion.
4. To capitalise the achievements of the school.
5. To act as a means of unifying the school.
6. To express the idealism and reflect the spirit.
7. To encourage and stimulate worthwhile activities.
8. To aid in developing right standards of conduct.
9. To promote understanding of other schools.
10. To provide an outlet for student suggestions for the betterment of the school.
11. To develop better inter-school relationships.
12. To increase school spirit.
13. To promote cooperation between parents and school.

Factors Essential for the Success of the School Magazine: Contributions from the students should be corrected before their publication. The school magazine should include a variety of articles. Not only short stories, essays, poems, titbits but current news, school news about curricular and co-curricular activities, photos, designs and cartoons, etc. should also find place in the school magazine. Student editors should be carefully appointed. Prize for the best contributions may be given to the students to give them an incentive to write. The teachers should not make the school magazine as their organ.

The teacher in-charge of the magazine should be a man of vision, of literary taste and well versed with the current events.

In schools where the number of students is small and the financial position does not permit the publication of a full-fledged magazine, it will be advantageous to take resort to wall-magazine.

Blackboard or wall-magazine greatly helps in the preparation of the printed magazine. News on boards may be written every day in the morning. Daily news should be illustrated with the help of a map. Important places where important events take place should be shown on the map. Other boards dealing with facts and figure regarding our natural resources, development projects, inspiring thoughts from religion, history or ethics may be prepared weekly or fortnightly as the case may be. The students should be made responsible for preparing these boards.

VI. Scouting and Girl Guiding

Values of Scouting: Prof. Bertrand Russell has very beautifully commended the value of scouting: "The naturalist may praise it for its success in putting the boy close to Nature's heart, the moralist for its splendid code of ethics, the hygienist for its method of physical training, the parent for its ability to keep his boy out of mischief; but from the standing point of educator, it has marvellous potency for converting the restless, irresponsible, self-centred boy into the straight-forward, dependable, helpful young citizen. To the boy who will give himself to it, there is plenty of work that looks like play, standard of excellence which he can appreciate, rules of conduct which he must obey, position of responsibility which he must occupy as soon as he qualifies himself, in a word: a programme that appeals to boy's nature".

Another writer, Dr. L.D. Coffman writes: "Scouting gives us no lecture on vocational guidance, and yet it teaches the meaning, the importance of the dignity of work; it operates no bank and yet it teachers the meaning of thrift; it contains no jails and yet it teaches the meaning of self-control; it does not preaching and yet it teaches devotion to a cause and loyalty to a purpose; it is founded upon no religious creed or sectarian doctrine and yet it emphasises above all things the importance of religion. It is universal in appeal, natural in its methods, progressive in its outlines, strengthened and cemented by the bonds of fellowship and the idealism of the movement.

Following are some of the important contributions of scouting:

1. Social service training.
2. Developing spirit of fellowship.
3. Inculcating the value of dignity of labour.
4. Sublimating instincts.
5. Developing love of nature.
6. Fostering a spirit of adventure.
7. Promoting practical efficiency.

History of Scouting: Sir Robert Baden Power (1857-1941) founded the Boy Scout Movement in 1908. However, in India, the movement was introduced in 1911 at Bangalore. Many rival organisations such as the 'Seva Dals', 'Bharat Youth Sangha', Seva Samiti, Boys Scout Association and finally, the Hindustan Scout Association, came into existence.

Badel Powell had served the army in India, Afghanistan and then in South Asia.

In India it was considered for long that the movement was alien in its character.

The movement has received a great setback with the starting of N.C.C. and other organisations.

The movement is non-political, non-official and voluntary.

VII. Student Participation and Student Self-Government

A school is considered to be an ideal place for training in citizenship and democratic values. Student's participation in running some of the administrative functions is also known as a sort of student self-government. Self-government on a large scale by the pupils is not possible even in well established progressive schools in our country There are nevertheless practical undertakings in the schools to train pupils for citizenship. The organisation of co-curricular activities offers a field in which student government to a considerable extent could function very effectively. The simple Council Type of self-government is easy to practise.

To start with, a school may have school Sabha. Each Class or section elects one representative to the Sabha. Some talented students may be nominated by the head of the school in consultation with the staff adviser. The Sabha may have six committees under it and the members may be elected from among the elected representatives. One staff member may act as an adviser to each committee. The following activities may be undertaken by these committees.

(a) Games and Sports Committee.
(b) Health and Sanitation Committee.
(c) A committee for organising activities like debates, dramas, magazines, hobbies, etc.
(d) Discipline Committee.
(e) Committee for social welfare activities like Adult Literacy Campaigns, Flood Squads, Labour Weeks, etc.
(f) School Cooperative Store Committee.

No rigid rules can be laid down for the range of activities to be undertaken by the Sabha. Every type of activity which has some educational significance may come under its purview.

H.C. McKown has given a list of 147 activities which can be undertaken by the Sabha or the Council. Some of these activities are given here:

1. To welcome new students.
2. To supervise and help in the maintenance of good sanitary conditions in the school.
3. To decorate the classrooms and the school premises.
4. To visit sick students.
5. To meet and welcome the visiting teams.
6. To provide assistance to the weak and handicapped students.
7. To plan campaigns—courtesy, safety, punctuality, etc.
8. To organise contests and competitions.
9. To publish school magazine and school bulletins.
10. To organise and manage a lost and found department.
11. To promote better lunch-room and cafeteria manners.
12. To promote good manners at athletic contests.
13. To look after library and reading-room.
14. To promote good behaviour at assembly, public events, before and after school.
15. To arrange lectures.
16. To organise exhibitions.
17. To organise the school store.
18. To organise the school bank.
19. To introduce students to new movements in education.
20. To promote and arrange inter-school visits.
21. To arrange inter-school sports tournaments.
22. To promote inter-home room programme exchanges.

23. To hold academic contests.
24. To organise excursions and trips.
25. To provide for publicity of commendable school work.
26. To promote good dress and neat appearance.
27. To collect material for school museum.
28. To supervise ventilation.